Perspecta 49
Quote

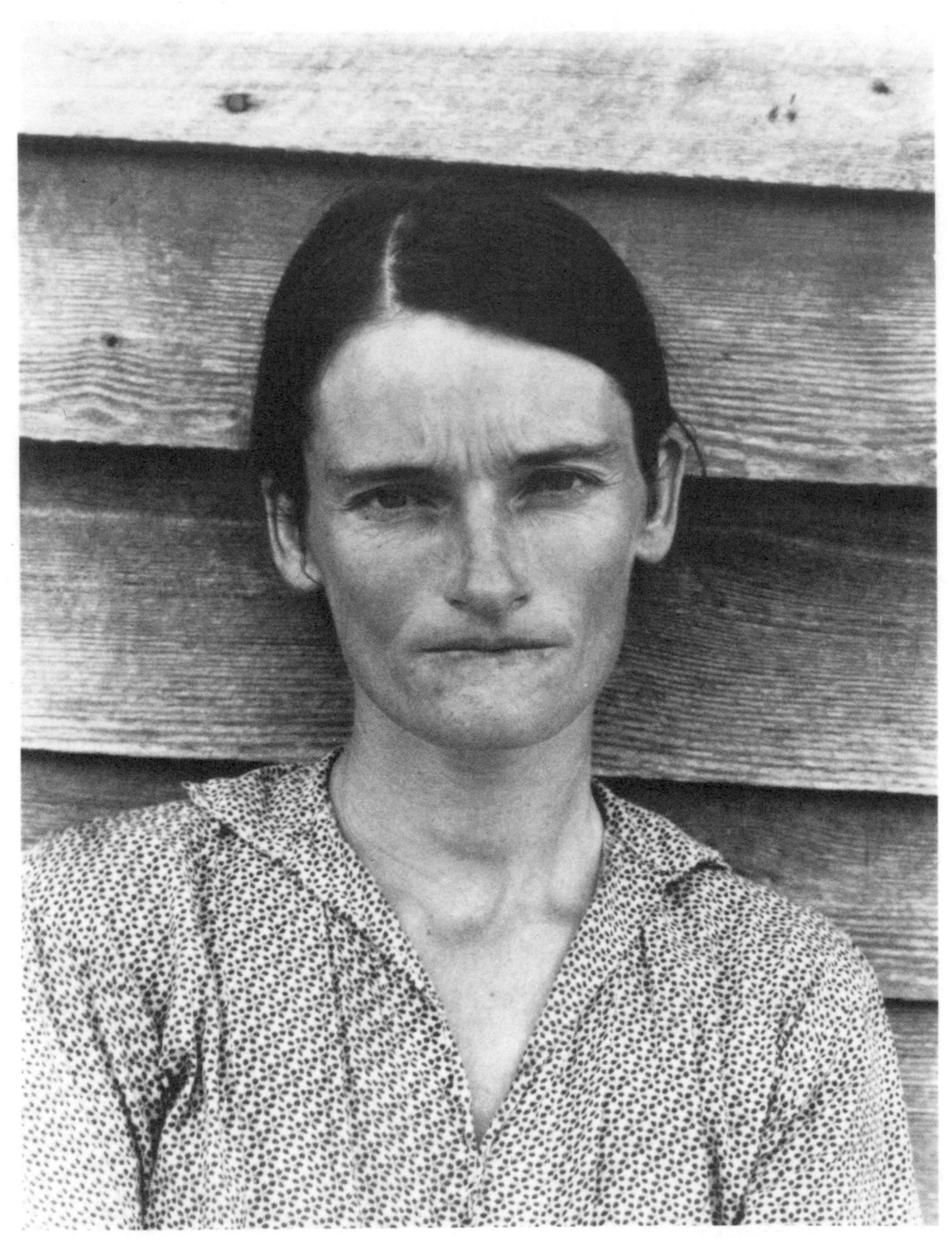

Sherrie Levine, *After Walker Evans*: 4,
gelatin silver print, 5 1/16 x 3 7/8 inches, 1981.

page 4
Eiffel Tower, Tianducheng.
Francis Fukuyama, “The End of History?” 1989.

Editors' Statement

Every intellectual endeavor relies upon an existing body of knowledge, enduring and primed for reuse. Historically, this appropriation has been regulated through quotation. Academics trade epigraphs and footnotes while designers refer to precedents and manifestos. These citations—written or spoken, drawn or built—rely on their antecedents and carry a stamp of authority.

In the field of architecture, appropriation is faster, easier, and more conspicuous than ever, but also less regulated. These displacements are no longer self-referential games: operative framings and apocryphal attributions conflate authorships and confuse copyrights. Buildings are copied before construction is completed. Digital scripts are downloaded, altered, and re-uploaded, transposing the algorithm, not the object itself. Design bloggers curate texts and images—copying and pasting, copying and pasting. In the sea of memes and GIFs, tweets and retweets, quotations are innumerable and viral, giving voice to anyone with access to these channels.

Traditionally, the practice of quotation has inoculated the author against accusations of plagiarism. Today, the quicksilver nature of contemporary communications obscures chains of reference. Must we jettison conventions of authorship or will we establish new codes of citation?

This issue of *Perspecta* explores the uneasy lines between quotation, appropriation, and plagiarism, proposing a constructive reevaluation of the means of architectural production and reproduction. Although architecture is a discipline that prizes originality and easily ascribed authorship, quotation and its associated operations are ubiquitous, intentional, and vital, not just palliatives to the anxiety of influence. These are perhaps the most potent tools of cultural production, yet also the most contested.

Perspecta 49 welcomes the contest.

A.J.P. Artemel
Russell LeStourgeon
Violette de la Selle

The end of history will be a very sad time. The struggle for recognition, the willingness to risk one's life for a purely abstract goal, the worldwide ideological struggle that called forth daring, courage, imagination, and idealism, will be replaced by economic calculation, the endless solving of technical problems, environmental concerns, and the satisfaction of sophisticated consumer demands. In the post-historical period there will be neither art nor philosophy, just the perpetual caretaking of the museum of human history.

‡

“Most of the buildings did not seem to amount to much more than bad copies, or copies of copies.”

‡ Eeva-Liisa Pelkonen

When Modern Architecture Went Viral

We now commonly use the term *viral* to refer to the phenomenon where a post on the Internet—whether a film clip posted on YouTube or a notorious tweet—has been rapidly shared and viewed by millions. Going viral is usually good news, bringing notoriety to the author as well as to the field pertaining to the subject dicussed, whether in the realm of culture, commerce, or politics. We could just as well refer to viral architecture in terms of certain formal idioms that are so common today around the globe. Yet while architects have been busier than ever during the building booms of recent decades, it is hard to get too excited about the outcome: think of all the bland curtain-wall office buildings and skyscrapers that you encounter in any region of the world. If dropped randomly somewhere in the world you might not immediately realize in which country you have landed. It is hard to evaluate or categorize contemporary buildings, which often amount to nothing but a mash-up of motifs taken from various styles. Even buildings that look like something we once referred to as Modern architecture don't quite seem to fit the bill, not least because they no longer adhere to the socio-aesthetic mission that gave birth to the Modern movement. Something gets lost when architecture goes viral.

Revisiting *Transformations in Modern Architecture* (February 21–April 24, 1979), one of the most controversial architecture exhibitions in the history of the Museum of Modern Art, offers an early diagnosis of the cause behind the condition. On display were photographs of no less than 403 buildings by 270 architects from 16 countries—most structures rather unknown and resembling the ones next to it. The sheer quantity of projects on view underscored the fact that none of the buildings were in any way remarkable or trailblazing. When viewed together, they proved that second- and third-generation Modern architects seemed simply to repeat and exaggerate established Modernist formal idioms to the point of parody. Even the show's curator, Arthur Drexler, acknowledged that when it came to so-called "late Modern" architecture, quantity seemed to trump quality. An instant uproar within the profession was to be expected as many questioned why certain masterpieces and bigger names had been excluded in favor of such mediocrity. The most potent question came from Reyner Banham, who bluntly asked, "What was [the show] all about?"[1]

The title of the exhibition is a clue as to what Drexler might have had in mind when highlighting such apparent mediocrity in bulk: "Modern architecture," which the very same institution had helped to promote with its landmark exhibition *Modern Architecture: International Exhibition*, in 1932, was surely alive and kicking, yet somehow "transformed." The process of how the formal code of Modern architecture migrated from building to building across time and space, somehow transforming along the way, constituted the subject matter of the show, hence the abundance of examples. Clearly none of the featured buildings alone was worthy of study.

1–2 Installation views of the exhibition *Transformations in Modern Architecture*, 1979. The Museum of Modern Art Archives: Mali Olatunji.

By 1979 MoMA had clearly succeeded in its mission: Modern architecture had conquered the globe. To underscore this proliferation, Drexler densely packed some five hundred black-and-white photographs into four horizontal rows and mounted them on a slightly concave panel that wrapped around the perimeter of the room without giving any additional information about the name of the architect, location, or purpose of the project (fig. 2). The format created a somewhat dizzying effect; the viewer was enveloped by images, his or her eye wandering from photograph to photograph, forced to conclude that every project looked a lot like the one next to it. It was clear that the established tenets of Modern architecture were no longer valid. Indeed when it came to late Modern architecture, form was clearly no longer motivated by functional, material, or structural logic; instead form seemed to simply follow form. It was equally clear that the original meanings and ideals, if any, had been lost in the course of the various iterations along the way.

The climax of the exhibition took place in an octagonal room built in the middle of the gallery space, dedicated to curtain-wall buildings depicted on backlit photo transparencies affixed to the black walls (fig. 1). Here, loss of original meaning became fully apparent as the installation demonstrated how the once pioneering, now ubiquitous glass curtain-wall system had replicated itself throughout the globe. In Drexler's words, the "metal and glass cladding systems have been so refined as to communicate almost nothing."[2] The display format underlined that Modernism had proliferated simply by multiplying its own formal and material code fragment by fragment. The visitor was left to wonder whether this state of affairs was desirable since most of the buildings did not seem to amount to much more than bad copies, or copies of copies.

It is interesting to note that the show took place shortly after Richard Dawkins wrote the book *The Selfish Gene* in 1976, about how ideas, a behavior, or a style can go viral within culture. Appropriating a concept introduced in this text, Drexler identified the architectural "fragments," such as "parapets," that could be referred to as "memes" that form the "replicating entities," while sets of representational tools and dominant construction techniques acted as "sets of mutually-assisting memes," which facilitated the proliferation and ultimate domination of certain formal motifs over others.[3]

In more ways than one, *Transformations* was an unusual exhibition for MoMA, which like all museums is committed to the preservation and display of unique objects. The architecture department had previously fulfilled this mission by presenting each project thoroughly with models, plans, and photographs and by indicating the criteria for inclusion with appropriate narrative framing, whether biographical (e.g., *Aalto: Architecture and Furniture*, 1938), ideological (e.g., *Good Design*, 1951), thematic (e.g., *Visionary Architecture*, 1960), geographic (e.g., *Modern Architec-*

3 Ludwig Mies van der Rohe, view of model for Glass Skyscraper Project, 1922.

4 Foster Associates, Willis, Faber & Dumas Headquarters, 1970–75, Ipswich, UK.

ture: USA, 1965), or typological (e.g., *Architecture of Museums*, 1968). By contrast, *Transformations* did not seem to have clear criteria for why certain projects were chosen over others, thus further diluting the whole notion of a unique object and, along with it, a solid foundation of what constitutes good architecture altogether.

There was no question that something had changed since 1932, when the museum mounted its first architecture show, *Modern Architecture: International Exhibition*. The press release for *Transformations* termed it an "elaboration of ideas first propounded 30 or 40 years ago."[4] Drexler addressed the issue of legacy in the accompanying catalog, which came out a year later, as follows: "The history of architecture during the last two decades involves sorting out, developing, and transforming possibilities implicit in its beginning."[5] To illustrate this point some original "ideas" were identified and included, such as Mies van Rohe's Glass Skyscraper of 1922 (fig. 3), which appeared as the ur-father for all subsequent glass buildings. In the exhibition catalog Drexler acknowledges that during this process of transformation original reference points often got lost, along with the ideals they represented. This loss was most pronounced with some of the curtain-wall structures, such as Norman Foster's Willis, Faber & Dumas building, in Ipswich, England, with its curving all-glass wall: the main goal was simply to make an all-glass facade just for the hell of it (fig. 4).

Drexler unambiguously saw the second and third generation of Modern architects as mere information processors who designed by multiplying and mashing together the bounty of ideas and forms passed to them throughout history, sometimes rather randomly. The exhibition and catalog even included some slightly humorous examples, such as an office, store, and apartment building by the Passarelli brothers in Rome that an architecture critic from *Architectural Forum* called a "Lever House with [a] Paul Rudolph Architecture School on top," which was identified politely in the catalog as a "hybrid"[6] (fig. 5).

In an interview for *Skyline* magazine, Drexler did not hide the fact that a lot of the selected buildings were not all that great by stating that "the show is in many ways an analogue of the real world: bewildering, profuse, overloaded, contradictory, inconsistent, largely mediocre. The devaluation of once lofty and supposedly profound ideas." In the same interview he elaborated on the question he wanted to pose with the show: How do forms proliferate, and what happens to them on the way? The question of copying gains a polemical focus, and Drexler addresses it head-on:

> That question infuriates architects. "My work has nothing in common with Joe's and Jim's. Obviously unique, I have invented this all by myself." This, however, does not appear to be the case. Certain themes have developed over a twenty-year period, which is not to say that someone has copied from someone else. It simply means that an idea is in the air, people discuss it, and it is regarded as more or less common property.[7]

5 Vincenzo, Fausto, and Lucio Passarelli, *Store, office, and apartment building on the via Campania*, 1962–65, Rome, Italy.

6 Projects chosen to showcase the use of "parapets" in the exhibition catalog, 124–127. From left to right, top to bottom: The Richardson Associates, Sea-Tac International Airport Parking Terminal, 1969–72, Seattle, Wash.; Luigi W. Moretti with Fischer-Elmore Associated Architects, The Watergate Apartments, 1961–64/70, Washington, D.C.; Luigi W. Moretti, "San Maurizio" condominium apartment block, 1962–65, Rome, Italy; Paul Rudolph, New Haven Parking Garage, 1959–63, New Haven, Conn.; Ulrich Franzen & Associates. Alley Theater, 1966–68, Houston, Tex.; Michel Marot & Andre Minangoy, Marina Baie des Anges, 1968–78, Villeneuve Loubet, France.

Copying was indeed the central focus of the show—how the process works and what happens to the original formal motives along the way. The exhibition made it clear that the generations of Modern architects following the first tended simply to repeat, almost compulsively and to dizzying effect, the formal motifs inherited from their precursors without understanding where these ideas came from. Two spreads dedicated to "parapets" exemplify the situation, suggesting that Frank Lloyd Wright's Fallingwater fathered dozens of bizarre-looking monsters (fig. 6). Drexler conveys the process of somewhat meaningless copying through the treatment of structural elements, which traditionally represented the most solid foundations of Modern architecture:

> If the structural elements of a particularly striking work are too thin or too fat, the first wave of imitations will make them thinner or fatter; the second wave will try to do the same with the remaining elements. This process, perhaps unconscious, exerts a centrifugal force on coherent systems of design and ultimately reduces them to parodies.[8]

To be sure, Drexler had nothing against copying as such; his mission was simply to raise questions as to how such clueless, bad copies came about, especially considering that imitating and replicating formal ideas and tropes was in fact an integral part of how architecture had been conceived throughout history. To make the point that Modern architects had somehow lost this art, he began the inaugural talk of the exhibition by quoting Mies van der Rohe's lament: "We told them what to do and they did not do it."[9] The statement was particularly meaningful coming from Mies; while there were certainly plenty of "Miesian" buildings in 1960, when he made that statement, these were clearly not approved by the master. The case of Mies versus his followers exemplified the perfect paradox at the heart of the show: how the replication of an idea en masse can lead to its ultimate demise.

The question of what made Modern architects such bad copiers formed the subtext of the exhibition. Two previous MoMA shows offered historical points of comparison. *Architecture without Architects* (1964), curated by Bernard Rudofsky in collaboration with Drexler, celebrated the transmission of ideas and techniques, albeit within vernacular building traditions, while *Architecture of the École des Beaux Arts* (1975) shed light on an education system that used imitation as a pedagogical tool. Indeed, Modern architecture represented an anomaly against this historical background.

Drexler acknowledged that some Modern architects did a better job of copying than others. The catalog singles out three so-called second-generation architects who had mastered the art to perfection: Louis Kahn, James Stirling, and Robert Venturi. He praises, for example, how "Kahn opened a door to the past without engaging in historical revivalism. He seemed to have taken modern architecture apart and put it together again, making it a more subtle instrument." For example, the Richards Medical Research and Biology towers "recall the castles and Romanesque churches Kahn admired so much," while the "Phillips Exeter buildings make no outward display of modern structural technique, [...] although their predominantly vertical fenestration may have neoclassical overtones."[10] Drexler praises Stirling as follows: "More than other architects in the last twenty years, Stirling has drawn on the industrial vernacular and, to a lesser extent, on the prewar history of modern architecture as high art."[11] Venturi, he notes, "has been particularly skillful in ... rearrang[ing] motifs from the more sophisticated reaches of modernism, [and] contradict[ing] them by adding decorative moldings to frame some windows."[12] Drexler steers away from defining their process as "copying," instead using terms such as *recalling*, *drawing on*, and *incorporating* to suggest a more conscious and educated process of referencing not only forms but also their original meanings, while creatively reworking and reinventing the themes.

Drexler's thesis that all good architecture is based on reworking noteworthy precedents recalls Harold Bloom's book *The Anxiety of Influence: A Theory of Poetry* (1973), in which the famous literary critic differentiates between good and bad poetry by distinguishing between various poets' ability to handle the "influence" of previous work: weak work is simply derivative, while good writers are able to create original work not only despite but because of their ability to carry a deep intellectual struggle through existing literary tropes. "In ways that need not be doctrinal," Bloom writes, "strong poems are always omens of resurrection. The dead may or may not return, but their voice comes alive, paradoxically never by mere imitation but in the agonistic misprision performed upon powerful forerunners."[13] According to Bloom the problem with some contemporary poets was that they suffered from a misguided "anxiety of influence"; that is, when some lesser poets confuse original contribution with breaking loose from any influence altogether. Drexler makes a similar argument about architecture:

> Architectural ideas are models. Part of their value is that they can be imitated, varied, "improved." No matter how strongly the modern movement stressed the idea of approaching each problem without prior commitments—as if the wheel had to be perpetually reinvented—any successful solution to an architectural problem embodies a previous success, and is itself successful in that it can be imitated.[14]

Like Bloom, Drexler drew the conclusion that most of Modern architecture was mediocre because its architects avoided the confrontation with models inherited from their forefathers that leads at best to the kind of "agonistic misprisions" that mark all good work.[15]

In order to understand how Modern architecture got to this point, we need to look back to the early 1950s, when the second generation of Modern architects began to emulate and evaluate the formal language of their predecessors. Eero Saarinen made the frank assessment that there was no shame or stigma attached to being under the influence of the Modern masters:

> [Le Corbusier, Mies van der Rohe, and Frank Lloyd Wright] made the great principles which together form our architec-

ture. Mixed together, they make the broth which is modern architecture. In different parts of the world, the ingredients of the broth have different proportions. For instance, architecture in South America and Italy is primarily made up out of the fundamental principles plus Corbu. This forms a different product than that of the U.S. which has primarily Mies, comparatively little Corbu, and FLW as a spice.[16]

This generation of architects' production could be categorized based on their affinity to a particular Modern master (e.g., "Miesians"), and so it was first presented on the pages of *Progressive Architecture* in 1960 and '61, where contemporary architects were asked to answer questions about the state of Modern architecture. The dominant theme then was "chaotism", no clear sense of direction could be detected in the contemporary architecture scene. The answers veered for and against on the stylistic eclecticism of contemporary architecture. Philip Johnson, for one, endorsed the chaos: "Let the students have a different hero every day. Maybe it's good for them." At the other end of the spectrum, Mies famously answered, "Certainly it is not necessary or possible to invent a new kind of architecture every Monday morning."[17] Both endorsed imitation, the former open to experimenting with different idioms, the latter insisting on sticking to what he considered the universal principles of all good architecture, by which he certainly was referring to his own.

Around the same period various architects and scholars began to investigate how forms migrate through time and space. In *Search for Form: A Fundamental Approach to Art* (1948), Eliel Saarinen, father of Eero, talked about "form migration" and asked whether the appropriation of forms led to direct copying or whether forms could be invested with new meanings when adopted by different cultures. Yale art historian George Kubler, an expert on pre-Columbian and Ibero-American architecture, broke away from the conventional art historical approach that tied forms and artwork to the particular time and place of their creation. In his influential book *The Shape of Time* (1962), Kubler argued that art history, when reduced to the study of coherent styles, is unable to explain how forms circulate through time and gain new meanings in new contexts. To illustrate the dynamics of citation, he referred to the language of electrodynamics, a popular field at the time, likening art to "signals" that trigger other individuals to repeat them. "The sign itself becomes form, and in the world of forms it gives rise to a whole series of shapes that subsequently bear no relations whatsoever to the origin."[18] While Kubler acknowledged that form migration often leads to the separation of a form from its original meanings, it is a natural process in which forms acquire new meanings along the way.

Writing some fifteen years later, Drexler observed that the process of transmittal from past to present was no longer working. Believing that architecture could be studied like any cultural phenomenon, as a semiotic system governed by relationships between signs and the things to which they refer, he drew the following conclusion: "When systems fail, when unifying architectural theory has weakened ... [a]ttention shifts to fragments, to some isolated elements useful in design." Altogether these factors led to a "play of unnecessary forms."[19] The question then was what had caused the link between the sign and signified to erode to the point that forms no longer had the vitality celebrated by Kubler.

The answer to that question was embedded in the exhibition format, which simulated the increasingly media-rich environment the architect operated within. To recreate that state of affairs, at least, Drexler took the visitor into the architect's head to evoke how one might process all that imagery in a meaningful way. He believed that exhibitions exemplified how an image-infested semiotic system operates: "[This is what] exhibitions can do: surround you with images and put you in a different relationship to them. It can present to you far more images simultaneously than you can absorb in any other way." He goes on to explaining how an overflow of images might have played a part in the collapse of the "system": "enlarging the number of buildings the memory can deal with" explains "what [has] happened to architecture during the last twenty years."[20] To demonstrate that the mind operates primarily through association in such a saturated environment, Drexler placed similar-looking buildings next to each other, where the juxtaposition "must be instantly clear visually. The juxtapositions must not depend on words. Words can be used to help along the examination of images but cannot trigger the connections that the eye is meant to make." The point was to show that when surrounded by images the mind ceases to look for an extra-visual meaning behind the image and settles on making purely visual associations. Ultimately this process led to the "late Modern" condition, where there was no "meaning" behind the image, only a telescoping series of other images.

Drexler was by no means the first to use an abundant number of photographic prints in an exhibition. Nor was he the first to acknowledge that this made for a completely different way of absorbing information than mounting original drawings on the wall, for example. By laying the photographs out as an ever-expanding matrix, he was surely indebted to his MoMA colleague Herbert Bayer, who had pioneered the method in the 1923 Bauhaus exhibition. The canted wall plane seems like a direct reference Bayer's 1930 diagram demonstrating how human vision expands along the horizontal and vertical axes (fig. 7). Variations of photo walls were used in numerous subsequent exhibitions and installations, including the Finnish Pavilion at the 1939 New York World's Fair, designed by Alvar Aalto, where photographs were embedded in a curvilinear form, letting the eye wander from image to image while making connections between them along the way.

Drexler must have been aware of the contributions to display technology by George Nelson, who in his book *Display* (1953) called for a new enlargement of vision based on the argument that the "post-Atomic" man lived in an increasingly dynamic world and was constantly bombarded with information and images all around.[21] In exhibition designs such as *The New Landscape* (1951), Nelson infested both horizontal and vertical surfaces with images, thus inviting the viewer to make connections between art and nature while discovering both visual and theoretical links behind

7 Diagram by Herbert Bayer depicting an expanded field of vision, 1930.

8 Maurice Jarnoux, André Malraux choosing images for *Les Voix du Silence*, 1948. Detail of a photograph by for *Paris Match*.

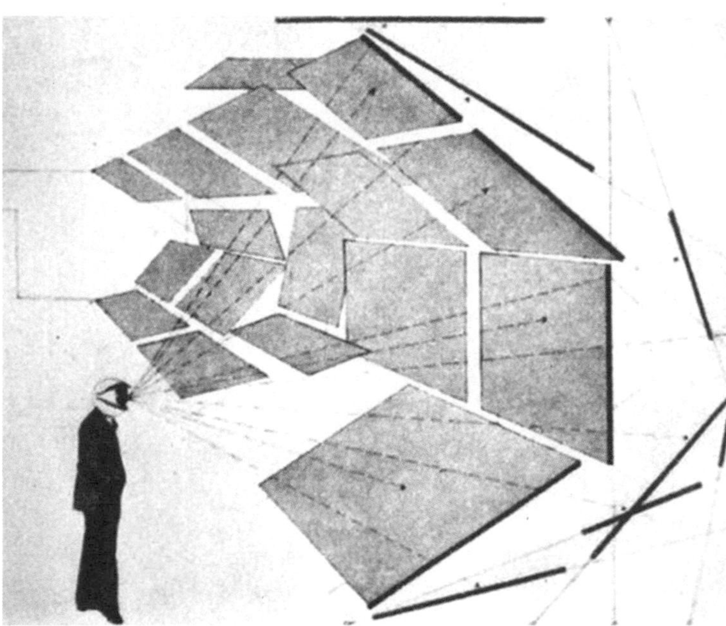

the phenomena.[22] It is important to note that Nelson enhanced the idea of such dynamic vision as well as that associations made by the viewer could be provisory and multiple.

It is also worth mentioning André Malraux's notion of a "museum without walls" or *musée imaginaire* centered around the idea that museums and publications using photographic reproductions had made it possible for the artwork to enter into the world of images and discourse by allowing it to transcend not only geographic and temporal boundaries but also well-defined historical and stylistic categories.[23] He also writes about the power of images to enter our consciousness without us being aware that we carry them in our minds, that they in turn affect our outlook and our perception of other images. As a mobile, reproducible medium par excellence, photography allows works to be compared, paired, and organized into categories according to formal and technical similarities, without additional knowledge. As Malraux noted: "…photography imparts a family likeness to objects that have actually but slight affinity. With the result that such different objects as a miniature, a piece of tapestry, a statue and a medieval stained-glass window, when reproduced on the same page, may seem members of the same family."[24]

A famous portrait of Malraux surrounded by photographs for the book *Les Voix du Silence* (1951) captures how photographic reproductions impact the consumption of art by facilitating the easy selection, combination, and pairing of images from across time and space. A coffee-table book is based on the fact that photographs facilitate pleasurable absorption rather than serious contemplation (fig. 8).

Unlike Bayer, Nelson, and Malraux, who seemed to have enthusiastically celebrated the new medium in the belief that modern man could pass educated judgment and create unity out of an increasingly image-saturated world, Drexler was not so sure. Architectural culture proved the point: the architect had become a somewhat passive conduit through which these images funneled into publications and media, proliferating into new buildings without judgment or control. If a good copy was based on a careful study of an existing built work through site visits, plans, and sections, a bad copy was often taken from a single photographic image. The problem identified in Drexler's exhibition was that bad copies proliferate with greater speed and quantity, often going viral, and when they do there is no way of stopping them.

This state of affairs could indeed be put in biological terms: Modern architecture goes viral when human beings, whether architects or users, become reduced to hosts. Like all viruses, the one carrying the genetic code of Modern architecture functioned by multiplying itself. *Transformations in Modern Architecture* demonstrated how the visitor's eye wanders from quote to quote, tracing and subsequently multiplying the effect of the viral load. The ultimate paradox is that the exhibition *Transformations in Modern Architecture* functioned as both critique and symptom of the phenomenon: it critiqued how Modern architecture had gone viral while disseminating further copies, and copies of copies.

The main culprit in the scenario was the seemingly harmless bad copy. Here we are reminded that around the time the exhibition took place, the HIV epidemic took hold, spreading a disease that drugs cannot cure but only mitigate the symptoms. This is because the HIV virus mutates by making "imperfect" or bad copies of itself. The current drugs work by attacking what could be called a "bad copy" problem by directing the virus to make "good copies" of itself that are more easily targeted. Considering this culture-nature parallel, it is perhaps no accident that medical metaphors were commonly used at the time to describe the state of Modern architecture. Charles Jencks, who in *Modern Movements in Architecture* (1963) had declared the "death" of Modern architecture, later wrote that "the architectural medics" had since ascertained that the "patient [i.e., Modern architecture] was supposedly restored to good health. Modern architecture we were told was again alive and well."[25]

Yet as Drexler noted, proliferation of ideas does not always account for their success, certainly not in terms of quality, especially when it comes to architecture. Indeed while in some other fields ideas proliferate and then disappear (think of music), the problem with architecture is that buildings stay with us for a long time. They cannot only go viral but adversely affect the well-being of individuals, communities, and even the planet as a whole. Looking at rapidly proliferating megacities, it is hard not to consider the proliferation of bad buildings, often copies of copies, as pathological. Could architecture then learn from medicine and figure out a way to stop bad copies from happening? Could architects, like doctors, perhaps figure out an ideal point of intervention? One thing is certain: we have not yet found a cure for the condition identified by Drexler in *Transformations in Modern Architecture*, where quantity too often trumps quality.

1 Reyner Banham, "MoMA's Architectural Mystery Tour," *AIA Journal* (December 1980): 56.

2 Arthur Drexler, *Transformations in Modern Architecture* (New York: Museum of Modern Art, 1980), 12.

3 See Richard Dawkins, *The Selfish Gene* (Oxford: Oxford University Press, 1976).

4 MOMA_1979_0007_7. Museum of Modern Architecture document, https://www.moma.org/momaorg/shared/pdfs/docs/press_archives/5707/releases/MOMA_1979_0007_7.pdf?2010.

5 Drexler, *Transformations*, 3.

6 See Drexler, *Transformations*, 101. He refers to the review in *Architectural Forum* in the opening lecture. Sound recording of opening lecture for *Transformations*, held at MoMA on April 10, 1979. Document number 79.29.

7 "Response: Arthur Drexler on 'Transformations,'" *Skyline* (Summer 1979): 6.

8 Ibid., 12.

9 Sound recording of opening lecture held at MoMA on April 10, 1979. Document number 79.29.

10 *Transformations*, 102.

11 Ibid., 106.

12 Ibid., 110.

13 Harold Bloom, *The Anxiety of Influence: A Theory of Poetry* (London: Oxford University Press, 1973), xxiv.

14 *Transformations*, 9.

15 Bloom also uses the word *swerving* to describe how great poets deal with influence.

16 Eero Saarinen, "Saarinen," *Perspecta* 7 (1961): 30.

17 See Thomas H. Creighton, "The Sixties: A P/A Symposium on the State of Architecture," *Progressive Architecture* (April 1961): 122.

18 George Kubler, *The Shape of Time: Remarks on the History of Things* (New Haven, Connecticut: Yale University Press, 1962), 9.

19 Sound recording of opening lecture. Quoted by Felicity D. Scott in *Architecture and Techno-utopia. Politics after Modernism* (Cambridge, Massachusetts: MIT Press, 2007), 91.

20 Sound recording of opening lecture.

21 George Nelson, "Problems of Design: The Enlargement of Vision," *Interiors* 111 no. 4 (November 1951): 108. My discussion of Nelson's text and his contribution to contemporaneous exhibition culture is informed by Isabelle Moffat's "A Horror of Abstract Thought: Postwar Britain and Hamilton's 1951 'Growth and Form Exhibition'." *October* 94 (2000): 89–112.

22 See Jochen Eisenbrand, *George Nelson: Ein Designer im Kalten Krieg* (Zurich: Park Books, 2014) for further discussion about Nelson's design philosophy.

23 Malraux first wrote about the condition in his three-volume book *La Psychologie de l'Art* (1947–49), which was condensed into the book *Les Voix du silence* (1951).

24 André Malraux, *The Voices of Silence*, trans. Stuart Gilbert (Garden City, New York: Doubleday, 1953), 21.

25 Charles Jencks, *Late-Modern Architecture* (New York: Rizzoli, 1980), 6.

§

“Similarities among architectural works are typically cloaked in apologies... But why not an architectural theory of sameness?”

§ Amanda Reeser Lawrence

Spin-Offs: The V.C Morris Shop and Self-Reflexivity in the Work of Frank Lloyd Wright

Interior Ramp, V.C. Morris Gift Shop, 1948.
Photograph by Julius Shulman, 1951.

1 V.C. Morris Gift Shop, 1948, San Francisco, CA.

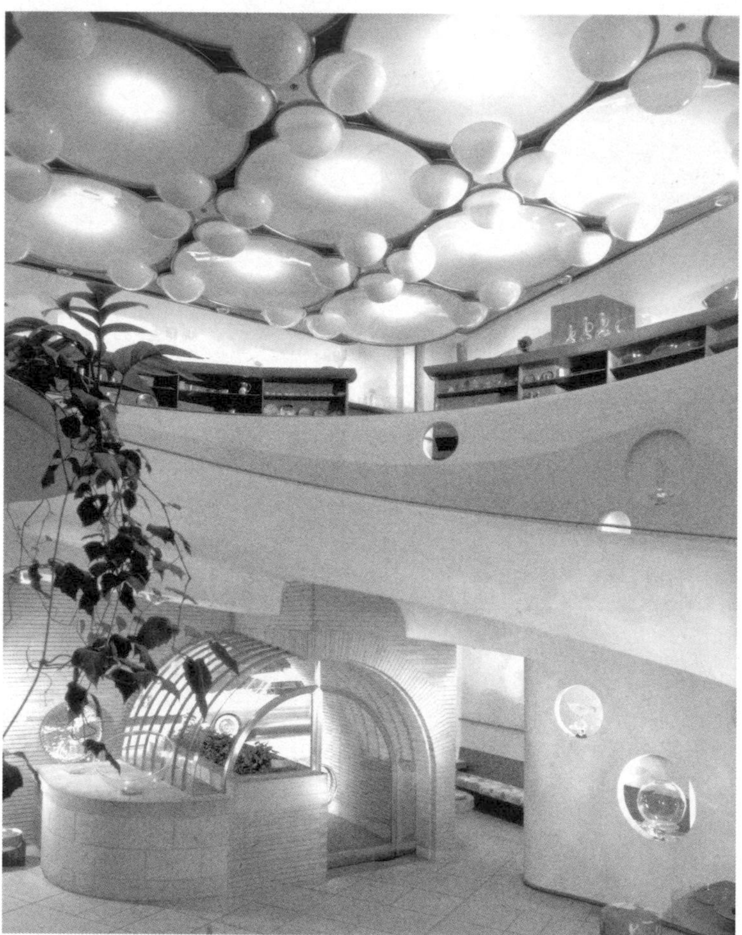

2 Interior, V.C. Morris Gift Shop, 1948. Photograph by Julius Shulman, 1951.

When Frank Lloyd Wright's V.C. Morris Gift Shop opened in 1949, the modest retail space was received as a compelling, if somewhat perplexing, project from "America's greatest architectural asset."[1] Located on a quaint side street off San Francisco's Union Square, its full-story brick facade, broken only by an arched opening, defied retail conventions prescribing glass window fronts (fig. 1).[2] Once beyond the rather foreboding facade, the prospective buyer was led through a short tunnel, with a barrel vaulted, half-glass and half-brick ceiling, and into a large central space lit from above through a panelized acrylic ceiling (figs. 2, 3). This space was wrapped by a spiraling ramp, which began a few feet to the right of the entrance and then ascended at a steep incline to the second floor mezzanine, with a continuous display of glass, silver, linens, and china along its outer edge (fig. 4).

The spiraling ramp was singled out as the most dramatic and remarkable element of the project, creating a sense of dynamism that pervaded the shop. As Arthur Drexler wrote in the catalogue for the 1952 MoMA exhibition, *Built in USA: Post-War Architecture*, it "shapes the space like an eggbeater stirring liquid in a bowl."[3] Reviews of the shop highlighted the ramp's sweeping form, noting its unique ability to display retail wares as well as its connection to Wright's longstanding interest in organic architecture.[4] More than anything the ramp was singled out for its similarity to another of Wright's projects—The Modern Gallery, as it was known at the time, which would eventually be named the Solomon R. Guggenheim Museum in New York. Although the Guggenheim wouldn't be built for another decade, its design had begun in 1943, and the interior spiral ramp within the "inverted ziggurat" was well known through publications and exhibitions (figs. 5, 6).[5]

Nearly all scholarship on the Morris shop, both at the time of its completion and more recently, falls back on its relationship to the Guggenheim.[6] In 1950 Elizabeth Mock is quoted describing the Morris shop as "an autobiographical sketch of its architect," including "the spiral ramp of the museum for New York."[7] Although Henry-Russell Hitchcock and Arthur Drexler include the Morris shop in their *Built in U.S.A.* exhibition, describing it as a "major building of Wright's" with "astonishing" "spatial effects," they too foreground its relationship to the museum: "The Morris store also gives us some hints of the effects Wright will obtain with the spiraling ramp and glass dome of his project for the Museum of Non-Objective Art."[8] A 1983 article in *Progressive Architecture* claims that the Morris shop is "famous chiefly as a forerunner of the Guggenheim Museum."[9] And in a 2009 essay Joseph M. Siry discusses the store—along with a number of other Wright projects—as "clearly looking ahead" to the Guggenheim.[10] Mark Anthony Wilson states the connection most forcefully in his book *Frank Lloyd Wright on the West Coast*: "there is no doubt that the Morris Shop served as a working prototype for the Guggenheim Museum; a trial run done on a much smaller scale."[11] These scholarly assessments inform popular ones as well; a recent Wikipedia entry on the Morris shop describes it as a "physical prototype, or proof of concept, for the circular ramp at the Solomon R. Guggenheim Museum."[12]

3 Interior, V.C. Morris Gift Shop, 1948. Photograph by Julius Shulman, 1951.

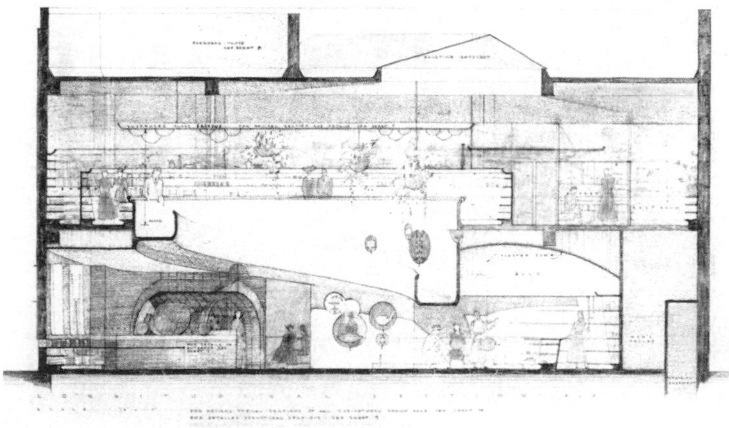

4 Section, V.C. Morris Gift Shop, 1948.

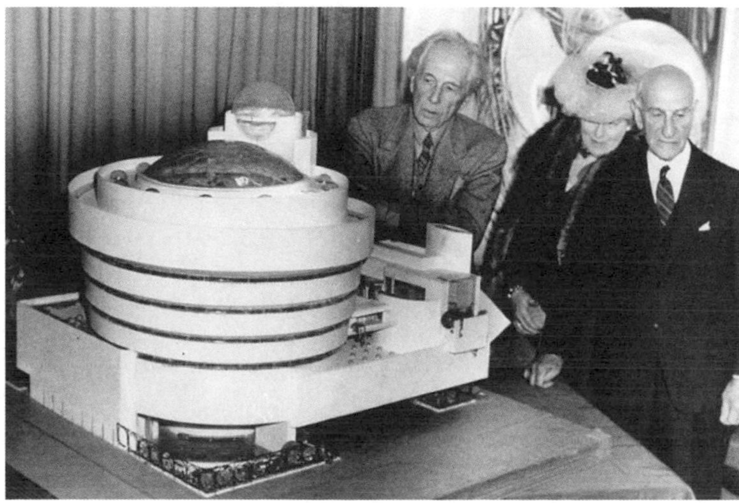

5 Frank Lloyd Wright, Baroness Hilla Rebay, and Solomon R. Guggenheim, 1945.

It would seem that the Morris shop exists solely in the shadow of the Guggenheim—a stepping stone on the way to the fully-formed glory of its more outsized relative. This presumption, however, elides what was in fact a complex sequence of design development. The overlapping chronology of the two projects obfuscates a clear demarcation of first and second positions—with the Morris shop both before (in terms of execution) and after (in terms of design). Asking which project is the original is both unanswerable and unproductive. At the very least something is surely learned from the Morris shop on the way to the Guggenheim, particularly given the myriad modifications and changes made to the Guggenheim design from the first version in 1943 to the completed building in 1959. Moreover the presumption of a linear design development, with the Morris shop as a "trial run" en route to the Guggenheim, at once precludes consideration of the store on its own terms and paradoxically prevents a more careful study of what exactly is shared between the two works.

Rather than attempting to locate a first and second, or a major and minor, this essay considers the Morris shop in conversation with the Guggenheim as well as other Wright projects as a launching point for an inquiry into architectural self-reflexivity. Similarities among an architect's works are typically cloaked in apologies, excused as unfortunate and/or necessary expedients, with the real analytical emphasis placed on the differences. But why not an architectural analysis of sameness? Studying similar examples from a single architect evades questions of plagiarism, at least in any legally binding sense (a point to which I return later in the essay), but it does not necessarily make the terms of evaluation any easier. Are resemblances among works intentional, or perhaps the unconscious results of an inadvertent signature? Do shared ideas within an architect's body of work reference one another, or earlier works, or other broader, more universal ideas? Does an architect's purported "genius," or their own admission of influences, impact our willingness (or reluctance) to see consistent motifs and repetitive gestures within their work? These questions remain largely unanswered, if not unasked, because aspirational originality remains a defining aspect of Modernism, and originality is still seen as antithetical to any form of reference or explicit relationship to the past, whether recent or remote, even if that past is an architect's own oeuvre.

My argument is that the core of Wright's inventiveness lay in his ability to reuse ideas and to rework and revise motifs through different projects and contexts. In considering acts of self-reflexivity in Wright's work, my aim is to expand the discursive possibilities for considering influence in architecture more broadly, and offer new ways of understanding the productive capacity of precedent. Thus this article tackles a largely unexplored, if not taboo, subject within architectural discourse that has taken on increasing urgency as questions of architectural plagiarism, the codification of architectural copyright laws, and a broader cultural shift toward sharing and reference all challenge long-held disciplinary notions about copies and originals.[13]

Spirals, Circles, and Other Sources

By most accounts there are six spiral buildings in Wright's oeuvre.[14] The first is the Gordon Strong Automobile Objective (1924–25), on Sugarloaf Mountain, Maryland. The conical building, which conceals a hemispherical dome and planetarium on its interior, is placed at the apex of the mountain; a double spiraling vehicular ramp on the exterior leads cars up and down the mountaintop (fig. 7). Over two decades passed before the spiral motif appeared again in the late 1940s, at which point there was a preponderance of spiraling forms in Wright's work. The Pittsburgh Point Park Civic Center (1947) and the Self-Service Garage for Pittsburgh (1949), both designed for Edgar J. Kaufmann, are large circular structures built of reinforced concrete with spiraling exterior automobile ramps (figs. 8, 9).[15] Neither was built. The remaining three spiral structures are the Guggenheim, the V. C. Morris Shop, and a house for Wright's youngest son, David, in Phoenix (1950–52) (fig. 10), all of which serve pedestrians, not cars, on their ramps. In the latter there are two spiral ramps: one wraps the exterior of the house and leads from the landscape to the elevated living space; a second, smaller spiral ramp encloses a circular kitchen tower and leads to the roof terrace.[16] An important seventh example, less frequently cited yet perhaps the most resonant with the Morris shop, is the Jaguar Showroom, designed for Max Hoffmann in New York (1954–55), in which a ramp similar in scale to the one in the Morris shop, also rising a single story, allows prospective buyers to move up and around the display of cars, which spin on a rotating platform at the center of the space (fig. 11).

In his 1993 assessment of Wright's Guggenheim and a broader discussion of his interest in the spiral, Jack Quinan writes: "All of the spirals, except the Gordon Strong, were created during the sixteen-year period that Wright worked on the Guggenheim and may be regarded as spin-offs from it."[17] Although Quinan dismisses the Gordon Strong project, we could certainly consider the Guggenheim (as well as the Morris shop) as a spin-off from Gordon Strong. Their differences, however, are numerous and consequential. Unlike the spiral at Gordon Strong, which was exterior to the building and diminished as it ascended (as in Pittsburgh Point) the Guggenheim spiral was inboard of the structure, and widened as it rose, an inversion of from the pyramidal ziggurat form at Gordon Strong.[18] If we consider the Guggenheim as Wright's first use of this interior ramp, the Morris shop (along with the Jaguar showroom) is indeed a "spin-off" of the Guggenheim. But here too the differences between the two spirals are significant: the Morris ramp rises a single story, the Guggenheim's ascends seven; the Morris ramp is circular, the Guggenheim's is spiral; the ramps at the Guggenheim and the Morris shop are made of different materials and deploy different structural systems; in the shop, movement was intended to begin to the right of the entrance and move upward, in contrast to the downward drift at the Guggenheim.

Going further, we might question the insistent focus on the spiral as the only or even the most significant point of similarity

6 Museum for the Solomon R. Guggenheim Foundation, The Modern Gallery, 1945.

7 Gordon Strong Automobile Objective, 1924–25, Sugarloaf Mountain, MD.

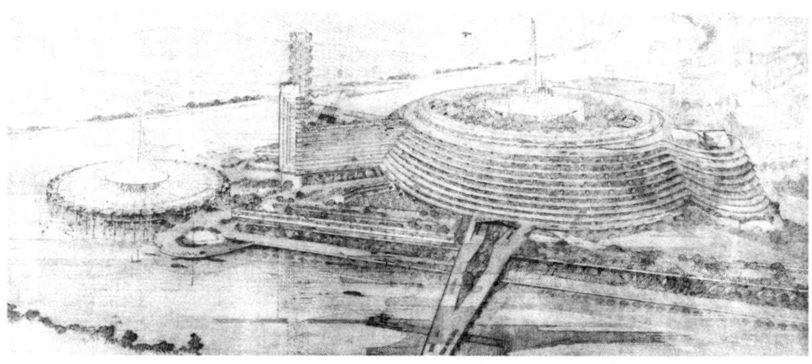

8 Civic Center at Point Park for the Allegheny Conference, 1947, Pittsburgh, PA.

9 Self Service Garage for Edgar J. Kaufmann, 1949, Pittsburgh, PA.

between the Morris shop and the Guggenheim. An arguably more striking resemblance between the Morris design of 1948 and the Guggenheim design of 1945 is the fact that both employ a pair of intersecting circles—one large and one small—as the dominant plan figure (figs. 12, 13).[19] In the Morris ground floor plan, the larger circle defines the ramp, the smaller delineates the rear display space. In the 1945 Guggenheim plan, the larger circle also defines the ramp (which at this point sits at the north end of the site), while the smaller circle, which contains a second ramp around its perimeter, serves as a lobby and information area, with a semicircular elevator tower at its center.[20]

As with the spiral, this intersecting circle motif tracks broadly across Wright's work at this time. An important example is the little-known Glen McCord house, whose plan is emphatically, even simplistically, rendered as a major/minor circle pairing (fig. 14). The plan of the second Jacobs House, built in 1948, also comprises a larger circle (though only a segment) with a smaller circle inset into the perimeter wall (fig. 15). We could expand this intersecting-circle plan family to include the Ralph Jester (Martin Pence) project (1938–40), comprised of a series of segmented circles, as well as the initial Morris house scheme, a tower of telescoping circles that culminates in the circular house itself, and its later version, which was redesigned for a lower area on the site and is also controlled by intersecting circles (fig. 16).[21]

Indeed circles were everywhere in Wright's work at the time, and they are everywhere in the Morris shop, "developed in endless variation"—from organizing plan gestures to ornamental tropes.[22] The display niches carved out of the curved plaster walls along the ramp are all variations on a circle: half-circles; full circles; some at eye level, others lower; some vertically aligned like bubbles rising from the surface; others individually floating and randomly positioned. At times a shelf protrudes—shaped as a segment of a circle. A planter suspended from the midpoint of the ramp is also a circle. The display table at the center of the space is a semi-circle. The ceiling is composed of a five-by-five grid of acrylic panels; at the center of each panel is a flat white plastic circle, with four smaller convex circles at its corners.

But circles and spirals aren't the only means through which to look for sources for the Morris shop. If we consider the shop through a different lens, as Robert Venturi does in *Complexity and Contradiction in Architecture*, the spiral form gives way to "strong contradictions between the inside and the outside—between the particular, private and the general, public functions," making it a rare example of a "traditional urban building," particularly for Wright, the "urbanophobe."[23] Venturi's precedents for the Morris shop are not the Guggenheim or other spiral-formed buildings, but pre-modern works such as baroque churches. On Venturi's terms, the Guggenheim, with an exterior volume that maps directly onto its interior plan, stands as the architectural opposite of the Morris shop, in which the spiral ramp is stuffed inside a rigid box.

These competing interpretations expose the complexity and, ultimately, the paucity of intellectual framing of the architectural precedent. Proof is elusive. Historians search for antecedents,

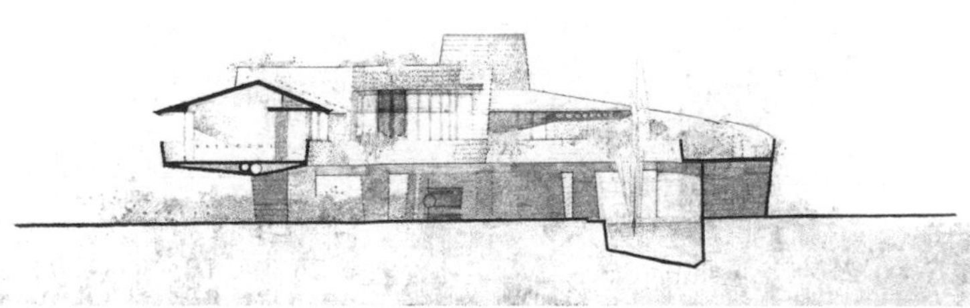

10 Section and Elevation, David Wright House, 1950–52, Phoenix, AZ.

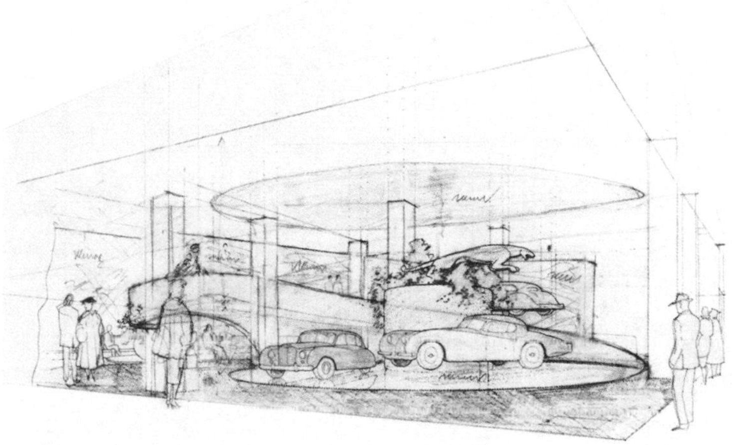

11 Hoffman Display Room for Jaguar, 1954–55, New York, NY.

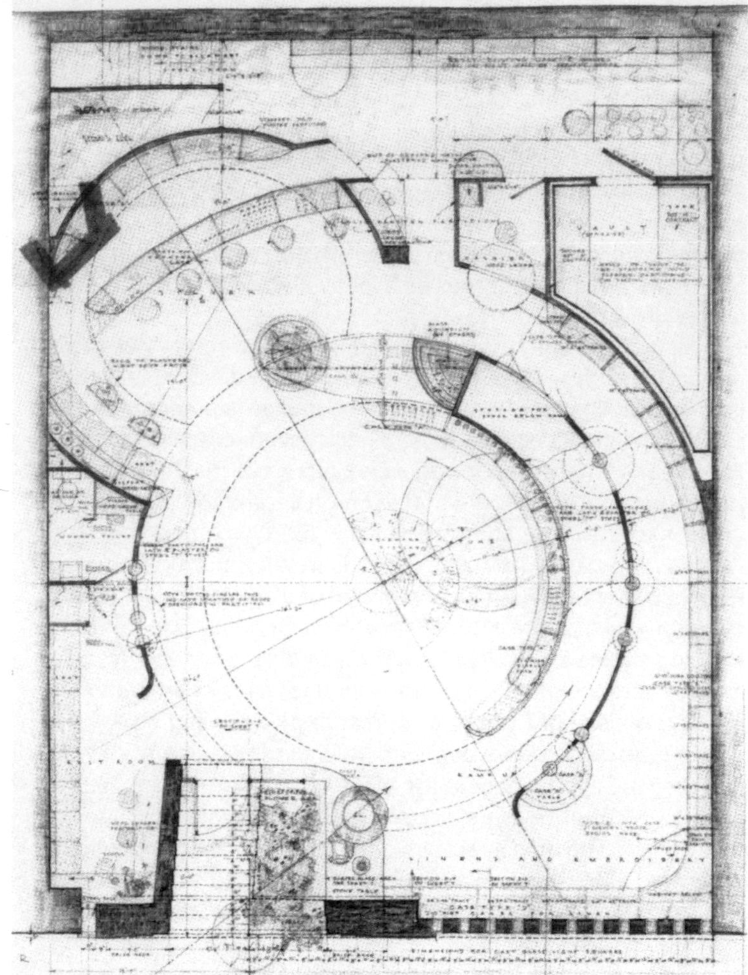

12 Ground Floor Plan, V.C. Morris Gift Shop, 1948.

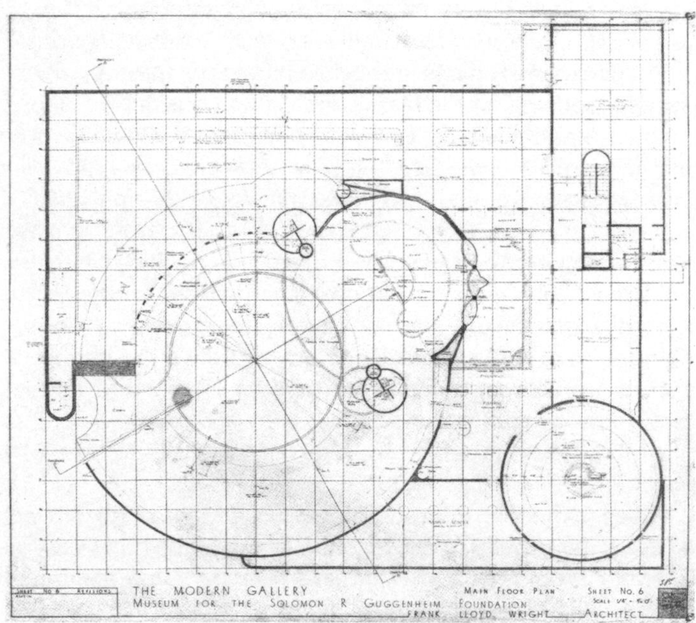

13 Plan, Museum for the Solomon R. Guggenheim Foundation, The Modern Gallery, 1945.

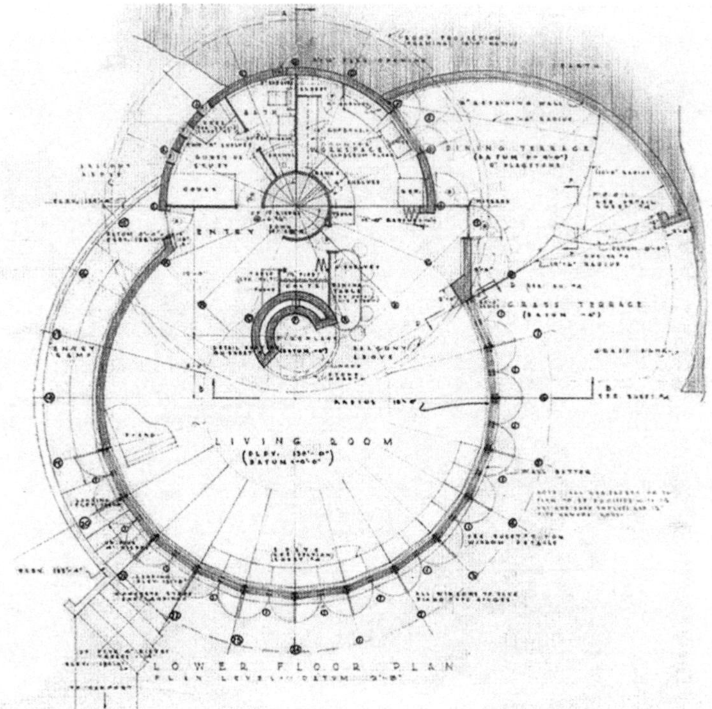

14 Glen McCord House, 1948, North Arlington, NJ.

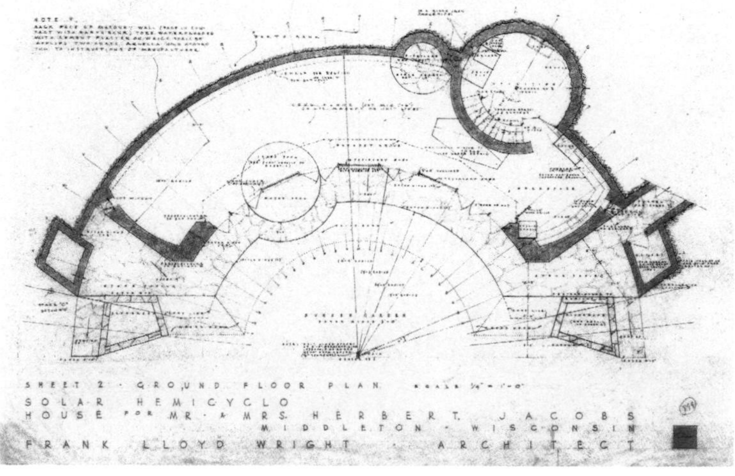

15 Plan, Herbert Jacobs House 2, the "Solar Hemicycle," 1948, Middleton, WI.

eager to demonstrate superior knowledge, to construct a specific historical narrative or advocate a particularly sensibility. The discovery of precedent is often an after-the-fact game, and is typically based on formal echoes. This search for similarity is typically framed with just enough difference to legitimize the later project. Moreover, this methodology largely sidesteps the question of architectural agency or intentionality. To what degree should an architect's own admission of sources (or lack thereof) contribute to the analysis of precedent and quotation within their work?

Beyond Influence?

Few architects so vehemently denied influence in any form as Wright did. "To cut ambiguity short: there never was exterior influence upon my work, either foreign or native, other than that of Lieber Meister, Dankmar Adler, and John Roebling, Whitman and Emerson, and the great poets worldwide," he wrote. "My work is original not only in fact but in spiritual fiber. No practice by any European architect to this day has influenced mine in the least. As for the Incas, the Mayas, even the Japanese—all were to me but splendid confirmation."[24] Vincent Scully writes that unlike Le Corbusier, who freely admitted influence, "Wright consistently refused to acknowledge that fact. His refusal to do so was partly based upon his own tragic need, which was to keep the romantic myth of the artist as isolated creator and superman alive in himself."[25] Ada Louise Huxtable notes, "The denial of any sources of influences other than his own ideas was one of his most assiduously practiced deceptions."[26]

And yet, while Wright so forcefully denied "exterior influence" on his work, he was quick to note the exceptions—in the quote above, he lists his former employers and mentor, an engineer, and two poets as "exterior influences" on his work. The remark seems baldly paradoxical; he claims to have no influences, then immediately lists a number of them. It is less contradictory, however, if we understand his listing of influences as a form of self-legitimization; he is asserting his own mastery through association with these established figures. Importantly he cites the influence of individuals, not specific projects. In this way he avoids the perceived instrumentalization of forms or even ideas, instead asserting himself as an equal.[27] I would suggest that this takes an even more forceful guise when he suggests that not just well-known individuals but entire cultures—the Incas, Mayas, and so on—"confirmed" his own discoveries. His architecture is equated with the artistic output of entire civilizations.

The mythification of Wright as a genius, both in his own terms and by subsequent historians, has profoundly affected the reading of influence in his work. Specifically it leads to an insistence on his use of universal ideas rather than his incorporation of any particular project or even the influence of a specific figure. In discussing Wright's use of the spiral, for example, historians often approach it as a mystical, foundational element—something that precedes a particular instantiation, what Kahn might have called "pre-form." Quinan argues that Wright's use of the spiral reflected his Unitarian and Transcendentalist beliefs, defining Transcendentalism as "current or energy which passes through and unifies all things in nature" and claiming that scholars "hold that the path of this current is a spiral."[28] He goes on to assert, "While Wright is nowhere explicit about what he derived from Emerson, it is difficult to imagine that the essential spiral that constituted the 'heart of his [Emerson's] aesthetic' was not imbedded in Wright's psyche at an early age, only to emerge as the crowning statement of his architecture at the end of his career in the form of the Guggenheim Museum."[29] He further discusses Wright's interest and "late exploration of geometry" as a proof of his "powerfully overdetermined" attraction to the spiral. In short, the spiral "is a transcendent form, and furthermore, the spiral can serve as a symbol of transcendency."[30] In Scully's brief analysis of the spiral in Wright's work, in which he includes the Morris shop and the David Wright house as well as the Guggenheim, he too focuses on a transcendental sensibility: "Here it was purely these mystical drives which formed the design ... like the pulsing sanctuary of a primitive cult drumming on Fifth Avenue."[31] David Watkin links Wright's use of the spiral to whirlwinds, the solar system and Milky Way, and the double helix of DNA.[32] In these characterizations, Wright is no longer merely a romantic figure or even a genius, but a deity.

But what if we consider Wright's use of the spiral or the circle not as a meditation on deeper spirituality or a testament to his Transcendentalist beliefs, but rather as a motif, something that allowed him to work more efficiently? What if we acknowledge Wright's use of precedent more broadly as constitutive of his work? What if Wright is "America's greatest architectural asset" not because each project is wholly and divinely original but because each is, to some degree, derivative? And not just derivative of any architectural works, but of his *own* projects?

A Legal Framework: Relevance and Precedent

Let us presume that the Morris shop was designed by someone other than Wright—Architect A—and that the Guggenheim was designed by another person—Architect B—in exactly the same form and at more or less the same time. Would we consider the Morris shop inappropriately similar to the Guggenheim? Going a bit farther, could Architect B sue Architect A for copyright infringement?

One of the few law review articles to tackle the question of architectural copyright asks precisely this question. In "Architecture and Copyright: Separating the Poetic from the Prosaic," Raleigh W. Newsam II writes: "The dispositive inquiry is whether his borrowing went so far as to constitute improper appropriation."[33] Newsam's article outlines the 1990 Architectural Copyright Works Protection Act (ACWPA), which was the first time in American history that constructed architectural buildings (as opposed to plans) were afforded copyright protection.[34] Architecture, he writes repeatedly, is a mix of "art and science," but ironically it was the "utilitarian" aspect that historically prevented architects—unlike artists or scientists—from traditional forms of copyright protection. The exceptions were building plans and albeit on a much smaller scale, the architect's handling of the two spiral ramps shows enough of a difference to militate against a finding of substantial similarity. Although the Morris Gift Shop architect may arguably have copied the spiral ramp concept from the Guggenheim, the dispositive inquiry is whether his borrowing went so far as to constitute improper appropriation. On these points, it would not seem that the original work was injured in proportion to the appropriation. Rather, the Morris Gift Shop architect arguably made effective use of the basic parti and several of other design ideas from the Guggenheim, but not to the extent that the latter was in any way diminished.[35]

16 V.C. Morris House, Scheme 1, 1945, San Francisco, CA.

drawings, which were seen as "writings" of the architect as author and as having a "scientific or technical character." The 1990 ACWPA legislation extended the definition of copyrightable architecture beyond the plans to any "tangible" expression of building, including drawings or the building itself.

Newsam's article acknowledges the challenge of separating the artistic from the utilitarian in architecture—a division that has proven as perplexing to the courts as it has intellectually challenging for architectural academics. His answer is to focus on the design process. This is in contrast to court cases in which substantial similarity between buildings was subject to the *ordinary observer* test: would an ordinary person think two buildings were substantially similar?

Newsam's argument focuses primarily on the common parti between the Guggenheim and the Morris shop—a central space wrapped by a ramp, where circulation and use are coincident; in other words, the ramp is the museum (or shop, in the case of the Morris). He concludes that the basic ideas of the Guggenheim, the "quantum or architectural expression"—including the spiraling ramp, its exterior helix form, and the skylighted dome—are all too general to be protected. By contrast, the elements that reflect "refinement" of this general idea of the ramp—the sloping exhibition wall, the slit of the skylight—are aspects that might warrant protection. And since these elements are not shared by the Morris and Guggenheim, he concludes that there would be no hypothetical case:

While the lay observer might reasonably conclude that the Morris Gift Shop has the "look and feel" of the Guggenheim,

Because Newsam's article looks only at the Morris shop as an allegedly improper appropriation of the Guggenheim parti, it doesn't tackle the myriad spiral or circular projects that have been discussed, nor does it consider the fact that the Guggenheim wasn't completed for another decade and underwent multiple design changes following the construction of the Morris shop. We could, for example, conceivably investigate whether the later Guggenheim designs derived ideas from the Morris shop. Could Architect A now sue Architect B for inappropriately borrowing "refinements" developed at the Morris shop in later designs for the Guggenheim?

The spiral, Newsam concludes, is too general an idea to be protected by architectural copyright—it passes the ordinary observer and commonsense tests as well. And yet the spiral as a highly specific architectural concept is precisely what allows us to link a series of Wright's projects together under a common theme. There would seem to be little value, for example, in discussing a Wright project with a rectangular plan as a "spin-off" of another Wright project—the notion of a rectangular building seems too commonplace, too "utilitarian." But is the spiral any less utilitarian than the box? The owners of the Morris shop described Wright's use of the spiral as "the easiest shape to negotiate."[36] In describing Wright's use of the spiral in the Self-Service Garage in Pittsburgh, Bruce Pfeiffer suggests that it was a logical solution: "Here the spiral is at its utmost utility; no other form or shape could have possibly solved the problem as well as it did."[37]

At the core of the dilemma is a question that Newsam doesn't address: What constitutes an architectural precedent? In his insightful writings on architecture and law, Peter Collins compares architectural precedents, which are formally defined and historically fixed, to legal precedents, which are based on rational and applicable methods, and remain valid only insofar as they are relevant.[38] A legal precedent is recalled for its continued validity; otherwise it is "mere" history. By contrast, an architectural precedent is typically considered as a singular and mute historical object, one that needs to be remade and updated by a later architect, and is recalled purely for its visual characteristics. And, of course, architectural precedents aren't binding. They are referenced only to the extent that an architect can establish a new context, use, or meaning for the past work.

Collins questions architects' reliance on formal similarity when considering precedents. I would argue, however, that his concept of relevance could be extended to formal solutions as well, insofar as they might be the most "rational" or "applicable" ideas, as Pfeiffer argues with Wright's spiraling ramp in Pittsburgh. More importantly, Collins's study suggests the possibility that architectural precedent could be considered as a productive tool rather than a fixed form, a means to identify past solutions that remain relevant today. In this way Wright's spiral buildings offer a proof of the validity and continued relevance of the form to solve myriad architectural problems across program types—a parking garage, a store, a museum. Rather than seeing these works as improper appropriations of one another, or looking to any particular source, or original, we can instead frame their sameness as proof of their continued relevance. Wright deploys his past discoveries as the basis for new solutions.

Positional Games

> In a large sense, one would say there is no pure originality. All minds quote. Old and new make the warp and woof of every moment. There is no thread that is not a twist of these two strands. By necessity, by proclivity, and by delight, we all quote. We quote not only books and proverbs, but arts, sciences, religion, customs, and laws; nay, we quote temples and houses, tables and chairs by imitation.
> —Ralph Waldo Emerson, "Quotation and Originality"

In "The Tyranny of the Skyscraper," one of his talks delivered at Princeton as part of *Modern Architecture: Being the Kahn Lectures for 1930*, Wright laments the continuing influence of Michelangelo's "first skyscraper," St. Peter's Basilica, in which he "hurled the Pantheon on top of the Parthenon." It wasn't so much the design itself to which he objected, but the fact that every state capital has since desired a dome on top to mark its significance. "From general to particular the imitation proceeds..."[39] In "Genius and Mobocracy," Wright recounts Louis Sullivan saying to him, "Frank, you have never been my disciple—but you are the only one who ever worked with me who understood. I couldn't do what you've done, nor could you have done what you've done but for me!"[40] He goes on to explain Sullivan's words: "He meant that though inspired by him I had not copied his work. I have never imitated him or anyone. He was great enough to be proud of me because I wasn't his disciple."[41] Whether or not we can locate Wright's imitations of Sullivan (and most surely we can) Wright's denial of copying, his distaste for imitation, and his acceptance of "inspiration" are all telling statements on modern architecture and its relationship to its past, and more specifically, the mechanisms through which that past might be acceptably reimagined or reused.

This debate around imitation and originality in architecture has more recently extended into the legal realm of protection with the passing of the AWCPA in 1990. Copyright is designed to protect creativity: the underlying notion is that no one will make original things if they fear that anyone can copy them without repercussion. But this focuses on difference alone as a marker for creativity, and on the presumption of a "genius" who creates novelty from past ideas, using "refinement" to establish distinctiveness. The model also presumes a linear model, which tracks ideas only from the past to the present. This model of influence, with its linearity and causality, precludes a study of more complex relationships between past and present. Moreover, it never allows that the present inevitably influences the past as well, reorienting our sense of what is valued and worth imitating, aligning certain works with others, or creating divisions or categorizations that allow us to see shared characteristics.

In his brief but powerful text "Excursus against Influence" Michael Baxandall challenges this conception of influence, which presumes a one-way movement of ideas from past to present.[42] Instead he offers the metaphor of a billiard table with many balls and no pockets; a game in which the strike of the cue ball—the creative act—reconfigures the other balls on the table, both in reference to each other and to the ball that was struck. "Arts are a positional game, and each time an artist is influenced he rewrites his arts history a little."[43]

Wright's V. C. Morris Shop is not simply a forerunner, prototype, or trial run any more than the Guggenheim is an original or a copy. Both projects feature a spiral ramp, an element that Wright quotes and requotes in his work beginning in the 1920s and continuing through the '50s. Wright's self-quotation demonstrates not only the relevance of the ramp as a generic notion but also the persistent reconfiguration—or what Baxandall would term "rearrangement"—of disciplinary history that occurs with each act of reference. Precisely because it isn't measured in terms of "improper appropriation," self-quotation highlights the broader axiom that the act of reference is at the core of architectural creation. In the words of Emerson, whom Wright includes among his acknowledged influences: "It is as difficult to appropriate the thoughts of others as it is to invent."[44] To Emerson's pithy remark I would add that it is equally difficult, and inventive, to appropriate one's own thoughts again and again.

Research for this article was supported by a Faculty Research and Creative Activity Incentive Grant from the College of Arts, Media and Design at Northeastern University. I thank Xavier Costa, George Thrush, and Jane Amidon for their support. I also thank the staff at the Avery Drawings & Archives at Columbia University. I am grateful to Neil Levine for reviewing a draft of this essay and for his thoughtful and thorough commentary.

1 Edgar Kaufmann Jr., "Three New Buildings on the Pacific Coast," *Architects Yearbook* 4 (1953): 55.

2 See "The New Curiosity Shop," *Architects Journal* 110 (10 November 1949): 512. Neil Levine argues that Wright's façade was a critique of the 'open front' store that typified modern retail design. Neil Levine, *The Architecture of Frank Lloyd Wright* (Princeton, NY: Princeton University Press, 1996), 370.

3 Arthur Drexler, *Built in USA: Post-War Architecture* (New York: Museum of Modern Art, 1952), 30. Drexler includes the Morris shop as one of only three of Wright's projects. The other two are the Johnson Wax Headquarters and the still-unbuilt Museum of Non-Objective Art in New York.

4 In addition to the *Architects Journal* and *Architects Yearbook* articles previously cited, the Morris shop was published as "China and Gift Shop by Frank Lloyd Wright for V.C. Morris, Maiden Lane, San Francisco, California," *Architectural Forum* 92 (February 1950): 79–85 and Edgar Kaufmann Jr. "Wright Setting for Decorate Art," *Art News* 48 (February 1950): 42–44.

5 See "Keeping Faith with an Idea: A Time Line of the Guggenheim Museum, 1943–59," in *The Guggenheim: Frank Lloyd Wright and the Making of the Modern Museum* (New York: Guggenheim Publications, 2009), esp. 144–157. Although Wright considered a hexagonal plan for the earliest schemes, by September 1943 the spiral shape predominated. The press was first shown the spiral model and design in 1945.

6 Levine is an exception; the Morris Shop launches his final chapter on Wright's post-war work. Levine, *The Architecture of Frank Lloyd Wright*, 365–374.

7 "China and Gift Shop by Frank Lloyd Wright," *Architectural Forum*, 82.

8 Arthur Drexler, *Built in USA: Post-War Architecture* (New York: Museum of Modern Art, 1952), 30. The Morris Shop is one of 43 buildings that they deemed "the most significant examples of modern architecture built in this country since 1945." The Museum of Modern Art Press Release 530 114-03, "'Built in U.S.A.: Post-War Architecture' to be Shown at Museum."

9 "Wright Restored: The V. C. Morris Store," *Progressive Architecture* 64 (1983): 40

10 Joseph Siry, "Wright's Guggenheim Museum and Later Modernist Architecture," in *The Guggenheim: Frank Lloyd Wright and the Making of the Modern Museum*, 44.

11 Mark Anthony Wilson, *Frank Lloyd Wright on the West Coast* (Utah: Gibbs Smith, 2014), 167.

12 "V.C. Morris Gift Shop," https://en.wikipedia.org/wiki/V._C._Morris_Gift_Shop, accessed June 19, 2015. See also Allison Meier, "Frank Lloyd Wright's West Coast Experiment: Ramping Up to the Guggenheim," accessed June 19, 2015, http://hyperallergic.com/185312/frank-lloyd-wrights-west-coast-experiment-ramping-up-to-the-guggenheim/.

13 An issue of *Perspecta* dedicated to the quote is certainly one reflection of this shift. For a more thorough discussion of the "crisis" around architectural replication, particularly as it relates to architectural pedagogy, see my essay "Radical Acts of Influence: Thoughts on Anxiety, History, and the Culture of the Copy," *Journal of Architectural Education* 69:1 (2015): 13–15. See also Ines Weizman, "Architectural Doppelgangers," *AA Files* 65 (2012): 19–20, 22–24; Wytold Rybczynski, "Architects Who Plagiarize," *Slate*, September 14, 2005; Bianca Bosker, *Original Copies: Architectural Mimicry in Contemporary China* (Honolulu: University of Hawaii Press, 2013).

14 Siry performs the most extensive analysis of Wright's spiral buildings, describing those listed above as well as precedents from other architects—including the spiral parking garages of Albert Kahn that Wright knew from the 1920s—and tracing the influence of Wright's spirals on later projects by Zaha Hadid, Frank Gehry, and Richard Meier. Siry, "Wright's Guggenheim Museum," passim.

15 The first of Wright's schemes for Pittsburgh Point featured a large circular building, nearly 175 feet high and a half mile in diameter, filled with civic programs including an opera house, stadium, planetarium, convention hall, and "Sky park," along with several smaller circular structures around the site, some of which also had traffic ramps around the exterior. In a second more "modest" scheme, the large circular building disappears but much of the circular geometry remains. See Richard Cleary, "Edgar J. Kaufmann, Frank Lloyd Wright, and the Pittsburgh Point Park Coney Island in Automobile Scale," *Journal of the Society of Architectural Historians* 52 (June 1993): 139–58.

16 See "Frank Lloyd Wright: His New Desert Home for his Son Is a Magnificent Coil of Concrete," *House and Home* (June 1953): 99–107.

17 Jack Quinan, "Frank Lloyd Wright's Guggenheim Museum: A Historian's Report," *Journal of the Society of Architectural Historians* 52 (December 1993): 477 n. 28.

18 For an extended discussion of this "logic of inversion" at the Guggenheim, see Levine, *The Architecture of Frank Lloyd Wright*, Chapter X, esp. 320–335.

19 Wright's fascination with the "seedpod" or "mandorla" shape, the space at the intersection of the two circles, became a fascination in its own right. In Wright's 1953 house for his son Robert Llewellyn Wright, the seedpod has grown and now subsumes the circle.

20 As the Guggenheim design evolved over the subsequent decade, the second smaller circle was effectively ejected, though its vestige remains in the convex balcony next to the elevator.

21 Frank Lloyd Wright was first contacted by Lillian and V. C. Morris in 1943 (the same year Hilla Rebay contacted Wright regarding the future Guggenheim.) The San Francisco couple hoped to build a house in the Sea Cliff neighborhood of San Francisco, just south of the Golden Gate Bridge overlooking the Pacific Ocean. In 1944 Lillian sent Wright confirmation of the purchase of two lots in Sea Cliff and arranged for a topographic map to be sent to Wright. A later design moved the house down closer to the water. Though the Morris house was never built, it led to the commission of the Morris shop.

22 "China and Gift Shop by Frank Lloyd Wright," *Architectural Forum*, 80.

23 Robert Venturi, *Complexity and Contradiction in Architecture*, 2nd ed. (New York, NY: The Museum of Modern Art in association with the Graham Foundation for Advanced studies in the Fine Arts, Chicago, 1977), 83–84.

24 Frank Lloyd Wright, "A Testament," in *The Essential Frank Lloyd Wright: Critical Writings on Architecture*, ed. Bruce Pfeiffer (Princeton, NJ: Princeton University Press, 2008), 17.

25 Vincent Scully, *Frank Lloyd Wright* (New York: George Braziller, 1960), 13.

26 Ada Louise Huxtable, *Frank Lloyd Wright* (New York: Lipper/Viking, 2004), xvi

27 We might also consider the possibility that his remark was intended to reorient our understanding of history through his work. Rather than understanding Wright as derivative of Roebling or Adler, we "re-see" Roebling and Adler through Wright.

28 Quinan, "Frank Lloyd Wright's Guggenheim," 470.

29 Ibid., 471.

30 Ibid., 474. He goes on to analyze Wright's own personality as analogous to the spiral: "For each of these reasons the spiral would have appealed to Wright, and in view of his deeply empathetic view of geometry it is very likely that Wright would have recognized something of himself in the eccentric, transcendent nature of the spiral." Quinan, "Frank Lloyd Wright's Guggenheim," 475.

31 Vincent Scully, *Frank Lloyd Wright,* 30.

32 Watkin argues that a 1958 presentation section drawing for the Guggenheim was intentionally misdrawn by Wright to suggest a double-helix form for the interior ramp. David Watkin, "Frank Lloyd Wright & The Guggenheim Museum," *AA Files* 21 (1991): 46.

33 Raleigh W. Newsam II, "Architecture and Copyright: Separating the Poetic from the Prosaic," *Tulane Law Review* 71. (1996–97): 1129.

34 Previous to this, Copyright Act of 1976 and the 1909 Copyright Act "gave virtually no protection to architectural structures, save for those few buildings which were purely monumental and served no utilitarian purpose, or where purely decorative elements could be conceptually severed from functional buildings." Newsam, "Architecture and Copyright," 1077–78.

35 Ibid., 1129.

36 "China and Gift Shop," 82.

37 Bruce Brooks Pfeiffer, *Treasure of Taliesin: Seventy-Seven Unbuilt Designs* (Portland, Oregon: Pomegranate Communications, 1999), 104.

38 Peter Collins, *Architectural Judgement* (London: Faber, 1971), 24.

39 Frank Lloyd Wright, "The Tyranny of the Skyscraper," in Bruce Pfeiffer, ed., *The Essential Frank Lloyd Wright: Critical Writings on Architecture* (Princeton, New Jersey: Princeton University Press, 2008), 198.

40 Wright, "Genius and the Mobocracy," 107.

41 Ibid.

42 Michael Baxandall, "Excursus against Influence," in *Patterns of Intention: On the Historical Explanation of Pictures* (New Haven and London: Yale University Press, 1985), 58–62.

43 Baxandall, "Excursus against Influence," 60.

44 Ralph Waldo Emerson, "Quotation and Originality," in *The Portable Emerson* (Viking Press, 1945), 295.

⌘

“The discipline of architecture is composed of, and multiplied by, constant projections onto its own archives.”

⌘ Ana Miljački

Project_Rorschach: On Architectural Memes and Self-Analysis

Once meticulously printed on a single antique press in Switzerland, the ten images of the contentious Rorschach test were sold only to licensed therapists. After expiring from copyright protection in the U.S., the test images are now available on Wikipedia for all to contemplate.[1] Invented by Herman Rorschach in 1921, such that they eschewed references to any culturally codified images, the test images have themselves become a meme in recent cultural production, with references appearing in music videos, commercials, art, and fashion. The cards were devised initially as a very specific diagnostic tool that invited the examinee's imagination to manifest itself in their methodically recorded interpretations of the blots. The test would eventually place over one million people somewhere on the psychogrammatic spectrum traversing between normalcy and pathology. Project_Rorschach remakes the test's ten cards as an invitation to see anew images of contemporary architectural tropes.[2]

In 1976, evolutionary biologist Richard Dawkins coined *meme* as a contemporary, biological notion of mimesis, offering "memes propagate themselves in the meme pool by leaping from brain to brain via a process which, in the broad sense can be called imitation."[3] Dawkins defined memes as ideas which repeat, transform, and vie for attention in the broad viscous medium of culture. The term has been eagerly appended to the similar ways in which material circulates on the internet, and Dawkins has in fact acknowledged the internet usage of the term *meme* as fairly correct.[4]

The idea that one's will and rationality become mere vehicles for the propagation of culture is directly opposed to the standard definitions of architectural authorship. From Alberti's use of orthographic projection to ensure the production of buildings that perfectly corresponded to his ideas, until perhaps this very moment, the architect has been conceptualized as the primary originator of ideas.[5] Theories of the architectural object as a cultural product are deeply historically and socially codified, yet the architect is still safely understood as a self-aware author. What architect, after all, would want to see themselves as a mere medium for channeling and transforming architectural memes?

Treating architectural tropes as memes begins to acknowledge the speed and the medium of their transmission. Architectural images presented in 72 dpi screen resolution, most often framed by Iwan Baan's camera lens, circulate on Archinect, Archdaily, Dezeen, Twitter, Pinterest, Instagram, and Facebook. The catchiness of a meme, whether it lives in the medium of a jingle, a rhyme, an image, or an architectural parti, may be its most fascinating aspect for a cultural critic. It is in this very space of fast enjoyment, imitation, transformation—of cultural evolution—that Project_Rorschach introduces some friction, or at least a wink and a nudge.

In Project_Rorschach, meant both as a commentary and a humorous diagnostic, ubiquitous images of architecture are grouped by memes and layered into ten revised Rorschach cards. No longer inkblots proper, but retaining the symmetry formerly constitutive of their process of figuration, these architectural Rorschach images are super-saturated compositions of chimneys, robotic bricks, cantilevers, house piles, hyper-towers, circles, phalluses, beany blobs, single surfaces, dia-grids and stacks. They are assembled precisely from the artifacts found in web archives and are allowed to operate in the low-res flatness that is their currency.

Although the inkblot revisions still might send the chance image signal, Project_Rorschach does not provide any means for authorial evaluation of the imaginations projected onto it. Instead, as an aesthetic intervention in its own right, it propels an open-ended string of interpretations of some of architecture's contemporary haunts. Its key and most hopeful offering is that nudge towards self-awareness of the collective disciplinary appeal of certain architectural tropes and the inertia with which they sweep the field. Relying on the Rorschach test's already existing cultural mystique, visual power, and tantalizing promise of evaluation, Project_Rorschach invites architectural self-analysis while simultaneously making visible the fact that the discipline of architecture is comprised of, and multiplied by, constant projections onto its own archives.

Project_Rorschach:
Ana Miljački and Lee Moreau (Project_)
with Sarah Hirschman

Team:
Oliver Wuttig, George Xinxin Lin, Alexander William Marshall, Andrew Manto, Clay Anderson, Sean Capone | The Supernature

1 See "Rorschach Test," https://en.wikipedia.org/wiki/Rorschach_test.

2 Project_Rorschach was produced for Design Biennial Boston 2013, curated by over,under at Boston Society of Architects Exhibition Space, from February to May 2013. We are grateful to the biennale jury and over,under for providing a perfect alibi for this project. Project_Rorschach was also exhibited at the Institute of Contemporary Art, Maine School of Art, Portland, from August to October 2014. The installation of the Project_Rorschach included: ten double-sided cards printed on a letter press; a tench (table-bench) produced in dialogue with Gerrit Rietveld's Z-chair; and chez-lounge whose function was to both deliver the cards and provide seating for the contemplation of a video projection of the slowly morphing Project_ Rorschach cards.

3 Richard Dawkins, *The Selfish Gene* (Oxford: The Oxford University Press, first 1976, 30th anniversary edition 2006), 192.

4 Olivia Solon, "Richard Dawkins on the internet's hijacking of the word 'meme'" *Wired*, June 20, 2013, http://www.wired.co.uk/news/archive/2013-06/20/richard-dawkins-memes.

5 Mario Carpo has discussed the way in which the contemporary processes of architectural production might be closest to the pre-Alberti and, thus pre-architect as draftsmen and author era. See Mario Carpo, *The Alphabet and the Algorithm* (Cambridge, MA: The MIT Press, 2011).

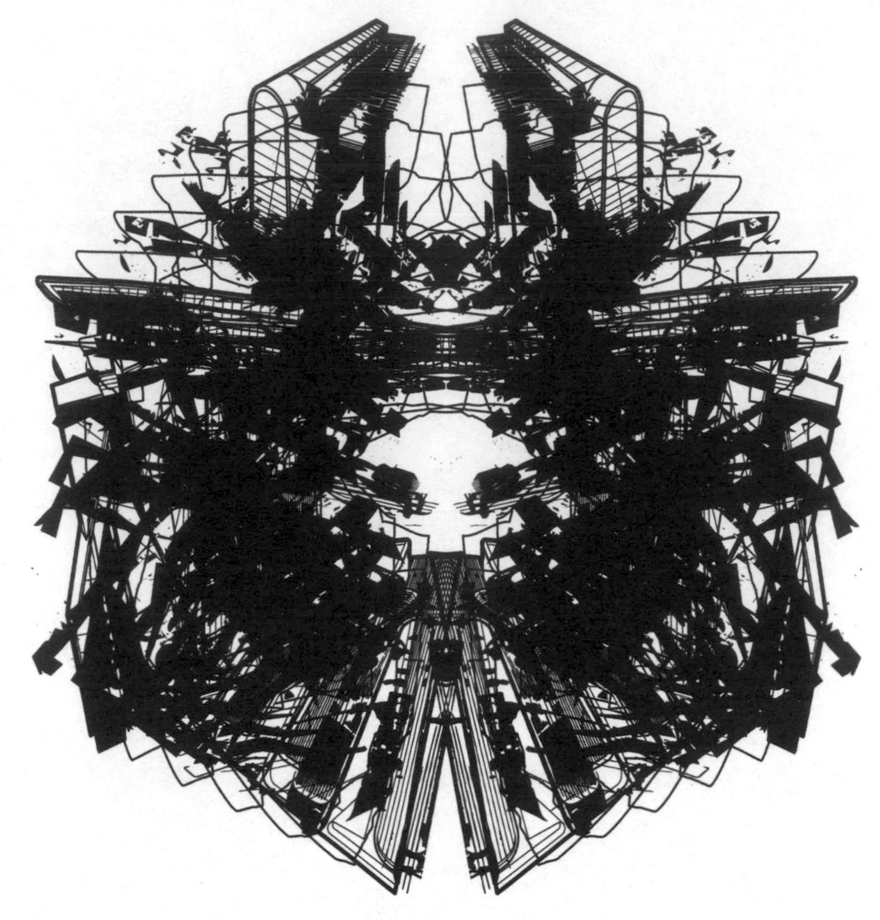

Card 10
pages 32–33

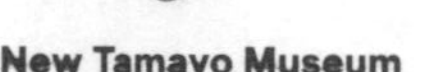

New Tamayo Museum
Rojkind Arquitectos and BIG, 2009, Mexico City, Mexico, www.archdaily.com/22625/new-tamayo-museum-rojkind-arquitectos-and-big/127257078_big-rojkind-tamayo-viz-exterior-2/

WoZoCo
MVRDV, 1997, Amsterdam, Netherlands, www.archdaily.com/115776/ad-classics-wozoco-mvrdv/

Utriai Residence
Architectural Bureau G. Natkevicius & Partners, 2006, Utriai, Vežaičiai, Klaipėda, Lithuania, www.archdaily.com/78438/utriai-residence-architectural-bureau-g-natkevicius-partners/

Hemeroscopium House
Ensamble Studio, 2008, Las Rozas, Madrid, Spain, www.archdaily.com/16598/hemeroscopium-house-ensamble-studio/

Guthrie Theater
Jean Nouvel, 2006, Minneapolis, MN, USA, www.nytimes.com/2008/03/31/arts/design/31prit.html

Card 2
page 34, top

Institute of Contemporary Art
Diller Scofidio + Renfro, 2009, Boston, MA, USA www.archinnovations.com/featured-projects/museums/diller-scofidio-renfro-institute-of-contemporary-art-boston/

Images and Audio Museum
Diller Scofidio + Renfro, 2009, Rio de Janeiro, Brazil, www.archdaily.com/31828/diller-scofidio-renfro-win-competition-for-the-new-image-and-audio-museum-in-rio-de-janiero/

M-Preis
Peter Lorenz Architekt + Partner, 2001, Telfs, Austria, archidose.org/wp/2004/06/14/m-preis/

Eyebeam
Diller Scofidio + Renfro, 2004, New York, NY, USA, www.arcspace.com/features/diller--scofidio--renfro/eyebeam/

Educatorium
OMA, 1997, Utrecht, Netherlands, www.architectureguide.nl/project/list_projects_of_architect/arc_id/804/prj_id/1021

Card 4
page 34, bottom

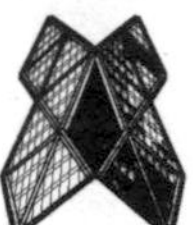

Hearst Tower
Foster and Partners, 2006, New York, NY, USA, www.archdaily.com/204701/flashback-hearst-tower-foster-and-partners/hearst10/

0-14
Reiser + Umemoto, 2010, Dubai, United Arab Emirates, www.archdaily.com/273404/o-14-reiser-umemoto/

Seattle Central Library
OMA + LMN, 2004, Seattle, WA, USA, www.archdaily.com/11651/seattle-central-library-oma-lmn/1162672709_seattle-central-library-fdoherrera-018/

Prada Store
Herzog and de Meuron, 2003, Aoyam, Tokyo, Japan, us.zinio.com/sitemap/ArtPhoto-magazines/El-Croquis/129-130-HERZOG de-MEURON-2002-2006/cat1960012/is-373646068/pg-208

Card 6
page 35, top

Graz Kunsthaus von Schlossberg
Peter Cook, 2003, Graz, Austria, www.archdaily.com/89408/bix-light-and-media-facade-at-moma/

Ordos Art & City Museum
MAD Architects, 2011, Ordos, Inner Mongolia, China, www.archdaily.com/211597/ordos-art-city-museum-mad-architects/

Galaxy Soho
Zaha Hadid Architects, 2012, Beijing, China, www.archdaily.com/287571/galaxy-soho-zaha-hadid-architects/

Meiquan 22nd Century
Zhang Xin (developer), 2012, Chongqing, China, www.dezeen.com/2013/01/02/zaha-hadid-building-pirated-in-china/

Residential Housing Tower
Contemporary Architecture Practice, 2004, Dubai, United Arab Emirates, www.amazon.com/Digital-Architecture-Now-Global-Emerging/dp/0500342474al-Emerging/dp/0500342474

Card 7
page 35, bottom

Doha Office Tower
Jean Nouvel, 2013, Doha, Qatar, www.dezeen.com/2007/04/25/jean-nouvel-in-doha/

30 St. Mary Axe
Norman Foster, 2003, London, UK, www.architizer.com/en-us/blog/dyn/3559/london-loves/#.UQR9ar80V8E

Zhengzhou Greenland Plaza
SOM, 2013, Zhengzhou, Henan, China, www.archdaily.com/319809/zhengzhou-greenland-plaza-skidmore-owings-merrill/50f81387b3fcb316d0001100_zengzhou-greenland-plaza-skidmore-owings-merrill_014-jpg/

Torre Agbar
Jean Nouvel, 2004, Barcelona, Spain, archinect.com/features/article/98177/in-focus-jordi-miralles

“It is no small irony that the coming together of two of the most well known signatures in the LA cultural scene… opened up a black hole of confusion into which their joint production disappeared.”

Sylvia Lavin

Double or Nothing: Architecture Not in Evidence

In 1981, Peter Arnell and Ted Bickford opened the Arnell/Bickford Advertising Agency. The kickstart for their business was a contract with Rizzoli to produce six monographs on architects.[1] The two had met while working for Michael Graves on Alessi products where the opportunities to capitalize on the growing audience for post-modern design were clearly on view. Arnell/Bickford stepped rapidly from architecture to product placement and advertising to the marketing of architects as products.[2] By the early 2000s, architectural monographs had proliferated far beyond Arnell and Bickford's six and had taken shape as a discernable genre within a long history of books about architects. One noted feature of these volumes was the exponential increase in their size. This expansion reflects not merely the growing scale of production by what were then called signature architects, nor merely the growth of the signature itself as it mutated into various forms of ever more global fame and celebrity. Instead, monographs grew larger because an increasingly wide range of material came to be considered pertinent to the subject of architecture. From the number of air miles flown in a year to passing mentions in the media, almost every possible aspect of architectural production was ultimately deemed essential, and no piece of information too irrelevant for inclusion.[3] While the post-modern monograph helped produce the signature architect, it simultanously subsumed that signature within an increasingly depersonalizing terrain of information in which the signature was one data point among many.[4]

The post-modern monograph is distinguished from other chapters in the history of the type not by its relation to self promotion—Claude-Nicolas Ledoux famously spent his prison years redrawing his pre-revolutionary work in order to remove aristocratic insignia and make himself more marketable to a post-revolutionary clientèle—but by the way it constitutes the subject of architecture.[5] The Rizzoli monographs all adhere to the same basic structure: each volume begins with the architect's name alone centered mid-recto, followed by his portrait on the verso. These opening pages define the architect as a specific person worthy of close attention, uniquely responsible for the work to follow. If the initial elements of the Arnell/Bickford series establish a mechanism for formatting singularity, the books all terminate in an opposing structure that takes the form of lists. Beyond the anticipated list of buildings and projects, the mono-

INDEX

17

Michael Graves, Buildings and Projects, 1966-1981 (New York: Rizzoli, 1985), cover and page 17.

graphs contain lists of others things: lists of awards, bibliographic lists, lists of staff members. It is precisely the proliferating list that distinguishes the post-modern monograph from models such as Le Corbusier's *Oeuvre Complète*, which contain only a single list of works.[6] The multiple back matter lists are presented neutrally, without comment or argument, in either alphabetical or chronological order. They are apparently impersonal and self-evident—not only in their structure but in their being: that a monograph would now include lists of data that had not hitherto been construed as belonging to the same order of things as the architectural works, required no comment. The effect of these lists, however, was radically to distend the single architect into a larger world of labor, discourse, and judgment.

The Arnell/Bickford monographs divide the architect into two different kinds of subjects: the first is a person of whom a portrait can be taken, who speaks casually and personably in an interview, or writes in the first person. The other architect is a subject who emerges from lists and whose distinctive features are constituted as a formal summary of data. Through this distinction between the architect who can be pictured and the architect who can only be indirectly described by tabulations and lists, the Rizzoli monographs call attention to the emergence of two mutually irreconcilable views of the architect as subject: on the one hand, a singular and autonomous creator known by a proper name and, on the other hand, a statistical anomaly or data point at the intersection of multiple data sets. Not only do they reflect a schism between views of the architect as a particularly expressive being and as an information operator—as a series, the monographs convert the very distinctiveness of the five different names of architects they were produced to celebrate into the same flat list of buildings and projects—the monographs quite literally place architecture inside the epistemological gap that divides them. Between the portrait of the unique creative talent and the profile delineated through tabulated data lay an increasingly unspecified field called architecture.

For the reader, the means of navigating this field offered by the monograph series was, not surprisingly, a list—the eponymous *list of buildings and projects*. Yet rather than provide a consistent way of accessing information about the buildings and projects, the lists vary from one monograph to another and some are internally conflicted. For example, in the first of the series, the monograph on Michael Graves, the list is called an *index* and appears as part of the front matter on page 17, rather than the back matter which is a far more typical site for an *index* in American publishing. Front matter lists are normally called *tables of contents* and are generally thematic, unlike indexes that can, in their simplest form, be no more than lists of names or places organized alphabetically, provided as a means of locating information. In today's publishing environment, tables of contents generally remain the responsibility of the writer, while book packagers, professional indexers, or software generate indexes. Tables of contents, in other words, belong to the domain of authors, arguments, and portraits while indexes belong to the order of automata, algorithms, and profiles. Not only was architecture placed in between these epistemic systems, but the very tool provided to manage the schism was itself riven by the same incompatible structures.

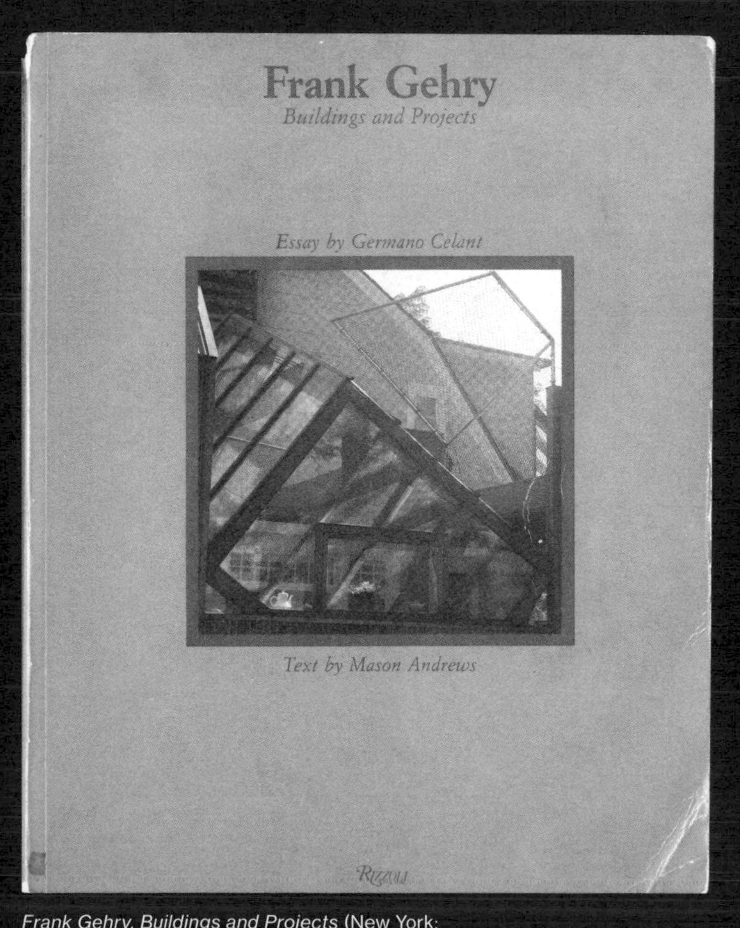

Index of Buildings and Projects

The following is a complete chronological listing of all projects undertaken by Gehry's office. Listings of those projects illustrated in this volume are followed by the page number on which they are illustrated.

Romm House 1954
Los Angeles, California

David Cabin 1958
Idylwild, California

Steeves House 1959
Brentwood, California
Page 18

Resort 1960
Clifton Springs, Australia
Page 20

Marais & Miranda House 1961
Hollywood, California

Hillcrest Apartments 1962
Santa Monica, California
Page 20

Kay Jewelers [illegible]ices and Warehouse 1963
Los Angeles, California
Page 22

6th & Hill Apartments 1963
Santa Monica, California

4th & Pier Apartments 1963
Santa Monica, California

Kenmore Apartments 1963
Los Angeles, California

Kay Jewelers Store 1963
Redondo Beach, California
Page 22

The Challenge of Our Cities and Towns 1963
New York World's Fair
Page 28

Steeves Office Building 1963
Santa Monica, California
Page 24

Faith Plating Company 1964
Hollywood, California
Page 24

Hauser-Benson Health Resort 1964
Desert Hot Springs, California

Kline House 1964
Bel Air, California
Page 26

Kay Jewelers Store 1964
Buena Park, California
Page 22

Planning Study 1964
Los Angeles County Museum of Science & Industry

Atkinson Park Recreation Building 1964
Santa Maria, California
Page 26

Urban Renewal Study 1964
Newburgh, New York

Danziger Studio and Residence 1964
Hollywood, California
Page 30

Art Treasures of Japan 1965
Los Angeles County Museum of Art
Page 36

Kay Jewelers Store 1965
San Fernando Valley, California

420 Rodeo Drive 1965
Bel Air, California
Page 34

Schottland & Miller Medical Building 1965
Torrance, California

Assyrian Reliefs 1966
Los Angeles County Museum of Art

Merriweather Post Pavilion of Music 1967
Columbia, Maryland
Page 34

Reception Center 1967
Columbia, Maryland
Page 37

Public Safety Building 1967
Columbia, Maryland
Page 38

Norton Simon Sculpture Installation 1967
Los Angeles County Museum of Art

Rockdale Urban Renewal Study 1967
Atlanta, Georgia

Ahmanson Gallery Planning Study 1967
Los Angeles County Museum of Art

Frank Gehry, Buildings and Projects (New York: Rizzoli, 1985), cover and pages VII–XI

The effects of this aporia became increasingly acute as the Arnell/Bickford series unfolded and are particularly evident in one of the last volumes to appear, *Frank Gehry: Building and Projects*.[7] Despite variations in design and nomenclature, each of the five other volumes in the series link buildings and projects included in the principal list to pages in the book.[8] The Graves *index*, for example, is divided into three columns: page number on the left, name of project in the center, and year of the project on the right. Every project on the list has a name, a date in the chronology, and a place in the book. Some projects may only occupy a single page, but every building or project in the index is represented by at least one image. The Gehry monograph's *list of buildings and projects*, in contrast, is laid out in two columns but individual entries have either two or three lines. The first line of all entries begins with the name of the project in bold, immediately followed by a date. The second line is a place name, for the most part. The third line, if there is one, contains a page number. Un-sited projects, fish lamps commissioned by a linoleum manufacturer for example, have only two lines, but the second contains the page number rather than a place. This index, in other words, is obfuscatory and difficult to comprehend. The editors, furthermore, knew it was not self-evident. Recognizing that the list required clarification, they prefaced it with an explanation: "the following is a complete chronological listing of all projects undertaken by Gehry's office. Listings of those projects illustrated in this volume are followed by the page number on which they are illustrated."[9]

While indexes are devices intended to simplify the management of information, the details of their design reflect more complex epistemologies, including types of information resistant to managerial simplification. The Gehry index needed an explanation precisely because it includes, without acknowledging as such, a mysterious category of work that is presented by project name, given a date, and sometimes a location—"the Golden Cover Shopping Center, 1976, Palos Verdes Estates, California," for example—but not assigned a page number. There is no additional material in the book on these projects. Their presence in the index is therefore purposeless, in the sense that the entry is a dead end rather than the beginning of a path toward additional information. Other monographs in the series acknowledge the category of listed but unrepresented work, but maintain the clarity both of the distinction and of the listing arrangement by dividing them into two separate lists. Robert Stern's monograph, for example, contains both a *Chronological List of Works*, which is precisely that and no more, as well as a list of *Selected Works*, which refers narrowly to those works documented in the volume by images and project descriptions. Only the Gehry monograph contains the particular aporia of works that are included and excluded at the same time, making the list itself simultaneously complete and incomplete.[10]

Every pageless project is no doubt the beginning of an untold story, but one in particular stands out. The entry reads "Ed Ruscha House, 1977, Los Angeles, California."[11] The name, date, and place triangulate around what was then a significant center of architectural thought. By 1977, Ruscha's work had been of considerable interest to English speaking architects for some time, Los Angeles had become the principal occasion for thinking about the post-metropolitan city, and Ruscha's books on the built environment of Los Angeles had brought the two interests together. Architects had particularly and repeatedly referred to *Twentysix Gasoline Stations* (1963), *Thirtyfour Parking Lots* (1967), and *Every Building on the Sunset Strip* (1966) both directly and indirectly.[12] Denise Scott Brown wrote about Ruscha as early as 1969, using detailed analyses of his books to describe and establish what she considered an important new way of seeing the environment—not in the pictorial tradition of landscape views but through the scientific methodology of geographic and quantitative surveys.[13] It is well known that the fieldwork for the research that ultimately produced *Learning from Las Vegas* began not in Nevada but in Ruscha's studio, where Scott Brown took students prior to their departure for the desert. She and Robert Venturi had students explicitly imitate Ruscha's linear collage of photographs of the Sunset Strip in their analysis of the Las Vegas strip, which during the second phase of their fieldwork they saw not only by car but by helicopter—an essential component of the apparatus Ruscha used in the production of *Thirtyfour Parking Lots*.[14] Indeed, Venturi and Scott Brown's adoption of Ruscha's documentary photographic style and his use of the helicopter to establish a vantage point for recording the urban environment substantially augmented Venturi and Scott Brown's representational strategies.

More telling than their interest in Ruscha's visual vocabulary and the complex machines he used to produce it, however, is the fact that Scott Brown referred to Ruscha's publications not as art books but as scholarly monographs.[15] Indeed, most of her discussion of Ruscha's work emphasizes the quality that in her view made it scholarly: a means of analysis that allowed the material to "speak for itself."[16] This definition of the scholarly as an objective method that deployed techniques for recording and transcribing data without comment or judgment, would become the most radical element of Venturi and Scott Brown's pedagogy, and an essential component in their development of what they began to call a *research* rather than *design* studio.[17] Research was scholarly in the degree to which it was merely a mode of transmission, lacking in either judgment or art. As a result, for Ruscha to serve as a proper model for enabling data to speak for itself, it was necessary for Ruscha not to appear to speak on the data's behalf. While it was precisely his reputation as an artist that led Scott Brown to Ruscha's studio, turning him into a scholarly authority required diverting attention away from the way he converted information into art. It was, in turn, by assuming what she had construed as Ruscha's *scholarly* posture—objective and unmediated by artistic sensibility—that Scott Brown could equate representation with information and architectural analysis with research.[18]

This process of turning Ruscha the artist into an information resource was not promoted by Scott Brown alone but was indicative of a broader transformation in the way architecture constituted knowledge for and about itself. For example, Reyner Banham discusses Ruscha in his very first text on Los Angeles of 1968.[19] Ironically, while celebrating what he called the triumphant art of flamboyantly "doing your own thing," Banham praises Ruscha's cool paintings and books as impersonal—imposing

Bubar's Jewelers 1980
Santa Monica, California
Page 188

United States Chancellery 1980
Damascus, Syria
Page 176

World Savings Bank 1980
North Hollywood, California
Page 192

Connections 1981
Architectural League, New York
Page 194

Lafayette Street Lofts 1981
New York, New York
Page 196

AFTRA Offices 1981
Los Angeles, California

Westlake Office Park 1981
Westlake–Thousand Oaks, California

14th Street Housing 1981
Atlanta, Georgia
Page 198

Benson House 1981
Calabasas, California
Page 200

House for a Film Maker 1981
Santa Monica Canyon, California
Page 206

Indiana Avenue Houses 1981
Venice, California
Page 208

Feibleman House 1981
Los Angeles, California

Baldwin Studio 1981
Los Angeles, California

Seventeen Artists in the 60's 1981
Los Angeles County Museum of Art
Page 214

Paramount Theatre Shell 1981
Oakland, California
Page 212

IX|X

Billy Al Bengston, *Ed Ruscha Studio*, 1970.

neither judgment nor comment.[20] Because he argued it refrained from criticism shaped by aesthetic predetermination, Banham considered Ruscha's work to offer a model for urban analysis of cities, like Los Angeles, filled with things like parking lots that Banham wanted to present as themselves unmediated by design or aesthetic shaping. Parking lots, according to Banham following Ruscha, just do "their parking lot thing."[21] By using Ruscha to present parking lots and commercial structures as facts—*a priori*, self-evident, and suited to being fully and adequately described through the medium of a list—Banham propelled architecture into a terrain where judgment was not subjective but rather absolute and irrefutable.

Precisely by not criticizing, Ruscha becomes for Banham a new kind of architecture critic, a role Banham cast Ruscha to play in his film, *Reyner Banham Loves Los Angeles.*[22] Banham introduces Ruscha to the film's audience as an artist, but Banham does not ask Ruscha about his artwork. Instead, Banham asks Ruscha to offer direct statements of fact about the city: what buildings to see and why. Banham's diversionary tactics that limit his reader's ability to recognize Ruscha's artistry takes its most deliberate form in Banham's own list-making: when Banham brought together various previously published texts and lectures as *Los Angeles: The Architecture of Four Ecologies*, he chose Ruscha's 1968 *Hollywood* as the book's final illustration. Although unmentioned in the text itself, the caption lists Ruscha as the artist of the work, as does the list of illustrations.[23] But when Banham uses photographs of parking lots, the very photographs in Ruscha's *Thirtyfour Parking Lots*, which Banham does three times, the illustration captions do not credit Ruscha. Indeed, no artist is credited in these captions. The difference between using Ruscha as an artist with a signature who makes fine art and as an anonymous source of images of anonymously produced features of the city is only revealed in the fine print of the list of image credits. Artists' names are included in the title while photo source credits are contained within parentheses.[24] The moment he severed their producer in two, Banham was able to determine the order of things to which the images belonged: work of art or document. Relying on the ostensibly non-judgmental nature of the list—his flamboyant style nothwithstanding—Banham managed his data such that it invisibly regulated what could be known, made his criticism appear to rely on facts, and therefore constituted his opinion as knowledge rather than personal judgment.

Architects continued to break Ruscha into two kinds of subjects well into the the 1970s. John Margolies invited Ruscha to contribute to a special issue of *Design Quarterly* devoted to conceptual architecture in 1970.[25] The contributors were asked to provide whatever they considered to be an example of conceptual architecture, a biography, and a portrait of themselves as well as to design the layout of their pages. Ruscha provided five images of women, numbered and named—and hence turned into a data set—and covered the photograph of himself with his CV, explicitly staging the conversion of portrait to profile.[26] By 1972, architects were writing to ask him for information about parking lots.[27] In 1973, students from the Architectural Association made seeing the Mohave Desert from a helicopter part of their architectural research. And finally, by the mid-1970s, Environ-

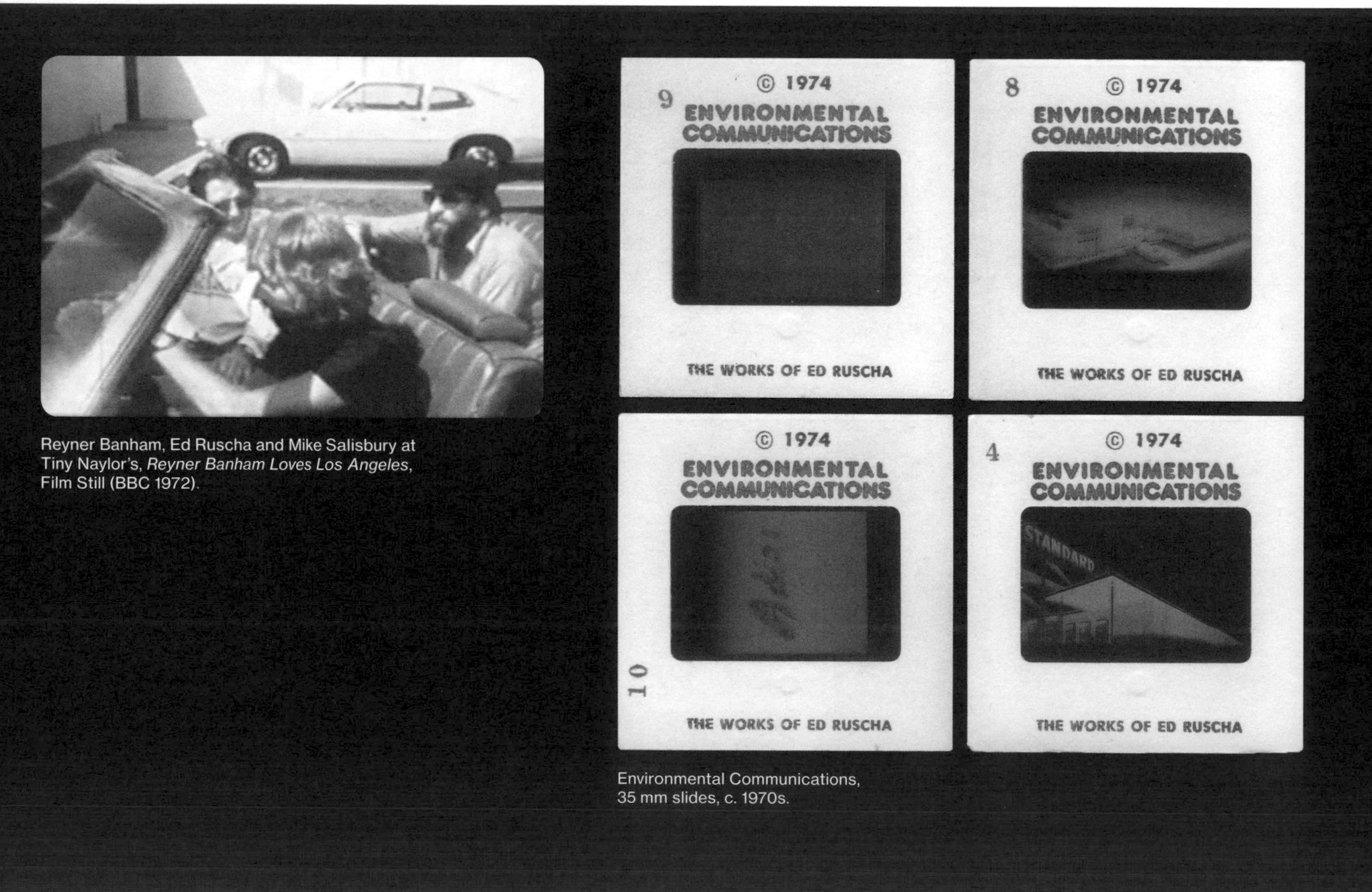

Reyner Banham, Ed Ruscha and Mike Salisbury at Tiny Naylor's, *Reyner Banham Loves Los Angeles*, Film Still (BBC 1972).

Environmental Communications, 35 mm slides, c. 1970s.

mental Communications, a collection of Los Angeles based architects and urbanists, had transformed the Ruscha-derived idea of using commercial means of disseminating documentary images of LA into a successfully operating slide distribution company as its own form of critical architectural practice.[28] They issued a set of twenty-five slides devoted exclusively to Ruscha's paintings and silkscreens, which they updated and re-curated as Ruscha produced more work. At the same time, Environmental Communications also began distributing Ruscha's books. As had Scott Brown and Banham, Environmental Communications divided Ruscha's production into parts defined not in terms of medium, paintings versus books, but as distinct ontological categories. The slide sets were devoted to art, while Environmental Communications promoted the books as a resource for architects—writing in their sales catalog that "in his books, Ruscha proves to be an extremely alert observer who succeeds in giving his photographically registered impressions a cool, yet deadly accurate typographic form. His books are among the most penetratingly graphic visual information of the West Coast (Los Angeles) one can wish for."[29]

Architecture worked hard to turn Ruscha into information, a ruse that Ruscha was happy to play along with—even to abet. Not only did he willingly play the role of guide to Los Angeles in Banham's film, Ruscha helped shape the proper mode of reception of his books by creating the Information Man, an imaginary person whose function was to generate an endless data stream about the afterlife of his books: how many had been read, how many had killed mosquitoes, how many had been smelled, etc.[30] Ruscha invited his audience to use the books to produce additional information and architects did just that by using Ruscha as a fantasy figure on whose confabulated authority a new logic of facticity could enter the discipline. By 1977, it had become possible to conceive of architecture the way Ruscha conceived of his books, as "simply a collection of facts," which, detached from artistic sensibility, could be fully represented by items on a list.[31]

The inclusion of the Ruscha house on the Gehry index is evidence of the persuasiveness of this rhetoric of factuality precisely because everything else about the index functions to emphasize a decidedly counterfactual definition of architecture. The *list of projects* as a whole, but page X on which appears the Ruscha house in particular, recounts the slow but steady overcoming of what Gehry specifically called the architecture of matters-of-fact.[32] Gehry argued that overcoming facts is what enabled him to make work expressive of his personal artistic sensibility, and Page X, devoted to the period between 1976 and 1978, covers the most pivotal examples this effort. Projects listed on this page were given space in the book in relation to the degree to which they corroborate this account of how one kind of architecture became a different kind of architect: neither the Familian House nor the Gunther House were built, but they were each given multiple pages that include documentary materials, sketches, construction documents and models in order to flesh out how each specifically contributed to Gehry's pursuit of a personal signature. Harper House, fifteen stories of condominiums built in Baltimore, receives only two pages largely devoted to photographs of the completed building—a matter

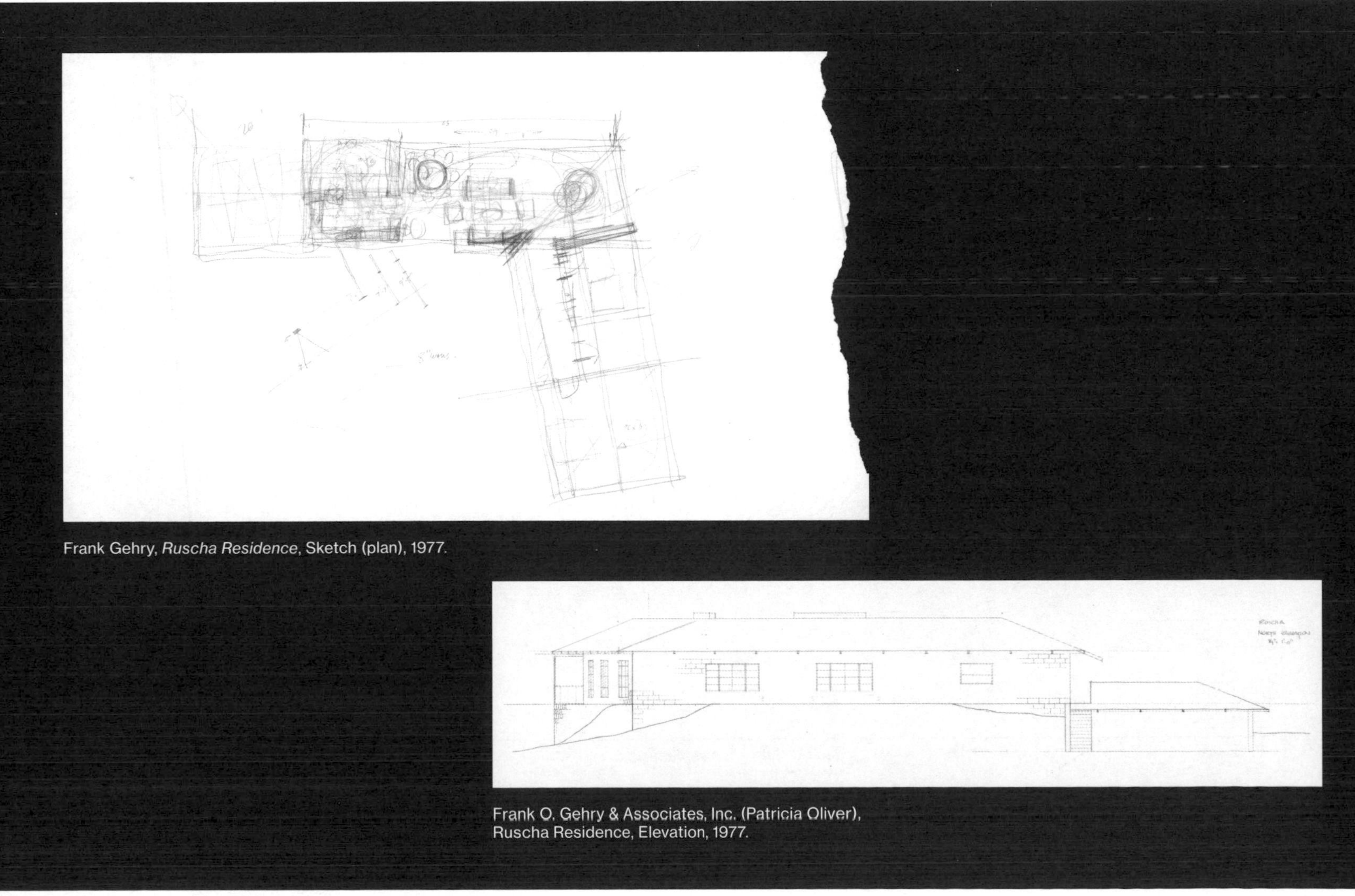

Frank Gehry, *Ruscha Residence*, Sketch (plan), 1977.

Frank O. Gehry & Associates, Inc. (Patricia Oliver), Ruscha Residence, Elevation, 1977.

of fact presentation that reinforces the understanding of it as a matter of fact building. Gehry's own house receives the greatest number of pages not only on the 1976–1978 page but in the book as a whole, using the space in order to substantiate it as the place where the architect of matters-of-fact was reborn as an architect of matters of art. "My house was a turning point," after which "I had do start over—literally start over again."[33]

Without meriting anything beyond the listing of its name as a fact, the Ruscha house neither proves nor disproves the claims transcribed into the medium of the index. Why, then, include it all? The answer lies in the logic of the monograph itself, which Arnell described as consisting of an "unretouched" presentation of "raw data."[34] The purity of the data was essential to Arnell's capacity to claim that the monograph was an unmediated transcription of the architect into book form. In other words, as distinct as the Rizzoli monographs and their association with advertising have been understood to be from the research studios of academe, they both adhered to what Scott Brown called the scholarly method. The Ruscha house could not be omitted because the house was linked to evidence in the form of documents that could not be suppressed without undermining the very possibility that something called raw data might exist.[35] The line in the index is neither an error nor a symptom but rather a simple registration of the existence of a paper trail, a tube of drawings in the Gehry archive containing what Arnell referred to as raw data. It is beyond the scope of this essay to demonstrate how the construction and maintenance of an archive free enough from judgment to contain records of projects considered unworthy of publication belongs to precisely the same logic of facts and evidence that is the subject of this essay. In this context, it must suffice to state that there is a Gehry archive and in that archive is a tube labeled Ruscha House and in the tube are several different kinds of drawings; two freehand sketches of plans on trace made with pencil; one measured drawing labeled north elevation, also made on trace; and two working drawings on vellum, one showing a floor plan and one combined roof and site plan. There are blueprint copies of the latter. The drawings are marked Frank O. Gehry and Associates, Inc., are all labeled Residence for Ed Ruscha, dated Dec. 7, 1977 and identified as Project No. 77-2100.

While the number of drawings is small compared to other Gehry projects of the period, they nevertheless provide a wealth of information. The elevation shows a pitched roof, posted fence and square casement windows. The freehand sketch plans describe a not perfectly V-shaped structure, where the dining room furniture is to be put, and where the closets are. Extra graphite is deposited at the notch of the plan, as if the notch required extra thinking and hence extra drawing. The problematic notch makes the V-shape appear not as an *a priori* figure but as the result of a bar being bent or an ell widened to accommodate something irregular in the terrain. The site plan gives particular attention to the septic tank: a piece of printed paper cut out from an external source on septic tanks is glued to the large sheet. The need for the septic tank, despite the fact that the monograph sites the house in LA, suggests that the house was intended for someplace without access to standard plumbing. The working drawings are properly detailed with smoke detectors

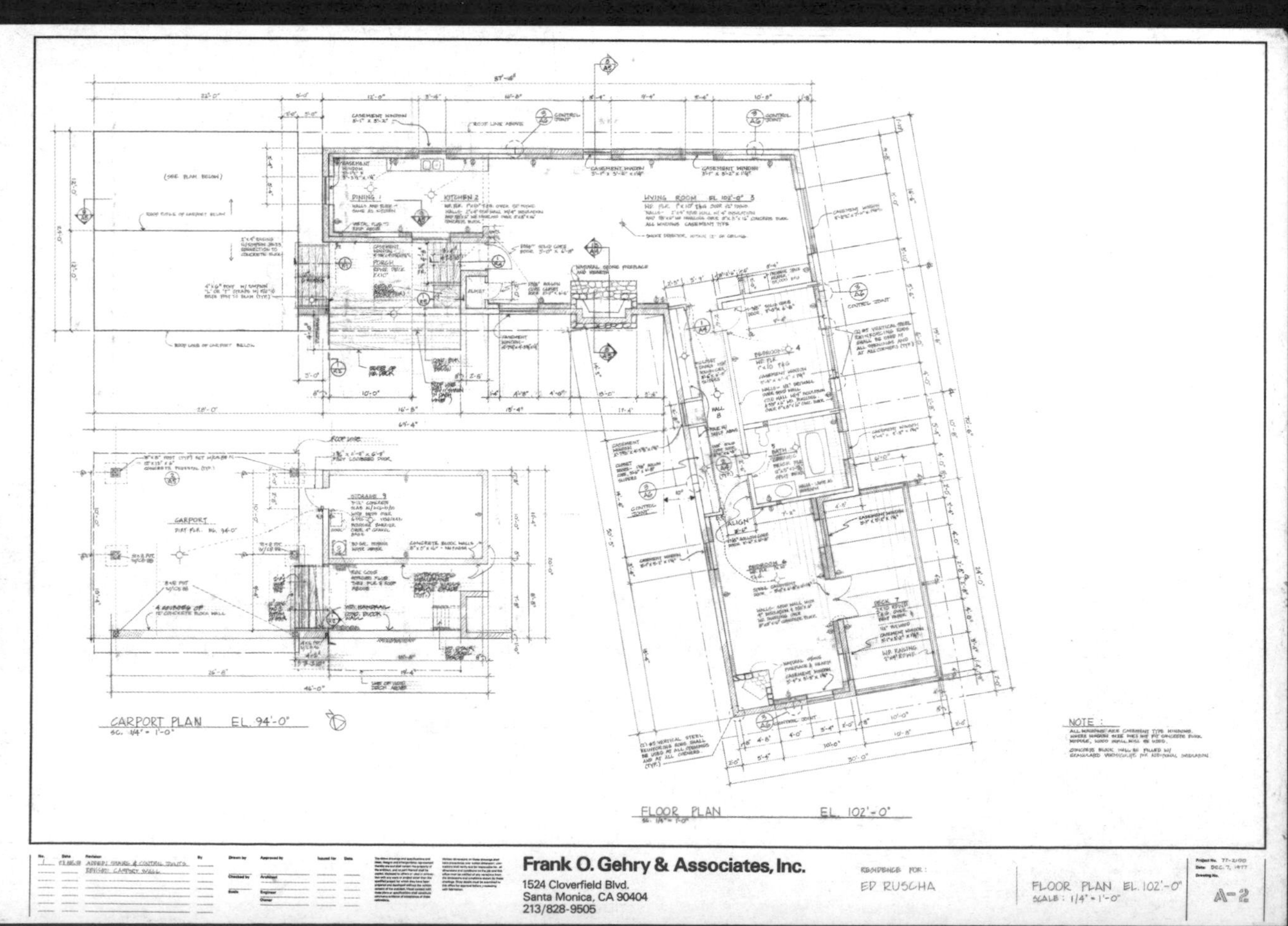

Frank O. Gehry & Associates, Inc., Ruscha Residence, Construction Document (plan), 1977

and interior finishes called out. In other words, while few in number, the drawings stretch across a range of types, from preliminary sketch to presentation drawing to working drawing. They are in fact a set, complete if not robust, on the basis of which it is plausible to conclude that a two-bedroom residence with bath was sited, designed, and detailed thoroughly enough that a house could have been built.

What neither the tube nor the project number, nor any other point of access to the Gehry archive provides, however, is any indication of whether the house was built or not. The drawings clearly and unequivocally link Gehry, Ruscha, and a house, yet like much eyewitness testimony they are also, in and of themselves, incomplete as evidence. The drawings and the archive contain no particulars. There are no payment records, contracts, or photographs. The drawings provide no address and few qualities that specify the person or persons who made them, or the person who might inhabit the house. There are no models of the house in the Gehry archive (by 1977, model making had generally come to be understood as the quintessential design tool in the production of Gehry's "expressive" work) and no mention of a Gehry/Ruscha house in the architectural press. From the perspective of an architectural audience, the house does not exist. It is a fact not in evidence.

Paper trails, however, like indexes, are always more than they first appear to be, most immediately because they cannot help but trail out into different directions: every piece of paper is connected to its own production—the paper mill, its labor force, the materials used—which in turn weaves it into a widening network of agents. Paper documents in the modern era, in particular, belong to trails that inevitably refer to more paper. For example, the site plan notes, "for all survey information refer to survey drawing prepared by William H. Warner, Warner Engineering." Various William Warners had been topographical engineers since the Mexican-American War and many of them, including William Henry Warner, worked in the California desert and in Yucca Valley.[36] In turn, the identification of Warner Engineering in Yucca Valley gives significance to the fact that no street address but only geographical coordinates are included in the drawings. Undeveloped in the 1970s, that area of the desert was literally off the grid, without power, water, and roads. As a result, real estate was identified by coordinates rather than by street address. All these data points embedded in irrepressible data of documents, situate the house in a location that not only corroborates the need for the septic tank but, when linked to the name Ruscha, yields a substantial body of evidence attesting to Ruscha's attachment to the Yucca Valley Desert, in particular.

Ruscha liked to go to the desert, to simply lie down, take long walks, watch baseball on TV, or pose for photographs dressed as a cowboy.[37] One of his books, *Royal Road Test*, documents precisely one such journey.[38] Critics liked to go with him. In fact, if Arnell/Bickford went to the archive to find raw data to use as evidence to make a case for architects, art critics have typically gone to the artist's studio for the same purpose.[39] In Ruscha's case, since he made much of his work on the go, the *topos* of the studio visit was frequently replaced with that of the ride-along. The term refers to a situation in which a civilian is allowed to ride

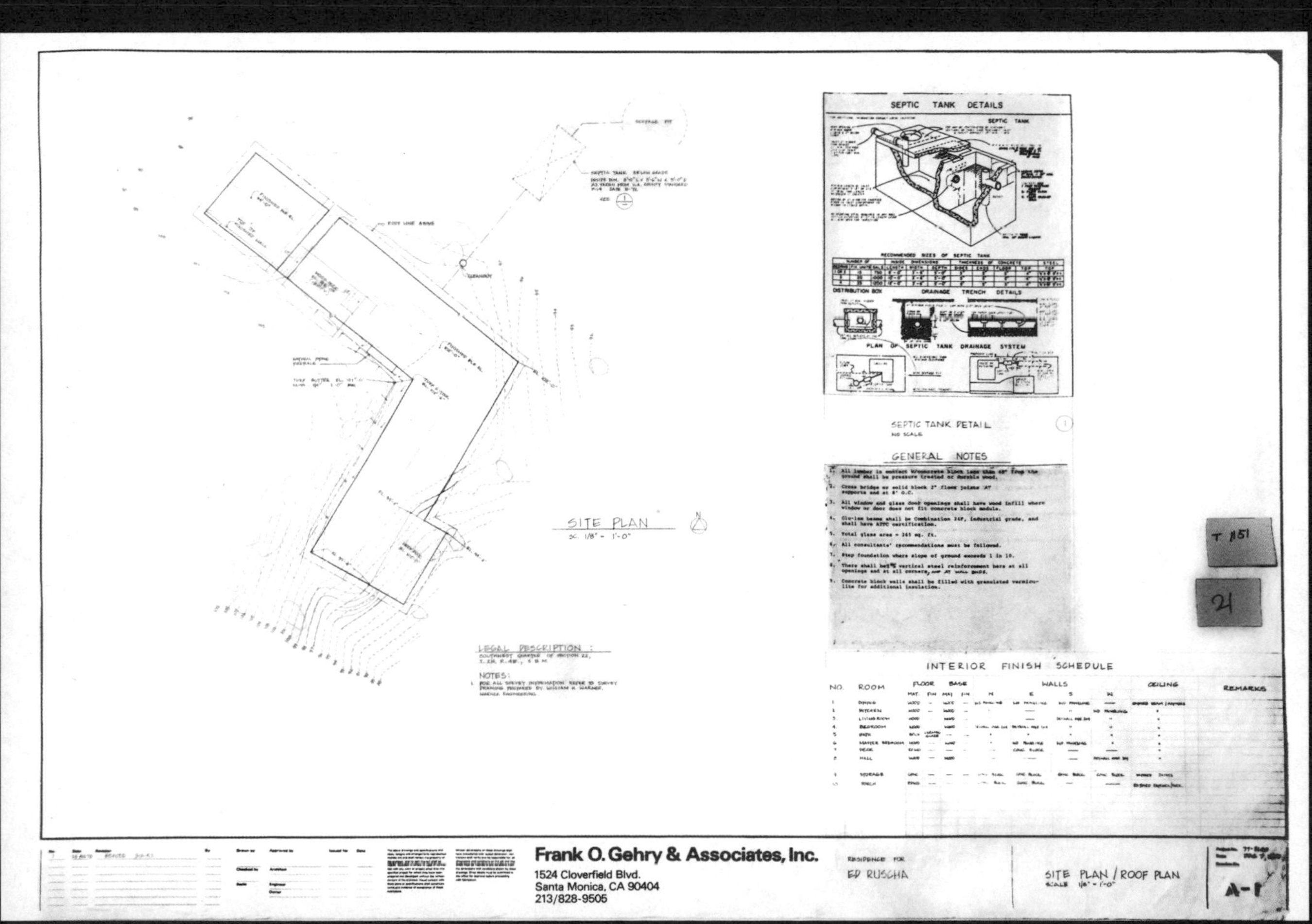

Frank O. Gehry & Associates, Inc., Ruscha Residence, Site Plan, 1977

along as a passenger in a police car observing the police at work. At least since Banham interviewed Ruscha from the back seat of a car in his film, the ride-along has reinforced not only the common view that Ruscha's work is inseparable from the built environment that it documents, including most particularly its emphasis on transportation and the mobilization of viewers and images, but Ruscha's own view that his work is factual, like "a police report."[40] One such ride-along essay was published in *Vanity Fair* within a few months of the publication of Gehry's monograph.[41] The author, art critic Peter Plagens, had written a scathing review of Banham's *Architecture of Four Ecologies* where he argued that not only had Banham gotten all the salient facts wrong, but that he had not even understood what a fact proper to a discussion of things like the impact of cars on LA might be.[42] Plagens contrasts what he calls Banham's "insidious propaganda for freeways" to his own statistically based understanding of the chemical constituents of smog, number of days per annum with smog alerts, and how many people living near freeways have emphysema.[43]

Plagens' essay on Ruscha begins with an overabundance of coordinates:

> The artists' hideaway is about ten miles from Pioneertown, which is eight miles from Yucca valley, which is thirty miles north of Palm Springs, which is a hundred miles east of his residence in Los Angeles.

Plagens goes on to describe the "mile-long serpentine driveway" and the residence it leads to in some detail:

> a weird conglomeration of materials (cinder-block walls, a Spanish tile roof, and a knotty-pine interior), expenditures (secondhand timbers from a collapsed Malibu water tower, and reclaimed steel window casings which had to be reconditioned for what new ones would have cost, because, in the words of the artist, "I like the idea of them"), and aesthetics (the house is elegantly plain, like a zoning reject from Palos Verdes Estates, but wonderfully set among the stones). I compliment Ruscha on the siting of his home, which notches around a huge boulder.[44]

The location of the house, the casement windows, and the knotty-pine interior are all verbal descriptions of the information described visually in the Gehry & Associates drawings. The huge boulder coincides with the notch in the plan, just as the plain elegance of the building sited with particular attention parallels the minimalist elevation drawings and the distribution of graphite on the plan sketches. Plagens is even attentive to construction labor, quoting Ruscha's description of an archetypally desert-rat-like neighbor who had been "instrumental in building the house."[45] Plagens, in other words, produces a virtually comprehensive description of a house: its materials, its site, its mode of construction, its layout, and its aesthetic—establishing a chain of evidence that makes it possible to conclude that the Ruscha house listed in the Gehry monograph was built. Plagens' survey of the house is just as complete as the drawing set in the Gehry archive. However, Plagens' survey was also just as incomplete as the drawings in the tube because it fails to mention what one

Evelyn Hofer photographs from *Vanity Fair*, February 1968.

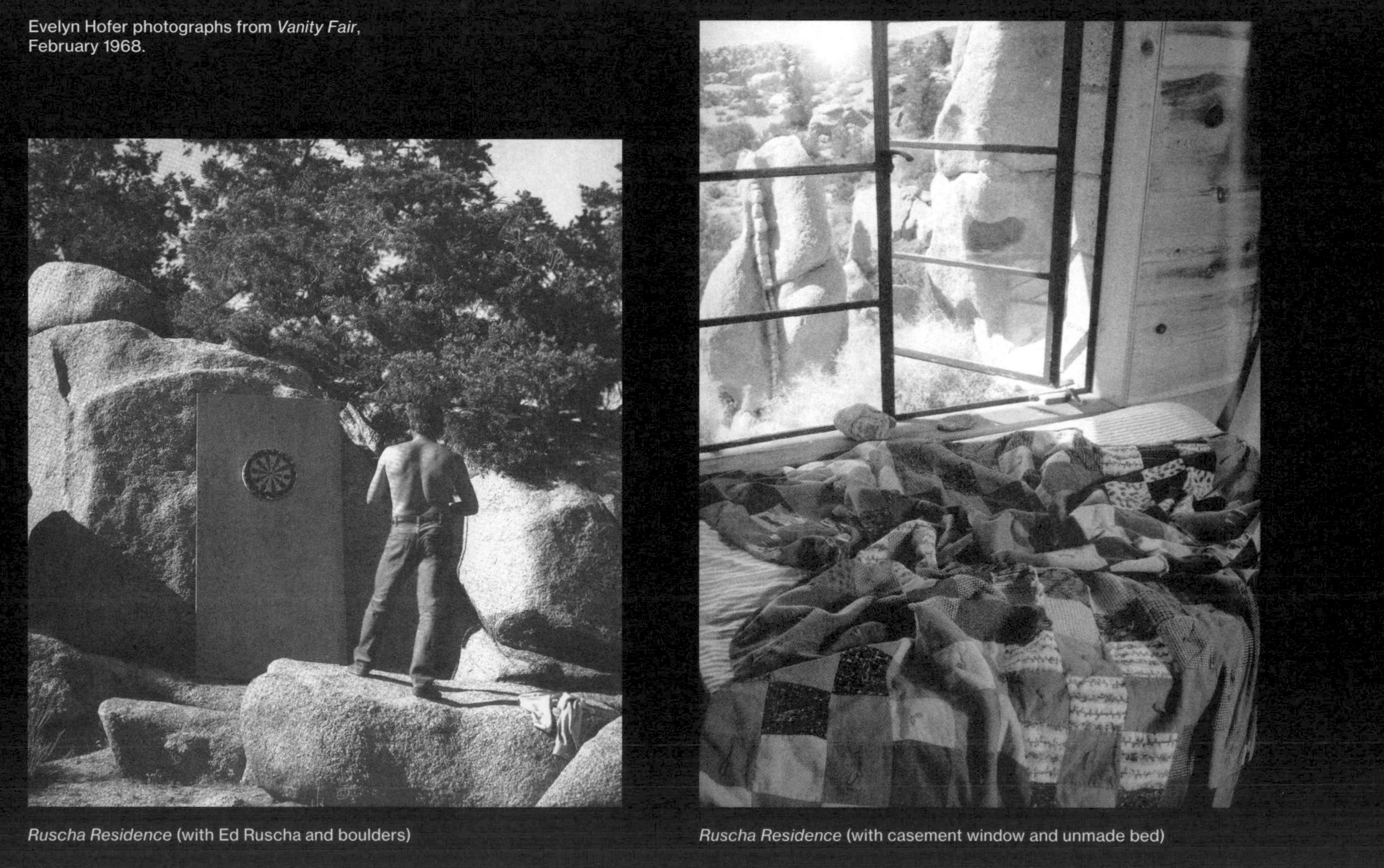

Ruscha Residence (with Ed Ruscha and boulders)

Ruscha Residence (with casement window and unmade bed)

would normally expect to be an irrepressible raw data component of the house: Plagens neglects to mention Gehry. He describes an architectural totality but makes no mention of either an architect or of architecture: the components and activities of both are present in fact but they themselves are, once again, not in evidence.

Or rather, there is too much evidence about the house and no single concept of architecture that can hold it together. There is evidence that Ruscha spotted the land while in a helicopter looking for property to buy.[46] There is evidence that Ruscha collected architectural parts and pieces, casement windows, bowling alley floors, and Spanish tiles, and wanted them to come together in the form of a stock image of a Western house, just as he put images of houses, palm trees, and parking lots together into things that look like regular books. There is evidence that for Ruscha, Gehry played the role of the photographers who often shot the images he used in his books: as Ruscha has famously said, "it's not really important who takes the photographs ... I don't even look at it as photography."[47] There is evidence, in other words, that Ruscha considers himself to be the architect, evidence that most importantly takes the form of this statement by Ruscha: "I designed the house myself." [48]

There is also evidence that Gehry & Associates were the architects of this house and that much effort was exerted to turn Ruscha's brief—form my bits and pieces into a house that looks like no one made it—into a building. The casement windows, for example, were irregular and did not fit precisely into concrete block construction. Every window, instead of a matter of fact was a historical memento, warped by time and the flows of material life. Patricia Oliver, a new employee at Gehry & Associates who was assigned Project No. 77-2100, had the task of figuring out how this would work. Her job was literally to fill the gap between Ruscha's fantasy of being off the grid, isolated, and free to look at the world through standard, industrially produced casement windows, and the regulatory and procedural standards that inevitably ferret out irregularities and demand that they be accounted for. Rather than inert, her apparently perfunctory elevations exquisitely render the schematic quality of a false front, just as the command to use nonstandard timbers and manage boulders required extra planning effort—the "grind" into the paper that Gehry said typified his drawings of this period. [49] There is evidence, in other words, that a full range of architectural services were provided by Gehry & Associates, including an entry—however anomalous—on his list of buildings and projects. Nevertheless, Gehry disclaims the design, saying "I didn't do anything."[50]

It is no small irony that the coming together of two of the most well known signatures in the LA cultural scene not only did not double the notoriety of their collaboration, but opened up a black hole of confusion into which their joint production disappeared. It is also no small irony that Gehry and Ruscha came together at all since each is associated not only with different but with mutually irreconcilable views of what it means to be a creative producer, with Ruscha insisting on the facts and Gehry insisting on their overcoming.[51] But there is a great deal of evidence about the effects disappearing things have had on our

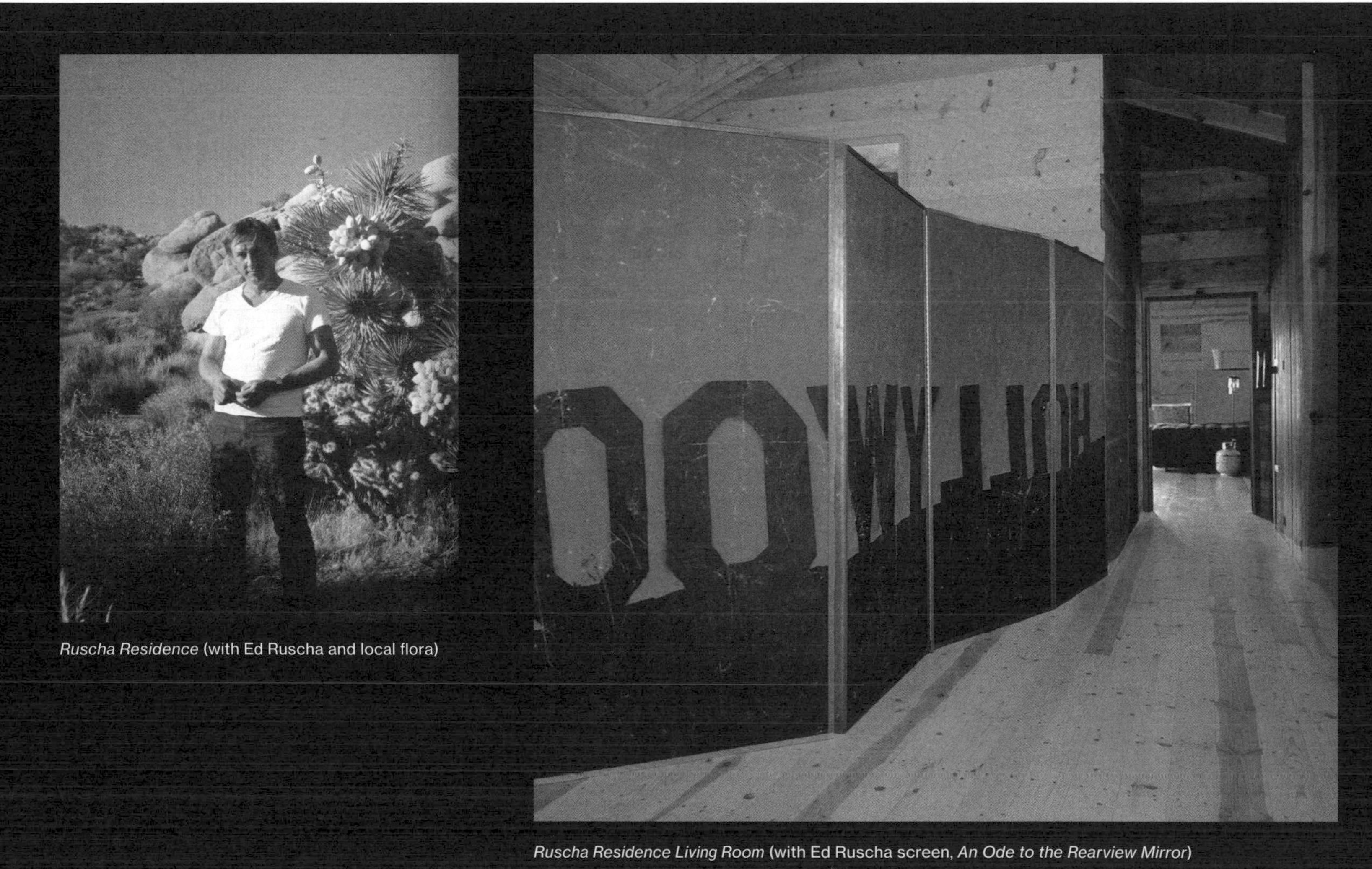

Ruscha Residence (with Ed Ruscha and local flora)

Ruscha Residence Living Room (with Ed Ruscha screen, *An Ode to the Rearview Mirror*)

capacity to know the subject of architecture. The conflict that appears to put Gehry and Ruscha at odds actually demonstrates the way in which the forms of production that architecture both represented and induced exposed an epistemological conflict in the definition of creative work as such.

By the mid-1960s, architects actively aligned themselves with creative practices and worked equally hard to align architecture with the emerging information episteme. These mutually contradictory efforts produced myriad logical inconsistencies because they required that architects develop both new skills in the management of data as well as ways of minimizing how they shaped that data into argument. For example, early layouts of *Learning From Las Vegas* credit Ruscha in the captions for the photomontage that imitated his *Every Building on the Sunset Strip*, but the attribution is eliminated in the published book allowing what had at first been conceived of as art, and subsequently been reconceived of as documentation, to return as architecture.[52] Banham similarly deployed a set of bureaucratic protocols about where and how to credit Ruscha that, while apparently trivial and without effect on the visibility of his work—all four Ruscha images are printed at the same resolution—fundamentally determined the definition of the work. Using nothing more than a parenthesis, Banham divided the images into two non-coincident categories, art of intention and acts of information. This differentiation, however, was precisely the distinction he was at pains to undermine in relation to architecture. *Frank Gehry, Buildings and Projects* contains both working drawings (which neither the Stern nor the Graves monographs do: technical documents were not the norm in monographs during the 1980s) as well as highly personal sketches, while simultaneously arguing that these two forms of architectural production belong to ontologically different categories. The result of these irreconcilable classifications is not only a house that has two architects and apparently no architecture, but the subsumation of a complexly orchestrated aesthetics of information into a residue of research protocols, indexes and documents that architecture continues to value only in the degree to which they are understood to be purely prosaic forms of production—lacking precisely the forms of creative judgment and personal opinion that gave rise to them in the first place.

If architecture's design of Ruscha reflects a deepening conflict about the possibility of creative work in architecture, Ruscha's design of architecture reveals the same conflict. For example, in 1965 Ruscha photographed some apartments in Los Angeles and put them together in a book called *Some Los Angeles Apartments.* The buildings are identified only by street address and the photographs themselves are prosaic and perfunctory in their generic frontality, indifferent print quality and what has been called amateurish framing. That same year, Ruscha selected ten of these photographs and drew them with soft spreading graphite, carefully expunging antennae and sharpening color contrast to intensify their apparently automatic manufacture.[53] The doubling produces the paradoxical effect of making the machine image appear more natural than the hand made image, even though Ruscha himself asserted that drawings always "give a touch of the hand" and retain something of the personal in them.[54] The drawings and photographs, while almost

Ed Ruscha, *Beverly Glen*, from the book *Some Los Angeles Apartments*, 7 x 5½ x 3⁄16 inches, 1965. © **Ed Ruscha**.

isomorphic, not only rely on different working methods but produce fundamentally irreconcilable definitions of the work of art. Leo Steinberg, describing the art of the late 1960s, distinguishes the work of "the data-ingesting mind of the technician," and that of what he called "the artist in the fullness of his human interest."[55] Ruscha took a lot of pictures and made a lot of drawings too, but it is the subject of architecture that compelled him to do both and to be simultaneously Steinberg's computer and his person.

Ruscha and Gehry agree about everything except the facts of the case of the house in the desert.[56] Ruscha claims the concept of the house, but the house itself, in his view, makes no claim on architecture.[57] Conversely, Gehry makes no claim to the design but includes the house on his list of works. The conflict over attribution lies less in the question of authorship itself than in the question of whether this house has any architecture to claim or disclaim. Ruscha's goal was to build an edifice made out of the raw data of the commercial landscape, without signature or comment.[58] Gehry's goal was to distance himself as much as possible from buildings that did not properly bear his signature. Both goals were predicated on the notion that one could clearly distinguish between architectural matters of fact and architectural signatures, or between building and architecture, or even between architecture and art. It was precisely these distinctions, however, that were being eroded as a new logic of information increasingly took over in the form of proliferating lists, lists that could be assembled and reassembled in infinite ways, and that, in turn and with each reassembly, eroded the difference between indexes and septic tank instructions, between project numbers in archives and surveys of every building on the sunset strip. Every document, utterance, drawing, and caption embedded in the Gehry/Ruscha case bears witness to the fact that it was not possible for matters of fact to assemble themselves into a house just as they testify to the fact that no single signature could account for them all.

The strange case of the disappearing house is highly dependent on its historical situation. Any earlier and the archival impulse would not have been strong enough to preserve the record of a job considered to be negligible—the ideal of raw data would not have been compelling enough to countermand the clarity of a list, nor would there have been an artist's work so elastic in definition that it could be reclassified with a tool as modest as a parenthesis. Any earlier in the development of architecture's shift into the information era, and the house would in fact have disappeared. Any later, however, and new platforms like Instagram would have geo-tagged the images of the house precluding any possibility that it could be off the grid, and the celebrity of both Ruscha and Gehry would have combined to produce an irrepressible architectural spectacle. Any later, and the house could not have been anything but overexposed.

The strange case of the disappearing house, however, also reflects broad and still not fully decipherable shifts in architectural definition with salience that exceeds the anecdotal traces of a single house. The modern systems of production and exchange that yielded casement windows and concrete block also yielded a form of knowledge based on the predictable rationality of facts divorced from the whims of human intentionality. Ruscha's "I

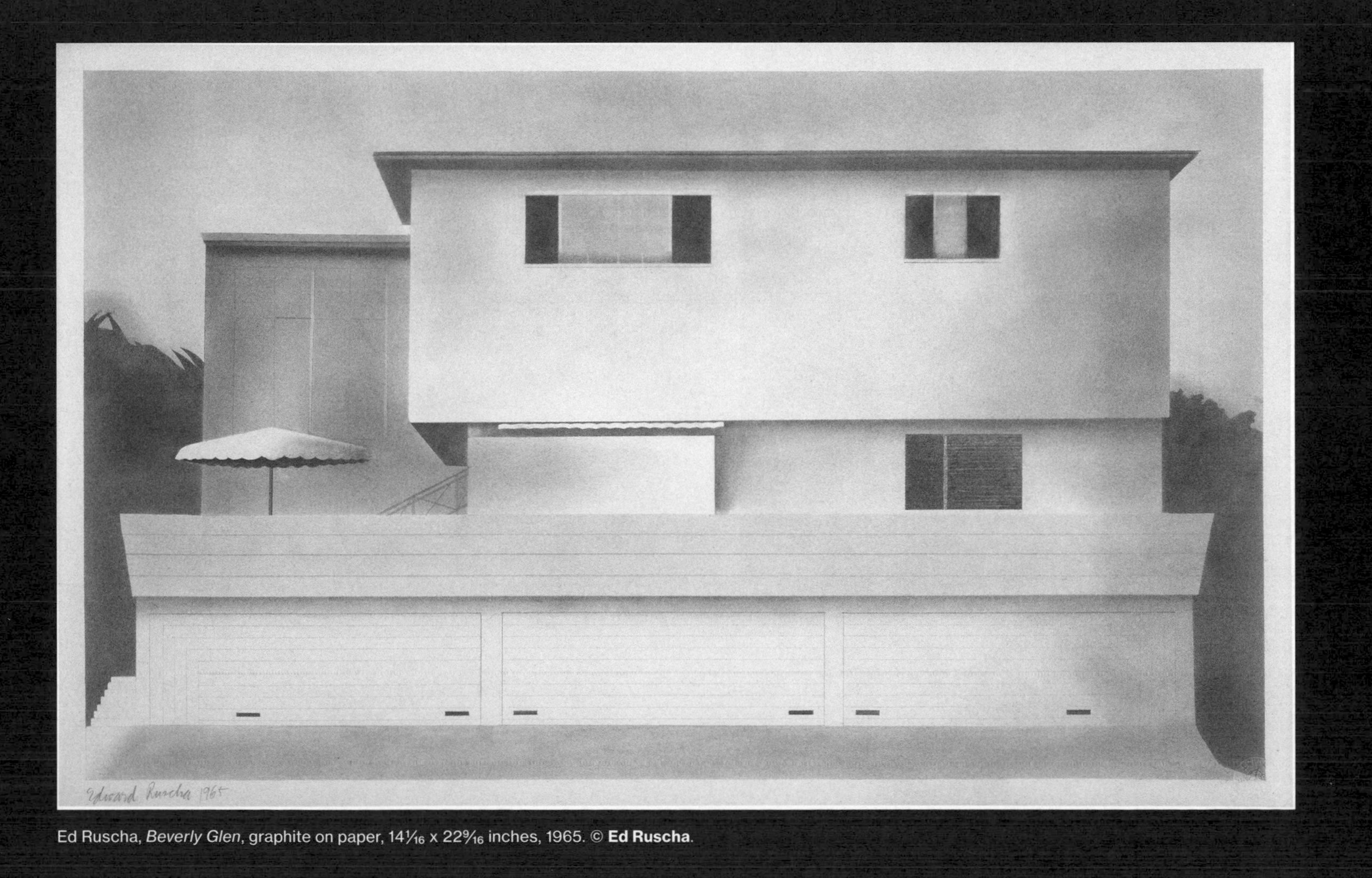

Ed Ruscha, *Beverly Glen*, graphite on paper, 14$\frac{1}{16}$ x 22$\frac{9}{16}$ inches, 1965. © **Ed Ruscha**.

designed it myself" was uttered as a statement of this kind of fact, untainted by uncertainty about what *to design* could entail and what *its* product might be. This epistemology, however, simultaneously produced an array of devices, diagrams and desires—from archives and lists to parentheses—that not only belie the impersonality of these facts but that reveal the almost infinite number of decisions and calculations that produced them. As archives open and investigations unfold, the rapidly accumulating data about these facts is indeed becoming increasingly raw, not because it is truthful but because it is revealing wild forms of incongruity in the very logic of post-modern architecture. As a result, the ordinary can no longer be defined as such nor neatly opposed to the extraordinary: Project No. 77-2100 and Ruscha's house are one and the same thing and simultaneously utterly incongruous.

Furthermore, and for the same reasons—because its every move and moment of intuition is captured, documented and measured—artistic genius is increasingly tied to an ever expanding bureaucracy of production. As the ubiquity of paperwork transgresses categories like sketch and document, matters of fact and matters of signature reveal themselves to be not different in nature but, instead, the result of different kinds of arguments made from the same evidence.[59] Architecture was certainly not alone to come face to face with how much its definition would change as more and more data about every detail of its production would be tracked, accounted for, profiled and claimed. Nevertheless, architecture's long standing understanding of itself as constituted by both art and *techné*—and as therefore constituted by the differences between them—made it especially alert to their collapse. No definition of architecture has yet emerged to enable these worldspaces to be coincident, and without definition, architecture cannot be in evidence. As the case of the disappearance of the Gehry/Ruscha house indicates, not being in evidence also means that architecture cannot be fully claimed or managed, and in that aporia, strange marvels manage miraculously to thrive.

(While the Ruscha Residence was under construction, Ruscha made Rocky II*, a fiberglass boulder that he placed among real rocks in an undisclosed desert location, never to be seen again. There is a massive manhunt for that rock, about which, like his Gehry house, Ruscha has remained totally silent.*[60] *Plagens concluded his description of the boulders around which the Ruscha house notches with the following sentence: "I tell you, it was a helluva job, trucking that big rock in here," he [Ruscha] lies, smiling with eerie earnestness." An image of the mold for Rocky II has recently been unearthed, an irrepressible archival fact.*[61] *An art collector who owns property once owned by Ruscha and very near to the house in question, suspects that Rocky II remains where Ruscha left it, sitting as a cover to the septic tank.*[62] *Given that for many, including Vitruvius, the distinctive feature of architecture is that it has toilets, the question is not what are the facts of this case but what are the effects of compiling the facts this way or that.)*

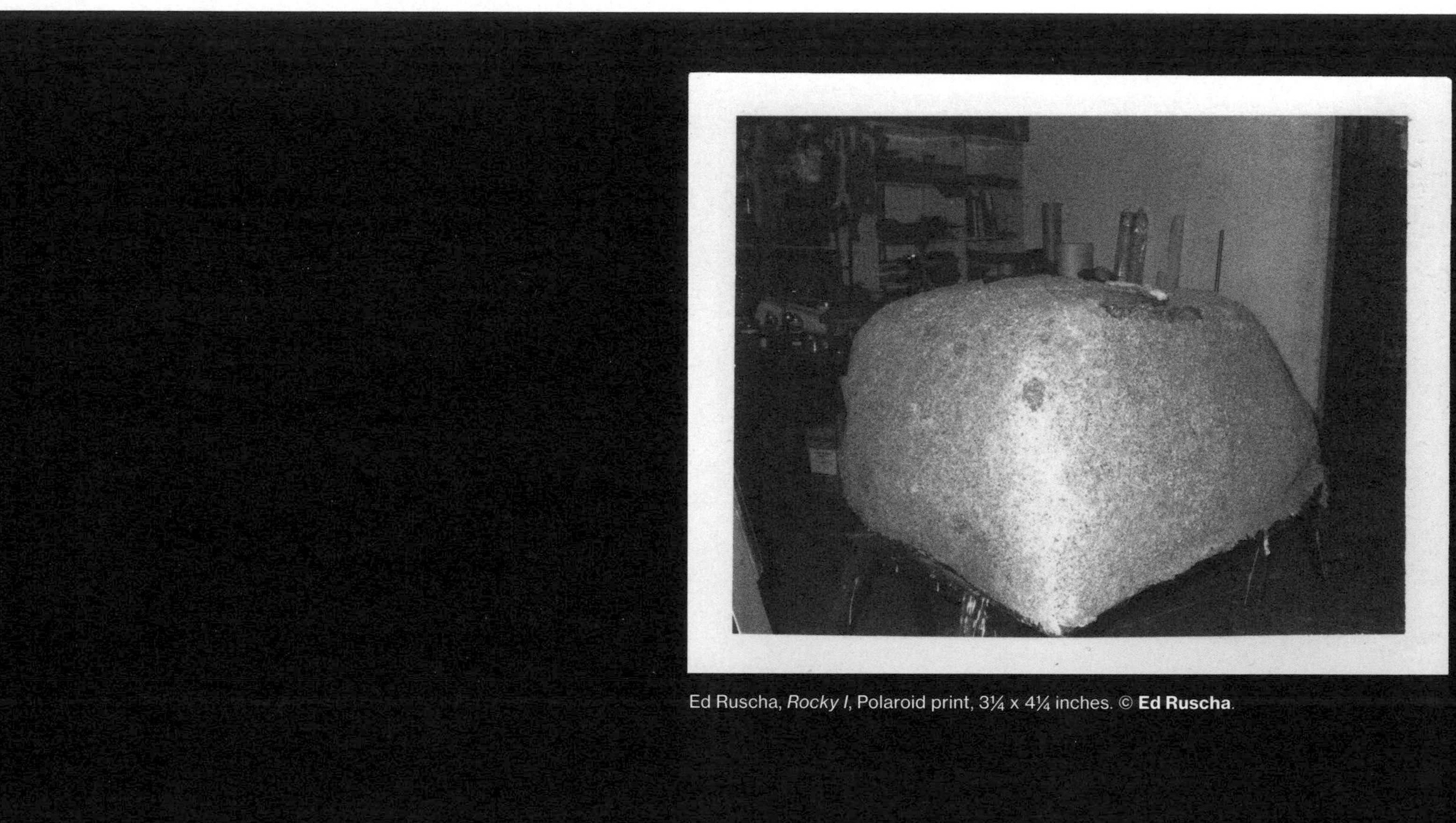

Ed Ruscha, *Rocky I*, Polaroid print, 3¼ x 4¼ inches. © **Ed Ruscha**.

1 Philip Dougherty, "Advertising; Arnell/ Bickford Agency on the Move," New York *Times*, July 22, 1986. Accessed August 17, 2015. http://www.nytimes.com/1986/07/22/business/advertising-arnell-bickford-agency-on-the-move.html.

2 The first volume of the series was on Robert Stern, published in 1981. Monographs on Michael Graves (1982), James Stirling (1984), Aldo Rossi, (1985), Gwathmey Siegel (1984), and Frank Gehry (1985) followed. Arnell went on to be involved with other publications on architects and is still active in architectural branding.

3 While there is quite a bit of Internet chatter on the contemporary architectural monograph (see, for example, Mrinal Rammohan, "The Architectural Monograph is Here to Stay," ArchDaily, June 16, 2015. Accessed November 3, 2015. http://www.archdaily.com/640615/the-monograph-is-here-to-stay/; Martin Fuller, "Commentary: Is the architect's monograph our latest endangered species?" Architectural Record, February 15, 2011. Accessed November 3, 2015. http://archrecord.construction.com/features/critique/2011/1103commentary.asp) there is little scholarly literature on its historical emergence. Nevertheless, certain key features can be discerned if one considers Le Corbusier's *Oeuvres Complétes* and Rem Koolhaas's *S,M,L,XL* to constitute two ends of a process of that restructured the genre. They differ not in number of pages—*S,M,L,XL* has fewer pages than the *Oeuvres Complétes* as a set, which is how it was conceived—but principally in the number of different types of information included.

4 Although the many more recent platforms that permit self publishing, from little booklets to Instagram, have introduced new qualities—today's monographs have more in common with McLuhan than with McMillan—the genre continues to produce a specific kind of architectural subject and to define what we know about and how we know the subject of architecture.

5 On this aspect of Claude-Nicolas Ledoux's *Architecture Considérée sous le rapport de l'art, des moeurs et de la legislation* (1804), see Svend Eriksen, *Early Neo-Classicism in France*, trans. Peter Thornton (London: Faber, 1974), 66; Anthony Vidler, *Claude-Nicolas Ledoux: Architecture and Social Reform at the End of the Ancien* Régime (Cambridge, Massachusetts, and London: The MIT Press, 1990).

6 On the history and theory of lists in particular, see Umberto Eco, *The Infinity of Lists: An Illustrated Essay*, trans. Alastair McEwan (Rizzoli, 2009); Jack Goody, "What's in a List?" *The Domestication of the Savage Mind* (Cambridge: Cambridge University Press, 1977), 74–111. For a broader understanding of the list as one of many similar tools for managing information in the context of modern bureaucratic and scholarly protocols, see Lisa Gitelman, *Paper Knowledge: Toward a Media History of Documents* (Durham and London: Duke University Press, 2014); Peter Becker and William Clark, eds., *Little Tools of Knowledge: Historical Essays on Academic and Bureaucratic Practices* (Ann Arbor: University of Michigan Press, 2001); John Guillory, "The Memo and Modernity," *Critical Inquiry* 31, No. 1 (Autumn 2004): 108–132.

7 After the Arnell/ Bickford series of six was completed, Rizzoli continued to produce monographs on architects. It is interesting to note that in 1987 Rizzoli published *Venturi, Rauch & Scott Brown* by Stanislaus von Moos. This book could be considered more 'old-fashioned' than those by Arnell/Bickford in that it is organized around argument and theme rather than chronology and includes a range of textual analyses.

8 It is worth noting that the monographs on the European architects included in the series, Stirling and Rossi, both use the term "Schedule" as title for the list of works while the lists of works by the American architects are called "Indexes." Typically, a schedule relies on chronology while an index relies on the alphabet as means of organizing information. Schedules are devices used in office management and the management of building construction while indexes belong more to the vocabulary of books and research. Since technically the Gehry and Graves indexes are more like schedules or chronologies than indexes, the use of terms in the series appears to be both random and telling, the result of micro-decisions by Arnell/ Bickford about the appropriate rhetorical shaping needed to generate the proper brand identity for each architect.

9 Arnell/Bickford, *Frank Gehry Buildings and Projects* (Rizzoli, 1985), viii.

10 This aporia leads to others, particularly with respect to the decision making process in the production of the monograph. For example, the question of who made the decision to organize the list in this way is raised by the "aside" but also left unclear: its language leaves responsibility for the compilation and its lacunae in a strange limbo between the Gehry office and the volume editors. The monograph is also indeterminate in its authorship, with Gehry's name appearing more as a title, Arnell and Bickford as editors, Germano Celant the producer of something called an "essay" that had to be distinguished from something called "text" produced instead by Mason Andrews. In other words, there is no *mono* in the *graph* typically assumed to substantiate the common view of Gehry as architectural auteur.

11 This entry is on page X of the index, a page that begins with the entry on "Harper House, *1976, page 94*" and ends with "Arts Park, *1978, page 152.*"

12 It is current art historical practice to present these books as artworks and hence to identify them with titles in the main text rather than through publication data in footnotes. It was common architectural practice, to refer to them as books. For more on this point, see below.

13 Denise Scott Brown, "On Pop Art, Permissiveness and Planning," *AIP Journal* 35 (May 1969): 184–189. All three images included in this article are from Ruscha's artist's books.

14 Much of this is well documented in Alexandra Schwartz, *Ed Ruscha's Los Angeles* (Cambridge: MIT Press, 2010), particularly the third chapter, "Learning from Ed Ruscha," as well as in Martino Stierli, *Las Vegas in the Rear-view Mirror: The City in Theory, Photography and Film,* t rans. Elizabeth Tucker (Los Angeles: The Getty Research Institute, 2013).

15 Scott Brown, "On Pop Art, Permissiveness and Planning," 186, where she writes of *Every Building on the Sunset Strip* as "a scholarly monograph with a silver cover and slip-on box jacket, it could be on the piazzas of Florence..." See also her "Learning from Pop," *Casabella* 359–360 (December 1971): 14–23.

16 On Scott Brown's notion of things that speak for themselves and how she developed this notion through Ruscha, see Schwartz, *Ed Ruscha's Los Angeles,* 156; Deborah Fausch, "Ugly and Ordinary: The Representation of the everyday," in *Architecture of the Everyday,* Steven Harris and Deborah Berke, eds. (New York: Princeton Architectural Press/Yale Publications on Architecture, 1997), 75–106.

17 There is a great deal of literature on the research studio as well as Venturi and Scott Brown's role in its development. Much of it emphasizes textuality as such rather than its relation to the emergence of an information-driven epistemology. See Steven Izenour, "Education in The 1970s: Teaching For An Altered Reality," *Architectural Record* 10 (1970): 130; Scott Brown, "Education In The 1970s: Teaching For An Altered Reality," *Architectural Record* 10 (1970): 133; Scott Brown, *Having Words* (London: AA Publications, 2009); Scott Brown, "With People In Mind: The Architect-Teacher at Work," *Journal of Architectural Education* 35 (1981): 43–45; Beatriz Colomina, "Radical Pedagogies In Architectural Education," *Architectural Review*, September 28, 2012. http://www.architectural-review.com/today/radical-pedagogies-in-architectural-education/8636066.fullarticle; Hilar Stadler and Martino Stierli, eds., *Las Vegas Studio: Images From The Archives Of Robert Venturi And Denise Scott Brown* (Zurich: Scheidegger & Spiess, 2009); Kazys Varnelis, "Is There Research In Studio," *Journal of Architectural Education* 61 (2007): 11–14.

18 Scott Brown pays particular attention to the development of new research tools, design analysis and their relation to data in "Learning from Pop," *Casabella* 359–360 (December 1971). The apparently objective nature of photography, particularly as used by Ruscha, was essential to her understanding of visual research and clarifies her virtual silence on Ruscha's paintings and works in other media. Ruscha's paintings were apparently less amenable to being transformed into a scholarly tool for presenting urban analyses as empirical data.

19 Before publishing *Los Angeles: The Architecture of Four Ecologies* in 1971, Reyner Banham first presented his ideas about Los Angeles during a series of radio broadcasts that were then published as "Encounter with Sunset Boulevard," *The Listener* 80 (August 22, 1968): 235–36; "Roadscape with Rusting Rails," *The Listener* 80 (August 29, 1968): 267–68; "Beverly Hills, Too, Is a Ghetto," *The Listener* 80 (September 5, 1968): 296–98; and "The Art of Doing Your Thing," *The Listener* 80 (September 12, 1968): 330–31. The latter is particularly concerned with Ruscha.

20 Banham, "The Art of Doing Your Thing," 331.

21 Ibid., 330.

22 Reyner Banham, *Banham Loves LA*, dir. Julian Cooper (BBC, 1972). For more on the film, see Edward Dimendberg, "Reyner Banham on Los Angeles as a Mobile Metropolis," *Urban History* 33, no. 1 (2006): 106–125.

23 Reyner Banham, *Los Angeles: The Architecture of Four* Ecologies (Berkeley and Los Angeles: UC Press, 1971), 223. It is worth remarking that even though Banham makes it clear he considers it to be a 'work of art' in the way he captions it, that he also makes no mention of the work in the text, treating it as a mere illustration, suggests additional ambivalence about its status.

24 Punctuation plays a large role in establishing credit in this context. The names of those whose function is merely documentary are placed within parentheses while those given creative credit and author status for works represented in the illustrations are without parenthetical framing. Ed Ruscha and Charles Eames (whose photograph of the Watts Tower is Banham's image 58b) are the only two names to appear in both ways.

25 Ed Ruscha, "Five 1965 Girlfriends," *Design Quarterly*, no. 78/79 (1970): 47–53

26 This feature is consistent across all the contributors to the *Design Quarterly,* no. 78/79, bio pages and in fact had become something of a trope within conceptual art publications.

27 Schwartz, *Ed Ruscha's Los Angeles*, 133.

28 On both the relationship between the trip made to Los Angeles by students from the AA to Ruscha and for more on Environmental Communications, see my exhibition

catalog *Everything Loose Will Land, 1970s Art and Architecture in Los Angeles* (Vienna: MAK Center and Verlag fur Kunst, 2013). Exhibition catalog.

29 *Environmental Communications* (1976). Sales catalog. The group physically separated the two facets of Ruscha's production in their 1976 sales catalog; page 46 is devoted to the Ruscha slide set of images of his paintings and silkscreens, while it is not until page 63 that they advertise the sale of Ruscha's books.

30 Ed Ruscha,"My Books End Up in the Trash," Interview by A.D. Coleman, originally published in the *New York Times*, August 27, 1972 and reprinted in Ed Ruscha and Alexandra Schwartz, *Leave Any Information at the Signal: Writings, Interviews, Bits, Pages,* (Cambridge, MA: MIT Press, 2002): 46–50.

31 Ed Ruscha,"Concerning *Various Small Fires,"* Interview with John Coplans originally published in *Artforum* (February 1965) and reprinted in Ruscha and Schwartz *Leave Any Information*, 26. For additional comments on Ruscha's own manipulation of images, captions and credits, see Susanna Newbury, *Thirtyfour Parking Lots* in the Fragmented Metropolis," in Lavin, *Everything Loose,* 50–55.

32 Frank Gehry and Peter Arnell, "No I'm an Architect," A Conversation, in Arnell/Bickford, *Frank Gehry Buildings and Projects*, xviii. This introduction to the Gehry monograph is an important early statement of what has since become a commonly repeated narrative of Gehry's development.

33 Arnell/Bickford, *Gehry Building and Projects*, xiv.

34 Ibid., xiii.

35 One could surmise that another reason to semi-include the Ruscha house was that by 1985 Ruscha was well known outside of Los Angeles, well enough known for association with him to be valuable, particularly for an architect for whom it was important to be associated with artists. However, there is no evidence for this conjecture and Ruscha, while long since friends with Gehry, is not among the group of artists to whom Gehry frequently refers when describing the intimate circle of artists friends that were in his view important to his life as an architect. Those, instead, were Billy Al Bengston, Ed Moses and Robert Irwin.

36 See "The History of US Topographic Engineers," the U.S. Corps of Topographical Engineers website, http://www.topogs.org/History.htm. Accessed May 12, 2016.

37 On the trope of the desert in relation to Ruscha, see Emily Eliza Scott,"Wasteland: American Landscapes in/and 1960s Art." (PhD diss., UCLA, 2010), esp. 72–77 on Ruscha. I'd like to thank Susanna Newbury for her generous assistance with Ruscha bibliography in relation to the desert.

38 Ed Ruscha, *Royal Road Test.* (New York: G. Wittenborn, 1967).

39 On the artist's studio in this context, see Caroline A. Jones, *Machine in the Studio: Constructing the Postwar American Artist,* (Chicago and London: University of Chicago Press, 1998), particularly Chapter 2, "Filming the Artist," 60.

40 Ruscha and Schwartz, *Leave Any Information at the Signal*, 29.

41 Peter Plagens, "Ruscha's Landscape." *Vanity Fair* (February 1986): 88–95.

42 Peter Plagens, "Los Angeles: The Ecology of Evil," *Artforum* 11.4 (1972): 67–76.

43 Ibid., 74.

44 Plagens, "Ruscha's Landscape," 89, 94.

45 Ibid.

46 This information was given to me in a telephone interview by Patricia Oliver (May 23, 2012) who was working at the Gehry office in 1976 and given the job of overseeing the Ruscha Residence. Various writers have made references to the location of the house and the history of the property. None of the references confirm nor contradict each other except insofar as they all place the house near Pioneertown, originally built as a western movie set. According to the Plagens profile in *Vanity Fair*, Ruscha first visited the Yucca Valley desert with Harry Cohn.

47 Ruscha, "My Books End Up in the Trash," 49.

48 Email from Ruscha studio to Kimberli Meyer, Oct. 1, 2012. The email also states that Gehry provided drawings out of "friendship and kindness," which I presume means without a fee. The notion that Ruscha designed it himself is repeated in Calvin Thomkins "Ed Ruscha's LA," *New Yorker,* July 1, 2013.

49 See *Gehry, Buildings and Projects*, xv. Gehry addresses in some detail the change in his drawing technique both required and produced by his turn away from the architecture of fact to the architecture of expression. In his early period, Gehry focused on developing a high degree of technical facility in producing realistic renderings and perspectives, even working as a professional renderer for architects like John Portman. After the shift, according to Gehry, his drawings were no longer representational but process oriented and involved actions like grinding, cutting, scratching etc.

50 Gehry has said this to me on numerous occasions.

51 Gehry and Ruscha did quasi-collaborate once. Gehry designed the installation for Billy Al Bengston's solo exhibition, *Billy*, at LACMA in 1968 while Ruscha designed the catalog.

52 Schwartz, *Ed Ruscha's Los Angeles*, 154–155.

53 Virgina Heckert, *Ed Ruscha and "Some Los Angeles Apartments"* (Los Angeles: Getty Publications, 2013) and the catalog to the exhibition *Ed Ruscha Los Angeles Apartments* held at the Kunstmueum Basel in 2013, edited by Christian Müller.

54 When asked if drawings are equivalent to photography, Ruscha responded "No, no because the drawing gives a touch of the hand to it.... drawings would never express the idea—I like facts facts, facts are in these books. The closest representation to an apartment house in *Some Los Angeles Apartments* is a photograph, nothing else, not a drawing, because that becomes somebody else's vision of what it is, and this is the camera's eye, the closest delineation of that subject." Ruscha, "My Books End Up in the Trash," 49.

55 Leo Steinberg, "The Flatbed Picture Plane," in *Other Criteria: Confrontations with Twentieth Century Art* (Chicago: University of Chicago Press, 2007), 55–92.

56 In the context of legal discourse, "the facts of the case" are generally understood to be those facts on which both the prosecution and defense agree.

57 Nor does Ruscha claim the house as a conceptual work of art, as did many other artists working on building-like works during the mid-1970s. It is beyond the scope of this essay to address in full how the many and well-known intersections between art and architecture in the 1960s and 1970s produced the epistemological confusion that has continued to surround architecture. However, it is important to note that many works that share the Ruscha Residence's complex relation to utility, authorship and architectural inexpression are commonly defined as works of art. Gordon Matta-Clark's *Food*, for example, is typically considered a conceptual work of art. There is no reason that the Ruscha house could not be similarly defined, particularly if one understands the difference to entail the presence or absence of a parenthesis rather than some essential quality.

58 Interview with Ralph Rugoff originally published in *LA Weekly,* June 16–25, 1987, and reprinted in *Leave Any Information at the Signal*, 260. It is worth emphasizing that while the house was clearly intended to mimic a developer logic, Ruscha did not see his own property as a form of development. The distinction is implicit in the following remarks made while discussing a parcel of land on Mulholland drive and not Yucca Valley. Ruscha described his interest in escaping the city and his nostalgia about places that were undeveloped: "It used to be just a piece of wild land that was sort of like my private little national park. I could hike up there and meditate or do whatever, and no one ever went up there at all. Of course, the city just had to sell it to some developer... I guess any vacant parcel of land out these is considered something of an eyesore. It's like stagnant land, and they're determined to make use of everything."

59 A few relevant texts on evidence and argument include Lorraine Daston, "Marvelous Facts and Miraculous Evidence in Early Modern Europe," *Critical Inquiry*, Vol. 18, No. 1 (Autumn, 19919): 93–124; Bruno Latour, "Atmosphère, Atmosphère," in *Olafur Eliasson: The Weather Project*, ed. Susan May (London: Tate, 2003): 29–41 and Latour, Bruno. "Visualisation and Cognition: Drawing Things Together." *Knowledge and Society: Studies in the Sociology of Culture Past and Present* 6, (1986): 1–40.

60 Pierre Bismuth is currently making what he calls a fake fiction feature film on his quest to fine this object called "Where is Rocky II?" See Chris Campion, "Where is Rocky II? The 10-year desert hunt for Ed Ruscha's missing boulder," *The Guardian*, February 11, 2015, http://www.theguardian.com/artanddesign/2015/feb/11/where-is-rocky-ii-ed-ruscha-mojave-desert-film-pierre-bismuth.

61 See archivist Anne Kofmehl's account of this 'discovery' in the Ruscha papers at the Ransom Center at the University of Texas at Austin. http://blog.hrc.utexas.edu/2016/01/06/ed-ruscha-and-the-mysterious-rocky-ii/

62 Telephone interview with Jerry Sohn, April 10, 2016. Ruscha owned a cabin on land that Jerry Sohn has further developed with cultural projects, including viewing pavilions by Arata Isoaki. See Peter Zellner, "Between Heaven and Earth." *Domus* 947 (May 2011) 40–49.

“If there is a quintessential discourse of power, it is law. And if there is a quintessential manifestation of power, it is architecture.”

Sergio Muñoz Sarmiento

Primary Structure: Law, Power, Architecture

Artistic originality has only its own self to copy.
—Vladimir Nabokov

Quotation

In its essence a quotation[1] contains the already said and, perhaps, the said-better. This is the basic structure of the quotation. To quote is to copy, to repeat, to reference, to cite, to monumentalize, to index, to decontextualize, to clone, to violate, and to appropriate—yet not always in good faith. This essay does not intend to be all-inclusive or comprehensive of all architectural and artistic relations to the law. Rather it is in the spirit of critical debate that I explore the legal, theoretical, and historical questions concerning the act of copying within the nascent and complex field of activities that are now related under the practical, theoretical, and speculative spaces of art and law.

For the act of copying to be in relation to the law *and* have artistic purpose and meaning, copying must be inherently upheld by artistic intent. This is not to say that legality and artistic intent are synonymous. There are certainly architectural and artistic practices that are quite rigorous in purpose and meaning and yet outside of the law. To be artistic does not necessarily mean to be lawful. Conversely we have witnessed architectural and artistic projects that are well within the boundaries of law but lack substance and rigor—that is, no critical links to architectural and artistic practices and histories, social purpose, or legal-economic interrogation.

If architects and artists are to produce and engage the aesthetic via practices of copying and appropriation without falling pray to infantile and nihilistic acts of appropriation, they must practice within the discourses of art and architecture, and within the space of law (i.e., there must be intent). To appropriate with complete disregard for the law is to believe that true dissent needs no First Amendment protection. The belief in so-called "outlaw" practices is perfectly commensurate with being an architect or an artist, at least in a historical sense, and I fully endorse this notion. However, to engage in this type of practice one must be ready to succumb to any legal and social repercussions.

A scrutinizing reader might ask, What is an essay about law as doctrine, material, and medium doing in an architectural journal? Yet it is wise to remember that the analysis of property, both tangible and intangible, and its relationship to aesthetic production is not only imperative but fundamental for understanding the relationship of culture to the social, political, economic, and the juridical. Indeed engaging in polemics over aesthetics and its relationship to rights, liberties, duties, and obligations is of the utmost political, economic, and social importance.

If we seek to analyze the dialogue between art and law, it is essential that we focus attention to the *types of questions* we ask and *how we approach* an analysis/answer to these questions. It is my belief that to foster a new and rigorous understanding of contemporary artistic and architectural production, we (artists, architects, legal scholars, curators, critics, and historians) must investigate under the tutelage of a legal mindset and juridical framework: How would a legal practitioner (lawyer, law professor, judge) address and solve this problematic? To fully understand the nascent conundrum of art and law—and to create a new perspective and space from which to create culture—we must approach and assess cultural production through an understanding of legal structures and mechanisms.[2]

This new approach is hardly far-fetched, and neither is it radical or controversial. In fact, art historian Benjamin Buchloh foreshadowed my argument when he highlighted Marcel Duchamp's seminal twentieth-century artistic gesture and its relation to law:

> Beginning with the readymade, the work of art had become the ultimate subject of a legal definition and the result of institutional validation. In the absence of any specifically visual qualities and due to the manifest lack of any (artistic) manual competence as a criterion of distinction, all the traditional criteria of aesthetic judgment—of taste and of connoisseurship—have been programmatically voided. The result of this is that the definition of the aesthetic becomes on the one hand a matter of linguistic convention and on the other the function of both a legal contract and an institutional discourse (a discourse of power rather than taste).[3]

Buchloh cites Duchamp's hiring of a notary to certify that his 1919 subversion of a reproduction of Leonardo da Vinci's *Mona Lisa* (otherwise known as *L.H.O.O.Q)* was *the* authentic and original readymade. Buchloh contends that Duchamp's readymades eviscerated the concepts of authenticity, authorship, and the belief in the autonomy and self-sufficiency of the art object.[4] However, what I argue is that this seemingly innocuous linguistic inscription—the notarization on Duchamp's "Mona Lisa"—did not just do away with traditional studio aesthetics of handmade production. Rather, this linguistic-legal maneuver also reinstated the belief in and market value of authenticity and authorship. The re-emergence of authenticity and authorship would soon be upheld

1 Quotation as defined by *Blacks Law Dictionary*: (17c) 1. A statement or passage that is exactly reproduced, attributed, and cited. 2. The amount stated as a stock's or commodity's current price. - market quotation (1847) The most current price at which a security or commodity trades. 3. A contractor's estimate for a given job.—Sometimes shortened to *quote*. See *Black's Law Dictionary*, 10th edition, 2014.

2 As an apt example, the author recalls a conversation with artist and teacher Michael Asher on the similarities between Asher's post-studio course taught at the California Institute of the Arts and the trial processes in a court of law. Both the author and Asher noted the importance of addressing the making and object of art through endless focused questions based on the Socratic method, with the intent of arriving at clear artistic intent. This conversation transpired around 2005. For an interesting example of the relationship between artistic and legal writing, particularly the synthesis of bare facts with little to no superfluous information, see Michael Asher, *Writings 1973–1983 on Works 1969–1979*, ed. Benjamin H. D. Buchloh (Halifax: Press of the Nova Scotia College of Art and Design, 1983).

3 See Benjamin H. D. Buchloh, "Conceptual Art 1962–1969: From the Aesthetic of Administration to the Critique of Institutions," *October* 55 (Winter 1990): 117.

4 Ibid., 119.

5 Buchloh, "Conceptual Art."

6 In the late 1960s and early '70s.

and legally sanctioned through Conceptual Art practices and eventually by certificates of authenticity. In effect, both Conceptual Art and certificates of authenticity made the art object a simple *lieutenant*.

If, as Buchloh argues, it was conceptual art after the readymade that established "an aesthetic of administrative and legal organization and institutional validation,"[5] we can conclude that by the time conceptual art was well underway[6] the definition of "author" and "art" shifted from the aesthetic to the legal. It was no longer the signature of the artist that authored and authenticated an art object, but rather the legal instrument (e.g., bill of sale, contract, and certificate of authenticity). And thus the definition of art and art "making" in contemporary art shifts from the artist's studio to the legislative chambers;[7] from art criticism and art history to legal briefs and judicial opinions;[8] from art school critiques to law school seminars and Socratic analysis.[9] In essence, if art and architecture are now to be defined and understood by legal and administrative discourses and institutions, so must the definitions of *author, authenticity, originality, copy*, and *appropriation*, among other terms. Ironically, artists are now faced with the daunting task of having to challenge and contest a legal order that artists of the twentieth-century helped put into place.

Yet definitions are not to be seen as enemies of architecture and art, for it is through the understanding of a foreign (and yet ever present) lexicon that individuals can mobilize and immobilize power through force and force through power. If there is a quintessential discourse of power, it is law. And if there is a quintessential manifestation of power, it is architecture.[10] Until we inhabit a different spatial order and social structure, we cultural producers will be forced to read and write contemporary architectural and artistic practices through the prism of the law.[11]

7 See, for example, the U.S. Visual Artists Rights Act of 1990, which protects only those works of art that fall under the classic definition of sculpture, painting, drawing, photography, and print. Installation art, site-specific art, performance, mixed-media and video art, and other new genres are not included. This exclusion perpetuates the need for lawyers versed in art and architecture, and for artists and architects to leverage their knowledge through legal structures and argumentation.

8 See, for example, seminal American art law cases such as *Rogers v. Koons*, *Blanch v. Koons*, *Cariou v. Prince*, *Chapman Kelley v. Chicago Park District*, and *Massachusetts Museum of Contemporary Art v. Christoph Büchel* as clear examples of judges acting as art critics. Given the increase of litigation concerning artistic production and consumption, one cannot underestimate the need for legal professionals to understand modern and contemporary art.

9 See, for example, the growing number of art law courses taught in law schools, with the subject matter growing beyond trust and estates and the appropriation of cultural artifacts to discourses of appropriation art and intellectual property, authentication, contractual disputes, artists estates and foundations, free speech, production and reproduction of artworks after an artist's death, property rights, and moral rights.

10 The author is well aware of Michel Foucault and his extensive thoughts on "power" and assumes that the reader is too.

11 This is more true if we choose to think of art as a legitimate business and thus necessarily within the bounds and under the protection of law.

Part I: Architecture

> It is fine to take from the same well—but not from the same bucket.
> —Zaha Hadid[12]

Influence and inspiration are inevitable. Yet we are currently witnessing an increase in unfettered copying coupled with a desire to protect creative works from unlawful appropriation and exploitation. What leads certain artistic individuals to believe that they can copy without consequence? Why are a growing number of artists increasingly seeking to protect their creative works through legal channels?

The main arguments in support of unbridled copying and appropriation are anchored in the cultural-historical (art movements and styles such as cubism, collage, Dada, pop art, the Pictures Generation); the sociocultural (a zeitgeist and/or "This is the culture in which we live"); and techno-architectural inventions (the photographic medium, the moving image, video recording such as Betamax recorders, the Internet, and other digital technologies). Reasons given by the *information wants to be free* constituency—what we can call the *free content* lobby—include the fantastical idea that originality and creativity are oppressive fictions, or more precisely capitalist fictions, that must be defied, subverted, and deconstructed at all costs.[13]

The free-content lobby argues that we live in an age where copy-and-paste, screen grabbing, scanning, and downloading are synonymous with jaywalking and selling loosies on a street corner: a sign of the times. Its adherents promote a disturbing and intellectually dishonest belief that nothing is or can be original; that we are all simultaneous authors/creators (albeit dead ones, presumably), constantly taking, mashing, regurgitating, and remashing preexisting, unoriginal, and omnipresent culture. This community also believes that when it comes to defining the concept of *author* we must begin and end with Post-Modernism's whimsical theory that the author is dead—across the board in all disciplines, institutions, and discourses—and thus of course expect that the law's definition and application of author follow suit. Ironically the critical theory and free-content establishments want us to believe that their fictional definition of author is normative. What they fail to reason is that their erasure of authorship is authoritarian in and of itself.

As professor Lionel Bently notes in his review of David Saunders's book *Authorship and Copyright*,[14] "Authorship in copyright is not, even in its historical foundations, equitable with authorship in literature and, therefore, a critique of literary authorship need not necessarily strike at the roots of copyright law."[15] Bently adds that poststructuralist critiques have no necessary implications for copyright law.[16] In fact, Bently continues, even if Roland Barthes was correct in proposing that the author is dead, law does not have to accept this "truth."[17] Just because Barthes proclaims the death of the author does not mean that publishers will "suddenly stop administering their copyrights or paying author royalties."[18] In fact, Bently concludes, if "there is a gap between the legal concept of authorship and the understanding of authorship in literary circles [it] simply does not matter."[19]

12 See "Seeing Double: What China's Copycat Culture Means for Architecture," *Guardian*, January 7, 2013, accessed November 3, 2014, www.theguardian.com/artanddesign/architecture-design-blog/2013/jan/07/china-copycat-architecture-seeing-double.

13 Eminent American jurist and law professor Richard A. Posner explains: "Notions of genius, of individual creativity, and of authorial celebrity, which inform the condemnation of plagiarism, make the leftist uncomfortable because they seem to celebrate inequality and 'possessive individualism' (that is, capitalism). Debora Halbert, professor at the University of Hawaii at Manoa, asserts that 'for the feminist and postmodernist, appropriation or plagiarism are acts of sedition against an already established mode of knowing, a way of knowing indebted to male creation and property rights.'" See Richard A. Posner, *The Little Book of Plagiarism* (New York: Pantheon Books, 2007), 94–95. For an in-depth treatise on the right to private property, see Jeremy Waldron, *The Right to Private Property* (Oxford: Clarendon Press, 1988). I note Waldron's text due to the overwhelming lack of knowledge on the doctrine of property

To put the death of the author silliness to rest, let us note law professor Jane C. Ginsburg's[20] lucid proclamation:

> More recently, however, the claims of authorship, indeed the concept of authorship in copyright law, have encountered considerable skepticism, not to say hostility, and not only from postmodernist literary critics. Many of the latter contend that copyright, or *droit d'auteur*, obsoletely relies on the Romantic figure—or perhaps fiction—of the genius auteur. But we know today, indeed we probably have always known, that this character is neither so virtuosic, nor so individual, as the "Romantic" vision suggests. Artistic merit has never been a prerequisite to copyright (at least not in theory), and authors are not necessarily less creative for being multiple. As a result, the syllogism "the romantic author is dead; copyright is about romantic authorship; copyright must be dead, too" fails.[21]

I do not mean to argue that there are no valid reasons for copying and appropriation in art and architecture. There are—criticism, parody, teaching, scholarship, research, commentary on the underlying work—and they fall squarely within copyright law's fair-use doctrine.[22]

When the student is ready, the master will appear.
—Mabel Collins[23]

We can guess correctly that when Thomas Shine first encountered the quote above the last things on his mind were plagiarism and copyright infringement. And surely David Childs never imagined that a former graduate student at the Yale School of Architecture would allege that he copied that student's architectural design when he proposed an architectural design for New York City's 2003 Freedom Tower. But that's exactly what happened. For a quick background, let's rewind to 1999, when Shine was studying architecture at Yale and Childs was a consulting design partner at Skidmore, Owings & Merrill (SOM). For an advanced design studio, Shine conceptualized and created a design proposal for a theoretical monumental high-rise that would be built in Manhattan and used by the media during the 2012 Olympic Games. Shine's design was titled "Olympic Tower" and included another preliminary design, "Shine 99." The facts, according to the New York District Court, are as follows:

> On or about December 9, 1999, Shine presented his designs for Olympic Tower to a jury of experts invited by the Yale School of Architecture to evaluate and critique its students' work. During a 30-minute presentation to the panel, Shine explained his tower's structural design, and displayed different structural and design models (including Shine 99), renderings, floor plans, elevations, sections, a site plan, and a photomontage giving a visual impression of the tower's exterior. Defendant Childs was on the panel, and he praised Olympic Tower during the presentation, as did the other luminaries[24] evaluating Shine's work. When the review was completed, Shine was applauded by the jury and other visitors, which, according to Shine, is "highly unusual" at a student's final review. After the presentation, Childs approached Shine, complimented Shine's color pencil rendering of Olympic Tower, and invited Shine to visit after his graduation.[25]

Clearly Childs was impressed with Shine's architectural designs. In fact he was quoted in *Retrospecta*, Yale School of Architecture's journal of student work,[26] which featured Shine's Olympic Tower, as stating that Shine's design was a "very beautiful shape. You took the skin and developed it around the form—great!"[27]

In summer 2003 World Trade Center developer Larry Silverstein asked Childs to begin working as design architect and project manager for the tallest building at the proposed new site as conceptualized by Daniel Libeskind—the building that would later be called the "Freedom Tower."[28] Childs's design for the skyscraper was completed within six months and was presented to the public at a press conference in Lower Manhattan in mid-December. At this presentation Childs and SOM displayed six large computer-generated images of the Freedom Tower, two scale models, and a computer slide show detailing the design principles, and distrib-

law by artists, curators, art critics, and art theorists. With the overwhelming trajectory of Marxist thought in liberal art departments and art schools, architects and artists would be well advised to review Waldron's text.

14 Published by Routledge in 1992.

15 See Lionel Bently, "Copyright and the Death of the Author in Literature and Law," *The Modern Law Review* 57 (November 1994): 979, accessed January 18, 2011, http://onlinelibrary.wiley.com/doi/10.1111/j.1468-2230.1994.tb01989.x/pdf.

16 Ibid., 977.

17 Ibid., 982.

18 Bently, "Copyright."

19 Ibid.

20 Jane C. Ginsburg is the Morton L. Janklow Professor of Literary and Artistic Property Law at Columbia Law School.

21 See Jane C. Ginsburg, "The Concept of Authorship in Comparative Copyright Law," *DePaul Law Review* 52 (Summer 2003): 1063, 1064–65. In this article Ginsburg comments on the lack of academic, judicial, and legislative sources concerning the doctrine of authorship. She further argues that the author is at the heart of copyright and in fact, "refocusing discussion on authors—the constitutional subjects of copyright—should restore a proper perspective on copyright law, as a system designed to advance the public goal of expanding knowledge, by means of stimulating the efforts and imaginations of private creative actors."

22 17 U.S. Code § 107 - Limitations on exclusive rights: Fair use

23 Mabel Collins, in *Light on the Path* (London: George Redway, 1886).

24 In addition to Childs and Shine's professor Cesar Pelli, the jury included Yale professor and urban planner Alexander Garvin, architecture writer and critic Paul Goldberger, and Robert A. M. Stern, dean of the Yale School of Architecture.

25 See Shine v. Childs, 382 F.Supp.2d 602, 605 (2005).

26 *Retrospecta* is the annual journal of student work at the Yale School of Architecture. According to the New York District Court, "because Childs is an alumnus of the Yale School of Architecture, he presumably received a copy of this issue of *Retrospecta*. However ... Childs denies that he ever saw a copy of the issue referenced by Shine in the Complaint."

27 See Shine v. Childs, 606.

28 Shine v. Childs.

29 Ibid., 606–607.

30 Ibid., 607.

31 The Court also noted, however, that because "the alleged infringing design may never be constructed, Shine's actual damages in this action may be reduced, and he may be unable to show the need for an injunction." Shine v. Childs, 607.

uted a press packet containing six images of the proposed structure.

Shine was not flattered with what he thought to be a clear rip-off of his Olympic Tower design. In fact he was not the only one to notice similarities between his designs and Childs's Freedom Tower.

> According to [Shine's] expert, Yale Professor James Axley, several days after Childs unveiled the design for the Freedom Tower, one of Shine's original models for Olympic Tower "was retrieved from archival storage and placed on the desk of the Dean of the School of Architecture."[29]

Shine filed a copyright infringement lawsuit against Childs and SOM in the Southern District of New York on November 8, 2004, claiming that they copied Olympic Tower and Shine 99 without his permission or authorization, and stating that Childs and SOM distributed and claimed credit for his designs "willfully and with conscious disregard" for his rights on his copyrighted works.[30] Although Childs's original design for the Freedom Tower was eventually scrapped for security reasons, the New York court noted that "because [Childs's] original design for the Freedom Tower remains in the public domain, Shine's infringement claim" remained valid.[31]

Architectural Works under the United States Copyright Act

To clarify the issues behind Shine v. Childs, a brief overview of U.S. copyright law related to architectural works is in order.[32] Copyright protection originates in the U.S. Constitution under Article 1, Section 8, Clause 8.[33] Of particular importance is the fact that although copyright statutes have protected literary, musical, and dramatic works; pictorial, graphic, and sculptural works; and compilations and derivative works, the law was silent when it came to protection for architectural works.[34] Although blueprints and models were protected under U.S. copyright law,

> most authorities concluded that plans were not infringed by using them, without the architect's permission, to construct the building they depicted. Moreover, the prevailing view was that an architect's rights did not extend to the actual building derived from his or her plans. A building, as a useful article, could be protected by copyright only to the extent it had artistic features that could be identified separately from, and were capable of existing independently of, the structure's utilitarian aspects.[35]

It was not until 1990, when Congress passed the Architectural Works Copyright Protection Act ("AWCPA") in adherence to the Berne Convention for the Protection of Literary and Artist Works, that copyright laws were updated[36] to provide

> full protection to works of architecture by establishing them as a new category of protectable subject matter ... and defining an architectural work as: 'the design of a building as embodied in any tangible medium of expression, including a building, architectural plans, or drawings. The work includes the overall form as well as the arrangement and composition of spaces and elements in the design, but does not include individual standard features.'[37]

It is thought by some[38] that within the nascent doctrine of architecture and copyright, Shine v. Childs is the most important infringement case to date, as it shed light on previously unanswered questions over the scope and meaning of the AWCPA. However, it is not simply the alleged copyright infringement of a student's design that is of concern to us, but also the concept or gesture of quoting—or more specifically, the difference between quoting and plagiarism.

32 Of the five intellectual property protections (copyright, patents, trademark, right of publicity, and trade secrets), copyright is believed to be the most important with respect to architectural works. See Manuel R. Valcarcel IV, "Copyright Issues in Architecture," *Southeast Real Estate Business*, October 2004, accessed December 13, 2014, www.southeastrebusiness.com/articles/OCT04/feature6.html. See also Rashida Y. V. MacMurray, "Trademarks or Copyrights: Which Intellectual Property Right Affords Its Owner the Greatest Protection of Architectural Ingenuity?," *Northwestern Journal of Technology and Intellectual Property* 3 Northwestern Journal of Technology and Intellectual Property Law (2005), accessed December 13, 2014, http://scholarlycommons.law.northwestern.edu/cgi/viewcontent.cgi?article=1031&context=njtip. Regarding the protection of landmark buildings through intellectual property, see Keri Christ, "Edifice Complex: Protecting Landmark. Buildings as Intellectual Property—A Critique of Available Protections and a Proposal," *The Trademark Reporter* 92 no. 1041 (September–October 2002).

33 "To promote the Progress of Science and useful Arts, by securing for limited Times to Authors and Inventors the exclusive Right to their respective Writings and Discoveries."

34 17 U.S.C. Sec. 102(a)(8)(1990). See David E. Shipley, "The Architectural Works Copyright Protection Act at Twenty: Has Full Protection Made a Difference?," *Journal of Intellectual Property Law* (Fall 2010): 3. "It was well established that plans, blueprints, and models were copyrightable writings under the 1909 Act's category of 'drawings or plastic works of a scientific or technical character,' and then as 'pictorial, graphic, and sculptural works' under the 1976 Act. The scope of an architect's copyright protection was, however, quite limited." See also Xiyin Tang, "Narrativizing the Architectural Copyright Act: Another View of the Cathedral," 21 *Texas Intellectual Property Law Journal* (2013) 33, 34: "Europe had recognized copyrights in architecture for quite some time."

35 See Shipley, "Architectural Works," 5.

36 Copyright scholar William Patry spent a year studying whether to extend copyright protection to architectural works. "The 1990 Architectural Works Copyright Protection Act was the end result [of the study]. It is a statute I have tremendous fondness for, both because it is a subject matter I truly love ..., because it was the only non-fast track statute I worked on that never changed once it left the House subcommittee, because it reflected pure policy, and because I lived deeply the history of its passage through battles in the Copyright Office and later in drafting the legislation." See William Patry, "Twisting in the Wind," *The Patry Copyright Blog*, accessed December 14, 2014, http://williampatry.blogspot.com/2005/08/twisting-in-wind.html.

37 See Shipley, "Architectural Works," 5.

38 See Andrew Baum and Britton Payne, "Protecting Architectural Works: Breaking New Ground with Familiar Tools," *Construction Lawyer* 27 (Fall 2007): 23. See also Shipley, "Architectural Works," 6: "Cases like Shine v. Childs are the exception, not the rule."

1-2 Oliver Edmund Freundlich

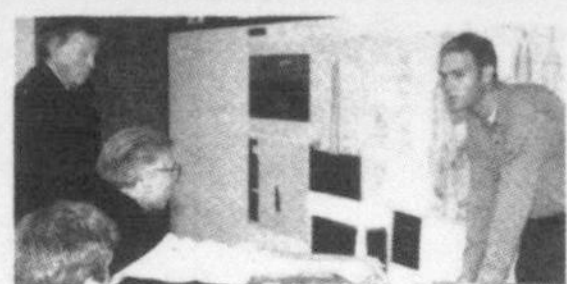

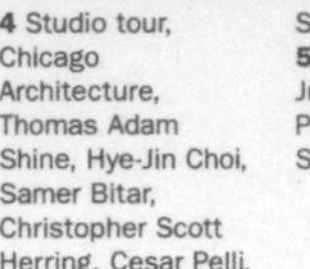

4 Studio tour, Chicago Architecture, Thomas Adam Shine, Hye-Jin Choi, Samer Bitar, Christopher Scott Herring, Cesar Pelli, Stanley Tigerman
5 Vincent J.Scully, Jr., Alexander Purves, Christopher Scott Herring

Thomas Adam Shine: The building appears as just another tall building as a silhouette from far away in New York City. The form changes depending on the angle as you get closer and closer to the building. Driving down 11th Avenue the building slowly unwinds as you see the facade and the light reflecting off the window mullions. You might see something that may appear as a flame going up slowly. Moving in closer to the building a secondary system takes over which is the skin of the building based on triangulating the form and breaking it down so you get a reading of both the mass of the building and the height. The building starts on the Manhattan grid, with the form generated by a twist shifted off center and then aligned. Rather than having horizontal and vertical bracing, I just crossed the entire building so there are no vertical columns apart from the core in the building – it is all slightly diagonal.
David M. Childs: It is a very beautiful shape. You took the skin and developed it around the form – great!
Alexander D. Garvin: It is totally different no matter where you are, because of the surface modules, which is oddly contextual.
Paul Goldberger: Can you tell us a little about the base and the entrance?
Thomas Adam Shine: The idea was to mark the entrance. So you come into the lobby and you see not just the skin of the building, but the solid mass of the building. It is aligned so the three elevator cores, at least on the ground floor, line up with the three entrances of the building so there is a continuous reading through the skin.
Paul Goldberger: We have seen a whole lot of buildings that are essentially not entered. Here, not only is there an entrance, but the entrance derives from the themes he is playing with in the façade.

6

7

Page from the Yale School of Architecture's *Retrospecta* 1999–2000 showing Shine's Olympic Tower.

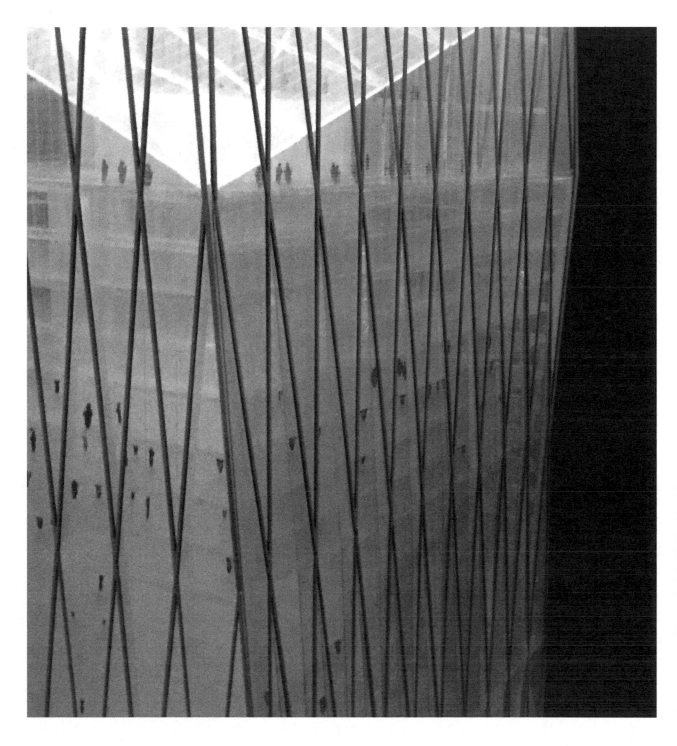

Architectural models of the 2003 scheme for the World Trade Center, designed by David Childs with Daniel Libeskind.

comparisons between the two structures in their Reply Memorandum. See Def. Reply Br. at 12, 18, 21, and 24. Although defendants offer these comparisons to point out what they claim are significant differences between the two towers, "[i]t has long been settled that 'no plagiarist can excuse the wrong by showing how much of his work he did not pirate.'" Tufenkian, 338 F.3d at 132 (quoting Sheldon v. Metro-Goldwyn Pictures Corp., 81 F.2d 49, 56 (2d Cir. 1936) (L. Hand, J.)). Any lay observer examining the two towers side by side would notice that: (1) each tower has a form that tapers and twists as it rises, (2) each tower has an undulating, textured diamond shaped pattern covering its facade, and (3) the facade's diamond pattern continues to and concludes at the foot of each tower, where one or more half diamond shapes open up and allow for entry. These combination of these elements gives the two towers a similar "total concept and feel" that is immediately apparent even to an untrained judicial eye.

It is possible, even likely, that some ordinary observers might not find the two towers to be substantially similar because, as defendants note, there are differences between the Freedom Tower and Olympic Tower, including, inter alia, the number of sides of each tower that twist (the Freedom Tower's two versus Olympic Tower's four); the direction of each tower's twist (the Freedom Tower twists clockwise and Olympic Tower twists counterclockwise); the shape of each tower's ground floor (the Freedom Tower is a parallelogram and Olympic Tower is a square); and the various contrasting details of each tower's

25

Excerpt of Court Opinion and Order, Shine v. Childs, 382 F.Supp.2d (2005).

entrance and facade. See Def. Reply Br. at 11-24; see also Warner Bros., Inc. v. Am. Broad. Cos., 654 F.2d 204, 211 (2d Cir. 1981) ("[W]hile 'no plagiarist can excuse the wrong by showing how much of his work he did not pirate,' a defendant may legitimately avoid infringement by intentionally making sufficient changes in a work which would otherwise be regarded as substantially similar to that of the plaintiff's.") (quoting Sheldon, 81 F.2d at 56). However, it also is possible that a lay observer, applying the total concept and feel test, might find that the Freedom Tower's twisting shape and undulating diamond-shaped facade make it substantially similar to Olympic Tower, and therefore an improper appropriation of plaintiff's copyrighted artistic expression.

Because reasonable jurors could disagree as to the substantial similarity between Olympic Tower and the Freedom Tower, defendants' motion for summary judgment as to plaintiff's claims regarding Olympic Tower is denied.

Plagiarism vs. Copyright Infringement

In *The Little Book of Plagiarism*,[39] eminent jurist and scholar Richard A. Posner argues that not all plagiarism is copyright infringement, and not all copyright infringement is plagiarism.[40] Furthermore, Posner adds, plagiarism is not easily defined by the concepts of theft or borrowing,[41] necessitating another key factor: that of concealment.[42]

Yet for Posner adding concealment to the definition of plagiarism is still not enough. In order for there to be plagiarism, Posner continues, the copying must be "deceitful in the sense of misleading the intended readers,"[43] and this deceitful copying must also induce reliance by the same intended readers.[44] In other words, the reader must be induced to act based on the belief that the work she is viewing or reading is original. A good example would be a museum curator (the reader) providing an artist (the plagiarist) an opportunity to exhibit an artwork that the curator believes to be original, but in fact the artist has copied the idea and/or artwork from another creator.

Yet we still do not have an adequate and robust definition of plagiarism. According to Posner, the curator and viewing audience would then have to *care enough* about being deceived about the original author of the idea and/or artwork "that had he [the curator and viewing audience] known he would have acted differently."[45] The ultimate definition of plagiarism, Posner concludes, is "nonconsensual fraudulent copying."[46]

39 Published by Pantheon Press in 2007.

40 Posner, *The Little Book of Plagiarism*, 5.

41 Ibid., 11–12.

42 Ibid., 17.

43 Ibid., 19.

44 Posner, *The Little Book of Plagiarism*.

45 Ibid., 20.

46 Ibid., 33. I want to add that in Posner's other groundbreaking text, *The Economic Structure of Intellectual Property Law*, coauthored with William M. Landes, the authors argue that a "plagiarist and a copyright infringer are both copycats; the difference is that the plagiarist is trying to pass off the copied work as his own while the infringer qua infringer is merely trying to appropriate value generated by property that belongs to someone else." Published by Belknap Press in 2003.

Copyright Infringement

Under U.S. copyright law, in order for Shine to prevail in a copyright infringement claim he would have to prove ownership of a valid copyright and the copying of the original elements of his work. The U.S. District Court for the Southern District of New York acknowledged that Shine's copyright registration certificates were compelling and valid evidence of a copyright. For the copying element of infringement Shine had to prove that Childs had access to his design and that there was substantial similarity between his and Childs's design. Because Childs evaluated Shine's designs at Yale, he had to concede that he had access to Shine's design. Therefore the only remaining issue was whether the designs were substantially similar.

To decide the question of substantial similarity, the court debated how to compare and contrast the similarities and differences between the two designs. The court considered whether to apply the *separability* test[47] or the *total concept and feel* test, finding that the latter was "appropriate for architectural works because the AWCPA protects the 'overall form' of architectural designs in addition to their individual copyrightable elements."[48] The New York court found that using the total concept and feel test, "courts have taken care to identify 'precisely the particular aesthetic decisions—original to the plaintiff and copied by the defendant—that might be thought to make the designs similar in the aggregate.'"[49]

Applying the total concept and feel test, the New York trial court first found that although the design of Shine 99 was arguably protectable and original,[50] the idea of a twisting tower with a rectangular base and parallel sides was not unique and that there was no evidence to suggest that Childs would have thought of the idea only by viewing Shine 99. The court further found that Shine's own expert could not find similarities between Shine 99 and Freedom Tower substantial enough to warrant comment.[51]

However, as to Shine's Olympic Tower, the court did find that

> a lay observer, applying the total concept and feel test,[52] might find that [Childs's] Freedom Tower's twisting shape and undulating diamond-shaped facade made it substantially similar to [Shine's] Olympic Tower, and therefore an improper appropriation of [Shine's] copyrighted expression.[53]

The court noted:

> Any lay observer examining the two towers side by side would notice that: (1) each tower has a form that tapers and twists as it rises, (2) each tower has an undulating, textured diamond-shaped pattern covering its facade, and (3) the facade's diamond pattern continues to and concludes at the foot of each tower, where one or more half diamond shapes open up and allow for entry. The combination of these elements gives the two towers a similar 'total concept and feel' that is immediately apparent even to an untrained judicial eye.[54]

Interestingly the court also observed that it would be

> possible, even likely, that some ordinary observers might not find the two towers to be substantially similar because, as the defendants note, there are differences between the Freedom Tower and Olympic Tower, including, inter alia, the number of sides of each tower that twist (the Freedom Tower's two versus Olympic Tower's four); the direction of each tower's twist (the Freedom Tower twists clockwise and Olympic Tower twists counterclockwise); the shape of each tower's ground floor (the Freedom Tower is a parallelogram and Olympic Tower is a square); and the various contrasting details of each tower's entrance and facade.[55]

Given the possibility of different legal outcomes, the court allowed the case to proceed on the question of whether Childs's Freedom Tower design infringed Shine's Olympic Tower design, declining to allow the same question in regard to Shine's Shine 99 design. Unfortunately the case was settled in June 2006,[56] so we were left without a legal analysis and conclusion as to whether Childs infringed Shine's copyrighted Olympic Tower architectural design.

Plagiarism or Inspiration

Legal analysis aside, given the mentor-student relationship between Childs and Shine, the question of whether Childs plagiarized Shine's architectural designs is equally as important. Thus if we apply Posner's definition of plagiarism to that issue, would Childs's actions meet the requirements for plagiarism? As previously noted, one finding of the New York District Court was that a lay observer might find Childs's design to be substantially similar to Shine's. Given this judicial finding, it would not be far-fetched to conclude that Childs copied Shine's designs. Given that Childs did not credit Shine for the design, we can say that Childs also concealed his copying, therefore arguably leading developer Silverstein to believe Childs's designs were original. We can then say that these factors led to Silverstein's decision to award Childs the coveted status of architect and project manager for the tallest building at the proposed new World Trade Center site. The only remaining variable is the question of whether Silverstein would have cared enough about the concealment—whether he would have consented to fraudulent copying.

Remember that the New York court also found that it would be possible, even likely, that some ordinary observers might not find the two towers to be substantially similar. Given this scenario, our previous plagiarism analysis is turned on its head. Accusations of plagiarism quickly turn into acknowledgments of inspiration, and inspiration is certainly not an ethical or legal wrong. Furthermore, and given the power imbalance between Childs and Shine, a plagiarism allegation against Childs would most likely have earned Childs a slap on the wrist or, at best, a public shaming. So what other recourse, other than plagiarism, did Shine have to address his alleged injuries? It is here that we must highlight the increasing leveraging of law by cultural producers in order to alleviate perceived or actual wrongdoings, while keeping in mind that the appropriation and quoting of law and juridical structures by artists as both form and content has not always taken place in a court of law.[57] In the paragraphs that follow I highlight two artists whose artistic architectural projects engage the spatial and architectonic implications of the law. These two projects claim, create, and destroy spaces not unlike the practice of architecture or the law, and yet not necessarily successfully.

Part II: Law as Medium[58]

Not all architectural and artistic projects that appropriate law—as medium, content, subject matter, or physical manifestation—are aesthetically and intellectually rigorous. Nevertheless there are cultural gestures (some of them labeled *art projects*) that successfully analyze the law's fiction and force—with its attendant and real spatial and political consequences—without disregarding aesthetics. Artists such as Hito Steyerl, Christian Marclay, Mike Kelley, Felix Gonzalez-Torres, and Soda_Jerk[59] critically appropriate content as well as legal instruments, and through their laserlike focus examine legal-economic and legal-historical relationships related to the travel industry, gun rights, the ideological and pedagogical dissemination of American history, certificates of authenticity and conceptual art, and intellectual property.

Yet there are some art projects that appropriate law in a purely symbolic manner, and thus regrettably do not engage or incorporate the force and structures of law. In brief, these projects privilege aesthetics and the commodification of art at the disservice of analyzing the relationship between artistic and legal fictions, thus perpetuating a superficial and pedestrian understanding of law. These projects—art as art—do not help us to better understand the chameleonic and amorphous nomenclature otherwise known as law.

A clear example of this symbolic approach is Carey Young's *Declared Void II* (2013). According to the artist's press release, this project

> consists of a large-scale legal text in black vinyl with a wall drawing which delineates a corner of the gallery. The text

47 See Shine v. Childs, 613. "If the court were to follow the ["separability test"]...and separate out only those 'kernels' of expression that would qualify as original, that, as our [Second] Circuit has held, 'would result in almost nothing being copyrightable because original works broken down into their composite parts would usually be little more than basic unprotectable elements like letters, colors, and symbols.'" Brackets added.

48 Ibid., 614.

49 Ibid., 613.

50 Ibid., 610.

51 Ibid., 612.

52 Shine v. Childs.

53 Ibid., 615–16. Brackets added.

54 Ibid., 615.

55 Shine v. Childs.

56 See Andrew Mangino, "Freedom Tower Suit Resolved," *Yale Daily News*, accessed January 3, 2015, http://yaledailynews.com/blog/2006/09/26/freedom-tower-suit-resolved.

57 Artists have engaged and employed law in its physical manifestations (e.g., legal instruments otherwise known as contracts[78]) in order to refer back to the conditions that make art possible. These artists use written agreements as a medium, some more successfully than others. The unsuccessful ones tend to use the contract or legal instruments in symbolic form. But there are also artists such as Michael Asher, Hans Haacke, Adrian Piper, Felix Gonzalez-Torres, and Daniel Buren, who understand that it is not enough to simply pretend to use a contract or its structure for purely aesthetic or poetic reasons, or to simply index a functional structure in a nonfunctional manner. These artists keep the functional aspects of contractual agreements in conjunction with law's operative and forceful nature. Seth Siegelaub and Robert Projansky's seminal and groundbreaking artists' rights agreement of 1971, "The Artists Reserved Rights and Transfer Sale Agreement," is also indicative of the law's influence on the interpretation of art, artistic movements, and practices.

58 I align the term/concept "medium" here with Rosalind E. Krauss's notion of medium as defined in her seminal texts, *A Voyage on the North Sea: Art in the Age of the Post-Medium Condition* (London: Thames & Hudson, 2000), Reinventing the Medium, Critical Inquiry Vol. 25, No. 2, "Angelus Novus": Perspectives on Walter Benjamin (Winter, 1999), pp. 289–305, and Under Blue Cup, MIT Press, 2011.

59 Soda_Jerk (aka sisters Dan and Dominique Angeloro) is an Australian art collective based in New York.

60 See *Carey Young: Legal Fictions*, accessed February 20, 2016, www.careyyoung.com/carey-young-legal-fictions.

61 Volumes of legal scholarship have addressed the issues and difficulty of granting constitutional waivers. See Michael E. Tigar, "Foreword: Waiver of Constitutional Rights:

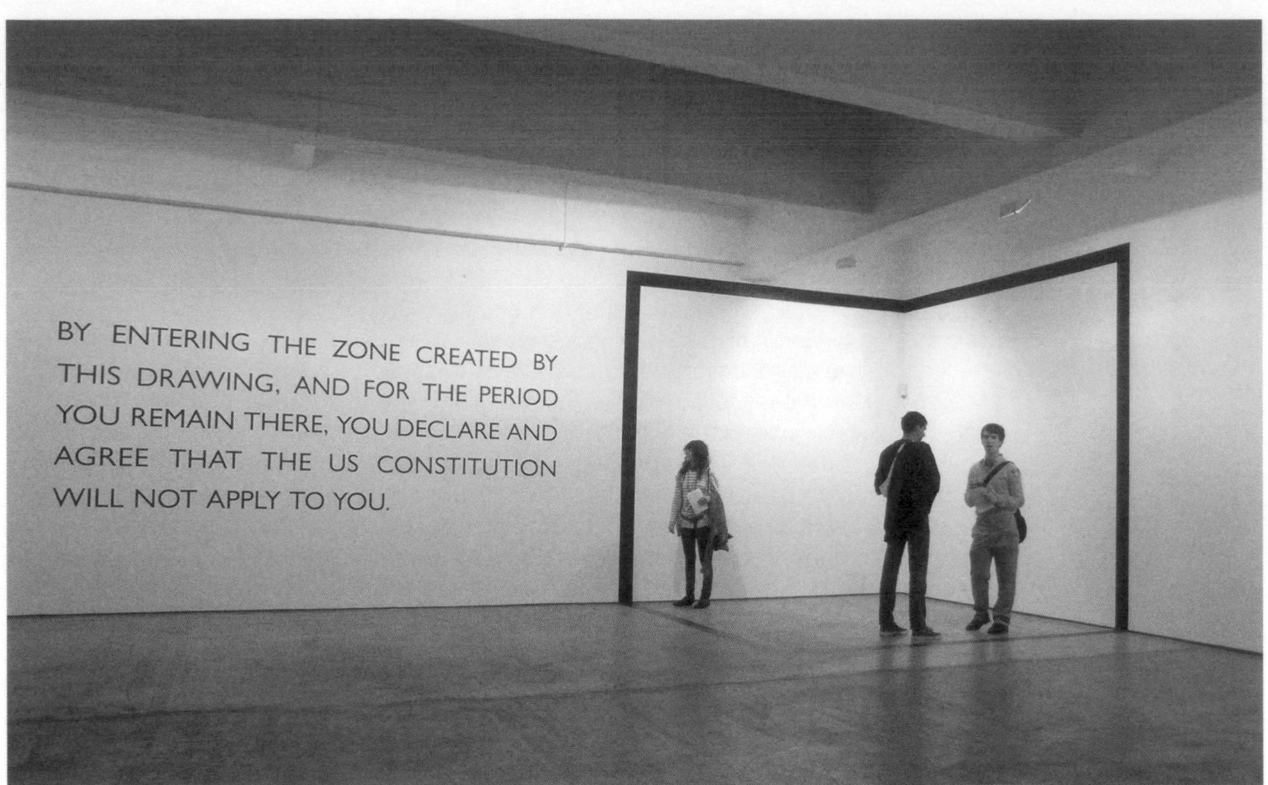

Carey Young, *Declared Void*, 2005, Vinyl drawing and text, Dimensions variable, 133 x 133 inches (337.8 x 337.8 cm) as installed. Vinyl band: 6 inches (15.2 cm); letters: 6 ¼ inches (15.8 cm) high.

takes the form of a contract in which American citizenship is offered to the viewer in return for the viewer entering the performative "platform" created by the work. While clearly a fictional proposition, the piece offers a contractual agreement with the artist in which the viewer can enter and share the artist's hallucinatory proposition. Developed from an ongoing interest in legal "black holes," in which law is used to create zones with unclear legal status and rights, the piece conflates the aesthetics of minimalism and conceptual art with ideas of migrancy and offers a potent political provocation.[60]

Take also Young's *Declared Void* from 2005, where the artist informs viewers that they will waive their U.S. Constitutional rights by stepping into a cubic space delineated by a thick black vinyl line applied to the walls and floor. Alongside the wall, Young adds the following text: "BY ENTERING THE ZONE CREATED BY THIS DRAWING, AND FOR THE PERIOD YOU REMAIN THERE, YOU DECLARE AND AGREE THAT THE US CONSTITUTION WILL NOT APPLY TO YOU." This quaint metaphor[61] pales in comparison to the ongoing situation endured by numerous alleged terrorists and enemy combatants at the Guantanamo Bay detention camp. Young was quite aware of this very real legal heterotopia.[62] As writer Brian Sholis notes, "In fact, while crafting the piece Young sought legal advice on how best to *re-create* the 'gray area' of the detainee prison at Guantánamo Bay."[63] Lawyer-curator Daniel McClean supported this artistic gesture by arguing, "A legal fiction, Young's work asks where legal territories apply and where laws and human rights are enforceable, a particularly pressing question in the context of Guantanamo Bay, where the U.S. Constitution was deemed by officials of the U.S. state not to apply in the torture of Al-Qaeda suspects."[64] Young's simplistic project is eclipsed only by McClean's willful ignorance masked as art criticism. Young's recreation, appropriation, and quotation did not comprise a legal fiction but rather a more

Disquiet in the Citadel," *Harvard Law Review* 84 (November 1970), accessed November 6, 2014, http://scholarship.law.duke.edu/cgi/viewcontent.cgi?article=5874&context=faculty_scholarship. Citing Johnson v. Zerbst, Tigar explains that for a waiver to be effective it must be an "intentional relinquishment or abandonment of a known right." He adds, "Whether the Court in fact has been willing to validate mythical consents and whether the image of the 'free man' is grounded in demonstrable reality remain to be seen." However, Tigar argues that "there may be some procedural incidents of the criminal process which the accused cannot waive. The Supreme Court has said that the right to jury trial, for example, is a right not only of the accused, but of the government, and that it would not be unconstitutional to require the government's and the court's concurrence in a waiver." See also Maurita Elaine Horn, "Confessional Stipulations: Protecting Waiver of Constitutional Rights," *University of Chicago Law Review* 61 (Winter 1994), citing Johnson v. Zerbst: "Although *Johnson* concerned the waiver of the Sixth Amendment right to counsel, it has been subsequently interpreted to apply to a defendant's constitutional rights generally. Also, *Johnson* creates a presumption against waiver. 'Courts indulge every reasonable presumption against waiver of fundamental constitutional rights and we do not presume acquiescence in the loss of fundamental rights.' The trial court should clearly determine that the defendant has made a valid waiver, and 'it would be fitting and appropriate for that determination to appear upon the record.'"

62 For a definition of *heterotopia*, see Michel Foucault, "Of Other Spaces," *Diacritics* 16 (Spring 1986): 22–27.

63 See Brian Sholis, "Carey Young," Artforum.com, accessed November 6, 2014, http://artforum.com/picks/id=24394&view=print. Italics mine.

gratuitous fiction, make-believe—without force, consequence, or import.

In *Declared Void II,* viewers are asked to pretend that they have been granted the highly-coveted U.S. citizenship within an art gallery space by the waiving of a magic wand and the drafting of a quasi-legal instrument (otherwise known as a contract). In *Declared Void,* Young's viewers—in New York's Chelsea arts district no less—are asked to imagine what it would be like to lose their constitutional rights—freedom of expression, the right to be secure against unreasonable searches and seizures, and the right to be protected against cruel and unusual punishment[65]—presumably while making dinner reservations via OpenTable and taking selfies on their iPhones. Clearly the architectural and legal differences between an art gallery and prison are not obvious to all, as is the fact that prisoners at Guantanamo Bay are not voluntarily waiving any of their civil and human rights.

No one within Young's art project will actually experience the schizophrenic physical, emotional, and psychological traumas experienced by detainees at Guantanamo Bay. Young's viewers will not exist in a state of legal limbo—stateless, homeless, lawless.[66] In short, Young's audience will not experience the asphyxiating force of law.

64 See Daniel McClean, "The Artist's Contract/From the Contract of Aesthetics to the Aesthetics of the Contract," *Mousse* no. 25 (June 2010), accessed February 20, 2016, http://mousse magazine.it/articolo.mm?id=607.

65 These are only three of many rights granted under the U.S. Constitution and the Bill of Rights.

66 For a clear exposé on Guantanamo Bay and its implications on due process, see Marc D. Falkoff's "Litigation and Delay at Guantanamo Bay," *New York City Law Review* 10 (Summer 2007): "Some day the prison will be closed and the term 'Guantánamo' will be reduced to little more than a cultural signifier, evoking the same kind of national shame that we feel upon hearing about Fred Korematsu and our Japanese American internment camps in World War II." For a wonderful analysis on post 9/11 suspension of law, see Giorgio Agamben, *State of Exception* (Chicago: University of Chicago Press, 2005).

I didn't want to be told what to do.
—Gordon Matta-Clark[67]

And yet there are art projects that successfully engage the law as medium with the intent to ask probing questions rather than provide moral claims. Take for instance Gordon Matta-Clark's 1975 sculptural-architectural project *Day's End*, installed—or perhaps deinstalled—on New York City's Pier 52. Much has been written about how Matta-Clark's breaking into closed-off city property led to his outlaw-fugitive status. But to my knowledge little has been written about the relationship between Matta-Clark's violent act and property law as well as the history of property contestation in the United States. Although volumes could be written about this relationship, here I will highlight two seminal texts that are key to analyzing the concepts of appropriation and intent in relation to *Day's End* and its appropriation of law: the fundamental property law case in the United States from 1823, Johnson v. M'Intosh,[68] and the law review article, "Property Outlaws,"[69] by legal scholars Eduardo Moises Peñalver and Sonia K. Katyal.

To Matta-Clark—and to his attorney—the artistic reasons for breaking into city property to carry out a sculptural project were key. Matta-Clark's attorney, advising him on the importance of an artistic statement—i.e., artistic intent—writes, "The statement should generalize about what you did and avoid descriptions, but you should amplify the artistic (in)tensions [sic] and relate it to your theories about art and this kind of art."[70] Equally important was Matta-Clark's conceptualization of this "trespass" as appropriation: "I simply appropriated the pier by keeping my crew of henchmen boarding and barbwiring up all the alternative entrances except for the front door in which I substituted my own lock and bolt."[71] Matta-Clark's intent was to create an overriding property right by aestheticizing a debased and abandoned structure.

> If in the midst of this state of affairs it would seem within the rights of an artist or any other person for that matter to enter such a premises with a desire to improve the property, to transform the structure in the midst of its ugly criminal state into a place of interest, fascination, and value.[72]

These same reasons were held paramount in Johnson v. M'Intosh: the need to put property occupied and used by Native American to so-called better use. Like the settlers need to create a fictional legal construct to override preexisting definitions of *property* and *property rights*, Matta-Clark employs the tools of a colonizer to discover unused property and question current property laws and property use. Peñalver and Katyal argue that the violation of property laws by outlaws can enhance the social order. In their view "the apparent stability and order that property law provides owe much to the destabilizing role of the lawbreaker, who occasionally forces shifts of entitlements and laws."[73] Matta-Clark's appropriation of private property—embodied by precision, focus, intent, and specificity—questions the ethical and moral dimensions of better use in an unauthorized taking of property.

67 See Corinne Diserens, ed., *Gordon Matta-Clark* (New York: Phaidon Press, 2003), 179.

68 Johnson v. M'Intosh (21 U.S. 543) granted Indian land to U.S. settlers under the court's ruling that the settlers be granted property rights due to their "discovery" of "untitled" land.

69 Eduardo Moises Peñalver and Sonia K. Katyal, "Property Outlaws," 155 *University of Pennsylvania Law Review* 1095 (2007).

70 See Diserens, ed., *Gordon Matta-Clark*, 8.

71 Ibid., 12–13.

72 Ibid., 12.

73 Peñalver and Katyal, "Property Outlaws," 1098.

Gordon Matta-Clark,
Day's End (Pier 52), 1975.

Conclusion

Power dynamics have never been more palpable. Although power structures and imbalances have historically been present, it is not until now that we are fully experiencing the materialization and exploitation of law to build new power structures and reinforce old ones. We are no longer simply witnessing the traditional power battles between corporations or corporations against individuals but also the birth of creative individual against creative individual.

The logical outcomes of this new manifestation are power oppositions between artist and artist, architect and architect. Given the late-twentieth-century rise in the use and appropriation of law and juridical structures by artists, it is only natural that architects and artists of all classifications leverage the bodies of law—and all their amalgamated linguistic and physical complexities—to empower themselves and their immediate constituencies. Perhaps the question is not that of obtaining a simple resolution to a dialectic between author and plagiarist or original and copy. Rather, our use and interrogation of law should be a tool for exposing the systems that create and perpetuate the powers that shape our built environment. This is not to say that law is our only hope. But neither is culture. It is only through quotation—with intent—of one through the other that we will begin to transform our spaces and languages into new and more inhabitable structures and modes of existence.

8

“If you want to scare me, give me piece of white paper.”

8 Interview with Richard Rogers

P49 What role do you think reference and influence play in your work and in the architectural profession?

RR Let's start by saying: I don't believe that ideas suddenly come out of the blue. Projects are not like Greek gods that rise out of your head. It doesn't quite work like that.

I think you are strongly influenced by what you see and what you do, by the people around you. Then it's in your mind, and the mind is a filing system. For instance, with the Pompidou Centre, lots of people say, "The sloping square looks rather like the Campo in Sienna." And it does. Had we studied Sienna very carefully? I hadn't, nor had Renzo [Piano]. But there's no question that we did know it. It was in our minds—it was part of our vocabulary.

P49 And yet the Pompidou doesn't look like any other building before it.

RR I wouldn't say it's original. If you look back at the Eames House and the California case study houses, or Bucky Fuller, you can see the inspiration they provided. In England, I was never interested in neo-Roman, neo-Greco, or neo-anything. When it comes to the England of the nineteenth century, for people like myself, like Norman [Foster], our interest was much more in the Crystal Palace, railway stations, and industrial buildings, because there you can see the beginning of structure, of open-ended structures. And they're open-ended because they had to deal with changing situations.

P49 So what makes your projects original or distinguishes them from their precedents?

RR In the case of the Pompidou, a powerful note can be found at the beginning of the concept report, "A place for all people, all ages, all creeds." And then it goes on and says, "a cross between the British Museum and Times Square."

In other words, we were looking for an open-ended form, not a static monument. At the time, everybody was looking for change—and very militantly.

Improvisation was very important to us. Think of modern jazz: if you have a beat, you can change the parts inside. The idea was that the Pompidou would be a machine which would respond to changing needs.

P49 Architecture stores ideas, but also transmits them across time and culture. The original Pompidou scheme had displays and screens on the facade. Were you using these media devices to magnify architecture's ability to broadcast information?

RR The original concept was all about communication. Those days were the beginning of a digital world.

The idea was for the building to actually show what was on at MoMA or at the British Museum. We wanted to make the building a useful tool for our client, the French Ministry of Culture.

Actually, we wanted it to go beyond that. We were in a moment of tremendous change: the intellectuals and the unions were just about to pull France to pieces and the U.S. was about to collapse with the Vietnam policies and so on. It was a crisis. If you look at the images on the concept elevation, it shows an image of Vietnam, it addresses the student revolution, it signals an intellectual turn. And we wanted it to. So you could use the screens in either way.

In the end, when everything was organized and we'd gotten the Electricité de France to pay for it, Pompidou died, and Giscard [d'Estaing] took over our building (as he was President) and he asked, "Who's going to control it?" I replied, "Oh, of course it will be controlled by culture." "Yeah? Which kind of culture? Left or Right?" In other words, he immediately saw it as a political communication system.In some ways, we were devastated about the loss but we hadn't accounted for how amazing the French are about their *promenade*. They started walking all over the "streets in the air." In other words, the facade became what it was always supposed to be: an extension of the *piazza*. The screens were replaced with people—with real people.

P49 It's interesting to think of architecture not as a formal statement, nor necessarily as a building itself, but as the design for a pattern of behavior.

We are all different individuals with different views, which allows us to develop our ideas for ourselves. For example, I am very interested in archi-tecture's ability to communicate one's visions.

Architecture operates for two clients: the user, primarily concerned with the function of the building, and the passer-by, attuned to its larger role. I am interested in what I call "democratic buildings": buildings that communicate their role to the public and engage with the larger context. Look at court buildings: these are actually schools for understanding what is right and what is wrong.

Architecture is a mixture of many different things. It's a mixture of different influences, different points of view, and different beliefs; it isn't static, it incorporates activities and time. At first, the Chairman of Lloyds had said they wanted [their new building] to house them for another century. They gave us a very detailed program to that effect, but this collapsed the day after we completed the project because the digital era set in and changed the whole idea of insurance. So we said (only half joking), "It's okay, you can always turn the building into a university."

It's a very flexible space: the service towers, which have a shorter life span, are on the outside and can be adapted, while the base of the building, which is more permanent, has uninterrupted floorplates and can be reorganized at will.

In the 1990s, I was a key defendant for a project by Mies van der Rohe that Peter Palumbo, a property developer, was trying to build. And the reason it didn't get anywhere was that it was too tall, it didn't fit with the historic heritage. Twenty-five years later, that criticism is no longer valid. Looking back now, it would have been too low! Today, there is not one single "original" building in the city of London, fifty percent of all the buildings in the City have been radically changed. So what are you trying to relate to?

With Lloyd's of London, we built the lower part to line up with the existing buildings around it and we used the uneven spaces of the medieval site boundary to locate our towers. Today there's nothing left: the context to which we responded in those days is no longer there.

Now, obviously, there's a medieval road pattern, and you still get some of the views from the hills on the periphery of London. I just want to point out that the context itself isn't static. History is not static.

When we built the towers on Lloyd's, we thought, why would all modern buildings have flat roofs when the church spires, turrets, and towers all around break up the skyline? I don't think you can say that our buildings don't have a sense of place, and you can't say that our buildings are not influenced by all the things we [the architects] are interested in. My point is that there is architecture that isn't influenced by place but it is still influenced by language. Language is very much about receiving ideas in your mind, and interpreting those ideas into form.

P49 You speak about language and, in many ways, the Pompidou was a development of your own language as a designer—a language that you continue to use and develop in your career.

RR We all have some kind of signature. I don't think there is such a thing as architecture with no signature or art with no signature. Of course, architecture has to work, it has to stand, but also it has to have the magic of art. That's, in a way, your signature.

P49 Could you talk a little about the collaborations that have marked your career?

RR I am a good collaborator, and I enjoy having a team. I met Norman at Yale, and we made up Team 4. Renzo, Norman, Ivan Harbour and Graham Stirk, Peter Rice, Laurie Abbott, and many others! They were all immensely influential in the work we did together, and even afterwards. So it is very much a joint effort, isn't it? I am very much a team person, I have always believed in it. It covers up some of my weaknesses!

Architecture is not about starting with a blank piece of paper. If you want to scare me, give me piece of white paper! You have to absorb and analyze influences. That begins in my opinion by having other people around you, and not just architects. There are still architects who think that architecture is about architecture. There's much more to architecture than architecture.

P49 Your work has been tremendously influential to us and an entire generation of architects. Do you ever think about that when you design?

RR Not really. I do love talking about architecture. I love arguing about architecture. So in that sense, I absorb some of your points, and you absorb some of mine. I like that conversation, that exchange. Teamwork: I love that word.

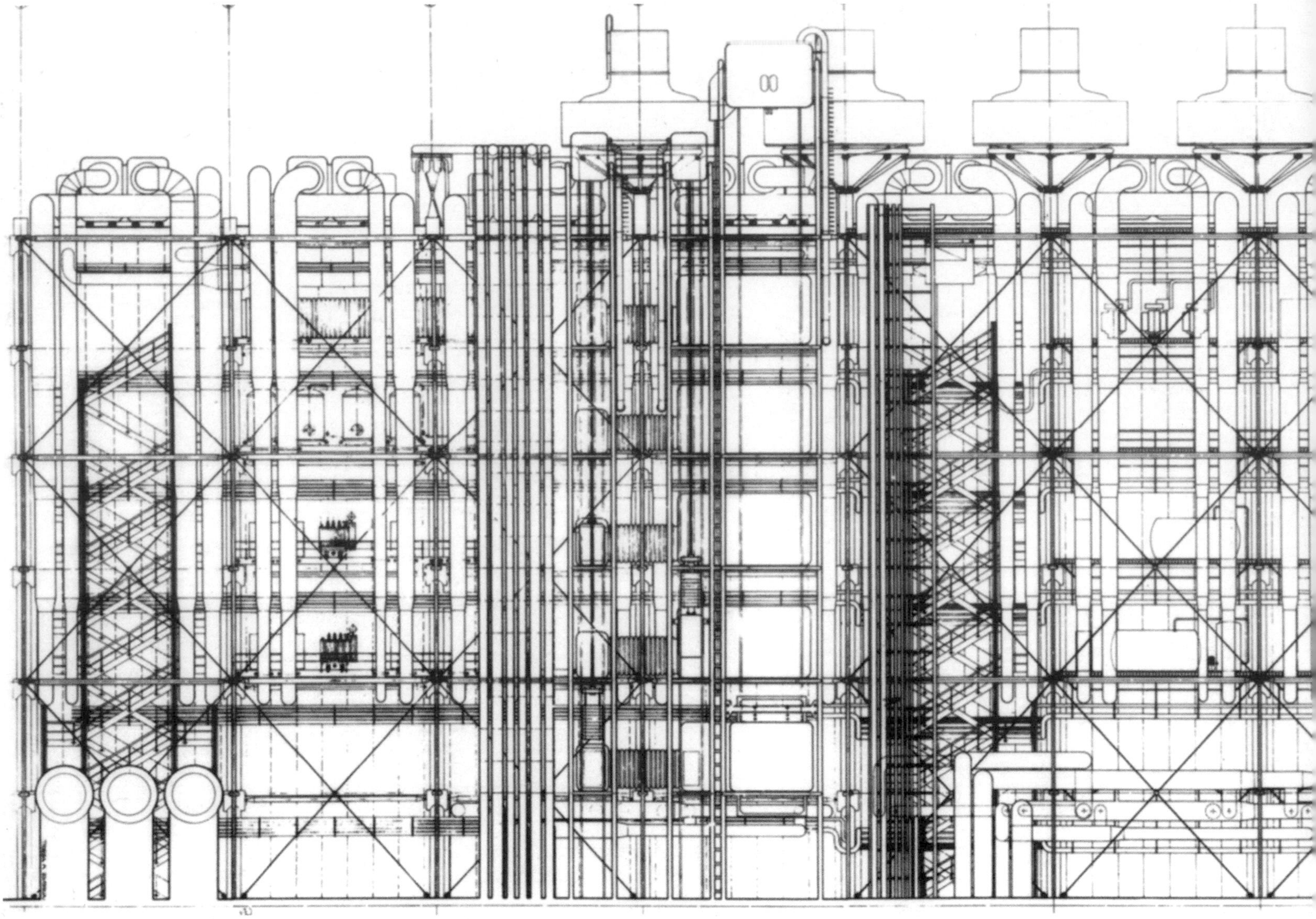

1 Building services are expressed on the facade. Elevation on the Rue du Renard: Piano + Rogers. The Centre Pompidou. Paris, 1971–1977.

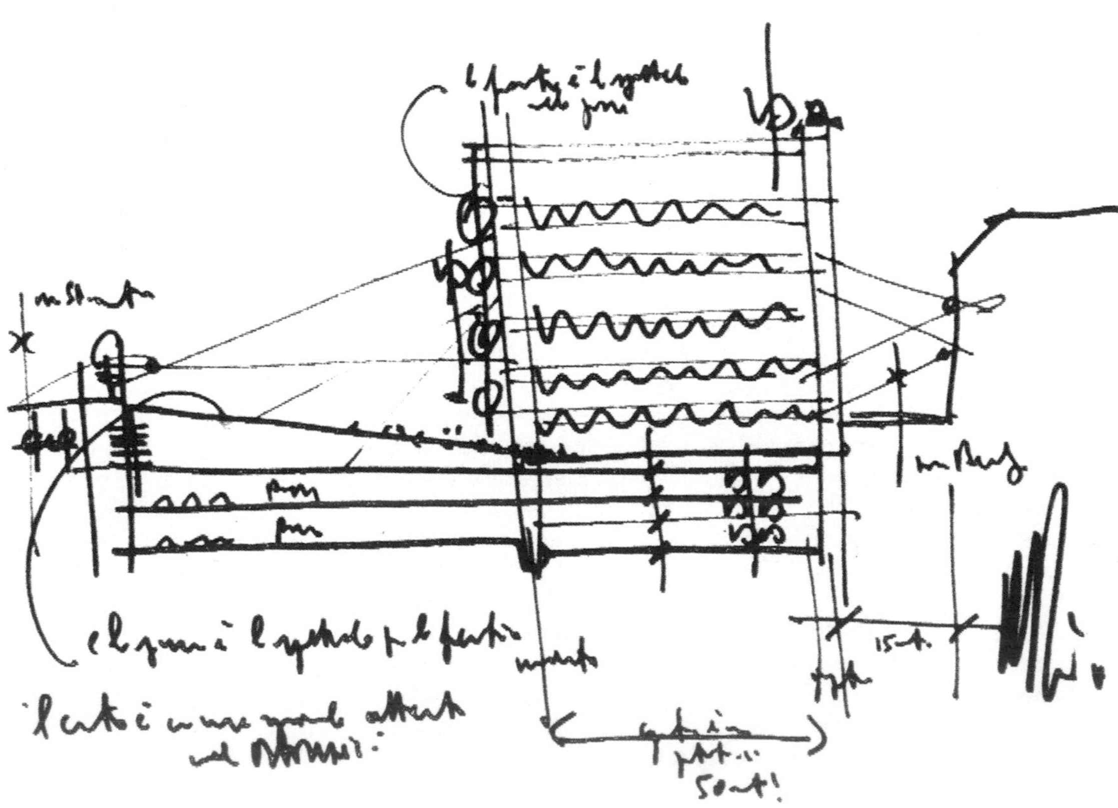

2 Concept sketch for the Centre Pompidou. Piano + Rogers.

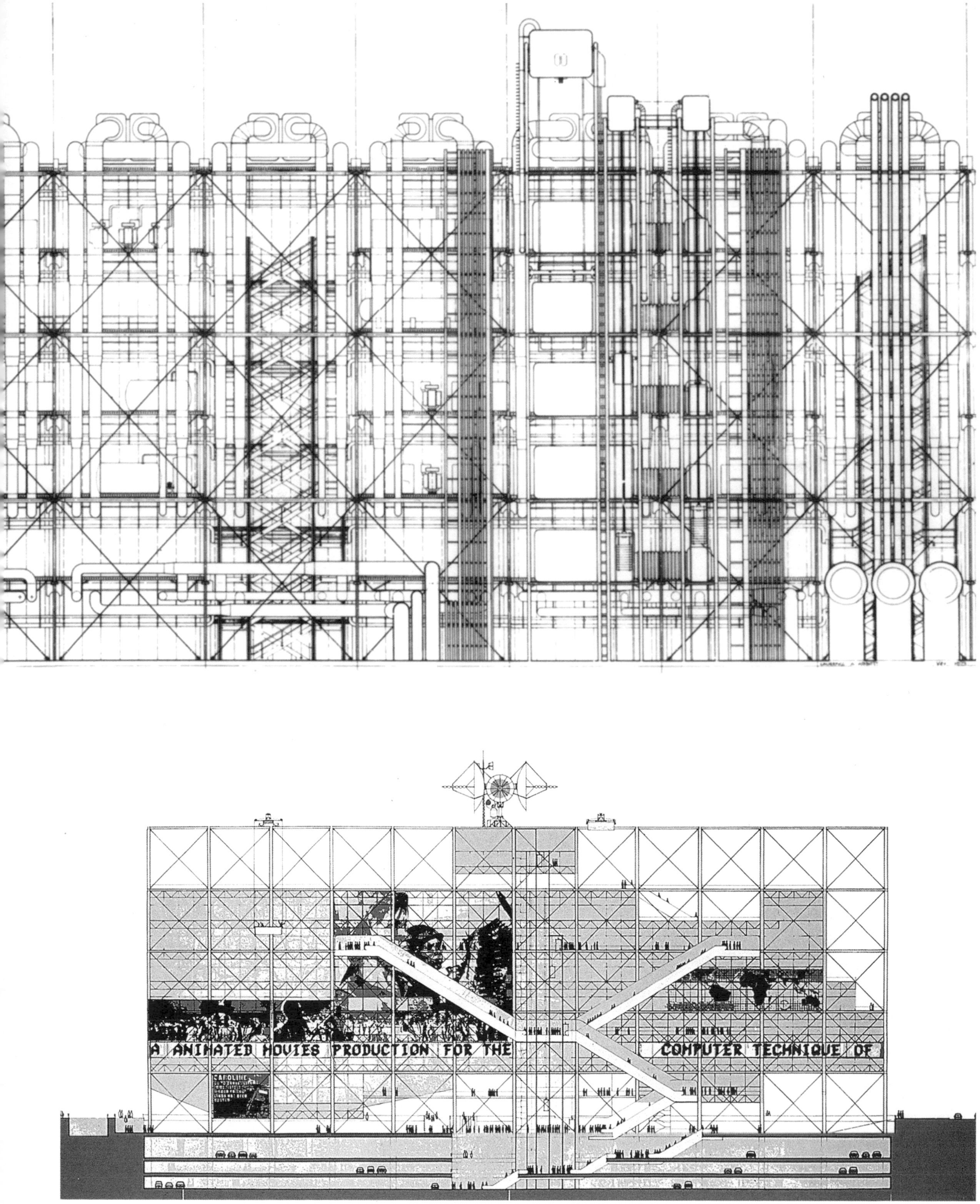

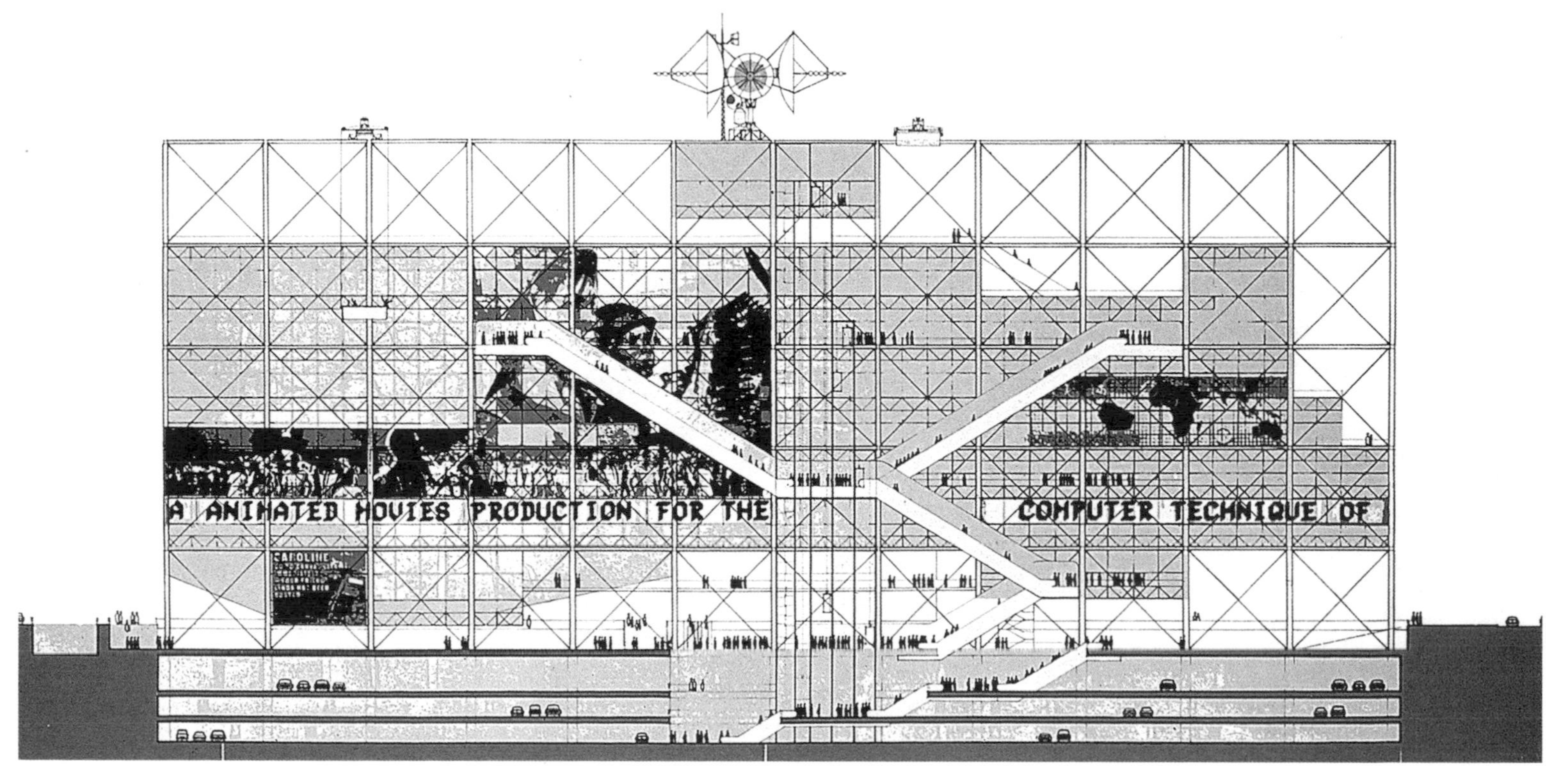

3 Elevation for the Centre Pompidou competition submission. Piano + Rogers.

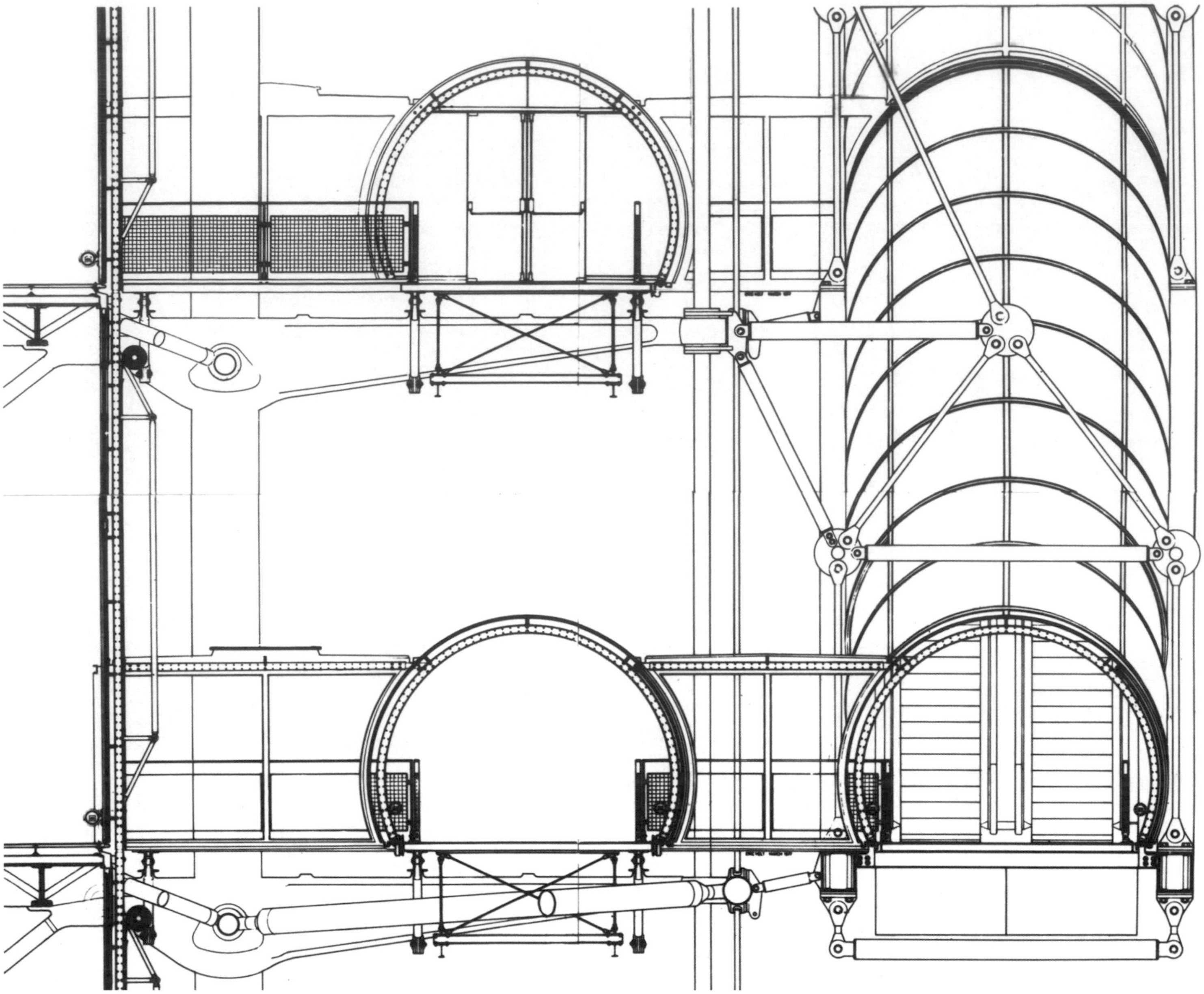

4

5

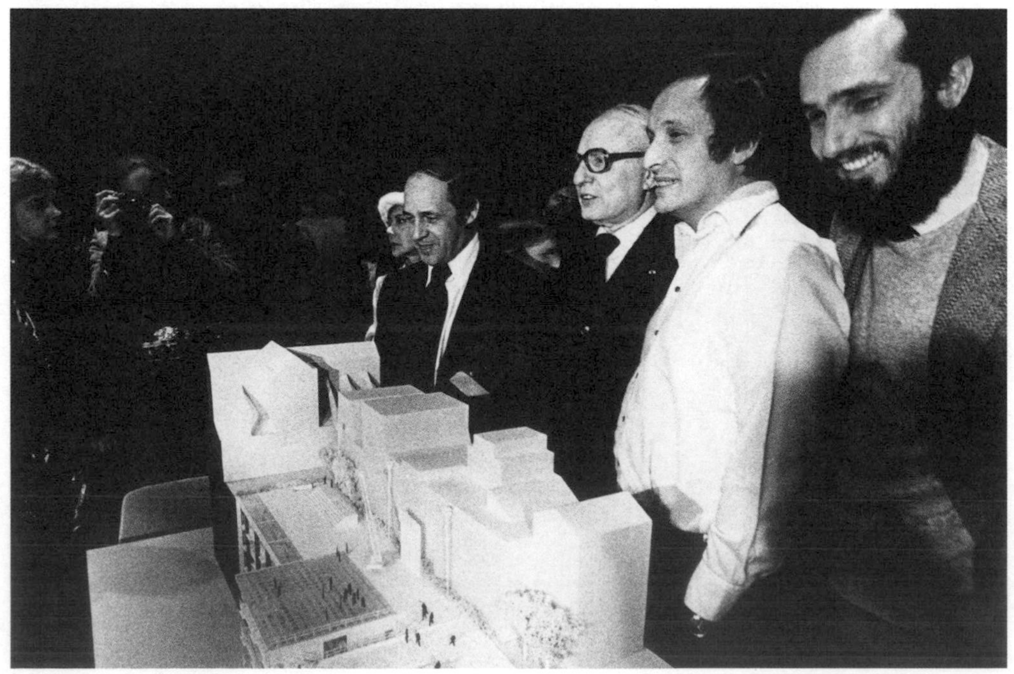

4 The Centre Pompidou's "street in the air." Section through the principal facade of glazed galleries and the escalator system. Piano + Rogers.

5 Collaboration. Press conference for IRCAM. (Left to right: Pierre Boulez, Robert Bordaz, Richard Rogers, Renzo Piano.) 1971.

6 The Centre Pompidou. Piano + Rogers.

7 Lifts and services on the exterior of the building. Richard Rogers Partnership. Lloyd's of London. 1978–1986.

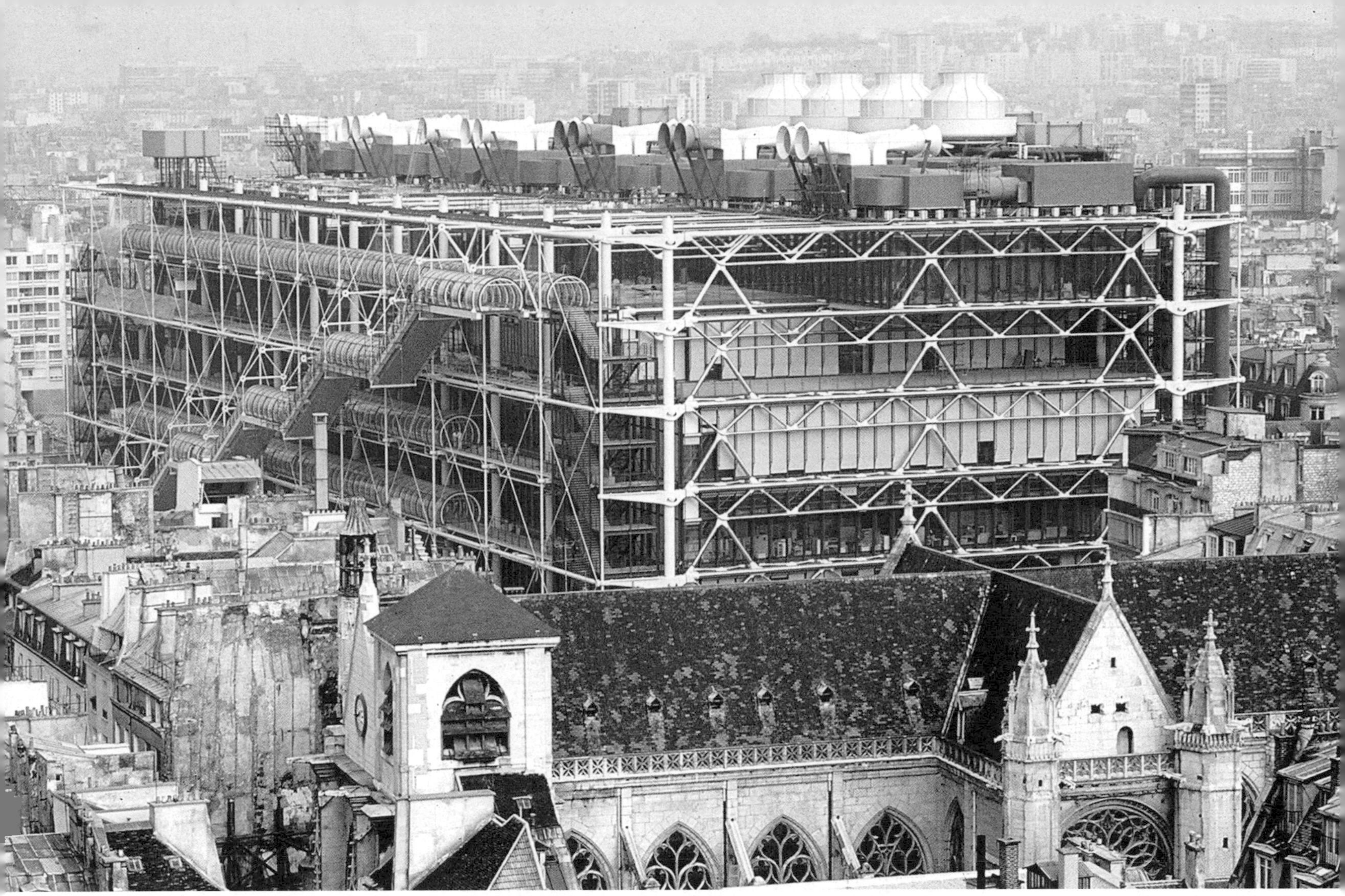

6

7

8 Lloyd's of London viewed from St. Mary Axe in the sunlight. Richard Rogers Partnership.

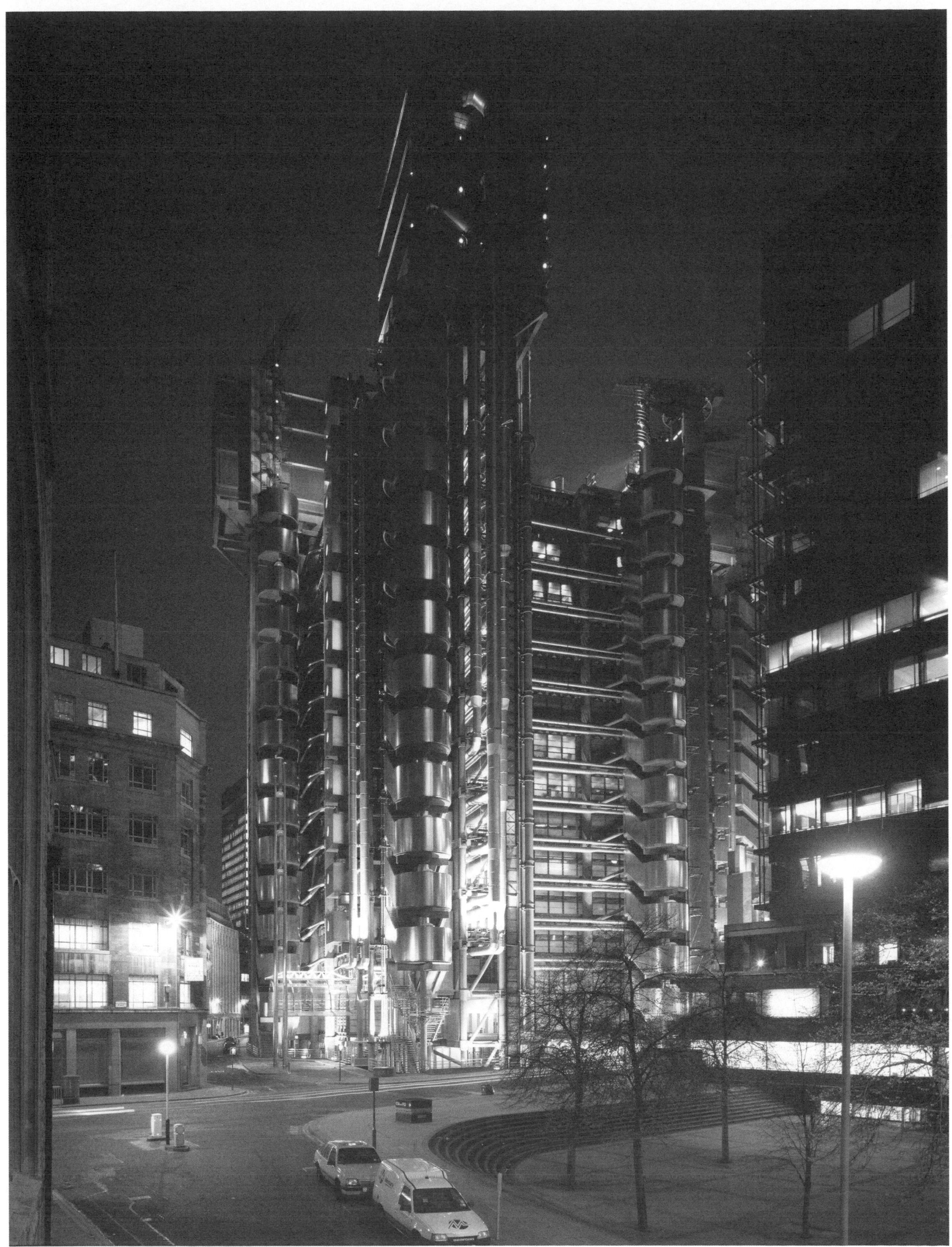

9 Nighttime view of Lloyd's of London. Richard Rogers Partnership.

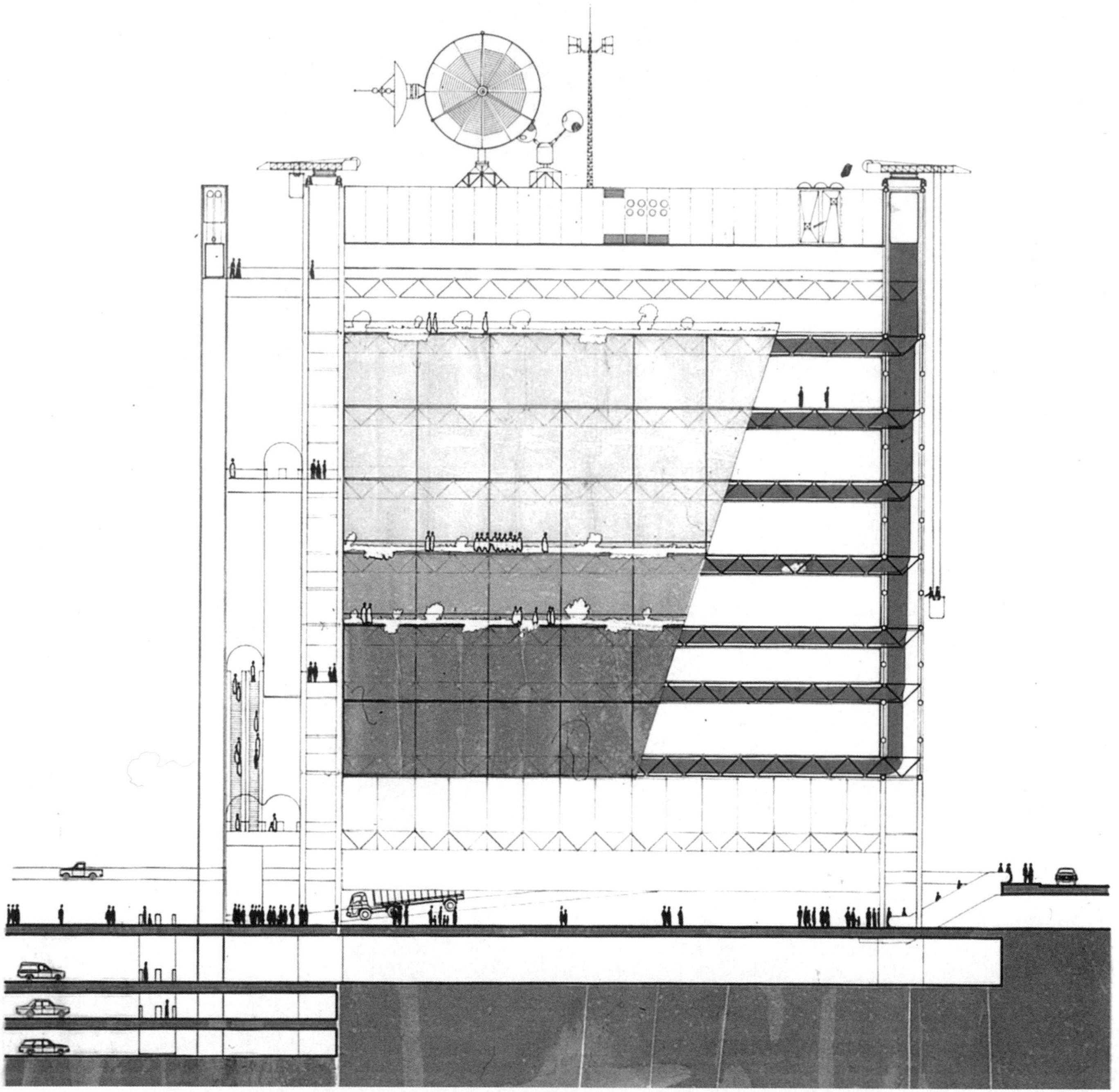

10 Wide spans allow for flexible spaces. Elevation of the Centre Pompidou on the Rue Saint Merri. Piano + Rogers.

♀

“Is it a copy, a replica, a reproduction, a substitution, a fake, a forgery, a surrogate, a double, a repetition, a clone, or maybe even a ghostly doppelgänger?”

♀ Mari Lending

Reciting the Tomb of Tutankhamen

In a small note in italics prefacing the 1970 printed version of a seminar on classical rhetoric given in Paris five years earlier, Roland Barthes touched upon the phenomenon of involuntary quotation. He presented the text simply as a transcription, a moment in the process of transposing an oral event into a "*texte de savoir*" heading toward audiences far removed from its place of origin. The transcription came with an apology: "Unfortunately, I can no longer (for practical reasons) authenticate the references of this scholarly text: I must write this manual in part from memory."[1] A conventional apology perhaps, yet this small confession threatens to destabilize the entire text that follows. The problem lies in the parentheses—the "practical reasons." This little insertion evokes a lack of accuracy that might compromise the text's scholarly authority.

The practical reasons Barthes alludes to are well known to every student and scholar struggling to get the quotes right and to adapt them to ever-changing conventions for proper referencing. Our books are in storage, the library is closed, our manically tagged copies of favorite books are lost, or we simply cannot locate the brilliant quote that we could swear appears in that exact text and that we habitually quote exactly from memory. Adorno provided some consolation when pointing to those short-lived moments of happiness when we believe we have finally tracked down favorite lines only to realize that we remembered them wrongly and have even improved them in our imagination. Books "worth quoting have lodged a permanent protest against quotation," he writes.[2] The phenomenon of not finding the required quote or realizing that it does not quite serve a purpose often leads to paralysis on the part of the author. Yet a certain distance from sources sometimes turns out to be unexpectedly liberating and productive, as was the case for two major twentieth-century books contemplating the European tradition. Fernand Braudel drafted his monumental work on Mediterranean culture while deprived of his archives and notes as a prisoner of war in Lübeck. Erich Auerbach similarly wrote his equally monumental *Mimesis: The Representation of Reality in Western Literature* while exiled in Istanbul, far from his Marburg library, during the same war.

Barthes's reason for not retracing the plethora of quotes in the transcribed manuscript was "practical" (citations that we can easily envision him sharing with his students by reading aloud from loads of books and notes, and of course reciting from memory), as was his reason for publishing this *aide-mémoire* in the first place. The idea, he writes, was simply to counter the lack of "a book, a manual, a memorandum of some sorts which might present a chronological and systematic panorama of that classical Rhetoric." The numerous entries were systematically, if idiosyncratically, divided into two parts ("A. The journey" and "B. The network"), with numbers spanning from "A.1. Birth of rhetoric" and "A.1.1 Rhetoric and property" through "B.3.11. *Compositio.*" Apologizing for the lack of proper references, he assures the reader that the subject matter is "commonplace learning." Nonetheless there are a few footnotes pertaining to the extensive text. Some of them contain excursuses continuing the discourse of the text; others supply more quotes with reference only to the name of the author ("Cicero"). A few are versions of the kind we use today to lend authority and transparency to our academic writing: "*Le Nouvel Observateur*, March 4, 1965," "Curtius, op. cit., pp. 414–416," and "Julia Kristeva, *Sèméiotikè*, Paris: Éd. du Seuil, 1969." However these footnotes are exceptions. Most of the innumerable quotes saturating the text are identified merely by a short and wonderfully disparate list of references, among them unspecified treatises on rhetoric from classical antiquity, "two fundamental books" (authors mentioned), and "several related readings, themselves incomplete and contingent." The eccentric list reads as an emblematic and profoundly hermeneutic definition of tradition, from which Barthes weaves fragments into a new fabric. This framework is preparation for something new that "may not yet have come into being" in a contemporary world that he famously characterized as "incredibly full of old Rhetoric."

Barthes's seminar and its printed transcription framed the publication of the hyper-canonized article "The Death of the Author," appearing in English in 1967 with the French original following the year after. In hindsight, however, the voluptuous dryness of the *aide-mémoire* appears as a more radical enterprise than the polemical article, with its dogged attack on origins, originality, intentions, and biographical authors. Today "The Death of the Author" reads as *doxa* in its assertion that it is languages that speak, not authors; that the birth of the reader must be ransomed with the death of the author; that the true locus of writing is reading; that every text is written here and now, and thus is always contemporary; and that literature is without origin, other than language itself ("the very thing which ceaselessly questions any origin"), to partly paraphrase and partly quote Barthes.[3] All of these insights, today exhausted from overciting, were anticipated in the rhetoric seminar. It dealt, at least on the surface, with the textual tradition *prior* to the birth of the author, the invention of originality, and the modern obsession with origins and authenticity. In its longing not only for pure contemporaneity but for the unforeseen, the *aide-mémoire* ties back to a world in which documents and manuscripts were continuously transcribed, captured by Erasmus in the early sixteenth century as "Friends Hold All Things in Common." For Erasmus quoting was about sharing something collectively owned; copying and copyright had not yet become a problem.[4]

Barthes presented his assemblage of voluntary and involuntary quotes as a collection and their commonplace sources as a compilation. As such, the short italicized preface evokes a past in which texts were worked by four closely related figures; elaborated and numbered but not hierarchized in the entry "A.6.2 The written text"—itself a full, perhaps involuntary, indeed unannotated Bonaventura quote.[5] The *scriptor* "purely and simply copies"; the *compilator* adds to what he copies, "but nothing that comes from himself"; the *commentator* "introduces himself into the copied text, but only to make it intelligible"; while the *auctor* "presents his own ideas, but always depending on other authorities." All figures are in play in the excessive unfolding of quotes in the manual, in which tradition is all about quoting, copying, and circulating fragments of the past. To this quadruple distinction Barthes adds yet two figures, closely related to the previous: the writer, not to be confused with an author, emerges in the Middle Ages in the *transmitter* (who "passes on an absolute substance which is the treasure of antiquity, the source of authority") and the *combiner* ("entitled to 'break' works of the past, by a limitless analysis, and to recompose them").[6]

Trying to make sense of a brand new impeccably annotated, spatial, three-dimensional, full-scale *texte de savoir*—namely an ancient Egyptian tomb reproduced from laser-scanned and recorded data of unprecedented accuracy and resolution—it struck me that the relation of this unforeseen fabric to the object it has painstakingly transcribed is exactly one of quotation, in fact perhaps even recitation. The work of the full entourage of premodern text producers catalogued in Barthes's *aide-mémoire* seems to be at play in the contemporary version of this ancient artifact, as a compilation and recomposition of both voluntary and involuntary quotations.

Experimental Preservation

In April 2014 a facsimile of Tutankhamen's tomb was installed at the entrance to the Valley of the Kings on the west bank of Luxor. A substitute for the original tomb, it is destined to become a tourist destination in its own right. Framed within the field of sustainable tourism, the new object marks a salvage operation in situ, replicating the real thing as the original is about to disappear, at least from public view.

The facsimile was produced by Madrid-based Factum Arte, which specializes in digital mediation of works of art and architecture. The studio is constantly developing and applying increasingly sophisticated technologies in the service of conservation and heritage, and its three-dimensional facsimiles of artworks, monuments, and architecture have become pivotal in the emerging field of experimental preservation. The extraordinary quality of the physical objects produced, restored, documented, performed, and displayed over the last decade helps us to see, look, and think differently about the material historicity of artifacts of the past. This corpus of works also prompts rethinking of a number of modern ideals, such as irreproducibility, aura, integrity, originality, origins, and authorship. "The cult of authenticity needs to be rethought," Factum Arte's founding director, Adam Lowe, says. "People need to start separating the idea of authenticity from that of originality."[7]

A key work in Factum Arte's production that has drawn global attention to shifting conceptions of originals and copies is the facsimile of Paolo Veronese's *Wedding at Cana,* recreated in its original setting in 2009. Andrea Palladio commissioned the painting for the refectory of the San Giorgio monastery in Venice in 1553. In 1797 the nearly 70-square-meter painting was cut into six when brought by Napoleon to the Louvre, where later it underwent a series of restorations. Given the compromised status of the original painting, the facsimile severely problematizes notions of originality. Presented in its intended architectural setting—without the gilded frame and glass, at the right height, and lit by the luminous reflection of the *laguna*—the new Venetian Veronese not only allows for a deeper understanding of the original painting but has changed forever the perception of its slightly tortured Parisian counterpart. As such, it demonstrates that copies cannot easily be separated from the works they evoke; they are artifacts that in their own right sign up for inclusion in the history of art and architecture.

Paolo Veronese, *The Wedding at Cana*, 1553, The Louvre, Paris.

Addressing the concerns of the present while giving voice to artifacts of the past, the Factum Arte staff of artists, conservators, archaeologists, art historians, and technicians digitize, create, recreate, and replicate spaces, surfaces, and objects in ways that tend to throw accustomed conceptions of chronological order into turmoil. Facsimiles of this eminence have the capacity to complicate time and temporalities of objects. Rather than fantasizing about pristine states or restoring away the work of time, the contemporary Veronese, with its microscopic surface topography, encompasses the full material history of the portable artifact—beyond its place of origin. A similar convolution of conventional perceptions of time and place was seen in Factum Arte's Piranesi facsimiles from 2010, presenting a series of latent nonexistent originals.[8] The transformation of two-dimensional design schemes from the mid-eighteenth century into three-dimensional objects of striking contemporaneity, estranged by their 250-year delay, constituted involuntary quotes in a Barthian sense, presenting entirely new and unforeseen fabrics. Works such as these testify to a defining moment in the moral and aesthetic valuation of high-quality facsimiles. "I would never exchange the facsimile for the original," said Pasquale Gagliardi of the Cini Foundation, who commissioned the Veronese facsimile. "I would be obliged to transform the refectory from a living and lived-in space into a museum, with the artificial, cold, uniform light of the museum."[9]

Reproductions, then, might bring art and architecture back to life in ways that original works, for many different reasons, are incapable of. While heavy-handedly restored original works of art and architecture risk disappearing, as Bruno Latour and Adam Lowe argue, "a well copied original may enhance its originality and continue to trigger new copies." [10]

Back in Luxor, the original to be salvaged and eventually replaced by its recently inaugurated facsimile dates back to the eighteenth dynasty and the fourteenth century BC. In comparison to its factual age, the ancient tomb is in fact something of a novelty. In terms of reception history it is a contemporary of Modernist classics such as T. S. Eliot's *The Waste Land* or Le Corbusier's Ville Contemporaine. In November 1922, after decades of obsessive excavation, British archaeologist Howard Carter finally uncovered the tomb of Tutankhamen, who ruled for less than a decade and died before he turned twenty years old. The burial chamber was opened on November 29, 1922, a press conference followed the next day, and a few weeks later the process of transferring its approximately 3,500 objects to museums started. Tutankhamen was catapulted into worldwide celebrity as a rock star of antiquity for the twentieth century. The myth of the mummy's curse was ignited in the popular imagination when Lord Carnarvon, who sponsored the excavation, died soon after in Cairo. The mummified pharaoh and his precious portables have kept their spell from the moment they were lifted out of an imagined eternity to a brutal historical reality. Seen by eight million visitors while touring America in the 1970s, *The Treasures of Tutankhamun* marked the invention of the blockbuster exhibition. Its grand finale came to the Metropolitan Museum of Art in New York, where it framed the celebration of the Egyptian gift of the Temple of Dendur, which due to Cold War geopolitics was relocated permanently to New York from Nubia.[11] In 2014 two new shows starring Tutankhamen premiered in England alone, proving that Tutmania was an inexhaustible phenomenon.[12]

Giovanni Battista Piranesi, Isis Tripod, from *Vasi, candelabri, cippi, sarcofagi, tripodi, lucerne, ed ornamenti antichi disegnati ed incisi dal Cav. Gio. Batt. Piranesi*, Vol. II, 1778–80.

The global flows of imagery and the young pharaoh's possessions have not diminished the allure of the tomb. While many tombs from the New Kingdom were plundered by robbers from the day they were sealed off and ultimately damaged by earthquakes, water and air leaks, salt crystallization, and other chemical processes that caused the plastered walls to crumble and fresco pigments to dissolve, Tutankhamen's relatively small burial

Factum Arte, facsimile of *The Wedding at Cana*, 2009, San Giorgio Maggiore, Venice.

chamber was intact when discovered more than 3,200 years after his death. But mass tourism has proven as destructive as natural phenomena. The effect of thousands of daily visitors for decades is evoked perfectly in Federico Fellini's 1972 movie *Roma*, in which amazed subway engineers break through the walls of a buried villa and watch intact frescos vanish before their eyes in the course of a moment. Mummies don't rot from worms, "they die from being transplanted from a slow order of the symbolic, master over putrefaction and death, to an order of history, science, and museums, our order, which no longer masters anything," as Baudrillard aptly put it in the 1970s, when it was discovered that Ramses II had severely disintegrated from a worm attack in a museum vitrine after three millennia of perfect preservation in his tomb.[13] It was inevitable that after less than one hundred years as a tourist destination Tutankhamen's tomb would have to close.

Reproducibility

As iconic monuments have disappeared from public view, facsimile tourism has emerged as a way to represent the lost object on or close to its site of origin. In 1963 the Lascaux cave in Dordogne was closed off as it was suffering from serious fungal damage only twenty-three years after its discovery. Two decades later Lascaux II opened, adjacent to the original cave. Its visitors far outnumbered those who got to see the more than 17,000-year-old Paleolithic paintings, until this replica remarkably repeated the deterioration processes of the prehistoric cave and had be shut down as well. Likewise the 2001 Neocave—adorned with copies of painted and carved bison and horses from the older Altamira cave in northern Spain, discovered in the 1870s and closed for the public a century later—has proven an esteemed tourist destination. In April 2015 French president François Holland inaugurated the biggest replica in the world, that of the 32,000-year-old Grotte Chauvet in southern France, sealed off since 1994 and already immortalized by Werner Herzog's 2010 *Cave of Forgotten Dreams*.

The Tutankhamen facsimile obviously belongs among such substitutes, offering visitors an experience that approximates the real thing in the very landscape of the original. Installed on the grounds of the recently renovated Howard Carter House, it will serve as part of a visitor center presenting the excavation history of the nearby tombs of kings, queens, and nobles. It will accommodate an estimated 500,000 visitors each year providing a comfortable alternative to the queues, security checks, and complicated ticket inspections required to enter the Valley of Kings under the hot Egyptian sun. Many Luxor tourists spend only a few hours around the monuments, as part of a ten-hour round trip by bus through the desert from the Red Sea resorts, and might find that the facsimile accompanied by a temple or two suffices for sightseeing of iconic Egyptian antiquity.[14]

Factum Arte, facsimile of the Isis Tripod, 2010.

While its position as a substitute is clear, the Tutankhamen facsimile attracts interest exactly through what distinguishes it from its relatives in Lascaux, Altamira, and Chauvet. The replica caves are site-specific, partly handmade singular objects constructed to imitate as far as possible the unapproachable prehistoric environments. They are irreproducible originals themselves, so to speak, of somewhat ambiguous status.

The Tut facsimile, on the other hand, is the result of scrupulously recorded and stored scientific data. In fact its most striking characteristic is perhaps its *reproducibility*, which gives the new object a projective quality that conceptually transcends its local Luxor context. The facsimile has the potential, like Barthes's transcribed cornucopia of quotes, to head toward new audiences, detached from its local place of origin, providing yet another variation on the unruly temporal effects of reproduced and circulating artifacts. Already its current position at the Howard Carter House raises the issue of distance from the original site as a charged new dimension. Does a nearby visitor center present a more authentic experience than, for example, a reproduction displayed in a museum on the other side of the world (or nearer, say, at the Red Sea coast, as archaeologists I met in Luxor proposed)? Does closer proximity to the source lend greater authority? Not only time but also place is a factor in constituting digitalized antiquities.

The Tutankhamen facsimile has already received massive global attention from critics univocally praising both its purpose and painstaking execution. A wide nomenclature has been suggested to pin down the epistemological status of the new object: Is it a copy, a replica, a reproduction, a substitution, a fake, a forgery, a surrogate, a double, a repetition, a clone, or maybe even a ghostly doppelgänger? These fluctuating notions obviously spring from the astonishment of the almost *unheimlich* resemblance of the copy to the original, based on a shared perception of the new object as an "exact copy." Seen as an isolated object, the Tutankhamen facsimile is indeed impeccably authenticated, and it gets the quotes right according to every thinkable scientific and academic standard. As such, it is apparently immune to the promiscuity of the involuntary quote Barthes evoked when refusing to track down all the bibliographical sources for his *aide-mémoire*. It is annotated in extreme detail, from the outline of the spaces, the colors of the murals, the reliefs of the walls, the granite appearance of the sarcophagus, and the deterioration, imperfections, and weathering of its surfaces all the way down to mundane site-specific paraphernalia such as the fire extinguishers, fans, and lamps that furnish every tomb and temple of the Theban necropolis. The characteristic yellow sign with black lettering in Arabic and English that marks every tomb in the Valley of Kings appears at the entrance of the facsimile, straightforwardly and rather boldly insisting "TOMB OF TUT ANKH AMUN." In concert, this exhibition of exactitude easily offers the conclusion "exact copy." Yet the facsimile invites reassessment precisely of the hackneyed dichotomy of copy and original, for the copying it performs happens way beyond the binary structure of a vanishing original and its bewildering perfect copy.

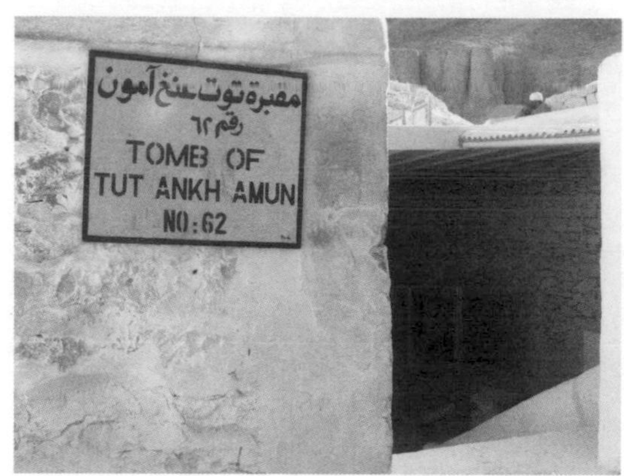

Entrance to the Tomb of Tutankhamen, ca. 2005.

Changing paradigms

Recording data is to a digital paradigm what quoting is to a textual. The digitally stored data that the Tutankhamen facsimile is produced from records, transcribes, and transmits—in short, quotes—large fragments of a monument as a high-resolution scan. Considered as a collection of quotes, indeed a whole recitation, the facsimile constitutes an original performance in its own right rather than a derivative that serves to document an ideal original. Just as in Erasmus's learned community, it ties back to a world in which friends held all things in common—as an emblematic definition of tradition, that is, before the dawn of authors and authorship, origins and originality. That does not make it an anachronistic occurrence—quite the contrary. Based on in-depth forensic studies and pushing the very limits of technological know-how, this state-of-the-art conservation piece within contemporary 3-D print culture rather hints toward a substitutional paradigm. According to Christopher S. Wood, that paradigm was brought to an end with modern print culture, when "copying was the normal way to make new things" and when the meaning of an artifact was both to be found and preserved "across a chain of mutually substitutable artifacts" rather than by the authority of historical origins and first versions.[15]

South wall of the Tomb of Tutankhamen, now lost, photographed by Harry Burton at the time of excavation, 1922.

Both unique and reproducible, the Tut facsimile is well framed within the history of things—including "both artifacts and works of art, both replicas and unique examples, both tools and expressions"—that George Kubler, in the early 1960s, launched in polemic contrast to the "bristling ugliness" of the concept of material culture favored by certain anthropologists and archaeologists to distinguish ideas from artifacts. The rethinking of art and architectural history by tracing objects through time, objects occurring as serialized editions derived from lost prime objects, artifacts unfolding by transmission, replication, and quoting all formed a Kublerian "shape in time": a conflation of ideas and objects expressed in visual form.[16] By repeating, reviving, and recovering what is lost or what might be lost, the Luxor facsimile transcends mere citation, or the transposing of a fragment from one text or context to another. Instead it seems to evoke recitation. It is a recitation that belongs in the trajectory of the object it has transcribed, evoking its past and anticipating its future.

Entrance to the facsimile of the Tomb of Tutankhamen, 2014.

Forever Anterior

Barthes's *aide-mémoire* comprises a poetic and scholarly manual that generously guides its readers through the territories of classical rhetoric. It also had a contemporary agenda, in detecting how new and unforeseen works of art might come into existence, resonating with the premodern practice of quoting and copying, and beyond the modern paradigm of authorship, originality, and origins. In fact it might also serve as a memorandum hinting at the way the Tutankhamen facsimile operates as part of a hermeneutic machine anchored in a world where unstable originals were produced rather than reproduced and preserved in transcription. The facsimile is about destinations rather than origins, and it revives a panoply of other texts.

Firstly, like the *scriptor*, resurfacing in Barthes's ideal modern writer, Factum Arte "purely and simply copies" by recording data from the ancient tomb. Secondly, the new tomb's documentary properties and its status as a tourist destination, substituting a vulnerable vanishing source, bring Factum Arte close to the *compilator*, who adds "to what he copies, but nothing that comes from himself." The *commentator*, in turn, "introduces himself into the copied text, but only to make it intelligible," lurking in the display of Harry Burton's photographs in the antechamber, documenting the opening of the tomb and the lifting of its treasures, and making the historical context legible for the visitor. The *auctor*, presenting "his own ideas, but always depending on other authorities," is matched by the scholarly and scientific expertise of Factum Arte's multidisciplinary team. More broadly, and beyond this specific edition, the work of the *transmitter*, passing "on an absolute substance which is the treasure of antiquity, the source of authority," relays the tomb's present and future, while the *combiner*'s effort is mirrored in the way it is based on a limitless analysis, breaking and recomposing a work of the past into a brand new work.

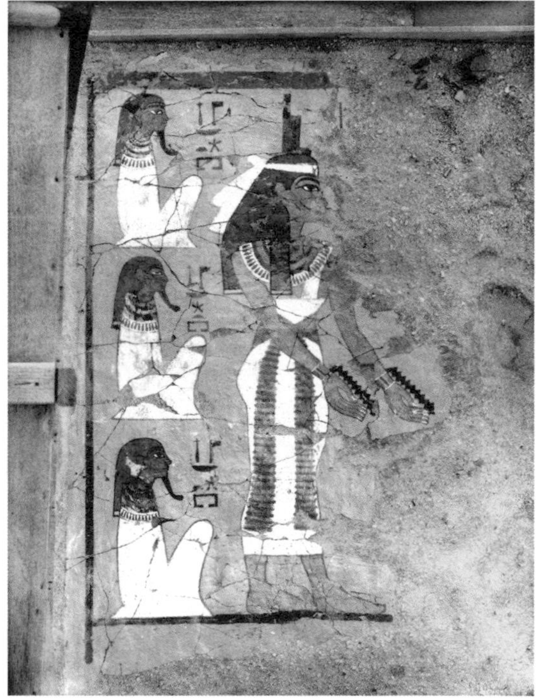
Reconstruction of the south wall, photographed by Alicia Guirao at Factum Arte's workshop in Madrid, 2012.

The "modern writer (scriptor) is born simultaneously with his text," Barthes says. "There is no other time than that of the utterance."[17] By repeating "a gesture forever anterior, never original," the facsimile aligns itself with the public performances of the ancient rhapsody, where substantial parts of itinerant yet uncodified texts were continuously disseminated to new live audiences. It comes as no surprise that Plato did his very best to corrupt the virtues of the professional rhapsodist. With his characteristic pedantry, irony, and evil logic, Socrates is confusing, tricking, and mocking the celebrated rhapsodist Ion from Ephesus, who has just arrived in Athens to compete in the rhapsodic contest at the Panathenaic festival by performing the same Homeric recitation that had just won him the golden crown in Epidaurus. As an inspired "interpreter of interpreters," however, even Plato had to acknowledge the rhapsodist as a mediator in the inspired oral interpretation of the divine eternal truths

The sarcophagus, ca. 1323 BC, photographed by Harry Burton in 1922.

interpreted by Homer, not dissimilar to the way the reproducible digitally stored data from the ancient tomb might be performed in other places, and in even more perfected—or inspired—versions.[18]

Reproductions were debated with passion in the nineteenth century, in discourses less inflicted by the ecstasy and madness in which Plato inscribed the arts. There is an obvious lineage from the oral rhapsodic tradition and premodern text producers to the contemporary 3-D high-tech facsimiles that runs via late nineteenth-century production, circulation, and recomposition of full-scaled architectural fragments and monuments. These plaster casts were produced by highly skilled *formatori* in collaboration with the most prominent European archaeologists, art historians, and museum directors at a time when museums renowned for their unrivaled collections of antiquities (among them the British Museum and the Louvre) proudly presented plaster casts among their most precious originals. Just as the rhapsodist memorized and performed poetry of the past, the "reproducer must know the masterpiece, every line and curve; he has to adjust details. And this he cannot and does not do properly unless he is well grounded in art, unless he knows its principles, unless he has a love for the thing he is doing, which gives him understanding and quick sympathy," an American critic stated in 1899. Until this prolific cast culture fell out of vogue due to Modernist aesthetics of authenticity, new conceptions of purity, and an increasing obsession with originality, a perfect cast was seen not only as "more than mechanical reproduction": "authentic casts made with care are more valuable than marbles or bronzes, not in material, but in what counts for more than that, in workmanship and understanding."[19] Value has long been tied to reproductions, and the Tut facsimile takes its cue from the noble tradition of casting—exactly "to reproduce and preserve the works of great masters of all times"—but with the uncanny accuracy that digital resolution offers, going from plaster to pixels, so to speak.

Making History

If one reproduces something that large and in meticulous detail, is it still a quote? When Jorge Luis Borges let fictitious author Pierre Menard—a successor of Poe and Baudelaire and a precursor of Mallarmé and Valéry—set out to write an identical new version of *Don Quixote*, he concluded that the endeavor was troublesome both practically and philosophically but not impossible. According to the narrator struggling to make a sensible inventory of the late Menard's utterly unruly, highly surreal, and mostly unpublished oeuvre, Menard never aimed at a mechanical transcription of the original, nor did he propose to copy it: "His admirable intention was to produce a few pages which would coincide—word for word and line for line—with those of Miguel de Cervantes."[20] The enterprise, itself Quixotesque in scope, was downscaled in the end. Menard decided to focus on two chapters and a fragment of a third. The inventive copyist's first and fruitless strategy was one resembling method acting (studying Catalonian, converting to Catholicism, fighting Moors and Turks, and erasing from his mind European history from 1602 to 1918), but this could only lead to anachronistic banalities and thousands of drafts torn into pieces for their lack of precision. Composing *Don Quixote* at the beginning of the twentieth century "is almost impossible," according to Menard, and the original was part of the problem: "It is not in vain that three hundred years have gone by, filled with exceedingly complex events. Amongst them, to mention only one, is the *Quixote* itself."

If the style of the new edition appeared, in the end, archaic and slightly affected compared to Cervantes's spontaneous prose, its first reader nevertheless found it "a revelation to com-

Facsimile of the sarcophagus, photographed by Alicia Guirao in 2012.

pare Menard's *Don Quixote* with Cervantes'." The course of history (such as the influence of Nietzsche) simply made the new edition subtler than its seventeenth-century precursor: "Cervantes' text and Menard's are verbally identical, but the second is almost infinitely richer. (More ambiguous, his detractors will say, but ambiguity is richness.)" The story encapsulates Borges's bid on the birth of the reader and the death of the author, again overturning modern notions of origins, originality, and authorship. But more important than Borges's hysterical twists on historicity is the way he pinned down the *timeliness* of a perfect reproduction. The new tomb of Tutankhamen undermines illusions of timelessness and demonstrates the critically *historical* status of reproductions. The facsimile evokes the historicity of both the old and the new by pointing to the way objects behave, change, move, work, fluctuate, and circulate in time and space. Likewise it addresses the question of perception and reception of history by highlighting, as did both Borges and Kubler, the biographies of things replicated in time: "Menard (perhaps without wanting to) has enriched, by means of a new technique, the halting and rudimentary art of reading." However fanatically reproductions copy, they carry an inherently productive and liberating distance to the sources that makes us think differently about artifacts of the past and their possible futures.

"It gleams like a mystic lamp in the evening of the aging world," the great German philologist Ernst Robert Curtius writes (in one of Barthes's two "fundamental books," from which innumerable of his involuntary quotes and examples were lifted) when describing the transmission of ancient authorities by the copying of manuscripts in European cloisters through the Middle Ages.[21] In Luxor, the original tomb is forever trapped in history; the 3,200-year-old artifact is heading for slow deterioration. The new tomb will weather and decay over time as well. The data recorded in spring 2009, stored in the form of an information file, are however somehow lifted from history as a latency that might yet be translated into new possibly more perfect versions of the ancient tomb by mediation technologies yet unseen. So while the sealed-off tomb in the Valley of the Kings continues its already millennial-long journey through time, the facsimile establishes a new past for the tomb in the future, a version of the past that is eternally 2009. Whether that past will ever be legible for preservation or recitation is open for speculation. Meanwhile the past, present, and future tombs glow in their frozen and fluctuating temporalities like little lamps in the trajectory of Tutankhamen's tomb.

page 84
Detail of the north wall, Tomb of Tutankhamen.

page 85
Printing the facsimile of the north wall.

1 The seminar took place at the École pratique des hautes études in the academic year 1964–65, and "L'ancienne rhétoric. Aide-mémoire" was first printed in *Communications*, no. 16 (1970). I have removed the quotation marks surrounding the words *scholarly text* in this first quoted sentence lifted from the English translation, appearing in Roland Barthes, "The Old Rhetoric: An Aide-Mémoire," trans. Richard Howard, in Barthes, *The Semiotic Challenge* (Berkeley and Los Angeles: University of California Press, 1994), 11–12. Significantly, the quotation marks do not appear in the French original, which reads: "Par malheur, ce texte du savoir, je ne puis plus (pour le raisons pratiques) en authentifier les références: il me faut rédiger cet aide-mémoire en partie de mémoire." Barthes, "L'ancienne rhétoric," 172.

2 Theodor W. Adorno, "Bibliographical Musings," in *Notes to Literature*, vol. 2, trans. Shierry Weber Nicholson (New York: Columbia University Press, 1992), 27.

3 Roland Barthes, "The Death of the Author," trans. Richard Howard, *Aspen*, no. 5–6 (1967). This first publication took place in the legendary "Minimalism" issue of the American journal that came as a white box, guest edited and designed by Bryan O'Doherty and accompanied by George Kubler's "Style and the Representation of Historical Time" and Susan Sontag's "The Aesthetics of Silence."

4 See Kathy Eden, *Friends Hold All Things in Common: Tradition, Intellectual Property, and the Adages of Erasmus* (New Haven, Connecticut: Yale University Press, 2001). For the invention of copyright and the Italian *privilegio* in the Renaissance, see Victor Plahte Tschudi, "Negotiating Time in Print," in Arrhenius, Lending, Miller, and McGowan, eds., *Place and Displacement: Exhibiting Architecture* (Zurich: Lars Müller Publishers, 2014).

5 "A man might write the works of others, adding and changing nothing, in which case he is simply called a 'scribe' (scriptor). Another writes the work of others with additions which are not his own; and he is called a 'compilor' (compilator). Another writes both other's work and his own, but with other's work in principal place, adding his own for purposes of explanation; and he is called 'commentator (commentator).... Another writes both his own works and others' but with his own work in principal place adding others' for purposes of confirmation; and such a man should be called an 'author (auctor)." Quoted from Elisabeth L. Eisenstein, *The Printing Press as an Agent of Change: Communications and Cultural Transformations in Early-Modern Europe*, (Cambridge, UK: Cambridge University Press, 1979), 121–22.

6 Barthes, "The Old Rhetoric: An Aide-mémoire," 30.

7 Peter Aspden, "Fit for a King: Tutankhamun's Replica Burial Chamber," *FT Magazine*, April 17, 2014.

8 *Le Arti di Piranesi: Architetto, incisore, antiquario, vedutista, designer* premiered at Venice's Fondazione Giorgio Cini in fall 2010 and has since been constantly traveling.

9 Quoted from Alison Gee, "Which would you rather visit—a fake tomb or a real one?" BBC World Service, November 8, 2013.

10 Bruno Latour and Adam Lowe, "The Migration of the Aura, or How to Explore the Original through Its Facsimiles," in Thomas Barthscherer and Roderick Coover, eds., *Switching Codes: Thinking Through Digital Technology in the Humanities and the Arts* (Chicago: Chicago University Press, 2011), 278.

11 For the "salvage" of temples that would have been flooded by the construction of the Aswan High Dam in the 1960s and their relocation to New York, Leiden, Madrid, and elsewhere, see Lucia Allais, "Integrities: The Salvage of Abu Simbel," *Grey Room* 50 (winter 2013).

12 Toby Wilkinson, "Touch screens and Tut-mania" (review of *Ancient Lives, New Discoveries* at the British Museum and *Discovering Tutankhamun* at the Ashmolean Museum), *Times Literary Supplement*, September 19, 2014.

13 Jean Baudrillard, "The Precession of Simulacra," in *Simulacra and Simulation* (1981), trans. Sheila Faria Glaser, (Ann Arbor, Michigan: University of Michigan Press 1993), 10.

14 Spinning tourists are not a recent phenomenon. While casting a huge portion of the frescos of Hatshepsut's temple in the Theban Necropolis in 1905 in collaboration with Canadian archaeologist Charles T. Currelly before tinting the surfaces of the casts, British painter Walter Tyndal reported on the flow of passing tourists: "Some parties passed through Der el-Bahri to see Hatshepsu's [sic] temple. They went to see the Tombs of the Kings first [...] After lunch the guide would rush them through Hatshepsu's shrine, and then start them off to see the tombs of Sheykh Abd-el-Gurna; the Ramesseum would then be visited, and with hardly a pause to breathe everyone would remount their donkeys or get into their litters to be rushed off to Medinet Habu. The Valley of the Queens might then be visited, and a long ride, with a short halt at the Colossi of Memnon, would take them to the Nile, to be crossed after sunset, before the Luxor hotels could be reached. I have no doubt that most of these good people were thankful when so fatiguing a day was well over, and vowed that no power on earth would ever induce them to go through it again. A week would barely suffice to get more than a cursory glance of all the sights which are crowded into this long day. The following day is usually devoted to 'doing' the Luxor temple, and being rushed through the ruins of Karnak." Walter Tyndal, *An Artist in Egypt* (New York and London: Hodder and Stoughton, 1912), 195. These casts were commissioned by the Metropolitan Museum of Art. A partly dilapidated if recently restored set of the incredibly beautiful casts from Luxor can still be admired in the penthouse of Paul Rudolph's Art & Architecture Building, at Yale University. They are survivors of Josef Albers's iconoclasm of the Yale cast collection. Rudolph found them in the basement of former premises of the school while designing the A&A building.

15 Christopher S. Woods, *Forgery, Replica, Fiction: Temporalities of German Renaissance Art* (Chicago: University of Chicago Press, 2008), 19.

16 George Kubler, *The Shape of Time: Remarks on the History of Things* (New Haven, Connecticut: Yale University Press, 1962), 8.

17 Barthes, "The Death of the Author."

18 Plato, "Ion," in *The Dialogues of Plato*, vol. 1, trans. Benjamin Jowett (Oxford, UK: Oxford University Press, 1891), 503.

19 Edna Harris, *Brush and Pencil: An Illustrated Magazine of the Arts of Today*, vol. 5, no. 2 (November 1899): 58, 59.

20 Jorge Louis Borges, "Pierre Menard, Author of the Quixote," trans. anonymous (that is, *Ficciones* was translated into English by "Emecé Editores, S. SA., Buenos Aires [sic]"), in *Ficciones* (1946) (New York: Grove Press, 1962), unpaginated Kindle version.

21 Curtius, *European Literature and the Latin Middle Ages*, trans. Willard R. Trask (Princeton, New Jersey: Princeton University Press, 1953), 401.

"To some degree all restoration turns an original into a reproduction of itself."

Adam Lowe

The Theban Necropolis Preservation Initiative

opposite
The installation of the facsimile of the Tomb of Tutankhamen, 2014, Luxor.

Based in Madrid, London, and Milan, Factum Arte consists of a team of artists, technicians, and conservators dedicated to digital mediation in the production of both works for contemporary artists and facsimiles as part of a coherent approach to preservation and dissemination. The collective employs bespoke equipment and software to obtain optimum results in recording and outputting digital information. Factum Arte's non-contact methodologies challenge conventional notions of conservation and define the role facsimiles play in the protection of our cultural heritage.

The tomb of Tutankhamen was discovered in near perfect condition in 1922. The only damage to the interior in more than three thousand years was the growth of microbacteria on the walls. Soon after its discovery Howard Carter expressed concern that the entry of visitors would damage the fabric of the tomb. In the years since the discovery of the tomb the young Tutankhamen emerged from obscurity and captured the public imagination. The tomb and its treasures are now among the most celebrated cultural artifacts in the world. Although built to last for eternity, the burial chamber was not meant to be visited by mortals. By 2009 the tomb was receiving approximately one thousand visitors each day, dramatically affecting environmental conditions in the space.

The creation of an exact facsimile of Tutankhamen's tomb was the first stage of a wider initiative to safeguard the tombs of the Theban Necropolis through the application of new recording technologies and the creation of exact reproductions of tombs that are now either closed to the public for conservation or in need of closure to preserve them for future generations. These facsimiles are renegotiating the complex relationship between originality and authenticity.

The work carried out in Tutankhamen's tomb was first imagined in 1988 by the Society of Friends of the Royal Tombs of Egypt. Factum Arte's involvement began in 2001, with the approval of a research project by Dr. Gaballah Ali Gaballah to develop the techniques needed to scan the tomb of Seti I. In 2002 Factum Arte produced an exact facsimile of the tomb of Thutmose III for the touring exhibition *The Quest for Immortality: Treasures of Ancient Egypt*, which opened that year at the National Gallery of Art, in Washington, D.C.

In spring 2009 the burial chamber and sarcophagus in Tutankhamen's tomb were recorded in 3-D and color at the highest resolution ever achieved on a large scale. Factum Arte used this imagery to complete an exact facsimile of the tomb by 2012. This data, also being used to monitor the gradual decay of the tomb and its contents, was made available to the public in 2011. Understanding the transformations occurring as the physical world is digitized and rematerialized is key to the production of a facsimile that aspires to forensic accuracy. The following images document the work required to record, mediate, transform, replicate, and install the tomb of Tutankhamen on its current site at the entrance to the Valley of the Kings.

Part 1— Recording the Burial Chamber of Tutankhamen

Through the application of digital technologies it is possible to record the surfaces and structure of the tombs in astonishing detail and reproduce them physically in three dimensions without significant loss of information.

3-D Scanning

A number of different 3-D scanning methods exist, each with their own advantages and limitations. The 3-D data can be recorded at long range, capturing general topographical information at low resolution, or at close range, with enough accuracy to document the flaking paint or carving on a surface, emphasizing marks that are not easily visible to the human eye. The diverse methods of capturing 3-D data are redefining the relationship between image and form. It is essential to use the most appropriate type of 3-D recording and safely archive and process the resulting data, which can then be used for academic, conservation, and research purposes.

Lucida Scanner

The most significant practical issues in laser scanning are the costs and design of both the recording systems and the software used to process the 3-D data. After extensive research into these issues, the Lucida scanner was designed by artist Manuel Franquelo and built by Factum Arte. The Lucida software controls the operation of the scanner and the processing of the captured data. It treats 3-D information as a tonal-depth map in a manner that is compatible with most existing image-processing software packages. The data can be viewed and retouched as a high-resolution tonal image and built into layered digital archives containing different types of information. Using this approach, dimensionally accurate high-resolution 3-D recordings can be viewed with the corresponding color, X-ray, infrared, ultraviolet, and multispectral data or merged with historical images to assist in condition monitoring.

NUB3D White-Light Scanner

Factum Arte's approach to date has been to use the white-light system in tandem with a laser scanner. All of the walls in Tutankhamen's tomb were recorded with a NUB3D Sidio white-light scanning system at three different resolutions: 200, 400, and 700 microns. Sidio employs a mix of optical technology, 3-D topometry, and digital image processing to extract 3-D coordinates from an object's surface. This technique is known as structured light triangulation. The 3-D information is acquired by analyzing the deformation caused when patterns of light are projected onto the surface of an object. A series of images is captured by a video camera integrated into the recording head. From these images the software calculates a coordinated XYZ point cloud relating to the surface of the object. It then generates dense point clouds of millions of points or polygon meshes that describe the surface of the scanned object with great precision.

Composite Color Photography

So far no single 3-D scanner can record color at the standard required to produce an exact replica. Thus high-resolution color photography is an important part of the recording process. To achieve this it is necessary to use a composite approach, in which large numbers of macro images are tiled together to form one vast file. For the recording of Tutankhamen's tomb, two different computer-controlled structures were used to place the camera at a fixed distance parallel to the surface of the wall. Over 16,000 photographs were taken to provide a complete photographic map of the surface with a resolution of 600–800 dpi at actual scale. The resulting photographic archive is approximately 300 gigabytes of data. .

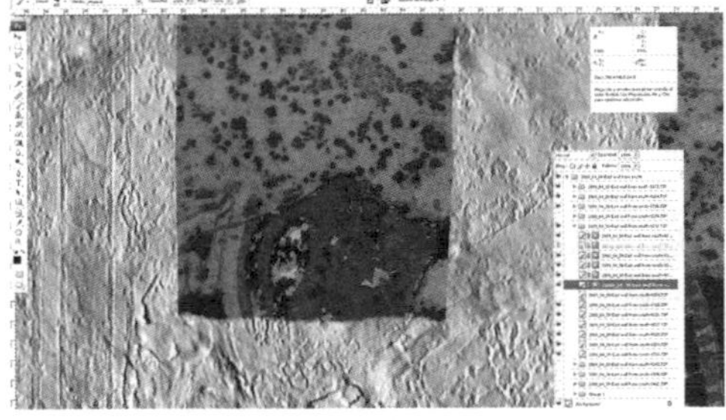

Data Archiving and Processing

The data was downloaded to an archiving hub, where it was organized and stored. The time-consuming work of processing was then done in a carefully planned and systematic way. As a rule of thumb, every hour spent recording in the field required one day of processing. Processing the digital information is a collective activity that grows rapidly into a vast archive. While the Factum Foundation is committed to promoting an open-source model, the data recorded in Tutankhamen's tomb belongs to the Egyptian Ministry of Antiquities. It was encrypted and made freely available for monitoring purposes and academic study with the ministry's permission.

Part 2—
Making an Exact Facsimile

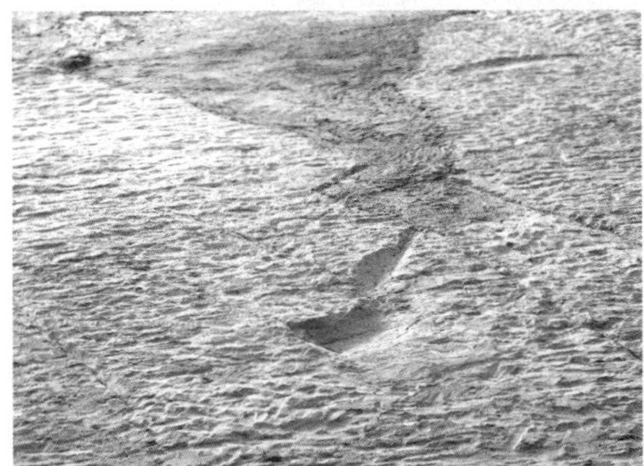

Routing

Many tests have been run to find the best and most economical way to turn digital information back into the physical object it depicts. There are now many forms of 3-D printing and new families of 3-D color printers in this rapidly developing field. Although currently the mix of resolution, scale, and cost makes 3-D printing prohibitive, these printers may one day provide a less time-consuming solution with comparable results.

In the meantime, the preferred option is to carve the surface into sheets of polyurethane or plaster using CNC routing machines. It takes approximately 400 hours to rout a one-meter-square panel in 3-D at a resolution of 260 microns. Routing the entire surface of Tutankhamen's burial chamber took more than six months using two machines. The walls were routed in one-meter-square sections that were then joined together. Once complete, these panels were cut into sections about one-and-a-half meters wide and the full height of the tomb that were then cast in such a way that they could be bolted together to produce invisible joins.

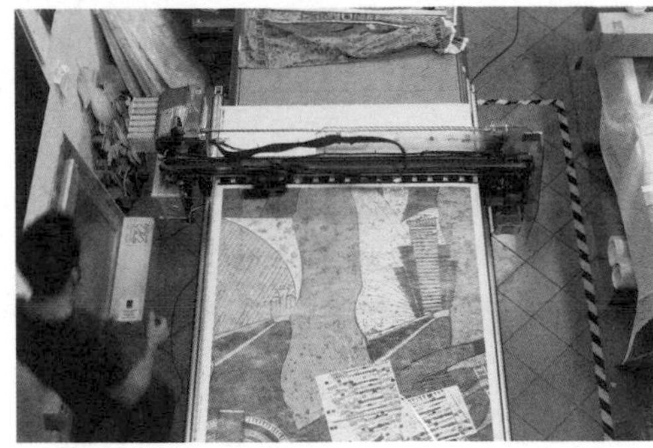

Printing the Walls of the Facsimile

Facsimile printing was done using a flatbed inkjet printer designed by Dwight Perry of Factum Arte. For many years this printer has been at the center of Factum Arte's approach to the production of facsimiles, closing the gap between the appearance of the original object and that of its copy. With this printer the image can be built from layers of color printed in perfect registration. This approach means that both the color and the tone can be controlled and locally altered to ensure a perfect match. The color is corrected both digitally and in the printing process.

Elastic Printing Support

An elastic printing media was prepared in direct response to a practical need: although Factum Arte's flatbed digital printer can overprint in perfect register, it cannot print a detailed and focused image onto an undulating surface. To solve this problem, Factum Arte developed a layered material that is ultra-thin, flexible, and slightly elastic and accepts pigmented ink without spread or loss of detail. The material is composed of two thin layers of inkjet ground backed with an acrylic gesso and an elastic acrylic support. It is built in seven layers rolled onto a slightly textured silicon mold. The skins have a short working life and need to be freshly made to ensure that they stretch to fit the surface correctly.

Once printed, the flexible skins are positioned and adhered using a slow-cure contact adhesive. Both sight and touch are essential to ensuring the exact relationship between surface and the color. Working with a raking light, the skin is positioned and repositioned until all details in the printing correspond to the underlying surface. The sharp edges of flaking paint or a defined crack provide clear registration points. In the case of the tomb, the slight relief and clearly defined edges of the microbacteria covering the walls provided the dominant positional guide. Once in the correct position on the rigid surface, the skin and the relief are put into a vacuum bag and pressure is applied evenly until the adhesive has cured.

Sarcophagus

The sarcophagus was scanned using both laser and white-light scanners. It was routed in sections into high-density polyurethane, joined together, and cast into a resin composite resembling the original red granite. The traces of paint and color were added by hand from photographs and notes made in the tomb.

The sarcophagus lid, made from a different type of granite than the rest of the sarcophagus, was scanned with the white-light scanner, routed, and cast in scagliola (a composite substance composed of selenite, animal glue, and natural pigments). With this process it was possible to recreate the crystalline character of the granite. Many tests were made to match the grain and color of the lid and ensure that the final result had the character of the original.

The Missing Wall Reconstructed

One of Harry Burton's black-and-white photographs, taken soon after the discovery of the tomb of Tutankhamen, shows a section of the south wall that was removed in order to empty the burial chamber. The location of this fragment is currently unknown. Working with the Griffith Institute in Oxford, Factum Arte used Burton's photograph to reconstruct a full-color replica of the missing fragment. The color information for the reconstruction was extracted from the high-resolution photographs of the south wall recorded in 2009 and mapped onto an enlarged version of Burton's photograph. The surface was carved by hand, prepared with plaster and gesso, and printed on the flatbed printer.

Part 3—
Installation of the Facsimile Next to Carter's House

Egyptian architect Tarek Waly designed and supervised the construction of a space to house the facsimile, an enclosure with the exact layout and dimensions of the existing tomb. The site was excavated down to the bedrock, and the entire structure was constructed below ground level. It was then buried to leave no visible trace other than a discreet door leading to a ramp. The facsimile begins from the ramp that runs into the antechamber to allow disabled access into the installation and for other practical reasons. The wooden floor, handrail, metal doors, and lighting systems are the same as those installed in the original tomb in 2009. The antechamber and annex are used as an exhibition space to inform visitors about the tomb, its discovery, and the problems of preserving a space never meant to be visited. This display will develop as new discoveries are made and new insights surface.

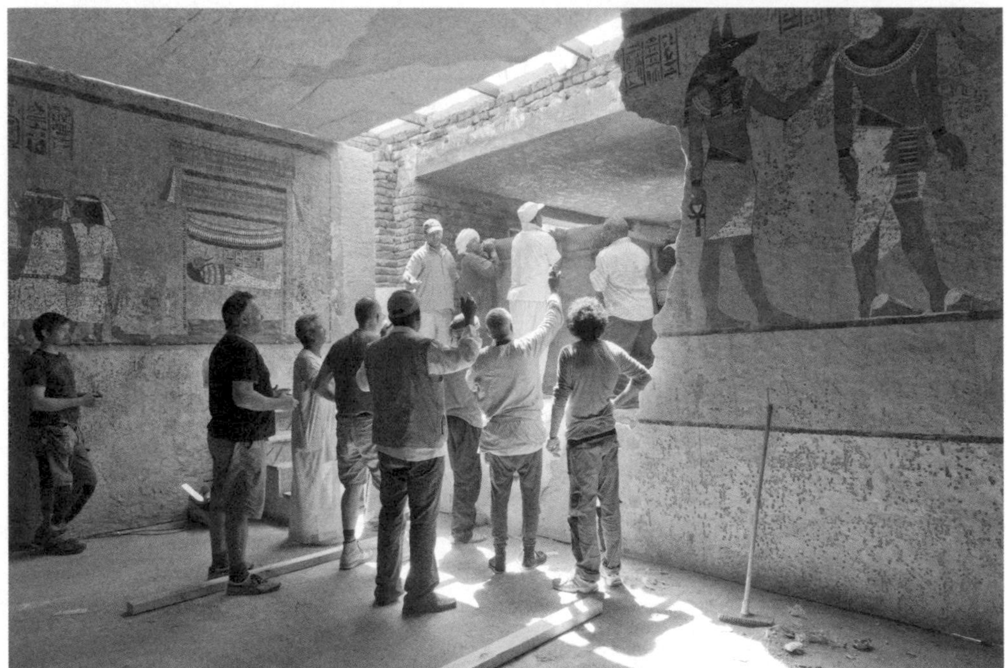

pages 95–96
The construction of the facsimile of the Tomb of Tutankhamen, 2012–2014.

To some degree all restoration turns an original into a reproduction of itself. Restorations reveal as much about the place and time in which they were carried out as they do about the original artifact. The facsimile of Tutankhamen's burial chamber demonstrates that digital technologies can record the surface of a complete heritage site and its contents, heralding a new era for forensically accurate study. In summer 2015 archaeologist Nicholas Reeves published his painstakingly detailed observations based on the 3-D data recorded by Factum Arte. He claims to have identified the traces of two sealed doors, one of which he believes will lead to the undiscovered tomb of Nefertiti. Recent thermal tomography and radar surveys appear to confirm that there is a void behind the north wall and a sealed door in the west wall. A technically advanced exploration of these voids seems inevitable.

We no longer think of art as static: the way it ages, transforming over time, becomes part of its trajectory. Thus even restorations become part of the biography of the work of art. Imagine Michelangelo walking into the Sistine Chapel today. Would he celebrate or be horrified? Imagine Leonardo encountering *The Last Supper* in Milan or Veronese seeing a painting he made on the wall of a monastic refectory in Venice visited by millions every year at the Louvre Museum. Imagine the people who built the tombs of the Theban Necropolis visiting the Valley of the Kings today. Have we altered their meaning and function in significant ways as we attempt to preserve and adapt them for thousands of visitors? Have we lost sight of their meaning and intention? Can we look beyond our temporally, culturally, and geographically conditioned perspective?

It has been difficult to raise money for the documentation and development of technologies to digitally record cultural heritage objects and sites. Sponsors and institutions prefer to support restoration projects and high-profile interventions. Yet as attitudes to originality and authenticity emerge from a century of Modernist ideology, the role of non-contact preservation and digital restoration are attracting attention. It is essential that we work together quickly to record as much as we can at the highest resolution realistically possible. The transcription of the Theban Necropolis is a clear example of this approach in action.

“We think of history in terms of use-value rather than quotation or classification.”

Precedent Pile

You can only quote something that already exists. No matter how recent the material cited is, it will always preexist the quote. Thus quotation inherently addresses the past, and this is particularly true in architecture; scholars have described the entire history of the field as an extended narrative of stylistic influence and quotation. Architects also tend to position their work in relation to previous practices, whether they want to invoke the authority of a distant era (as in the neoclassical fascination with ancient precedents), suggest continuity with recent movements (as in the postwar avant-garde's fascination with prewar Modernism), or even establish a break with history (as in the early Modernist rejection of nineteenth-century historicism). Architecture's forward progress, in other words, has long been understood through each successive generation's references to its predecessors.

Yet quotations of buildings have always been looser than those of language. Architects rarely achieve—indeed rarely aim for—the specificity and precision of the scholar or author. Because buildings tend to be large and complex, and rarely have identical programmatic requirements, producing an exact copy of another building would be impractical, if not actually impossible. So quotation in architecture has remained essentially a formal game played out on the level of aesthetic reference rather than strict likeness. This formal and visual emphasis, in turn, means that architectural quotation tends to work best on a (literally) superficial level: architecture is easiest to quote when treated as an image. Post-Modernism made this explicit; embracing historical reference was an effective critique of Modernism. Yet deploying architectural quotations as historical signs also produced architecture unprecedentedly dependent on the image—think of the "columns" flattened into the facade of Michael Graves's notorious Portland Building (1982), to name just one example.

Unfortunately, architecture also works best in that sense as a branding tool, and architects today are under enormous economic and political pressure to produce iconic images. Not coincidentally, the image-based approach of Post-Modernism is enjoying a renaissance. A new generation of designers is embracing a wide range of retro representational techniques—using hyper-dense line work and cartoonish doodles to depict everything from fragments of classical architecture to Rossi-esque Platonic solids, often with a dose of vivid color—in an apparent bid to reimagine architecture as a field of pure visual effects, not just a discipline rooted in representation. Ironically, this latest (re)turn to the image, which amounts to quotation of quotation, is often so facile that it has lost any sense of self-reflection. And when a historical reference no longer attempts to critically situate current practice it's no longer really a quotation at all—just pure style.

We started our practice at a moment when there was surprisingly little discussion of the architectural past. History seemed to have been tainted by its close association with theory, and advocates of the post-critical were doing their best to ignore both. At the same time digital design was ascendant, and its adherents, touting the liberating potential of the latest software, had once again declared a break with everything that came before. But we were sure that novel forms didn't necessarily make new architecture; in fact, the widespread fixation with formal innovation seemed to come at the expense of the more fundamental qualities that really make architecture: space, material, structure, and the complex social interactions that it can contain. As we looked around, we realized that digital design wasn't the only reductive, form-driven approach to architecture. An obsession with form making was behind everything from the diagram-based strategies supposedly rooted in program or performance to the sustainable design that was rapidly evolving into a full-blown symbolic language.

We've been trying to find a formless architecture ever since. As part of our search for alternatives to the trends of contemporary practice, we often look back into architectural history, but we see it as a fluid jumble of methods and techniques rather than a fixed library of images or formal precedents. Just as Georges Bataille, in his famous description of the *informe*, proposed that "a dictionary would begin as of the moment when it no longer provided the meanings of words but their tasks," we think of history in terms of use-value rather than quotation or classification. A column can be a historical artifact, or just another way of holding up a roof. Our approach is about process rather than form: we're looking for strategies that have pushed architecture's boundaries and rendered it, if not quite formless, then suggestively rough around the edges.

We're still not sure if there has ever been a formless architecture, and that's why we call these found methods "near misses." When we find one, we don't try to determine its historical meaning or fix it in a chain of semiotic reference; instead we try to put it to work for us, altering or exacerbating, scaling up or scaling down. Our approach certainly isn't an attempt at copying—if anything it's closer to the kind of mimicry that Bataille and Roger Caillois theorized as an entropic process, breaking down not just distinctions between object and environment but also hierarchies of thought. We see architecture from the past less as a precedent to follow than as another raw material to build with. The following are a few of our favorite near misses, spanning over four thousand years of architectural history:

Bent Pyramid
Dahshur, Egypt, 2600 BCE
Architect unknown

While most pyramids are by definition a kind of Platonic ideal of architectural form, this one is, famously, "bent." Its sloped sides climb from the ground at fifty-four degrees for nearly half of its approximately 350-foot height, then abruptly shift to a forty-three degree angle from there to the top. While archaeologists still debate the reason for this change, the most suggestive explanation is the theory advanced by physicist Kurt Mendelssohn in the 1970s. While other archaeologists have suggested that the pyramid's design was altered due to a lack of resources or to accelerate construction, he argued that it was an engineering problem: the nearby Meidum Pyramid, being built simultaneously, had undergone a catastrophic collapse, leading the designers of the Bent Pyramid to alter its geometry mid-construction to bolster its stability. The Bent Pyramid interests us not so much because of its aberrant shape (non-Platonic is not necessarily formless) but because its bend reminds us precisely that the pyramids are massive and potentially precarious accumulations of matter, not just geometric compositions. It suggests that construction entails not just the execution of an a priori design concept but a dynamic, contingent response to shifting material and environmental conditions.

San Carlo alle Quattro Fontane
Rome, Italy, 1646
Francesco Borromini

In his classic 1888 volume *Renaissance and Baroque*, Heinrich Wölfflin established Baroque buildings as legitimate objects of study for modern architectural history after previous scholars had seen them as degenerate perversions of Renaissance models. Here he built on the argument he had made in his dissertation two years earlier, that the physical process of making form was in itself the constitutive act of architecture, claiming that "the principle theme of architecture" is "a will that struggles to become form and has to overcome the resistance of a formless matter." But Wölfflin discussed Borromini's San Carlo alle Quattro Fontane and his other Baroque case studies in terms that made it sound increasingly like this struggle, rather than the final form, was of primary importance. In his description of San Carlo, Wölfflin writes, "The columns … looked as if they were perpetually twisting and turning. Each member seemed to have been seized by a wild frenzy. Everything was dissolved in decoration and movement." Our interest in the building lies in its eccentric plan, its cramped, even claustrophobic site, and its animated undulating surfaces—but most of all in the way it shifts the visitor's experience of architecture from a single moment of comprehension, in which the entire space is legible at a glance, to an ongoing process of destabilization wherein the space seems to transform continually as one moves through it, suggesting that a building might be inhabitable but ultimately unknowable. This is, after all, the church that famously inspired Richard Serra's *Torqued Ellipses*.

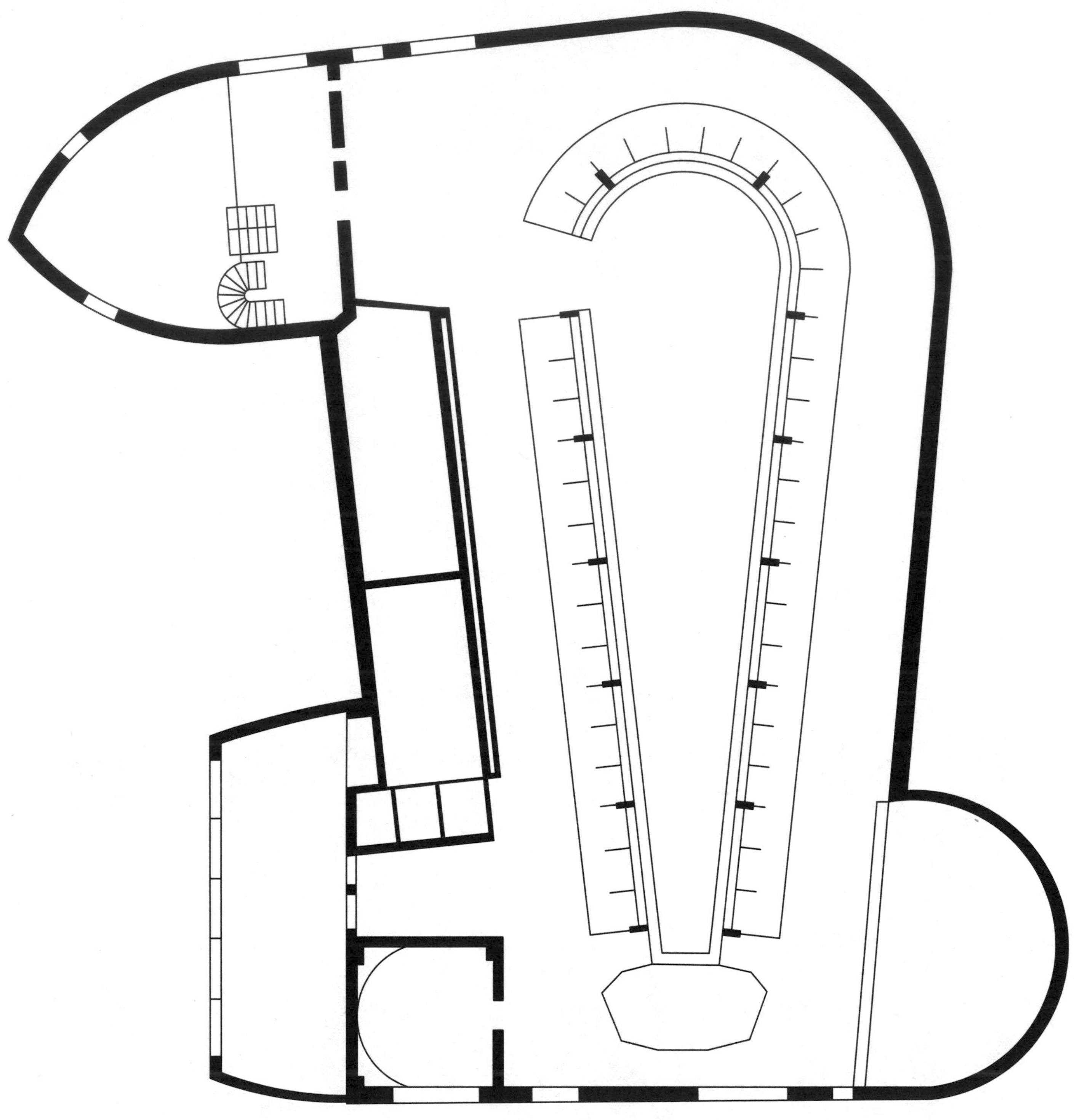

Gut Garkau Farm
Scharbeutz, Germany, 1926
Hugo Häring

Hugo Häring has become something of a cult figure in twentieth-century architectural history for championing a more organic Modernism in the face of the rationalist aesthetic we now associate with International Style, especially its postwar corporate manifestations. But while others associated with the same trajectory often tended toward expressionism and a kind of symbolic depiction of program, Häring's Gut Garkau Farm was literally organic—it was designed for animals, waste, raw material, and biological processes. The anomalous contours of the cowshed and barn, the rough materiality of the exposed concrete and brickwork, and some of the buildings' more eccentric features (our favorite is what Haring described as "a mechanical conveyor [that] delivers chopped turnips") were the result of architectural form being, in his words, "discovered" rather than invented in response to processes including "the distribution of rough fodder" and "the disposal of dung." If we now tend to associate Modern architecture with rational geometry and the abstraction of function into an idealized aesthetic, here is a different Modernism deeply grounded in the physical processes that unfold within the building.

Douglas Dam
Sevier County, Tennessee, 1943
Tennessee Valley Authority

Founded during the Depression, the Tennessee Valley Authority undertook the wholesale transformation of a regional landscape at a scale and pace unlike anything the world had seen. Over a quarter mile long and approximately two hundred feet high, the Douglas Dam was built in just over a year to meet increased power demands during World War Two and abruptly rendered a section of the French Broad River valley into a lake of almost fifty square miles. This dam and other large-scale infrastructure projects like it make a powerful statement about the current relationship between architecture and nature, but they haven't gotten much attention from architects. Today most conversations about architecture and the environment are dominated by the rhetoric of sustainability—which, however worthy its goals, tends to encourage a false dichotomy between architecture and the environment, assuming that nature exists in an ideal independent state and that so-called "green design" is the only approach that connects architecture to the environment. But the Douglas Dam is an example of the kind of hybrid landscape that defines our world: the uneasy amalgamation of the natural and the artificial that we see at so many different scales, from freeway overpasses and shoreline embankments to road cuts and drainage channels. These landscapes, neither fully organic nor fully man made, define the increasingly formless ecology of our contemporary condition: the result of an often awkward and even violent collision between the existing environment, flows of materials and waste, and man-made infrastructure. They remind us that, for better or worse, all architecture is already inextricably involved in an ongoing exchange with our environment.

"If nature,
in select instances,
produces organisms
capable of
transgressing
the assumed limits
of territory
and longevity,
why shouldn't
architecture
follow suit?"

Steven Lauritano A Remnant Vivarium

1 Karl Friedrich Schinkel, The Grand Pergola, as depicted in the *Sammlung architektonischer Entwürfe*, Blatt 171, 1835.

Nature's way was neither static nor an eternal return upon past occurrences. Language, human society, and the living organisms were conceived organically. They grew. Their life-course was a record of continued eruption of novelty, divergence from expectations, and strange remnants of past circumstances.
—William Coleman, *Biology in the Nineteenth Century*

Vivarium, in Latin, means quite literally place of life. The following essay seeks to elucidate the place of life in the architectural theory of Karl Friedrich Schinkel. When Schinkel wrote of architecture's "life-indicating requirements," what, precisely, did he mean? To begin answering this question, I have brought two projects into dialogue: Alexander von Humboldt's essay on the "Physiognomy of Plants" from his *Ansichten der Natur* (1808) and Schinkel's design for the Grosse Laube, or Grand Pergola (figs. 1 and 2), at the Court Gardener's House at Charlottenhof (1826–39). Through this juxtaposition, issues of quotation, classification, and the representation of fragmented remains (in nature and architecture) come to the fore. First I will extract a specific passage from Humboldt's text and consider its critical resonance in a variety of scientific, artistic, and architectural contexts. In the second part of the essay I will attempt to clarify Schinkel's natural-historical treatment of building remains through comparison with the study of ornament made by his contemporary Henry William Inwood. Finally, I will examine the conceptual affinity between Schinkel's work on the Grand Pergola and contemporaneous research on the physiology and survival strategies of microorganisms conducted by Christian Gottfried Ehrenberg at the University in Berlin. I will conclude the essay with a close physiognomic reading of Schinkel's pergola. Ultimately I hope that this body of evidence will help to distinguish Schinkel's material project of revivification, or *Wiederbelebung*, from other strands of stylistic revival.

2 The Grand Pergola, as depicted in an anonymous photograph, ca. 1907. Reproduced from Kurt Kuhlow, *Das Königliche Schloß Charlottenhof bei Potsdam*, Berlin, 1911, Tafel VIII, Abbildung 27.

§

The Parable of a Newly Raised Island

Picture the bleakest of nature's blank canvases: a barren rock face, piercing for the first time the surface of the sea in one of those periodic realignments of the planet's crust. This is the image Humboldt beckoned readers to conjure in 1808 as he sought to combat the stubbornly persistent belief in a *generatio spontanea*:

> If new lands are formed, the organic forces are ever ready to animate their sterile surfaces.... How are the seeds of life brought so immediately to these new shores? Whether by wandering birds, or the winds, or the rocking of the ocean, the distance from other coasts makes it difficult to decide. But no sooner does the naked rock of the newly raised island come into contact with the atmosphere than there is formed on its surface a web of velvety fibers, appearing to the naked eye as colored spots and patches. Some of these patches are bordered by single or double raised lines; others are run through with furrows and divided into fans. With increasing age the light color of the patches darkens. The bright yellow, once visible from afar, changes to brown, and the bluish-gray of the Lepraria transforms into a dusty black. The edges of the maturing patches run into each other; and on the dark ground thus formed there appear other lichens, of a circular shape and dazzling whiteness.[1]

Even as the nineteenth century approached its midpoint, many naturalists still subscribed to a doctrine of *Urzeugung*, or spontaneous generation, believing that certain lower organisms—algae, fungi, microscopic animalcules, and the like—could arise spontaneously from water, slime, dust, or an admixture of inanimate substances. A Prussian naturalist and geographer, Humboldt (1769–1859) counted himself among a small but growing group of scientists who hoped to dispel such notions.[2] Writing for a general audience in his essay "Physiognomy of Plants," Humboldt turned to the vivid image of a newly formed island in order to hammer home his message: Life does not originate from the nonliving; though the precise trajectories of airborne spores and seeds remain untraceable, their arrival, rather than any spontaneous emergence, is responsible for gradually populating the virgin rock with its colorful, organic layers (fig. 3).[3]

At various points in his essay, Humboldt invites readers to confront nature not only through the eyes of a naturalist but through those of a painter as well. In this context, his story of the newly formed island marks a moment of reversal. Suddenly it is nature herself who paints. With talk of raised edges and velvety patches, built up layer upon layer, daubs of yellow, brown and bluish-gray, fan shapes and circles expanding their borders, the excerpt evokes nothing so much as the actions of painting and the gestures of the brush.

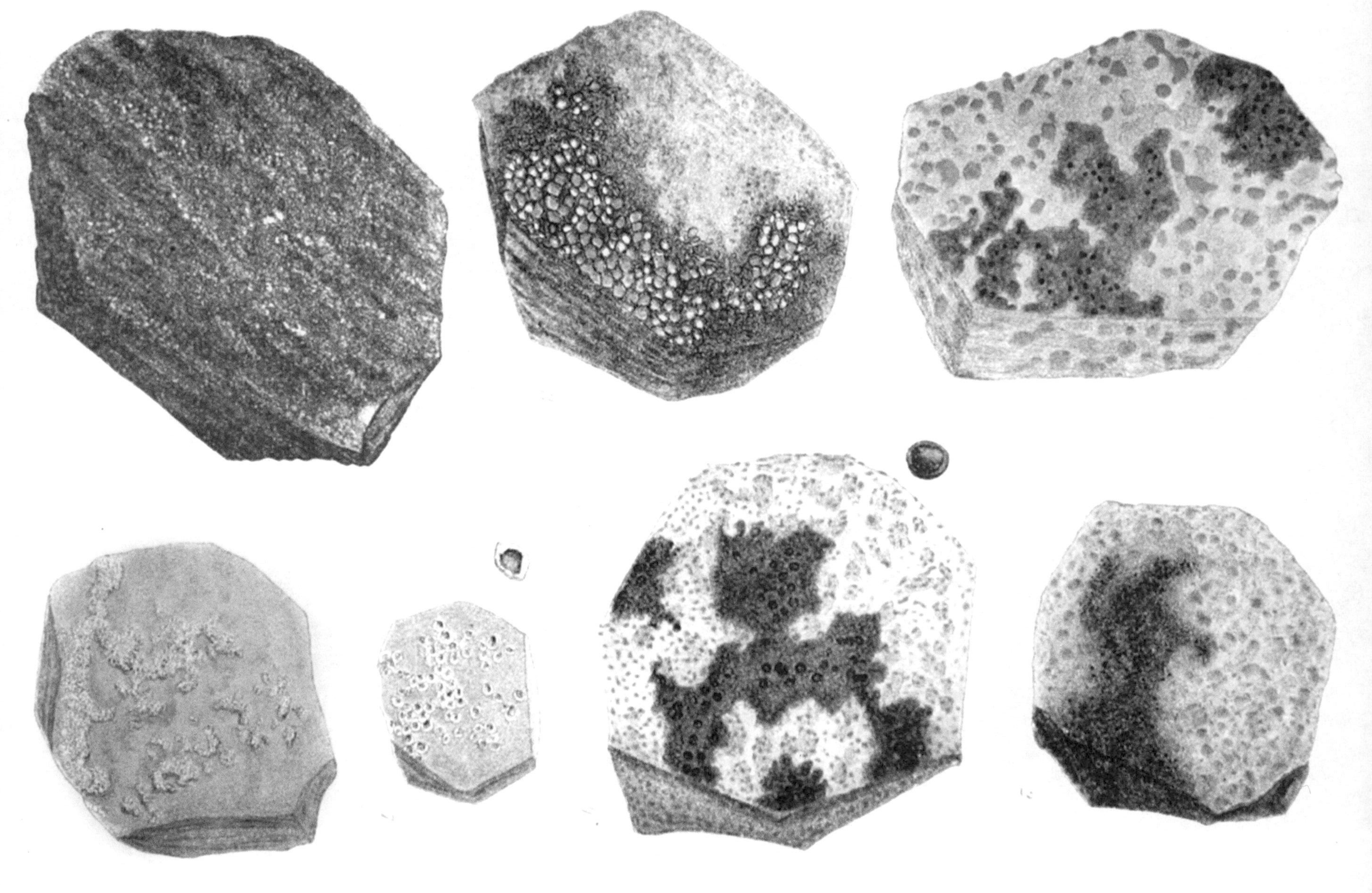

3 Walther Migula, “Lecanoraceae, Flechten,” (Lichens), Tafel 28 in *Kryptogamen-Flora. Moose, Algen, Flechten und Pilze*, Band IV. Flechten, 1. Teil, Berlin-Lichterfelde, 1929. Migula’s publication is a continuation (Band XII, Abteilung 1) of Otto Wilhelm Thomé’s, *Flora von Deutschland, Österreich und der Schweiz in Wort und Bild*, first published in 1885.

Barren rock becomes painted surface and Humboldt's passage performs a double function, as a commentary on the myth of spontaneous generation in biology and in the production of art. Indeed, contrary to the fantasies of some painters, an empty canvas is no more likely to find itself suddenly populated with images, in a flash of unsolicited inspiration, than a naked rock can expect to find its surface miraculously teeming with spontaneous fungal growth.

4 A picturesque fragment-arrangement on the grounds of Schloß Glienicke, 2011.

A year later Schinkel and Humboldt collaborated again, on plans for a new Palmenhaus on the Pfaueninsel in the River Havel, the latest addition to the Prussian royal pleasure grounds.[8] Alongside these personal interactions, Schinkel had the opportunity to absorb some of Humboldt's observations on the geographical distribution of natural forms at the celebrated "Kosmos" lectures, a total of seventy-seven presentations delivered by Humboldt to packed houses at the University of Berlin and the Singakademie between November 1827 and April 1828.[9]

Humboldt's parable draws attention to a subtle form of quotation that is common to nature and certain forms of art. It is not the learned quotation of the literary stylist who selectively replicates passages and makes clever allusions with the expectation that the original sources will become apparent to other readers in the know. To the contrary, the miniscule particles that travel from distant ecologies and touch down upon the naked island's surface remain all but undetectable, their origins anonymous. Pushing Humboldt's metaphor further, one might think of Caspar David Friedrich, a painter whose canvases present carefully joined fragments assembled from his experience of nature rather than reproducing specifically locatable views;[4] or the Jena Romantics, who published their textual *Athenaeum Fragments* as a collective and anonymous ensemble;[5] or Novalis, who referred to such fragments as "literary seeds," "granules," and "grains of pollen."[6] Humboldt's island parable shares an affinity with the creative projects of these contemporaries yet ventures into new territory by questioning the artist's ultimate control over the process of selection. In artistic systems dedicated to the meticulous assembly of quotations, the choice of inputs constitutes a creative act on which a large fraction of the artist's claim to authorship rests.

Humboldt's lichen-painted outcropping introduces the element of serendipity: the quotations of the natural world consist of three-dimensional material entities that find the new work, not the other way around. When control over the selection of inputs is ceded and outside agents begin to deliver quotations for use in a given project, how must the author adapt?

An avid follower of Humboldt's scientific writings, Schinkel had occasion to ponder such questions and to consider how nature's propagation systems might provide a model for the growth of new building practices, similarly predicated upon the arrival of architectural quotations as particles from distant shores. After Humboldt accepted the Prussian king's invitation to decamp from Paris to Berlin in 1827, Schinkel began to rethink his assumptions about building in response to a reading of architecture as an expression of natural historical forces.[7] When Humboldt organized the first annual convention of German natural scientists in 1828, he chose Schinkel's Schauspielhaus as the site for the opening ceremonies, and the two worked together on designs for a set of temporary decorations.

During this stretch of time Schinkel was busy working on preliminary designs for a project that would eventually take shape as a kind of architectural analog to the newborn island introduced in Humboldt's essay. Beneath the Grand Pergola, which stretches over the entrance to the Court Gardener's House at Charlottenhof, a small outcropping of stone rises above a sea of gravel to offer a space of repose (figs. 1 and 2). Its solid crystalline surfaces play host to an apparently growing assortment of architectural and sculptural quotations, deposited among specimens of active vegetal life. Some of the particles represent actual remnants of antiquity. There are segments of columns from Pompeii, the remains of a Roman sarcophagus, a Corinthian capital, and a finely carved antique console.[10] There are also classical vessels, most likely comprising a mixture of reproductions and genuine antiquities. These occupy the horizontal surfaces of the ashlar assembly, like fruits or seedpods fallen from the artificial troposphere of gridded beams and twining vines above. Replicated works of sculpture also appear beneath the pergola, including a miniature *Farnese Hercules* and contemporary pieces modeled after the antique: a *Herm of Bacchus*, by Karl Heinrich Möller, and three terra-cotta reliefs by Christian Daniel Rauch.[11]

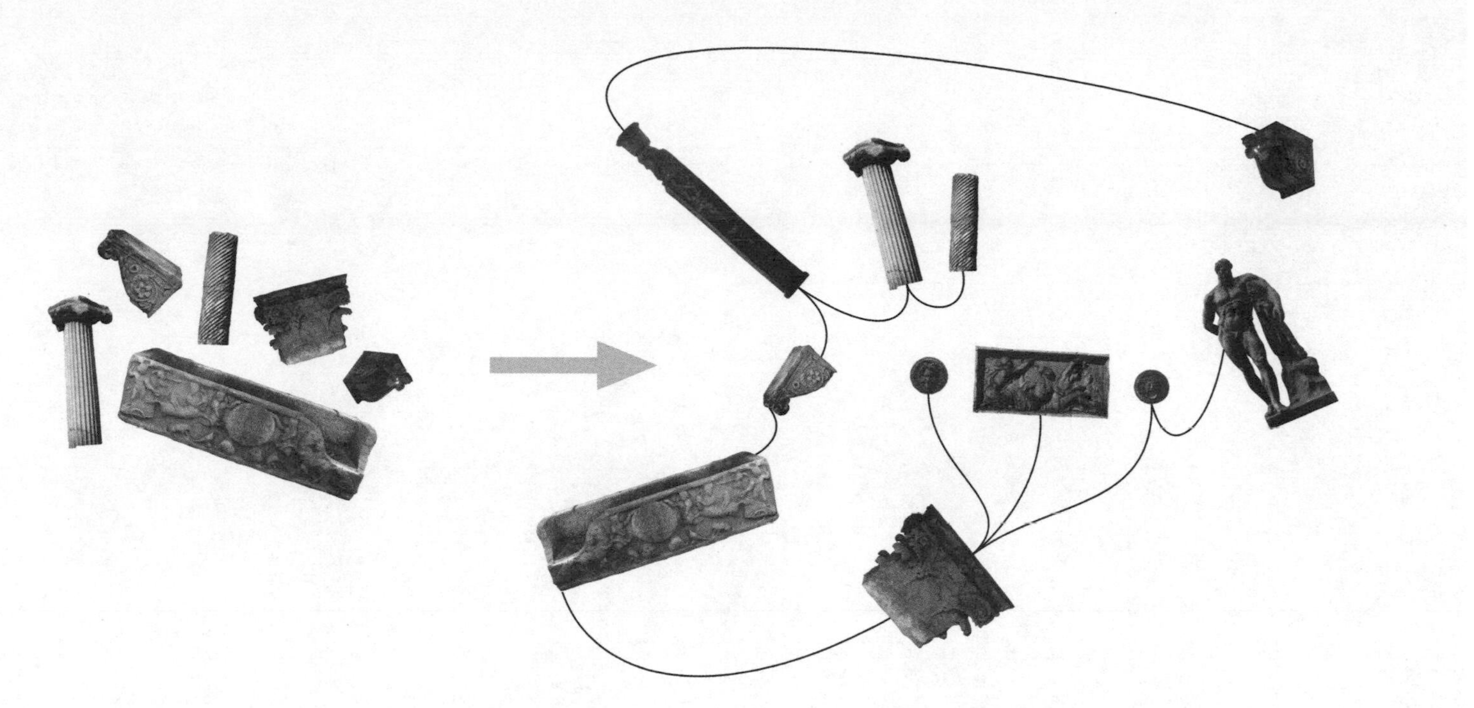

5 A new pattern of connectivity created by Schinkel for the antique remnants in the Grand Pergola at Charlottenhof (diagram by the author).

On a practical level, this Grand Pergola satisfied Crown Prince Friedrich Wilhelm's desire for an outdoor space where he could display his burgeoning collection of antiquities and art. The conceptual ramifications of Schinkel's architectural solution, however, far exceed the apparent simplicity of this program.

More than any other project in Schinkel's oeuvre, the Grand Pergola bears witness to a realization that framed his basic approach to design: architectural quotations do not perform the same way on paper as they do in the three-dimensional material world. Instead of relying on his considerable skills as a draftsman to assimilate the antique remnants into drawings, where they might find seamless integration alongside other replicated classical motifs, Schinkel called on living vines, stems, and leafy patches to weave together the disparate relics and join them in a flexible unity. Here one can actually observe Humboldt's vision of the "organic powers... incessantly at work in *reconnecting* with each other, the elements set free by death or dissolution."[12] Though in this case it is the death, or more precisely the *apparent* death, of ancient buildings and styles that makes possible a new hybridity, architecture physically joined with nature as the cycle of dissolution and subsequent recomposition unfolds through Schinkel's design.

Gone missing are the picturesque fragment piles, familiar a thousand times over in the "Vedute" of Piranesi. To transform the perception of these ancient moldering remains (fig. 4), Schinkel borrowed from the naturalist's understanding of revival, what might be termed *revivification*, or *Wiederbelebung*, to use a word from the contemporary scientific milieu. His design for the Grand Pergola preserves the material individuality of each architectural remnant while strategically implicating its form in an overlapping framework of structural, botanical, and irrigational flows (fig 5). The resulting composition approaches an experimental setup, a kind of microcosmic environment where Schinkel appears to have put his hypothesis to the test: when positioned within the proper set of environmental conditions, ancient architectural remnants can experience a kind of reactivation. By virtue of this *Wiederbelebung*, hidden aspects of a remnant's structure and effects have the potential to become visible once again.

In theory Schinkel could then apply these revealed structures to satisfy specific design challenges posed by contemporary buildings. As a site where such experimental work was carried out, the Grand Pergola announces a split in the project of architectural revival. It necessitates a differentiation between two modes of attempted quotation reanimation: one adhering more closely to literary tradition, devoted to the perpetuation of an established syntax and style, and another focused on the material, quasi-ecological, aspects of architectural survival.

Before exploring this divergence further it is necessary to point out one additional respect through which the Grand Pergola mimics the scenario of Humboldt's newly emerged island: despite being the primary architect in charge of design, Schinkel exercised only limited control over the selection of the pergola's constitutive elements. Remnants arrived from different directions, at different times, supplied by different agents. The crown prince provided the antique sarcophagus, which he acquired outside of Naples on his first trip to Italy in 1828.[13] Schinkel's assistant Ludwig Persius probably secured the Corinthian capital and the antique console sometime around 1831. Rauch supplied the terra-cotta reliefs and a cast-zinc fountain in the form of a fish by the end of 1834.[14] In 1835 Martin Hinrich Lichtenstein, a professor of zoology at the Berlin University, contributed one-half of a giant clam.[15]

6 "Gärtner Wohnung in Charlottenhof," a steel plate engraving by Ernst Friedrich Grünewald, after a design by Karl Loeillot de Mars, presented in Heinrich Spiker's *Berlin und seine Umgebungen im neunzehnten Jahrhundert*, Berlin, ca. 1840.

Thus the Grand Pergola project involved a specific mode of collaborative effort, not only in terms of the material inputs but in the overall design process as well.

The first drawing to depict the Gärtnerwohnung complex dates from 1826.[16] It is a small pencil sketch overlaid onto one of Peter Joseph Lenné's comprehensive plans for the grounds of Charlottenhof in the southeast corner of the Sanssouci Park. Whether this tiny sketch represents the work of Schinkel, the crown prince, or Lenné remains a matter of debate. After Friedrich Wilhelm III acquired the land in 1825, he gave the parcel to his eldest son as a Christmas present and a celebration of his marriage to Princess Elisabeth Ludovika of Bavaria. From that point on the crown prince actively involved himself in many facets of Charlottenhof's design (as the entire project came to be known), producing upwards of sixty sketches over the next several years. None of his drawings are dated, however, making it nearly impossible for scholars to disentangle the Gordian knot of the crown prince's own suggestions and requests from those of Schinkel, Persius, and Lenné.[17]

Even if such a chronology and accounting of the collective design process could be reconstructed, it would likely prove less insightful than the sum total of effects displayed in the Grand Pergola.[18] Schinkel staked a certain claim to authorship, or at least signaled his contentment with the resulting design, by representing the project among the final plates of his *Sammlung architektonischer Entwürfe*, the carefully managed monographic presentation he prepared to share and preserve his work.[19] In that same publication, Schinkel's descriptive caption for the Gärtnerwohnung suggests that ceding control over some aspects of the design was, in fact, part of his strategy:

> The entire genial construction of the villa, by its very instinct, allows for extensions and new additions in the same spirit as the different component buildings ... there is constant room for improvement and alteration, and in this manner, the possibility of a continuous joy in producing and creating is maintained.[20]

With this statement Schinkel rejects the Albertian paradigm that holds up the architect's final set of drawings as a complete and immutable instantiation of the design, to be executed exactly as represented.[21] In contrast, his caption frames the Grand Pergola as part of an architectural composition forever open to change. It is doubtful whether Schinkel could have arrived at such a position independent of Humboldt and his descriptions of nature's perpetually churning matter, especially those found in the essay "Physiognomy of Plants." Instead of anchoring the Grand Pergola in the perceived authority of past architectural traditions by imitating history's most esteemed models, Schinkel applied Humboldt's lessons about the incessant dissolutions and recombinations of organic life to the motley collection of antique remnants that he was provided, using these architectural particles as the very ingredients that open his structure to perpetual transformation. In this sense Schinkel's revivification of architectural quotations engenders a different kind of authority, one derived from the ongoing material effects periodically reactivated by the shifting forms of the adjacent plants (fig. 6).

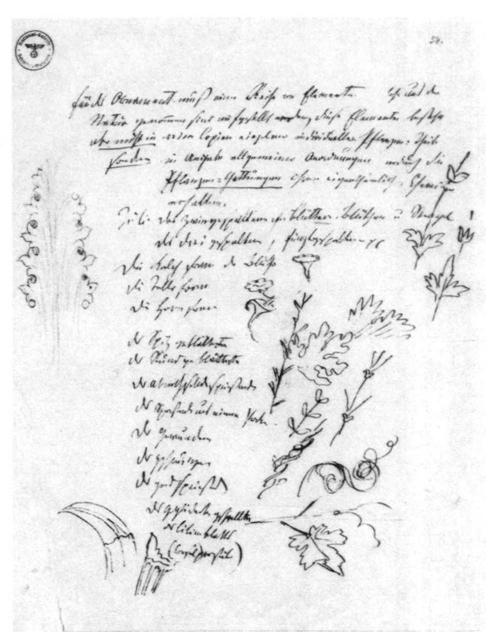

7 Karl Friedrich Schinkel, Notes on Vegetal Ornament ca. 1825, collection of the Staatlichen Museen zu Berlin, Nachlass Karl Friedrich Schinkel, "Heft IV, theoretische Schriften," Blatt 54.

§ §

Lebendige Quotations

Additions and modifications to the Grand Pergola and the larger Gärtnerwohnung complex continued even after Schinkel's death in 1841.[22] One person who was there to witness most of the subsequent changes was Humboldt. Long after he had challenged Schinkel to reexamine architecture through the lens of nature's organizing principles, Humboldt continued to bring his natural-historical meditations into close proximity with the Grand Pergola through his sheer physical presence. Once the construction of the Court Gardener's House was sufficiently complete, Humboldt convinced the crown prince to reserve a guest room for his use on the building's second floor.[23] That room provided one of Humboldt's favorite spaces for writing during the remaining years of his life. On more temperate days, one might very well find him within the bounds of the Grand Pergola itself, seated at its outdoor table among architectural remnants and their botanical counterparts. Perhaps Humboldt revised his "Kosmos" lecture notes on this very spot, or prepared the extensive endnotes for the later editions of his *Ansichten der Natur*. In either case, the Grand Pergola's commingling of nature and art would have surrounded Humboldt with a vivid reminder of the argument that underpins both of these texts—that painters, poets, and architects have something to teach the natural scientist because they are trained to see natural phenomena as part of a total impression. Such holistic visions, Humboldt wagered, might counteract the dissecting eye of the naturalist-classifier. "We must not follow the march of botanical systems," he had argued as early as 1808, "for they restrict the investigation too narrowly to the plant's reproductive organs, perianth parts, and fruits."[24] As a remedy to such selective analysis, Humboldt advocated a physiognomic approach, one that would grasp the specific character that an entire plant imparts to its immediate surroundings as it interacts with a host of environmental factors, including the color of the sky, the quality of the air, the intensity of the sunlight, and the density of shadows.[25] Put another way, the discernment of a plant's physiognomy demands consideration of its performance as part of a greater ecological whole.

Among Schinkel's loose-leaf notes and sketches there is a single sheet where his own thoughts on botanical classification, ornamental remnants, and the pursuit of something like an expressive physiognomy in building all coincide for a moment in the same theoretical space (fig. 7). "For ornament," Schinkel writes at the top of the page, "a range of elements must be deployed which are taken from nature. These elements, however, should not consist of pure copies from separate, individual plant-parts, but rather they should indicate the general structures through which the plant-types obtain their character."[26] To further clarify which general plant structures might be well suited for redeployment as architectural motifs, Schinkel provides a list and a set of corresponding diagrams:

> the bilaterally-divided in leaves, blossoms and stems
> the trilaterally-divided, quintuply-divided, etc.
> the goblet form of blossoms
> the plate-form
> the horn-form
> the pointed-leaf
> the rounded-leaf
> the alternately-sprouting
> the sprouting from a point
> the winding
> the coiling
> the oscillating
> the subdivided-swelling of the lily petal (console profile)[27]

Schinkel's first few entries reference familiar structural designations from the eighteenth century's classificatory schemes. Over the course of the list, however, a transition plays out. The static geometric categories give way to increasingly dynamic vegetal *actions*, a shift that parallels a transformation already well underway in the domain of science, namely the transition from natural history to the new discipline of biology. Schinkel's naturalist and zoologist colleagues increasingly redirected their attention from the ordering and naming project of the preceding two centuries to focus on the study of nature's vital processes.[28] In this sense Schinkel's list recalls the words of English physiologist William Lawrence, who declared that the time had come to "explore the *active* state of the animal structure."[29]

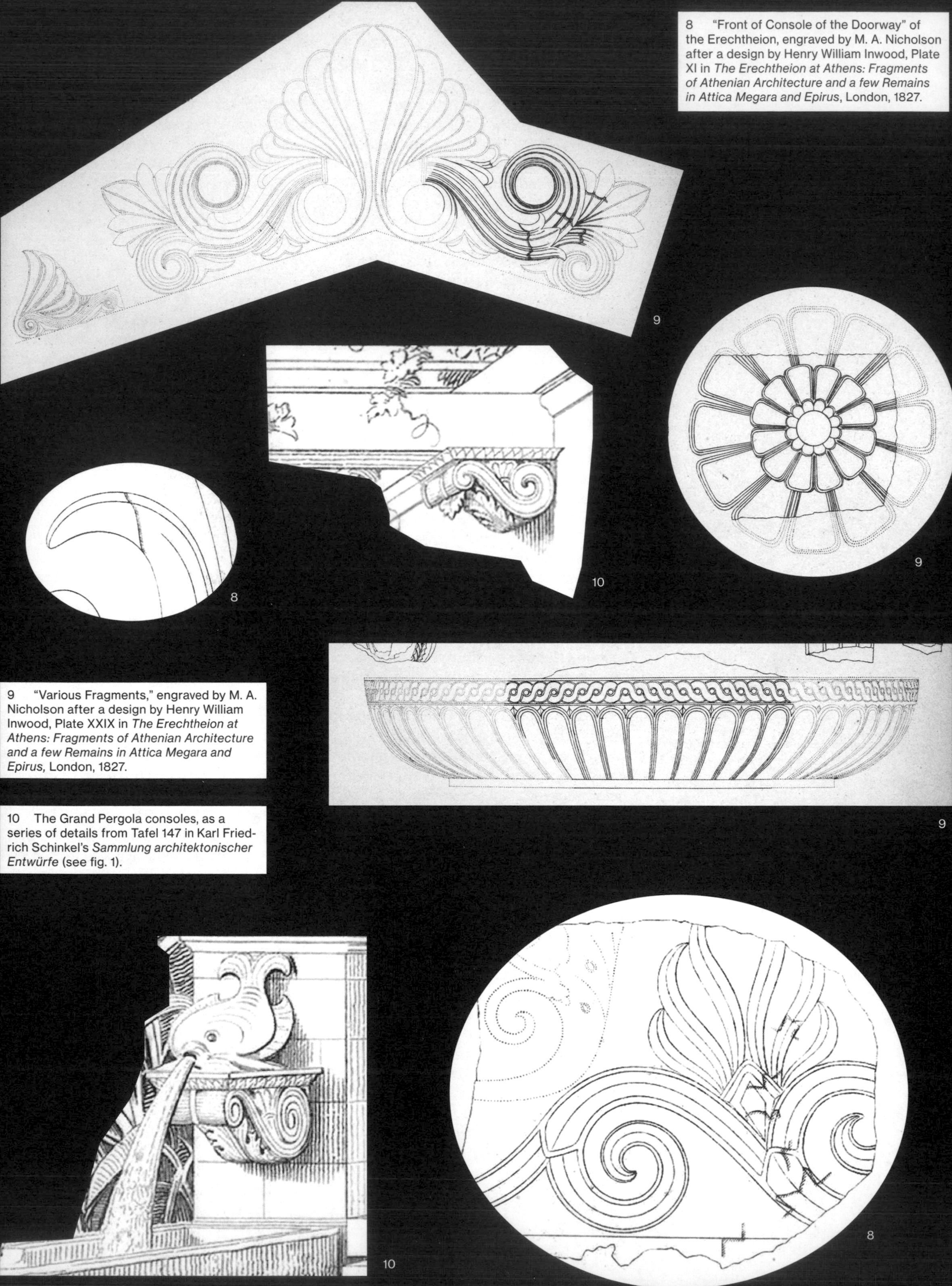

8 "Front of Console of the Doorway" of the Erechtheion, engraved by M. A. Nicholson after a design by Henry William Inwood, Plate XI in *The Erechtheion at Athens: Fragments of Athenian Architecture and a few Remains in Attica Megara and Epirus*, London, 1827.

9 "Various Fragments," engraved by M. A. Nicholson after a design by Henry William Inwood, Plate XXIX in *The Erechtheion at Athens: Fragments of Athenian Architecture and a few Remains in Attica Megara and Epirus,* London, 1827.

10 The Grand Pergola consoles, as a series of details from Tafel 147 in Karl Friedrich Schinkel's *Sammlung architektonischer Entwürfe* (see fig. 1).

For Schinkel the search for a discernibly active quality in architectural form transcended the relatively narrow problem of vegetal ornament. The notion of a *lebendigen*, or lively, character seems to have informed his selection of almost every building component, along with his determination of a building's overall parti:

> In architecture, as in every art, life must become visible.... The work of architecture must not stand there as a sealed-off artifact.... A striving, a sprouting, a crystallization, a coiling-up, a thrusting, a splitting, a joining, a pressing, bending, bearing, settling, nestling, coupling, holding, a laying and resting (the last of which, however much in contrast to the active qualities, also implies a deliberate and visible arrangement and to this extent must be thought of as a lively action), these are the life-indicating requirements of architecture.[30]

In this micro-manifesto espousing the need for built form to reveal signs of animation, or the *Lebendig*, Schinkel effectively outlines a proto-Semperian way of reading ornament.[31] This becomes especially evident at the Grand Pergola, where almost every one of Schinkel's life-revealing actions finds some form of expression. Because the design compels the individual remnants to interact physically with a combination of natural and architectural structures, the antique remains leave behind their "sealed-off" fossilized condition to press and to bear, to join and to coil once more.

Schinkel was hardly the only architect to pursue this line of investigation. The "study of nature in conjunction with that of the remains of classical antiquity" constituted one of the more popular theoretical subjects among architects during the first half of the nineteenth century.[32] However, Schinkel's emphasis on abstract botanical structures and the vital expression of organic action represents a sharp turn from the mainstream approach.

More often, architects and archaeologists sought to establish the correct correspondence between decorative motifs and their sources in nature. Beyond using visual comparison (of botanical and architectural specimens), authors of such studies frequently turned to antique textual sources hoping to find passages that might link a particular plant to a deity, a mythological figure, or a ceremony. This information could then be used to explain the vegetal ornament's application to a particular edifice based on its presumed dedication or functional use.

As a representative of this mainstream methodology, Henry William Inwood's 1827 study of ornament, "Fragments of Athenian Architecture," provides an insightful contrast to Schinkel's approach.[33] Though the text appeared during the earliest stages of the Grand Pergola's planning, its fundamental approach to classical remains could not be more distinct from that realized later at Charlottenhof. Inwood's publication presents material gathered during his trip to Greece in 1818–19.[34] Initially he focused his documentary efforts on the Erechtheion, perched on the Acropolis, but his attention soon turned to the urban fabric below and the various fragments he found embedded over doors and windows in the back alleys and courtyards of the city's labyrinthine streets. Like a botanist collecting samples, Inwood pried specimens from these architectural contexts and returned to England with a small collection of antique remains.[35] Once home, he set about the task of matching these classical motifs with their natural analogues. In his text he identifies multiple ornamental derivations of honeysuckle and lotus blossoms (fig. 8) as well as a range of motifs modeled after acanthus plants, fan palms, irises, reeds, roses, laurels, ivies, and thistles. In several cases Inwood backs up his posited botanical affiliations with literary citations from Vitruvius, Pindar, Euripides, and Aristophanes. Ultimately, however, such identifications merely served as a prerequisite for Inwood's broader project of visual comparison. Once a designation such as honeysuckle has been reasonably established, the particular specimen can find its place within a much larger series of similarly classified ornaments.

This in turn enables a secondary process of aesthetic judgment, based on criteria such as the elegance of petal arrangement, the proportional relationships, and the degree to which natural form has been preserved. Classification (of natural prototype) and aesthetic comparison go hand in hand. In Inwood's conception this two-step process encourages the development of taste, a goal he identifies as the true motivation for his project: "to cultivate, from contemplating the noblest remains of ancient art throughout the classic countries in which they arose, the refined genius and practical taste."[36]

In order to position his ornamental specimens within broader comparative series, Inwood relies on a constant stream of citations. He directs the reader toward an ever-growing bibliography of cross-referenced images, especially from the plates prepared by James Stuart and Nicholas Revett for *The Antiquities of Athens*, but also from the works of Piranesi, the publications of the Society of Dilettanti, the drawings of Charles Robert Cockerell, and publications by Sir George Wheler, Edward Dodwell, William Wilkins, and Lewis Vulliamy to name just a few.[37] One can picture a young architect pulling these volumes from the shelves of a well-appointed library and opening to the relevant pages to reveal the full range of honeysuckle motifs. If Inwood's aim was to improve the architect's ability to discern the best specimens, then the higher the volume of choices the better.[38] Further adding to the comparative pool, Inwood sends his readers to examine the genuine articles, citing a number of architectural specimens preserved in the Townley Collection, the Elgin Collection, Sir John Soane's Museum, the Cambridge Museum, and the private collections of Sir Sandford Graham and Sir Henry Englefield.[39]

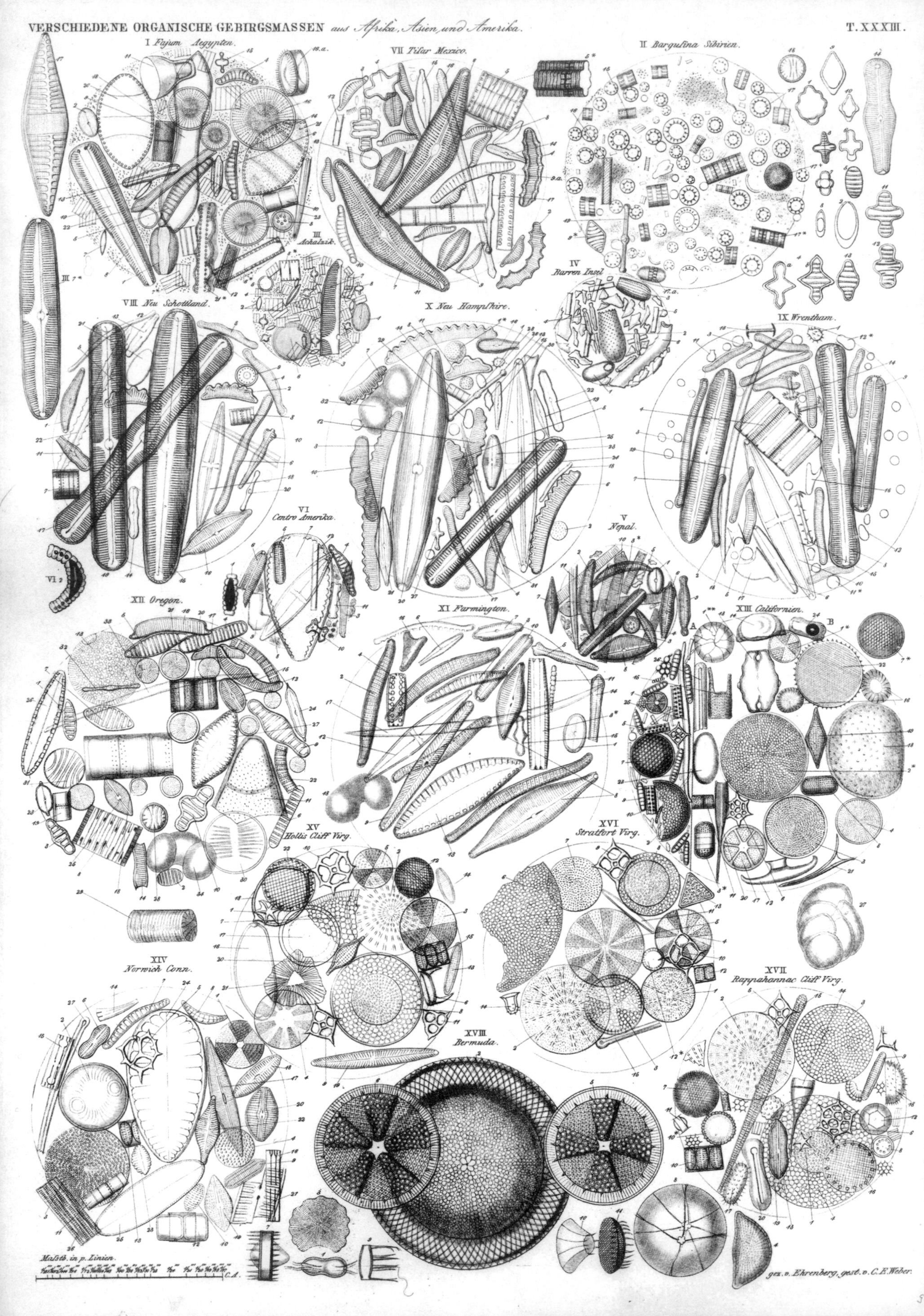

11 "Verschiedene organische Gebirgsmassen aus Afrika, Asien und Amerika" (Different organic rock masses from Africa, Asia and America), Tafel XXXIII in Christian Gottfried Ehrenberg's *Mikrogeologie*, engraved by C. E. Weber after a design by Ehrenberg, Leipzig, 1854.

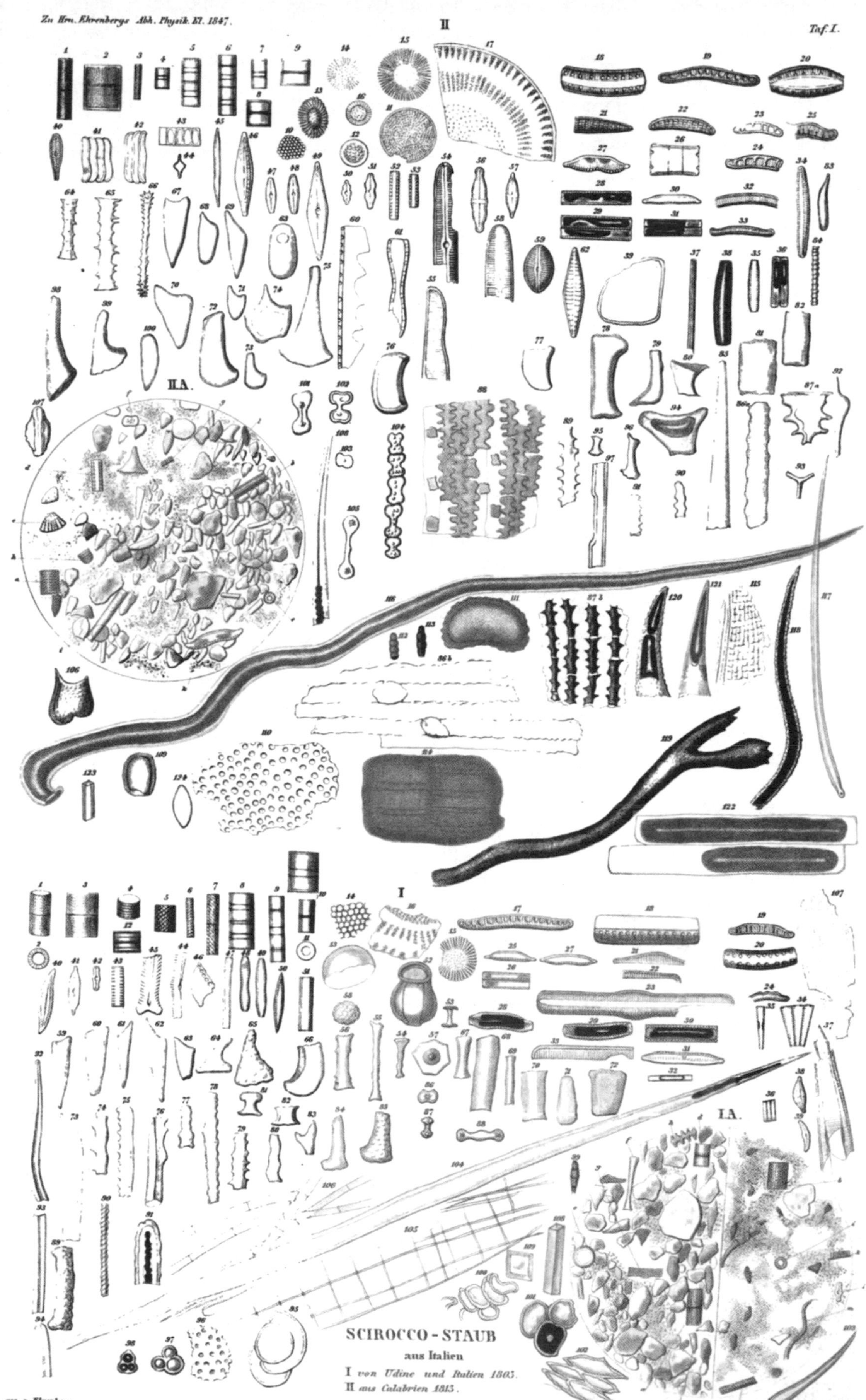

12 Tafeln I from Christian Gottfried Ehrenberg's *Passat-Staub und Blut-Regen. ein großes organisches unsichtbares Wirken und Leben in der Atmosphäre*, (Trade-Wind-Dust and Blood-Rain, a great organic invisible Activity and Life in the Atmosphere) published by the Königlichen Akademie der Wissenschaften, Berlin, 1849.

To summarize, Inwood removed his ornamental quotations from the material surroundings in which he found them and replaced that context with a new web of citations. His text connects each fragment back to nature, to ancient authors, and to ornamental motifs of the same species residing either in books or mounted on gallery walls. Through this process the architectural remains transition from existing as material remnants to surviving through a pattern of compilation and cross-referencing more common to literary quotations. Inwood exchanges the remnants' continuity with the built environment for a series of virtual continuities—proto-hyperlinks in a vast network that one might choose to call stylistic revival. In this new state the specific contours of the remnant's broken edges are rendered moot. Physical fragmentation, or a state of incompletion, poses no problem. Using rules of symmetry and proportion derived from the examples in the broader series, the absent portions of the antique fragments reappear in Inwood's illustrations virtually through the magical agency of the draftsman's dotted line (fig. 9).

By using this network of citations to join the fragments to their respective series, Inwood reframed the ornamental designs as products of repetition. They became repeatable, and completable, as parts of a pattern. Conceptually this is the very bedrock of architectural revivalism: not the belief that a direct copy of an ornament will impart meaning in the same way as it once did, but rather the notion that the practices of pattern making and recognition can be revived to establish a shared language of architectural quality. In theory, as more and more revived motifs are applied to the surfaces of new buildings, the public will come to recognize and respect the architect's role as a connoisseur of pattern with access to fine libraries and the dexterity to call up twenty or more honeysuckle specimens at a moment's notice.

Architectural remnants, on the other hand, have their own distinct relation to repetition. Their survival depends on versatility. They find new applications in different contexts, just as Athenians appropriated remnants of ancient structures to distinguish the entrances to their homes and Schinkel used them to articulate the architectural joints of an outdoor meeting place at the Court Gardener's House.[40]

Schinkel's treatment of one particular classical motif in the Grand Pergola demonstrates the conceptual divide between his attempt to reactivate remnants and Inwood's project of classification and comparison. In his list of vegetal structures suitable for expression through ornamental form, Schinkel refrains from positing any direct affiliations between plant species and specific architectural motifs with the exception of the last entry: "subdivided-swelling of the lily petal (console profile)." Schinkel's point, it would seem, is not to suggest a formal derivation of the architectural console from the lily petal (as Inwood would have done) but rather to point out an abstract sympathy between the organic membrane and the console's underside, where two curves break off from a centerline to evoke an active swelling, or unfurling growth.

Schinkel's placement of consoles at key junctures in the Grand Pergola assembly further clarifies his understanding of the classical motif's expressive potentiality (fig. 10). He employs two different specimens: one console dating from antiquity and another of more recent vintage, though the exact site and date of origin for each of the pieces remains unknown. Faced with Schinkel's pair of mismatched consoles, a strict revivalist would likely turn to processes of replication. According to established patterns consoles should be deployed as an identical pair, arranged symmetrically as a framing device for doors or other openings, or appear in a much longer series as decorative corbels beneath a cornice. Instead Schinkel assigned each of the formally distinct consoles a unique functional role. The more elongated antique remnant projects from a low masonry wall to form a shelf for the cast-zinc flounder fountain.

In the drawing of the Grand Pergola prepared by Schinkel for the *Sammlung architektonischer Entwürfe*, the fountain's plume of water tumbles out just beyond the console's outer lip. In this manner the "subdivided swelling" of the architectural ornament's underside acquires an added layer of expressivity, as a possible response to both the weight of the fish and the buildup of water that spills from the console's curling front edge. Schinkel brings the botanically inspired geometry of the console remnant into alignment with the motive force of the fountain's bubbling stream and its expressive structure becomes more visible by virtue of association.

On the other side of the pergola the second console acts as a solitary bracket for the arbor's central beam. A compact, more cubic variant of its nearby relative, this console articulates the key juncture in the pergola's structural assembly, securely binding the projecting framework to the solid wall. Once again the console's "subdivided swelling" is positioned as a visual index of collected force. Its ornamental scroll is held in tension between two surfaces of contact, like the flexing coil of a spring. In Schinkel's drawing, a tendril of grapevine nearby performs this same vegetal action, perfectly miming the console's scrolling geometry. These organic actions, some performed by real plants and others by their botanically structured architectural partners, hold the Grand Pergola together.

§ § §

"So too is the world of small things wonderful and grand."

Schinkel's quest to identify latent aspects of *Lebendigkeit* in even the smallest of architectural particles shares a conceptual affinity with the work of his contemporary Christian Gottfried Ehrenberg (1795–1876), a pioneering microbiologist at the University in Berlin. A scrupulous collector and observer of microscopic organisms, Ehrenberg was also recognized as a skilled draftsman with a talent for documenting the world beneath his microscope's lens. The fineness of line work and density of detail achieved in many of his drawings rivals even the most refined plates in Schinkel's *Sammlung architektonischer Entwürfe* (fig. 11). Throughout Ehrenberg's career, he championed the tiniest forms of organic life, repeatedly documenting and defending the sophisticated organizations and physiological activities of the infinitesimal organisms he observed.[41] "So too is the world of small things wonderful and grand" begins the simple inscription carved on his gravestone. "And from small things entire worlds are built."[42]

In much the same manner as Schinkel, Ehrenberg enjoyed a close friendship with Humboldt, who also served as a professional mentor.[43] The elder naturalist rarely missed an opportunity to praise the work of his younger colleague and repeatedly took measures to help advance his scientific career.[44] Ehrenberg received a major boon, for example, when Humboldt secured funding from the Berlin Academy to support his participation in an archaeological expedition conducted by Johann Heinrich Freiherr von Minutoli.[45] The journey to Egypt and parts of the Middle East (from 1820–25) was a grueling, underfunded endeavor, but Ehrenberg managed to collect thousands of specimens that formed the basis of his research over the next five decades.[46] Not surprisingly, many of the insights Ehrenberg generated were disseminated through Humboldt's popular scientific writings, particularly in the endnotes tacked on to later editions of his "Physiognomy of Plants."

Ehrenberg was also something of an amateur architect. During his travels he designed a villa for Abidin Bey, the governor of the Dongola province, in northern Sudan. This interest in architectural form shows up in his choice of research subjects, most notably in Ehrenberg's work on coral animals. When the Prussian expedition finally reached the shores of the Red Sea in 1823, Ehrenberg was captivated by the coral formations, which he saw as a kind of living architecture. Among his notes is a passage where he records how "the corals that lie deepest below the surface of the water … being magnified by the refraction of the rays of light, appear to the eye like the domes or cupolas of a cathedral."[47] When Ehrenberg later published his research,[48] he corrected a major misconception about these magnificent aggregated structures by demonstrating that the crystalized formations "must not be regarded as something extraneous to the soft membranes of the food-receiving animal."[49] In more architectural terms, Ehrenberg discovered that one should not think of the coral reef as a colony of organisms inhabiting a petrified ruin: each cell of the structure grows together with the miniscule animal inside as a single remnant-generating unit. As a consequence of this condition, Humboldt was quick to point out, pieces of coral that are removed "do not instantly lose their vitality, as does a forest tree when cut down."[50] This remnant-like mode of survival stems from the compartmentalization of the individual polyps. Certain species of coral not only survive this detachment but have the ability to enact it, to "detach themselves at pleasure."[51] This phenomenon prompted Ehrenberg to propose a classificatory distinction between the Phytocorals and the Zoocorallia, differentiating those coral animals that grow collectively and those capable of detaching themselves to roam free.[52]

Such coral polyps were not the only organisms with remnant-like properties that Ehrenberg studied. In the third edition of his essay on the "Physiognomy of Plants," Humboldt called attention to another phenomenon of extreme natural endurance documented by the younger scientist:[53]

> According to Ehrenberg's brilliant discovery, the yellow sand or dust which falls like rain on the Atlantic near the Cape de Verde Islands, and is occasionally carried even to Italy and Middle Europe, consists of a multitude of siliceous-shelled microscopic animals. Perhaps many of them float for years in the upper strata of the atmosphere, until they are brought down by vertical currents … still susceptible to revivification, and multiplying their species by spontaneous division in conformity with the particular laws of their organization.[54]

These tiny silica-clad creatures might be understood as nature's own building remnants (fig. 12).[55] Unbeknownst to Ehrenberg, he had stumbled upon a kind of retroactive model for a cultural practice being carried out by the architects and archaeologists around him: the displacement of small architectural particles from their sites of origin in Greece, Italy, and elsewhere to the cities of northern Europe. In his microbiological studies nature presented an unexpected rebuttal to proponents of a strictly autochthonous stylistic development, the kind of critics who asked as Friedrich Schlegel once did, "What can be more out of place than … Grecian or Italian columns in a strange land or climate?"[56] If nature, in select instances, produces organisms capable of transgressing the assumed limits of territory and longevity, why shouldn't architecture follow suit? To a designer like Schinkel, who was already well practiced in thinking of architecture as an extension of nature's ordering principles, such an analogy might have been welcome. Perhaps Ehrenberg's research offered him a kind of natural evidence to justify the out-of-place survival of architectural remnants on the sandy shores of the Spree and the Havel, hundreds of miles from their original ecologies.

Most vital to Schinkel's work, however, was the notion of an organism's susceptibility to *Wiederbelebung*, or revivification. The Infusoria and Rotifera observed by Ehrenberg survived their extended airborne journeys by entering a state of dormancy, becoming dry and solidified as their internal systems fall motionless. Yet as soon as these microorganisms come into contact with the right environmental conditions, they stir back into life.[57] Humboldt, acting once again as the disseminator of Ehrenberg's research, summarized as follows: "The apparent revivification of the Rotifera, as well as of the siliceous-shelled Infusoria, is only the renewal of long enfeebled vital functions—a state of vitality which was never entirely extinguished, and which is fanned into a fresh flame, or excited anew, by the appropriate stimulus."[58] The challenge for Ehrenberg—and for Schinkel in his parallel experimentation with revivified architectural remains—was to identify the correct stimuli.

For each of the experimenters the key ingredient turned out to be water.[59] Schinkel incorporated two separate fountains in the Grand Pergola design, in part to give the intimate space an atmosphere of refreshment, but also to elicit visual (and auditory) sensations of activity and motion.[60] It is not by chance that the plumes of water pass through and around all of the structure's ancient remains (see fig. 1, lower left). The small fountain in the center of the table, for example, rises up through the Corinthian capital that props up the horizontal slab.[61] As the tiny jet breaks forth through this surface, the cascading arcs of water rhyme visually with the carved ornamental cascades of sandstone below. Nearby a streaming plume of water leaves the mouth of the cast-zinc fish, spilling over the console into the cavity of a giant clamshell (a macroscopic zoological remnant in its own right).[62]

The water then trickles down into the rectangular volume of an antique sarcophagus and continues its course to the far end of the basin, where a crack at the corner forms a makeshift spout. Spilling from this crevice, the water finally ends up in a sunken channel, where it turns back toward the center of the pergola and disappears. In this manner Schinkel supplies his architectural remnants with all the sustaining moisture they could possibly need.

If indeed one accepts a reading of the Grand Pergola as a place where desiccated building remains reawaken upon contact with water, then the most beautiful description of the project comes not from the pen of an architectural historian or critic but from the pages (once again) of Humboldt's essay on the physiognomy of plants:

> The wind carries up Rotifera, Brachionidae and a multitude of microscopic creatures from the surface of evaporating waters. Seemingly inert and sunken into a state of suspended animation (*Scheintod*), the creatures float in the air until the dew brings them back down to the nourishing earth, dissolves the mantle enclosing their whirling, diaphanous bodies and (through the life-sustaining substance all water surely contains) incites new excitation in their organs.[63]

§ § § §

The Physiognomy of Schinkel's Pergola

Given the myriad ways in which the individual components of the Grand Pergola—from plants to remnants and replicas—interact, it is nearly impossible to capture the totality of the space through ekphrasis. Even Schinkel, in his textual description of the project for the *Sammlung architektonischer Entwürfe,* struggles to establish a fixed point of reference. His words wander in a run-on string of *Nebensäzten* through the Grand Pergola's concatenation of elements:

> In one of the corners under the broad pergola there is a stibadium arranged in the antique manner, with small steps leading up to it, where one finds a large table, supported by a Corinthian capital and surrounded by benches, and the table has at its center a shallow indentation, from which rises a bell-like plume of gently bubbling water. The walls surrounding this table are adorned with bas-reliefs, winding ivy, and a multitude of antique artworks, set on the parapet together with a row of small columns which support the pergola on this side; next to the small ascending steps, an antique sarcophagus collects water streaming forth from the mouth of a fish, which stretches out on a console at the base of the Bacchus herm's trunk and this water heightens the charming freshness of the place.[64]

As Schinkel demonstrates, it is supremely difficult to translate the Grand Pergola's compositional intricacy into words. If one sets out to describe a single element, the sentence rapidly grows to encompass two, three, four, or more. Finally one ends up trying to transcribe the mini-ecosystem in its entirety.

In the interior view of the Grand Pergola, presented in plate 171 of the *Sammlung architektonische Entwürfe,* the vanishing point selected by Schinkel fails to align with the pergola's central support, triggering a "wandering of the eye" that matches his wandering sentences. One's gaze darts back and forth between dueling foci, trying—and likely failing—to find a center before moving on to meander from one component to the next.

13 A Chronological Sampling of Vegetal Columns: a) Francesco di Giorgio Martini's tree column from the Saluzziano Codex, folio 15r, ca. 1485. b) Donato Bramante's tree column for the Canonica of S. Ambrogio in Milan, 1492. c) Philibert de l'Orme's tree column from the *Premier Tome de l'Architecture*, 1567. d) Detail from the frontispiece to the second edition of Abbé Laugier's *Essai sur l'Architecture*, designed by Charles-Dominiques-Joseph Eisen, 1755. e) Detail showing Schinkel's splitting vine column at the Grand Pergola from Tafel 147 in the *Sammlung architektonischer Entwürfe*, 1835. f) Hans Hollein's design for one of the columns in his Strada Novissima facade at the 1980 Venice Biennale. g) The chestnut tree column in Oswald Mathias Ungers's Deutsches Architekturmuseum, Frankfurt am Main, 1984. h) The tree column inside the Kunsthal, Rotterdam by OMA, 1992. i) One of 144 tree columns temporarily installed in the Neue Nationalgalerie by David Chipperfield, Berlin, 2014.

Schinkel might have had such an effect in mind when he scribbled down a short note on "relative order" in one of his sketchbooks. "Symmetry," he wrote, is something that "everyone can understand." "Relative order," on the other hand, "is understood only by those who know the conditions from which its law originates; these include the organization of *naturalien*-cabinets, of libraries (more or less) and several other architectural programs, both great and small."[65] Though these cursory remarks hardly provide a comprehensive definition, Schinkel appears to conceive of "relative order" as a pattern of organization that emerges variably as an adaptive compositional logic.

Symmetry does come easily to architects—whether reflectional, rotational, or translational—because it informs the very tools they use to draw. Nature, by contrast, has no need to rely on ruler or compass. Her creations follow a greater variety of ordering principles, some of them certainly "relative." One of Schinkel's objectives at the Grand Pergola was in fact to coax architecture into accepting some of nature's more dynamic organizational logics. In his own words, the goal was to "build up a diverse group of architectural objects that are capable of fusing (*verschmelzen*) congenially with the surrounding nature."[66]

Schinkel's choice of the verb *verschmelzen* speaks volumes. It connotes a merging, an amalgamation, or a melting together. If architecture and plants are truly to fuse and participate in shared systems, then architecture must adopt some of nature's relative order. Otherwise the human-made elements risk functioning as mere decor or "sealed off artifacts" not connected in any meaningful way to the surrounding environment. Such insulation would, of course, forestall any remnant's potential revivification.

One of the most striking examples of Schinkel's intended *Verschmelzung* plays out near the center of the Grand Pergola, where a thick stem rises from a burst of heart-shaped fronds to provide the main intermediary support for the pergola's network of beams. This vegetal column is an ambiguous tectonic and botanical entity. Its stem bifurcates before meeting the central beam, effectively transferring the gravity load from the structure above, through its shaft and into the ground below. Its branches terminate abruptly at the beam's lower surface, signaling perhaps that they have been cleanly severed to create a flat resting place for the horizontal spanning member. Given this cropping, some architectural historians have identified the vegetal member as a tree trunk modified to act as a column.[67] This identification places the Grand Pergola's central member in a long historical lineage (fig. 13), reaching back from the columns of Abbé Laugier's primitive hut to numerous Renaissance tree-columns, illustrated by Francesco di Giorgio, Filarete, Philibert de l'Orme, and Leonardo da Vinci, theorized in the writings of Alberti, and erected in stone by Bramante in the Canonica of Sant'Ambrogio, in Milan. Many of these arboreal columns followed Vitruvius's own description of the first building components felled in the primordial forest.[68] There is only one problem: the vegetal support planned by Schinkel for the Grand Pergola was not a tree trunk but rather the stem of a mature grapevine, which he had transplanted to the site.[69] Looking closely at the detail where this stem meets the beam, one notices that the third branching shoot does not appear to terminate at the horizontal member's surface but continues to climb up around it. This outgrowth then feeds the entire system of bifurcating, radiating tendrils, which spread over the gridded trellis and dangle between its gaps.

If the tree-trunk columns of architectural history collectively tell a story of nature appropriated, rationalized, and domesticated, the central vegetal support in Schinkel's pergola evokes a more complicated agency. Although its stem is modified to fit the architectural order, it reacts and adapts, sending out new offshoots to colonize the orthogonal system of overlapping beams.[70]

In the critical reception of the Gärtnerwohnung, the Grand Pergola's central vegetal member has frequently been tasked with bearing a heavy significance, as if it were a cipher capable of decoding all other choices made on the site. For architectural historian Iain Boyd Whyte it reveals the pergola's underlying narrative, based on "the tectonics of the simple hut ... becoming the vernacular house, and the vernacular house becoming the temple."[71] In his reading Schinkel used the Grand Pergola to reenact a story of "nature becoming building."[72] Barry Bergdoll likewise reads the Grand Pergola as "an image and experience of the evolution of structure" that models the "transition from nature to architecture."[73] Schinkel was certainly familiar with building projects like those described by Bergdoll and Whyte, designed to evoke a narrative of architectural progress, with Friedrich Gilly's proposed "Monument to Frederick the Great" standing foremost among them. Yet hardly any aspect of the Grand Pergola's composition suggests such a clear-cut linear development. There are moments in its structure where nature becomes a kind of architecture, but the overall assembly is just as capable of demonstrating architecture's ability to become more natural, or at least to have its organic performative capacities re-represented.

It seems most fitting to characterize the Grand Pergola as an attempt to show that nature and architecture can continue working on each other in perpetuity. Rather than following a one-way path from the felled trunks of the primitive hut to the rationalized purity of the Doric order, a more cyclical activity unfolds under the pergola's frame. If there is a temporal pattern to be observed, it mimics a trajectory closer to that of the helical tendrils that dangle from the pergola's creeping vines. Schinkel renaturalizes the ancient remnants and contemporary architectural components in the sense that their vitality, their capacity for organic action, is made visible again. This is the cyclical essence of the Grand Pergola's revivification. Schinkel does not ask the classical remnants to function in ways so radically different from their original purposes; he positions them in a manner and environment that heightens awareness of their active *performance* of those functional roles. That is why the notion of a vivarium matches the overall program of the Grand Pergola so well. Schinkel designed a space where lessons about the shared formal capacities of architecture and nature, and their underlying connectivity, might be learned (or relearned). As such, both architectural and natural specimens had to be kept alive. Like the terrariums and aquariums employed by his zoologist contemporaries, Schinkel's remnant vivarium provided a semicontrolled environment where he could observe the interaction of animate subjects.

§ § § § §

Postscript: Last of the Schinkelschülern?

On March 13, 1961, Philip Johnson delivered the keynote lecture at the 106th annual Schinkelfest in Berlin.[74] Focusing on the contemporary reception of Schinkel's surviving buildings, he titled his talk "Karl Friedrich Schinkel in the Twentieth Century: How We See the Great Architect after the Bauhaus-Corbusier-Revolution."[75] An analysis of the Gärtnerwohnung occupies the very heart of Johnson's homage, a fact that hardly comes as a surprise since the building held a special place in his architectural imaginary. Of all Schinkel's projects, the Court Gardener's House was the one Johnson identified as having exerted "the most profound effect" on him (rivaled only by the Museum am Lustgarten).[76] In the published version of the speech Johnson proceeds with characteristic agility through a sequence of tripartite comparisons, matching Schinkel's best-known projects with early-twentieth-century counterparts, then completing each analogical chain with a recent example from his own practice. The Court Gardener's House is juxtaposed with Mies's Barcelona Pavilion (fig. 14) and Johnson's own design for the Eric Boissonnas House, completed in 1956.[77]

Johnson's description of the Gärtnerwohnung pivots around its square courtyard (fig. 15) where the vertical jet of the central fountain forms an axis of rotation:

15 Karl Friedrich Schinkel, "Perspective vom Gartenhause in Charlottenhof bei Potsdam," copper plate engraving from the *Sammlung architektonischer Entwürfe*, Berlin, 1835, (Heft 24, Tafel 148). Reproduced from the 1858 printing by Verlag Ernst & Korn, Berlin (Tafelband IV, Tafel 172).

What I'd like to point out today is the extraordinary composition of the courtyard. For thirty-two years, from the time I first saw it, ideas about this courtyard have pursued me. Plainly speaking, it is a four-cornered plaza with the water jet fountain at center. But consider this plaza as a room and you will see how fascinating its four walls are. All sides are entirely different and yet they relate to each other harmoniously.[78]

Johnson then continues by describing each of the four virtual "walls" in further detail: to the south, the framed view of a "romantic" landscape, complete with pond and miniature island; to the east, a trelliswork vault reaching across the canal to form a tunnel for "mysterious boats"; to the north, the arcaded front of the Roman Baths; to the west, the villa itself, skirted by a long continuous pergola; and in the southwest corner, the temple teahouse, a compact jewel box of a building "whose own axis turns back along the water's edge."[79] The panoramic tour finally comes to a halt in the place where it began, at the center of the space, where "the sunken elevation of the garden court underscores the intimate and *centripetal* sense of the composition."[80]

In Johnson's speech this circling description unfolds without any reference to the Grand Pergola at the Gärtnerwohnung's entrance or its diverse remains. This ellipsis aside, his formal reading of the outdoor room reveals an essential continuity between the experimental pergola space and the compositional conceit behind the Court Gardener's House as a whole. The centripetal organization perceived by Johnson helps to establish the connection.[81] When taking in the building he was struck most of all by its ability to bring together several stylistically distinct elements and hold them all in place: though the selected components run into each other at ninety-degree angles, the composite effect is more harmonious. Johnson sensed a rotational, converging spatial flow. These are precisely the qualities evoked in miniature by the Grand Pergola assembly. In the reciprocal relationship between garden pergola and garden courtyard the unique role of Schinkel's remnant vivarium comes to light: the Grand Pergola forms a kind of microcosmic test bed for the Court Gardener's House design. Its rectangular tabletop stands in for the larger complex's sunken garden parterre, complete with a corresponding fountain.

14 Mies van der Rohe, Barcelona Pavilion, 1929–1930, reconstructed 1986.

Around this nodal point contrasting elements confront one another, abutting at right angles yet joined together by the circulating streams of water and stretching, clinging vines. Schinkel's project appears to be a rare example of a building that both contains and remains in dialogue with its architectural model. Then again, there is nothing miniature about the Grand Pergola's actual constitutive elements: they are full-scale architectural and natural components whose proximity has been intensified.

When passing through the Gärtnerwohnung's arched portal, a visitor makes the jump from microcosm to macrocosm, experiencing an architectural echo of Ehrenberg's biological thesis: just as the sophisticated organization of nature can be observed at all scales, from microscopic Infusoria to the largest creatures roaming land and sea, so too can architecture transmit a set of underlying organizational principles from its smallest configurations up along the chain. The special affinity between the Grand Pergola design and the larger courtyard suggests that Schinkel absorbed certain lessons by handling smaller material remnants and then scaled these insights up, applying them to assemblies of more complicated architectural quotations.

In the macro-composition of the garden courtyard space, Schinkel worked with an assortment of quotations as diverse as those of the Grand Pergola: the temple teahouse, apparently quoted from Stuart and Revett;[82] the espalier vault, said to come from an etching by Carl Wilhelm Kolbe;[83] the rustic Italianate tower, possibly transferred from Schinkel's own drawing of *San Lorenzo fuori le mura*;[84] the exedral bench, likely modeled after the *stibadium* at the Tomb of Mamia, near Pompeii. Though these larger building blocks lack the material uniformity and clear formal containment of the actual antique remains used in the pergola, they perform like remnants. Schinkel planned the overall composition in a way that preserves the individuality of the constitutive elements, even as they collide with each other and get swept up in the centripetal action that ultimately harmonizes and unifies the space. In this sense the Court Gardener's House signals a different approach to architectural historicism. The design moves well beyond the eighteenth century's isolated garden follies, with their historically evocative stylistic moods. Yet it avoids the facile stylistic mixing and matching that would come to characterize the late nineteenth century's urban facades. Instead Schinkel's vision of a remnant-derived architectural historicism takes its cues from nature, where an eclectic mingling of forms is an essential condition for survival.

1 Alexander von Humboldt, "Physiognomy of Plants," in *Aspects of Nature in Different Lands and Different Climates with Scientific Elucidations*, trans. Mrs. Sabine vol. II (London: Printed for Longman, Brown, Green and Longmans; and John Murray, 1849), 8–10. I have slightly modified Mrs. Sabine's translation. For the original German see Alexander von Humboldt, "Ideen zu einer Physiognomik der Gewächse," in *Ansichten der Natur mit wissenschaftlichen Erläuterungen* (Tübingen: in der J. G. Cotta'schen Buchhandllung, 1808), 164–67.

2 See for example Joseph Priestley, "Observations and Experiments relating to equivocal, or spontaneous, generation," in *Transactions of the American Philosophical Society* 6 (1809): 119–20. Louis Pasteur finally refuted the theory of spontaneous generation with his swan-necked flask experiments of 1859.

3 *Ansichten der Natur*, the collection of Alexander von Humboldt's essays that includes his text "Physiognomy of Plants," remained immensely popular throughout the nineteenth century. It was reissued in 1826, 1849, 1859, 1860, and 1889. The first French edition appeared in 1808 and the first English translation in 1849. The complete archive of editions is accessible online via *HumboldtDigital: Die Digitalisate Bibliographie*, www.avhumboldt.de/?page_id=469.

4 I am thinking here of Joseph Leo Koerner's work on Caspar David Friedrich, and his reading of two canvases originally titled *Aus der Dresdner Heide I* and *II* (*From the Dresden Heath I* and *II*). As Koerner points out, the German preposition *aus* "signals a movement away from origins," which I would oppose to the mode of literary quotation that involves reading backward, toward origins. See Koerner's Caspar David Friedrich and the Subject of Landscape [1990] (London: Reaktion Books, 2009), especially 15–20.

5 See Philippe Lacoue-Labarthe and Jean-Luc Nancy, *The Literary Absolute*, trans. Philip Barnard and Cheryl Lester (Albany: State University of New York Press, 1988), 14. As Lacoue-Labarthe and Nancy have rightly argued, the *Athenaeum* "does not claim to represent a rupture. It makes no pretense of starting out with a tabula rasa or of ringing in the new. It sees itself, much to the contrary, as a commitment to the critical 'recasting' of what is." See page 10.

6 In the original German, "*literarische Sämereien*," "*Körnchen*," and "*Blütenstaub*." See Novalis, *Blütenstaub, Fragmente* (1797–98), 114. See also Kurt W. Forster, "Warum Schinkel kein architektonisches Lehrbuch geschrieben hat," in Jörg Trempler, *Schinkels Motive* (Berlin: Matthes & Seitz, 2007), 17–18.

7 Barry Bergdoll, "Of Crystals, Cells, and Strata: Natural History and Debates on the Form of a New Architecture in the Nineteenth Century," in *Architectural History* 50 (2007): 1–29.

8 Barry Bergdoll, *Karl Friedrich Schinkel: An Architecture for Prussia* (New York: Rizzoli, 1994), 148.

9 Nicolaas A. Rupke, *Alexander von Humboldt: A Metabiography* (Frankfurt: Peter Lang, 2005), 39–42.

10 Kurt Kuhlow, *Das Königliche Schloß Charlottenhof bei Potsdam: baugeschichtlich und kunstgeschichtlich dargestellt unter besonderer Berücksichtigung der Handzeichnungen König Friedrich Wilhelms IV* (Berlin: Rheinhold Kühn, 1911), 41–43.

11 Kuhlow, *Das Königliche Schloß Charlottenhof bei Potsdam*, 42; Eva Börsch-Supan, *Arbeiten für König Friedrich Wilhelm III. von Preußen und Kronprinz Friedrich Wilhelm (IV.), Karl Friedrich Schinkel Lebenswerk*, vol. 21 (Munich and Berlin: Deutscher Kunstverlag, 2011), 594–95.

12 Humboldt, "Physiognomy of Plants" (emphasis added), 10.

13 Börsch-Supan, *Arbeiten für König Friedrich Wilhelm III*, 593; August Kopisch, *Geschichte der königlichen Schlösser und Gärten zu Potsdam. Von der Zeit ihrer Gründung bis zum Jahre MDCCCLII* (Berlin: Verlag von Ernst & Korn, 1854), 180.

14 Börsch-Supan, *Arbeiten für König Friedrich Wilhelm III*, 595–97.

15 Hans Hoffman, *Schloß Charlottenhof und die Römischen Bäder*, ed. Renate Möller (Potsdam: Generaldirektion der Staatlichen Schlösser und Gärten Potsdam-Sanssouci, 1985), 63.

16 Iain Boyd Whyte, "Charlottenhof: The Prince, the Gardener, the Architect, and the Writer," in *Architectural History* 43 (2000): 10–11.

17 On the difficulties involved in reconstructing the design process, see Bergdoll, *Karl Friedrich Schinkel: An Architecture for Prussia*, 137–41; and Whyte, "Charlottenhof," 10–11. On the crown prince's involvement, see Ludwig Dehio, *Friedrich Wilhelm IV. von Preußen: ein Baukünstler der Romantik* (Munich: Deutscher Kunstverlag, 1961). Even Schinkel's student August Stüler acknowledged the difficulty in parsing out the ideas of his teacher from those of the crown prince. See August Stüler, "Über die Wirksamkeit Friedrich Wilhelm IV. in dem Gebiete der bildenden Künste." Paper presented at the Schinkelfest on March 13, 1861, in Berlin, p. 19 (quoted by Whyte, "Charlottenhof," 10).

18 At least that is the stance I will take in this essay in order to slice, in my own way, through the Gordian knot of the Grand Pergola's multifaceted "authorship."

19 Schinkel's *Sammlung* originally appeared in installments between 1820 and 1837. The complete set of 174 engraved plates was later reissued in multiple editions. See Karl Friedrich Schinkel, *Sammlung architektonischer Entwürfe: enthaltend theils Werke welche ausgeführt sind theils Gegenstände deren Ausführung beabsichtigt wurde* (Berlin: Verlag von Ernst & Korn, 1858). The Grand Pergola is featured in plate 171 and also appears in a broader view of the Gärtnerwohnung complex presented in plate 169.

20 This translation is my own, but it draws in part on Karin Cramer's translation in *Collection of Architectural Designs Including Designs Which Have Been Executed and Objects Whose Execution Was Intended by Karl Friedrich Schinkel*, ed. Kenneth S. Hazlett, Stephen O'Malley, and Christopher Rudolph, trans. Karin Cramer (New York: Princeton Architectural Press, 1989), 53–54.

21 On the "Albertian paradigm," see Mario Carpo, *The Alphabet and the Algorithm* (Cambridge, Massachusetts, and London: MIT Press, 2011), 15–28.

22 The addition of the so-called "Roman Baths" marks the most significant extension (completed in 1840), though there were small changes among the constituent elements of the Grand Pergola itself, some of which I will discuss later in this essay. See also Börsch-Supan, *Arbeiten für König Friedrich Wilhelm III*, 594–96. After Schinkel's death, in 1841, the transformations tapered off, and today the ongoing production and creation is signaled more by the changing shape of the plantings and surrounding gardens than any modifications or substitutions in the architectural fabric.

23 Bergdoll, *Karl Friedrich Schinkel*, 153.

24 Humboldt, "Physiognomy of Plants," 17. I have slightly modified the translation. For the original German see Humboldt, "Ideen zu einer Physiognomik der Gewächse," 77.

25 Humboldt, "Physiognomy of Plants," 13–14.

26 My translation (underlining taken from the original), see *Nachlass Karl Friedrich Schinkel*, vol. 4, "Theoretische Schriften," Staatliche Museen zu Berlin, sheet 54 microfiche 0019, image 0242. Reproduced and transcribed in Goerd Peschken, *Das Architektonische Lehrbuch, Karl Friedrich Schinkel Lebenswerk*, vol. 14 (Munich and Berlin: Deutscher Kunstverlag, 1979, reissued 2001), illustration 78, 84.

27 My translation. See Peschken, *Das Architektonische Lehrbuch*, 84.

28 For an especially sophisticated reading of this moment in the history of science, see Chapter 5, "Classifying," in Michel Foucault, *The Order of Things: An Archaeology of the Human Sciences* [1966] (New York: Vintage Books, 1973), 125–65.

29 Sir William Lawrence, *Lectures on Physiology, Zoology, and the Natural History of Man, Delivered at the Royal College of Surgeons* (London: Printed for J. Smith, 1822), 53. Quoted in William Coleman, *Biology in the Nineteenth Century: Problems of Form, Function, and Transformation* (London, New York, Melbourne: Cambridge University Press, 1977), 2–3 (emphasis added).

30 My translation. See Peschken, *Das Architektonische Lehrbuch*, 32.

31 It is possible to read Gottfried Semper's writings on ornament from later in the century as a more fully theorized complement to Schinkel's own intuitions. See, for example, Semper's description of the vital organic forces that guide formal development in plants and Greek architecture in the sections on "Eurythmy" and "Symmetry" in the "Prolegomena" to *Style in the Technical and Tectonic Arts*; or, Practical Aesthetics [1860–1863], trans. Harry Francis Mallgrave and Michael Robinson (Los Angeles: Getty Research Institute, 2004), 85–90. Semper greatly admired Schinkel's work. In the "Prolegomena" he credits Schinkel as being the "coryphaeus" of a "Hellenistic" movement that was "creative from the start." (p. 79). According to Semper, "Archaeology can scrutinize the past as keenly and shrewdly as it likes, but ultimately it is left to the divining sense of artists to reconstruct something whole from the mutilated remains." (p. 79). Schinkel was one of those divinatory artists as far as Semper was concerned. The two architects met in Berlin sometime before 1834, and Semper concludes the first volume of *Style* with an appendix including the transcription of a letter sent to him by Schinkel recounting "the most pleasant personal conversations we shared during your stay in Berlin." (p. 428). The letter is dated June 19, 1834.

32 I have borrowed this description of the topic from an issue of *The Architectural Magazine and Journal of Improvement in Architecture, Building, and Furnishing, and in the Various Arts and Trades Connected Therewith*, conducted by J. C. Loudon, 2 (1835): 36.

33 Henry William Inwood, *The Erechtheion at Athens: Fragments of Athenian Architecture and a Few Remains in Attica Megara and Epirus* (London: John Williams Architectural Bookseller, 1827). During Schinkel's 1826 journey to England he made a point of visiting the St. Pancras Church, designed by Inwood with his father, William Inwood (erected between 1819–22). See Reinhard Wegner, *Die Reise nach Frankreich und England im Jahre 1826, Karl Friedrich Schinkel Lebenswerk*, vol. 16 (Munich and Berlin: Deutscher Kunstverlag, 1990), 114.

34 Roger Bowdler, "Inwood, Henry William (1794–1843)," *Oxford Dictionary of National Biography* (Oxford: Oxford University Press, 2004); online edition 2004.

35 Inwood's collection consisted of approximately forty objects, which he sold to the British Museum in 1843 for £40. See Bowdler, "Inwood, Henry William," 2004.

36 Inwood, *Erechtheion at Athens*, 42.

37 James Stuart and Nicholas Revett's *The Antiquities of Athens and Other Monuments of Greece* (London,

1762–1816) is by far his most common citation (see Inwood, *Erechtheion at Athens*, 4, 6, 11, 13–34, 48, 45). Other references include *The Antiquities of Ionia*, prepared by the Society of Dilettanti, in London, 1821 (see Inwood,15–16, 25, 27, 35); Piranesi's *De Romanorum magnificentia et architectura*, Rome, 1761 (see Inwood, 29); for Cockerell, see Inwood, 18, 24, 26); Sir George Wheler, *A Journey into Greece*, London, 1682 (see Inwood, 44–45); Edward Dodwell, *A Classical and Topographical Tour through Greece*, London, 1819 (see Inwood, 28, 35); William Wilkins, *The Antiquities of Magna Graecia*, London, 1807 (see Inwood, 31, 45); Lewis Vulliamy, *Examples of Ornamental Sculpture in Architecture*, London, 1823 (see Inwood, 30–31, 33); on Thomas Leverton Donaldson (see Inwood, 30); Lieutenant colonel William Martin Leake's *The Topography of Athens: With Some Remarks on Its Antiquities*, 1821 (see Inwood, 48).

38 On occasion Inwood even includes references to images that reproduce exactly the same ornaments as his own engravings, though usually it is to correct inaccuracies in the drawings of others. See for example Inwood, *Erechtheion at Athens*, 11, 14.

39 For the Townley Collection, see Inwood, *Erechtheion at Athens*, 22; for the Elgin Collection, see Inwood, 4, 16, 19, 23, 30, 33, 35–36, 38–39, 41; for Soane's Museum, see Inwood, 28; for the Cambridge Museum, see Inwood, 28, 35, 38; for the collection of Mr. Elliot at Cambridge, see Inwood, 36; for the collection of Mr. Gropius at Athens, see Inwood, 21, 36; for the collection of Sir Sandford Graham, see Inwood, 37–39; for the collection of Sir Henry Englefield, see Inwood, 38.

40 While Schinkel's work at the Grand Pergola clearly falls more in line with the material project of remnant revivification, by no means did he completely eschew the more pattern- and paper-based project of stylistic revival. Schinkel knew Inwood's book well and included its title on a list of eighteen recommended sources in the model book he developed with Christian Peter Wilhelm Beuth to cultivate taste among Prussia's emerging industrial designers and craftsmen. See *Vorbilder für Fabrikanten und Handwerker* (Berlin: Königl. Technischen Deputation für Gewerbe, 1821–30), 56.

41 See for example Ehrenberg's publications *Große Organisation in der Richtung des kleinsten Raumes* ("Great Organization in the smallest of Realms") (Berlin: Druckerei der Königlichen Akademie der Wissenschaften, 1834); and *Die Infusionsthierchen als vollkommene Organismen. Ein Blick in das tiefere Leben der Natur* ("Infusoria as Complete Organisms: A Peek into the Deeper Life of Nature") (Leipzig: L. Voss, 1838). Ehrenberg was also an early opponent of spontaneous generation. His dissertation, "Sylvae Mycologicae Berolinenses" (1818), offered evidence of the sexual generation of mushrooms through spores. Later he conducted research on the reproduction of lichens and molds.

42 This phrase also appeared as an epigraph to Ehrenberg's dissertation, "Sylvae Mycologicae Berolinenses." The translation is my own. See Rolf Bolling, "Das Leben und das Werk Christian Gottfried Ehrenbergs," in *Christian Gottfried Ehrenberg, 1795-1876* (Delitzch: Kreismuseum Delitzsch, 1976), 9.

43 I have been unable to locate any direct correspondence between Ehrenberg and Schinkel, although the two men traveled in the same social circles in Berlin. A letter written by Humboldt to Ehrenberg on January 14, 1842, suggests that the two families were well acquainted. In the letter Humboldt responds to Ehrenberg's earlier request that, following Schinkel's death, his widow should receive the appropriate financial support. Humboldt assured him that provisions had been made. See *Alexander von Humboldt Forschungsstelle, Berlin-Brandenburgische Akademie der Wissenschaften*, http://telota.bbaw.de/AvH-Briefedition/index.html.

44 After the death of Georges Cuvier, Humboldt went so far as to declare Ehrenberg "the greatest living zoologist." See Max Laue, *Christian Gottfried Ehrenberg. Ein Vertreter deutscher Naturforschung im 19. Jahrhundert* (Berlin: Verlag von Julius Springer, 1895), 167.

45 Bolling, "Das Leben und das Werk," 14–15; Harry Nehls, "Der Altertumsforscher Nicolaus Johann Heinrich Benjamin Freiherr Menu von Minutoli (1772–1846)," in *Forschungen und Berichte* (1991): 159–68. Schinkel also recommended a young architecture professor by the name of Ludwig Theodor Liman for the same expedition. Liman died quite suddenly after the traveling party reached Alexandria, and thus the expedition was left without a trained artist to document and inventory the artworks encountered. For Schinkel's correspondence recommending Liman, see "Angelegenheiten und Personal der Bauakademie, 1820–1823," Geheimes Staatsarchiv Preußischer Kulturbesitz, Inv: Nr. 69, I. HA Rep. 74, Staatskanzleramt, L IX Nr. 21, 2–3.

46 Bolling, "Das Leben und das Werk," 14–23.

47 A citation of Ehrenberg's manuscript notes in Humboldt, "Physiognomy of Plants," 67–68.

48 See Christian Gottfried Ehrenberg, *Über die Natur und Bildung der Coralleninseln und Corallenbänke im rothen Meere* ("On the Nature and Formation of the Coral Islands and Coral Reefs in the Red Sea"). Ehrenberg originally read the paper at the Königlichen Akademie der Wissenschaften in Berlin, on March 22, 1832, then revised the text for publication in February 1834 (Berlin: Druckerei der Königlichen Akademie der Wissenschaften, 1834). Once published, the research quickly garnered the attention of Charles Darwin, who praised the "excellent memoir" in his own work, *The Structure and Distribution of Coral Reefs* (London: Smith, Elder and Co., 1842). Ernst Haeckel also cited Ehrenberg's work on coral animals as an inspiration for his research. See Bolling, "Das Leben und das Werk," 21, 23, 36.

49 Humboldt, "Physiognomy of Plants," 62.

50 Humboldt, "Physiognomy of Plants," 63.

51 Humboldt, "Physiognomy of Plants," 63–64.

52 Humboldt, "Physiognomy of Plants," 63.

53 At the time of its publication Humboldt had recently returned from another expedition, accompanied by Ehrenberg and mineralogist Gustav Rose (who also happened to be Schinkel's nephew). At the invitation of Tsar Nicholas I, the trio traveled through northern Asia, to the Ural and Altai Mountains, and then back to the Caspian Sea. See Bolling, "Das Leben und das Werk," 25; and Gustav Rose, *Mineralogisch-geognostische reise nach dem Ural, dem Altai und dem kaspischen mere, von Gustav Rose* (Berlin: Verlag der Sanderschen buchhandlung (C. W. Eichhoff), 1837–42).

54 Humboldt, "Physiognomy of Plants," 4–5.

55 Ehrenberg eventually published this research in a 1849 text titled *"Passatstaub und Blutregen. Ein großes organisches unsichtbares Wirken und Leben in Atmosphäre"* ("The Trade Wind Dust and Blood Rain: A Great Organic, Invisible Activity and Life in the Atmosphere"), but his observations on the phenomenon date back much earlier, to the scientific expedition that launched his career (1820–25).

56 Friedrich Schlegel, *Kritische Friedrich-Schlegel-Ausgabe*. vol. 4: *Ansischten und Ideen von der christlichen Kunst*, ed. Hans Eichner (Munich, Paderborn, and Vienna: 1959); quoted in Barry Bergdoll, *European Architecture 1750-1890* (Oxford and New York: Oxford University Press, 2000), 147.

57 Antonie van Leeuwenhoek had reported on the ability of certain animalcules to survive desiccation and revivify upon contact with moisture as early as 1676, but it was not until the late eighteenth century that scientists began to submit Leeuwenhoek's observations to more rigorous experimental testing. Ehrenberg performed his own experimental work on the *Wiederbelebung* of Rotifera, and his publication on Infusoria contains a complete history of all previous investigations into the revivification of microscopic organisms. See Christian Gottfried Ehrenberg, *Die Infusionstierchen als vollkommene Organismen* (Leipzig: Leopold Voss, 1838), 492–96.

58 Humboldt, "Physiognomy of Plants," 50–51.

59 Multiple scholars have analyzed the important role played by water in the overall design of Charlottenhof. See for example Bergdoll, *Karl Friedrich Schinkel*, 160; Iain Boyd Whyte addresses the role of water in the Grand Pergola specifically—see "Charlottenhof," 16–18. M. Norton Wise takes a slightly different approach, focusing on steam; see "Architectures for Steam" in *The Architecture of Science*, ed. Peter Galison and Emily Ann Thompson (Cambridge, Massachusetts: MIT Press, 1999), 107–40.

60 Jörg Trempler, in his study *Schinkels Motive* (Berlin: Matthes & Seitz Berlin Verlagsgesellschaft, 2007), devotes an entire section to fountains (69–122). There he argues that the fountain, understood as an allegory of perpetually replenished artistic inspiration, played a key role in Schinkel's work.

61 Schinkel actually used two pilaster capitals joined together. The fountain's water bubbles up in the seam between the pieces. See Kurt Kuhlow, *Das Königliche Schloß Charlottenhof bei Potsdam: baugeschichtlich und kunstgeschichtlich dargestellt unter besonderer Berücksichtigung der Handzeichnungen König Friedrich Wilhelms IV* (Berlin: Rheinhold Kühn, 1911), 42.

62 The giant clamshell comes from a Tridacna gigas, the largest known bivalve mollusk, acquired in 1834 by Martin Hinrich Carl Lichtenstein, founder of the Berlin Zoologische Museum and professor at Berlin University. On the shell, see Hoffman, *Schloß Charlottenhof*, 63. It is not known precisely when the shell was added to the Grand Pergola assembly; Schinkel does not include it in his representation of the project in *Sammlung architektonischer Entwürfe*.

63 Humboldt, "Ideen zu einer Physiognomik der Gewächse," 66–67. My translation.

64 See Hazlett et al., *Collection of Architectural Designs*, 54 (original German edition, 10). I have altered Karin Cramer's translation substantially to better reflect Schinkel's somewhat cumbersome grammatical constructions.

65 These notes can be found in Schinkel's Sketchbook B, transcribed in Peschken, *Das Architektonische Lehrbuch*, 19–20. A similar passage is quoted in Bergdoll, *Karl Friedrich Schinkel*, 114.

66 Hazlett et al., *Collection of Architectural Designs*, 53. Again, I have modified the translation.

67 See for example Bergdoll, *Karl Friedrich Schinkel*, 156; and Trempler, *Schinkels Motive*, 170.

68 Vitruvius, *On Architecture*, ed. and trans. Frank Granger (London and Cambridge, Massachusetts: Harvard University Press, [1931] 1998), 77–83: "And first, with upright forked props and twigs put between, they wove their walls. Others made walls, drying moistened clods which they bound with wood, and covered with reeds and leafage, so as to escape the rain and heat."

69 Börsch-Supan, *Arbeiten für König Friedrich Wilhelm III*, 594: "ein Weinstock, fast stark wie ein Baum." The confusion results partly from

the fact that the thick organic support was replaced in 1841 by another herm, with a head modeled after a piece in the Prussian collection of antiquities. See Börsch-Supan, 596.

70 This sprouting action might actually make Schinkel's vegetal column a closer relative of the Renaissance *Broncone*—the representation of a dried laurel branch, capable of growing again—which functioned as a symbol for a kind of revivification. For example, when Lorenzo di Piero de' Medici used *Il Broncone* as an emblem, it symbolized his hope for the renewed vitality of the Medici family. See Carlo Pedretti, *A Chronology of Leonardo da Vinci's Architectural Studies after 1500* (Geneva: Librairie E. Droz, 1962), 119.

71 Whyte, "Charlottenhof," 20.

72 Whyte, "Charlottenhof," 20.

73 Bergdoll, *Karl Friedrich Schinkel*, 156, 160. Bergdoll also finds a similar phenomenon represented in the vestibule of the nearby Charlottenhof Villa, where he sees "the rise of architectural order from the accidental taming of natural plants" (p. 141), and at Schinkel's Schloss Glienicke Kasino, where he observes "the evolution of structural form, recapitulating in the vernacular that evolution from wood to stone, from simple structure to enclosed dwelling" (p. 126).

74 Johnson's address was originally delivered in German and later published by the A.I.V.B. See Philip Johnson, "Karl Friedrich Schinkel im zwanzigsten Jahrhundert. Wie wir den großen Architekten nach der Bauhaus-Corbusier-Revolution sehen." *Schriftenreihe des Architekten- und Ingenieur-Vereinz zu Berlin* 13 (1961). In a biographical sketch at the end of this volume Werner Gabler shares a telling anecdote: "A native Berliner once approached Philip Johnson in the dining room at the Four Seasons. The German visitor felt surprisingly at home in these foreign surroundings and he commented to Johnson that the room might as well have been built in Berlin, that perhaps, it might even be called 'Prussian' in the best sense of the word." Johnson agreed with this assessment and answered: "Didn't you know? I consider myself to be perhaps the last living student of Schinkel!" (p. 24).

75 The theme of "revolution" advertised in Johnson's title hardly makes an appearance in the body of the text. Instead he emphasizes the continuity in the formal strategies employed by select architects over the generations. In this sense Johnson's talk offers his own proposed genealogy of Modern architecture in the vein of Emil Kaufmann's *Von Ledoux bis Le Corbusier: Ursprung und Entwicklung der autonomen Architektur* (Vienna: Rolf Passer, 1933) and his essay on "Three Revolutionary Architects: Boullée, Ledoux, and Lequeu," in *Transactions of the American Philosophical Society*, no. 42 (October 1952). Johnson knew both Kaufmann texts well, and in light of this reading his evocation of a "revolution" in the Schinkelfest speech begins to make more sense. If there was a design revolution, Johnson wanted to afford Schinkel his due place at its outset. On the relationship between Johnson and Kaufmann, see Anthony Vidler, "From Ledoux to Le Corbusier to Johnson, to...," *Progressive Architecture* (May 1991): 109–10.

76 See Philip Johnson, "Introduction," signed "New York, 1980," in Hazlett et al., *Collection of Architectural Designs*.

77 See Johnson, "Karl Friedrich Schinkel," 15–20.

78 Johnson, "Karl Friedrich Schinkel," 16–17 (my translation). Philip Johnson's talk was eventually published in English, though it is not clear whether he made the translation himself, thus I have chosen to rely on the original German text. For the English version see Philip Johnson, "Schinkel and Mies" in *Program, Columbia University School of Architecture* (1962): 14–34, reprinted in Philip Johnson, *Writings* (New York: Oxford University Press, 1979), 164–181.

79 Johnson, "Karl Friedrich Schinkel," 17.

80 Johnson, "Karl Friedrich Schinkel," 17 (emphasis added).

81 Philip Johnson was not the only critic to sense the Gärtnerwohnung courtyard's centripetal organization. Barry Bergdoll, for example, identifies the "sunken garden parterre" as the "core" of the building complex: "an outdoor room around which the composition revolves." See Bergdoll, *Karl Friedrich Schinkel*, 156.

82 See Whyte, "Charlottenhof," 13; and Heinz Schönemann, "For the Enjoyment of Rural Life: Schinkel's 'Roman Baths' in Sanssouci Park," *Daidalos* 46 (December 1992): 100.

83 Schönemann, "For the Enjoyment of Rural Life," 101.

84 Schönemann, "For the Enjoyment of Rural Life," 99–100.

"By opening channels of design and construction to anyone with access to basic digital fabrication tools, WikiHouse proposes an architecture by and for amateurs."

WikiHouse New Haven

Project Portfolio

WikiHouse at Yale West Campus Urban Farm, 2014. Photographed in spring 2016.

WikiHouse, founded in 2011 by Alastair Parvin and Nick Ierodiaconou, is an open-source project for the design and construction of low-cost, self-built houses. Challenging traditional models of architectural authorship and enterprise, WikiHouse plans are Creative Commons licensed and can be downloaded and modified free of charge. WikiHouses are constructed of modular, pre-fabricated components, CNC milled from standard plywood sheets. The structure requires no bolts or fasteners, instead only utilizing layered mortise and tenon joints. As an open-source model, users are encouraged to adapt or improve the WikiHouse and upload modified designs to an online archive for others to use.

Yale School of Forestry and Environmental Studies student Peter Hirsch founded WikiHouse New Haven in 2014. Testing the sustainability of the WikiHouse model, Hirsch conducted a detailed life cycle analysis on each component of the structure. The project culminated in the construction of the first permanent WikiHouse in the United States, completed for the Yale West Campus Urban Farm in West Haven, Connecticut. Hirsch milled the 430 plywood pieces of the WikiHouse in eighteen hours and assembled the structure with a team of forty volunteers in a day. The WikiHouse is currently used as classroom and event space by the Yale Sustainable Food Program, Yale School of Nursing, and undergraduate clubs.

The architectural significance of WikiHouse rests not in the finished product, but rather in the model of its production. By opening channels of design and construction to anyone with access to basic digital fabrication tools, WikiHouse proposes an architecture by and for amateurs. While the first generation of WikiHouses do not approach the refinement of professionally designed structures, their crowd-sourced design is always revising, always improving.

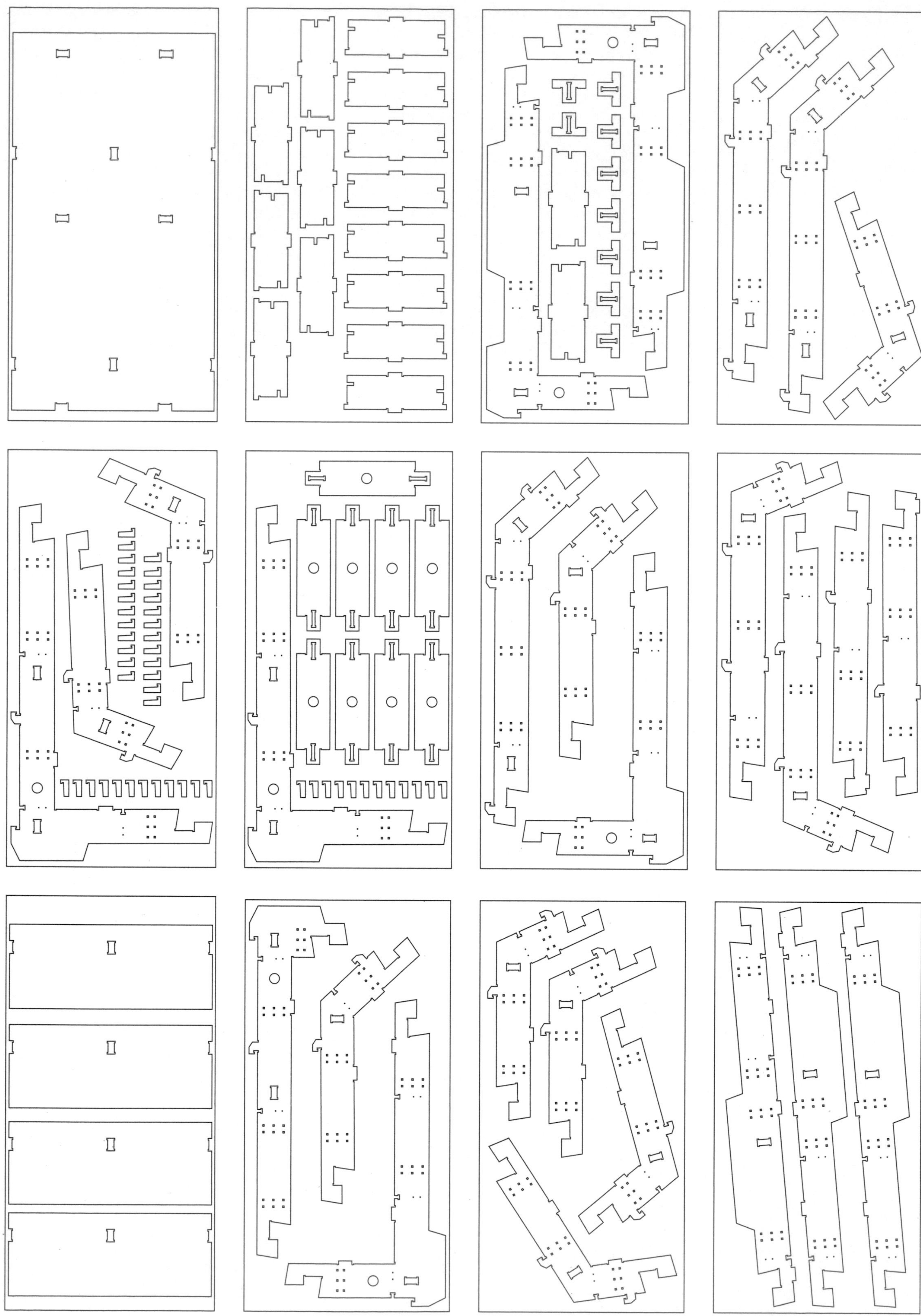

opposite
Twelve of the seventy-nine CNC mill templates, each designed for a standard 4' x 8' plywood sheet.

below
Perspective views of the 3-D WikiHouse model, designed in SketchUp.

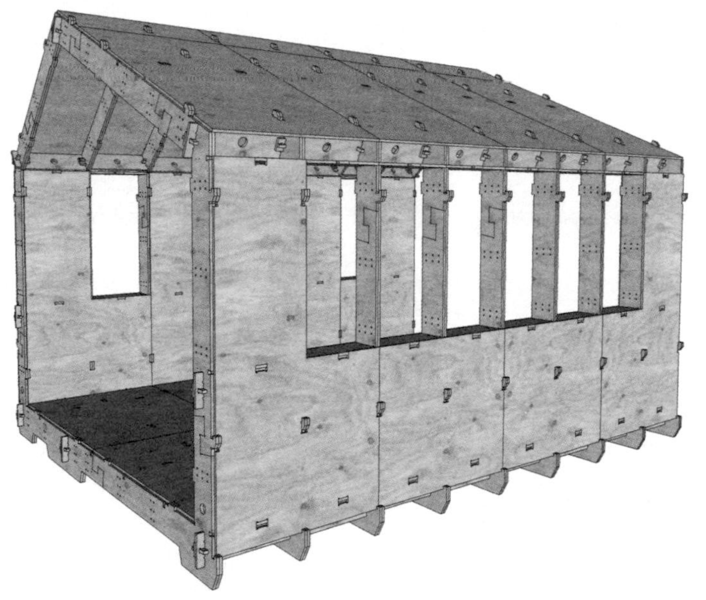

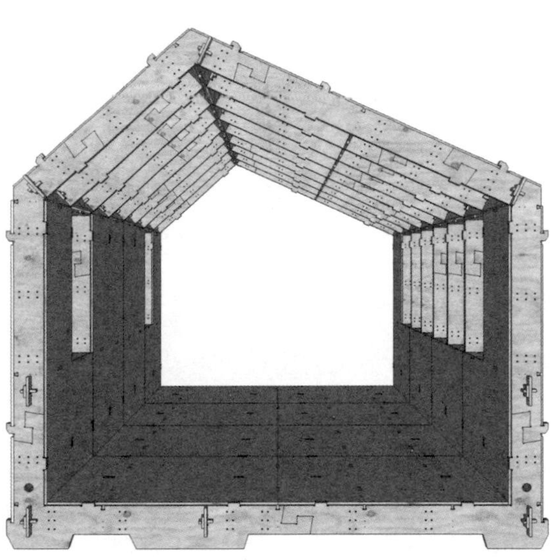

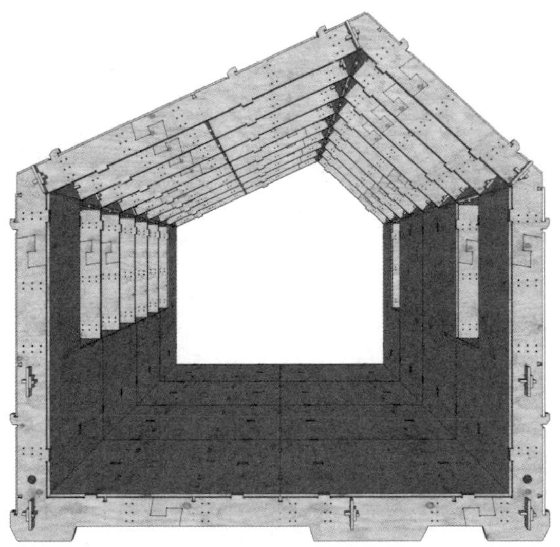

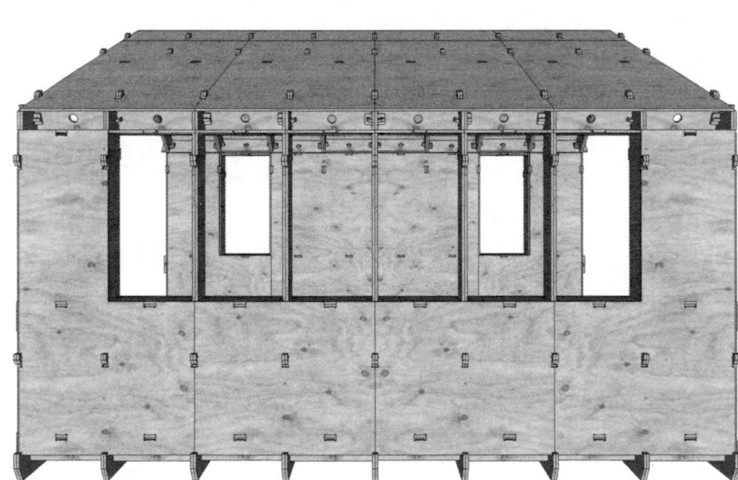

Construction of the WikiHouse at Yale West Campus Urban Farm, summer 2014.

"It is precisely by looking at the thing that does not fit that one can understand the norm."

Ines Weizman

The Exception to the Norm: Buildings and Skeletons in the Archive of Ernst Neufert

1

2

This is a story about the house of the man who devised the most widely known system of architectural norms intended for universal application. Since the house is not the most extreme embodiment of architectural rationality and systematization, its story falls out of the norm, but in a way that makes evident the perils and irrationality of spatial rigidity.[1]

Ernst Neufert (1900–1986) is one of the central figures in the practice and discussion of standardization in Germany. He is best known as the author of the *Bauentwurfslehre* (Architects' Data), a popular reference book for spatial requirements in architectural design that can be found in almost every architectural office and library. Neufert was also a practicing architect; he began his practice before the Second World War, realizing several successful projects for housing and commerce in the postwar period. The key to understanding his story and, by extension, the problematic history of standardization throughout his career, rests with one of his least known buildings: a house he owned and lived in.

Neufert designed the building while a professor of architecture in Weimar and oversaw its construction in 1929 in Gelmeroda, a nearby village. It was a house that responded to a specific brief and site, as well as the first he designed for himself. It was also an experiment in which he and his family were participants, testing it as a potential prototype for reproduction.

3

4

1 Ground floor stairway, Neufert House (Niclas Zimmer, 2014)
2 Ground floor, Neufert House (Niclas Zimmer, 2014)
3 Ground floor, Neufert House (Niclas Zimmer, 2014)
4 Retractable wardrobe, Neufert House (Niclas Zimmer, 2014)
5 Cellar, Neufert House (Niclas Zimmer, 2014)
6 Original hooks and wallpaper in wardrobe, Neufert House (Niclas Zimmer, 2014)

5

6

But buildings are, of course, also pieces of real estate: Neufert eventually moved on and started renting it out—and as is often the case, conflicts emerged between renters and landlord. This conflict would have been mundane were it not for the fact that it inadvertently revealed something about Neufert and his possible association with the Nazis during the war. There are other buildings like the Neufert House in Gelmeroda and throughout Germany—resonating with untold histories and cupboards full of skeletons—especially in areas such as Weimar-Thuringia, in the former East Germany, that were not accessible to their expropriated, deported, and sometimes murdered owners before the collapse of the Communist regime in 1989.

Neufert was one of the first students at the Bauhaus in Weimar (Staatliches Bauhaus Weimar) when Walter Gropius opened it in 1919. He clearly impressed Gropius as a student since the latter invited him to work at the architecture firm he ran in partnership with Adolf Meyer. Soon Neufert began to manage sites for projects such as the renovation of the Stadttheater Jena and the Fagus Factory, and had a major role in the design of the now iconic building for the Bauhaus school and the Masters' Houses in Dessau. Although Otto Bartning and Gropius had conceived of the Bauhaus together in 1919, the latter eventually took the lead. Seven years later, with Gropius departed to Dessau, Bartning wanted to direct a school devoted to the ideas of the Neues Bauen (New Building) and was keen to train architects in this method. After the forced relocation of the Bauhaus in 1926, Bartning was appointed director of the new Staatliche Hochschule für Handwerk und Baukunst in Weimar, which used the same building as the Bauhaus had in the campus designed by Henry van de Velde. Bartning offered Neufert a professorship in his school and soon made him director of its architecture department. It may have been an attempt at revenge on Gropius, and it certainly was interpreted by the Bauhaus director as such.

During his time in Weimar, at the heart of the functionalist agenda of the Modern movement, Neufert was particularly interested in the rationalization and systematization of the construction process. He developed a highly methodical teaching curriculum that concentrated on the spatial requirements for human movements in buildings.[2] While teaching, Neufert completed his first independent architecture projects for the university in Jena, the Abbeanum (1928), and the Studentenhaus (1929). His professorial income and a contribution from his mother-in-law allowed him to buy a plot in Gelmeroda, a village on the outskirts of Weimar, and he started to design his private house. In 1924 Neufert had married painter Alice Vollmer, a Bauhaus graduate and a student of Georg Muche and Paul Klee. By 1932 they had four children: Peter, Krista, Ingrid, and Ilas.

Besides building a home, Neufert understood the construction of the house as an opportunity to present his ideas for efficient planning, material resourcefulness, efficiency of movement, and time management. His meticulous preparation of the construction process, based on the American balloon-frame system, allowed him to erect the structure in an astounding two-and-a-half days, making the entire house ready for occupancy in only six weeks.[3] The family moved in during the spring of 1930.

7
8
9
GÄRTEN
MUSTERBEISPIELE
Gemüse
Müll
Sandkasten
Terrasse
Stauden
Rasen
N
4 Hausgarten mit 600 m² M. 1 : 500 nach G. Harbers
Hauptwindrichtung
Erläuterung:
1 Wohnhaus
2 Terrasse
3 Laube
4 Pumpenhaus
5 Wasserleitung
6 Stall
7 Wasserbecken
8 Rasen
9 Dungplatz
10 Wintergemüse
11 Gemüse
12 Himbeeren
13 Stachel- und Johannisbeeren
14 Blumen
15 Zier- und Schutzsträucher
16 Spalierwand
17 Hecken
18 Laubbäume
19 Obstbäume
20 Steinobst
21 Kernobst
22 Sickergrube
eingebautem Einfamilienhaus von Arch. A. Esch
NORD
77,49
44,00
45,39
86,23
15,60
17,38
22,04
41,50
113,10
Laufbahn
Sportplatz
Garage
Erweiterungsbau (Büro, Schule)
geschlossene, 2,0 m hohe Planke
7 Größere Gartenanlage mit Sportplatz vor Böschungen. Gegen sommerlichen Plankenwände.
Hühnerhof
Vorgarten
Gärten
vorräte
abstellraum
heizen
garage
waschküche
mädchen
wohnzimmer
bücherei
küche
arbeitszimmer
balkon
schlafzimmer
schlafzimmer grosselt
schlafzimmer kinder
bad
Abb. 45. Kellergeschoß.
Abb. 46. Erdgeschoß.
Abb. 47. Obergeschoß.
Abb. 43 bis 47. Holzskelettbau in Gelmeroda-Weimar.

The house was designed on a ten-by-ten-meter grid, both in plan and section. The timber-frame structure was meant to be visible from the outside: the eastern and western walls of the building presented large horizontal windows, whereas the supporting walls on the north and south sides of the house were almost windowless. While Neufert had studied how human proportions could be synthesized using various measuring and standardization systems, he experimented in this project with a scheme in which fixtures, cupboards, desks, beds, doors, and staircases, his family life, and his office were designed to fit within one-meter multiples to allow for a more efficient use of material, to make prefabricated building elements more compatible, and to make the entire house a prototype for reproduction.[4]

Shortly after the family (and a maid) moved into the new home, a coalition comprised of conservative parties and the National Socialist Party was elected to the government of Thuringia, which led to the closure of Bartning's modernist school. Paul Schultze-Naumburg, a member of the National Socialist Party and professed author of racist propaganda on "degenerate art," was now to direct the third iteration of the same institution within ten years, aiming to erase all traces of the previous two schools and to insist on traditional "Germanic" crafts and architecture. Neufert lost his job and left Weimar in 1932, taking up a position in the private school directed by Johannes Itten in Berlin.[5] One of the first Bauhaus master teachers, Itten had left the school in 1923 after disputes with Gropius over his teaching methods and established his own private school—but it, too, closed down under pressure from Hitler's regime, in 1934.

Meanwhile Neufert divorced his wife and began to travel and write about architecture in other places. He lectured and published articles in the architectural magazine *Bauwelt*, which took him to Scandinavia and England, places to which he later claimed he considered immigrating.[6] His biggest project during this time was the compilation of teaching material and research on the efficiency and standardization of building elements in construction: the *Bauentwurfslehre* was finally published in 1936, the first of many editions to come.[7] Neufert prepared the work with a team of architects, among them former Bauhaus student Gustav Hassenpflug, who had returned from the Soviet Union where he had been part of Ernst May's team.[8]

The well-known book is a combination encyclopedia, *catalogue raisonné*, guidebook for architectural practice, and manual with prescriptive guidelines on "correct" measurements in design. Neufert's data measure almost all routines and movements of human life, including the dimensions of quotidian objects, distances between furniture and people such as the measure of one marching man at 72 centimeters and four marching men at 1.80 meters, the size of hutches for rabbits (a Flemish Giant measures 40 centimeters in height when its ears are up), and instructions on how to trim blackberry bushes back to 35 centimeters in autumn.

Yet the book also presents plans of contemporaneous architecture projects as references for intelligent and functionalist design. These were projects Neufert admired, and certainly to publish them was a gesture of collegial friendship. We can assume that it was considered an honor to be included in the book. But even though the *Bauentwurfslehre*, as well as much of the work that went into it, predated the Nazi era and was to some extent antagonistic to its architectural ideals, the book was nevertheless published in a period in which many of Neufert's Jewish colleagues felt threatened or were forced to flee as they lost their jobs.

The book was republished with very few revisions throughout the war, when the exclusion of Jews from German social and political life turned into a violent reality and horrendous crime. An examination of some of these model projects lends insight into the contrast between the book and its social context.[9]

The 1936 issue includes, for example, Erich Mendelsohn's project for the Columbus House department store in Berlin, one of the architect's last projects before he emigrated to England in 1933. In *Berlin: The Politics of Order 1737–1989*, Alan Balfour proposed a striking history of the Columbus House, positioning Mendelsohn's department store as the index of dramatic changes in German history. The bankruptcy of the store's first owner left an incomplete construction site; the only thing completed was a facade composed of a giant billboard wall that aimed to compete with the colorful advertisement surfaces of vibrant 1920s Berlin.[10] Mendelsohn turned this wall into stone in 1932 and carved long horizontal windows into it. He was unwilling to place advertisements or neon lights in the spaces between the solid stripes or in the windowpanes. Only a few advertisements were allowed, including a small, awkwardly designed 1932 poster made especially to fit the facade which supported the reelection of President Hindenburg at a time when popular elections were still possible.

7 Neufert House, Gelmeroda (Niclas Zimmer, 2014)
8 *Bauentwurfslehre* (1936), page 153, which shows the plan of Neufert's own garden in Gelmeroda as a reference for garden design. This and all following images are from the Bauhaus-Universität Weimar, Archiv der Moderne / Neufert Stiftung.
9 Reconstruction of original plans for the Neufert House by Peter Mittmann in 1990, showing the cellar, ground floor, and the first floor.

following page
10 *Bauentwurfslehre* (1936), page 175, showing office buildings including Erich Mendelsohn's Columbushaus, 1930, Berlin.
11 *Bauentwurfslehre* (1936), page 143 showing housing projects by Moisei Ginzburg, Ernst Neufert, R.C. Reamer, Sven Wallander, and C. Fieger.
12 *Bauentwurfslehre* (1936), page 102, with diagrams of Margarete Schütte-Lihotzky's Frankfurt Kitchen.
13 *Bauentwurfslehre* (1936), page 227, showing Walter Gropius's Total Theatre, 1927.

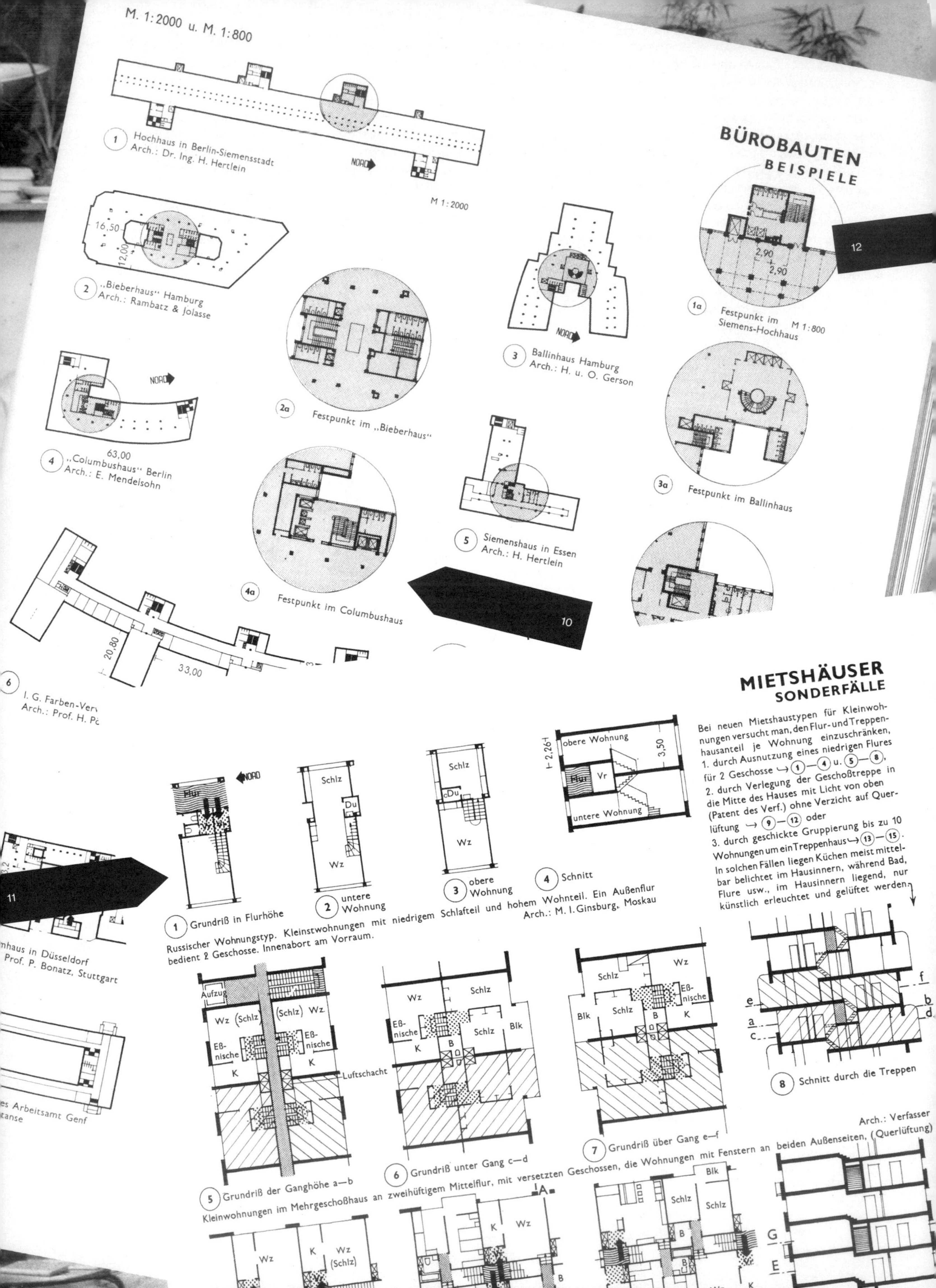

M. 1:2000 u. M. 1:800
BÜROBAUTEN
BEISPIELE
12
1 Hochhaus in Berlin-Siemensstadt
Arch.: Dr. Ing. H. Hertlein
NORD
M 1:2000
16,50
12,00
2 „Bieberhaus" Hamburg
Arch.: Rambatz & Jolasse
2a Festpunkt im „Bieberhaus"
3 Ballinhaus Hamburg
Arch.: H. u. O. Gerson
2,90
2,90
1a Festpunkt im Siemens-Hochhaus M 1:800
63,00
4 „Columbushaus" Berlin
Arch.: E. Mendelsohn
4a Festpunkt im Columbushaus
5 Siemenshaus in Essen
Arch.: H. Hertlein
3a Festpunkt im Ballinhaus
10
20,80
33,00
6 I. G. Farben-Ver
Arch.: Prof. H. Pö
MIETSHÄUSER
SONDERFÄLLE
Bei neuen Mietshaustypen für Kleinwohnungen versucht man, den Flur- und Treppenhausanteil je Wohnung einzuschränken, 1. durch Ausnutzung eines niedrigen Flures für 2 Geschosse → 1 — 4 u. 5 — 8, 2. durch Verlegung der Geschoßtreppe in die Mitte des Hauses mit Licht von oben (Patent des Verf.) ohne Verzicht auf Querlüftung → 9 — 12 oder 3. durch geschickte Gruppierung bis zu 10 Wohnungen um ein Treppenhaus → 13 — 15. In solchen Fällen liegen Küchen meist mittelbar belichtet im Hausinnern, während Bad, Flure usw., im Hausinnern liegend, nur künstlich erleuchtet und gelüftet werden.
11
Flur
Schlz
Du
Wz
obere Wohnung
untere Wohnung
Vr
2,26
3,50
1 Grundriß in Flurhöhe
2 untere Wohnung
3 obere Wohnung
4 Schnitt
Russischer Wohnungstyp. Kleinstwohnungen mit niedrigem Schlafteil und hohem Wohnteil. Ein Außenflur bedient 2 Geschosse. Innenabort am Vorraum.
Arch.: M. I. Ginsburg, Moskau
haus in Düsseldorf
Prof. P. Bonatz, Stuttgart
es Arbeitsamt Genf
tanse
Aufzug
Wz (Schlz)
(Schlz) Wz
Eß-nische
K
Luftschacht
Blk
B
e
a
c
f
b
d
5 Grundriß der Ganghöhe a—b
6 Grundriß unter Gang c—d
7 Grundriß über Gang e—f
8 Schnitt durch die Treppen
Arch.: Verfasser
Kleinwohnungen im Mehrgeschoßhaus an zweihüftigem Mittelflur, mit versetzten Geschossen, die Wohnungen mit Fenstern an beiden Außenseiten, (Querlüftung)
A
G
E

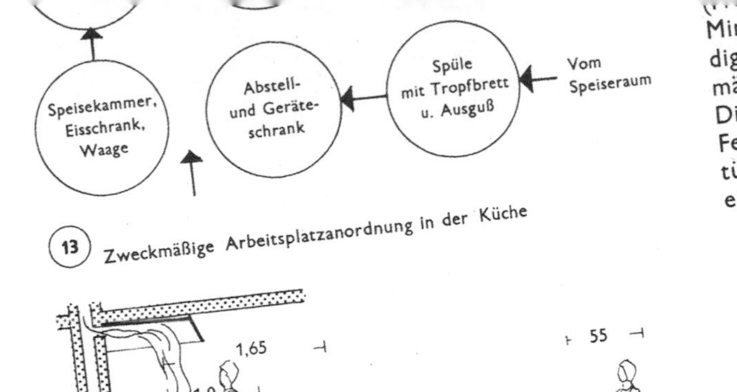

(13) Zweckmäßige Arbeitsplatzanordnung in der Küche

Mindestbreite 2,30 m. ... dige unterzubringen, wird die platzsparende Einr... mäßen Neubauten gleich mitgeliefert (sogar mit Elt-Kühlschrank). Die Oberflächen der Wände und Möbel sollen unempfindlich gegen Feuchtigkeit und abwaschbar sein, möglichst Schiebe- oder Rolltüren, die nicht platzraubend in den Arbeitsraum stehen. Am Herd ein Wrasenabzugsrohr zur Vermeidung von Schwitzwasserbildung.

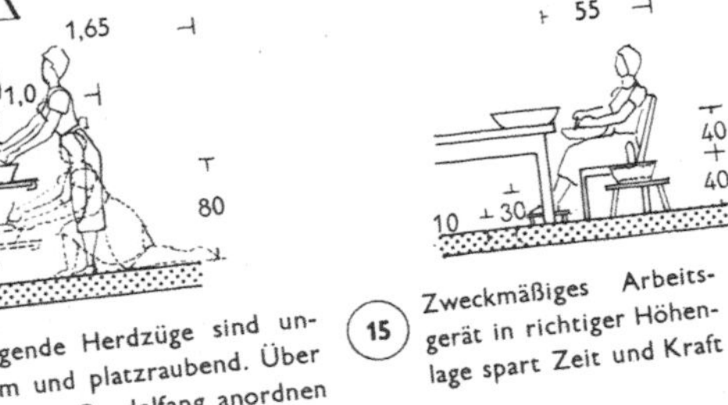

(14) Tiefliegende Herdzüge sind unbequem und platzraubend. Über Kochstellen Brodelfang anordnen

(15) Zweckmäßiges Arbeitsgerät in richtiger Höhenlage spart Zeit und Kraft

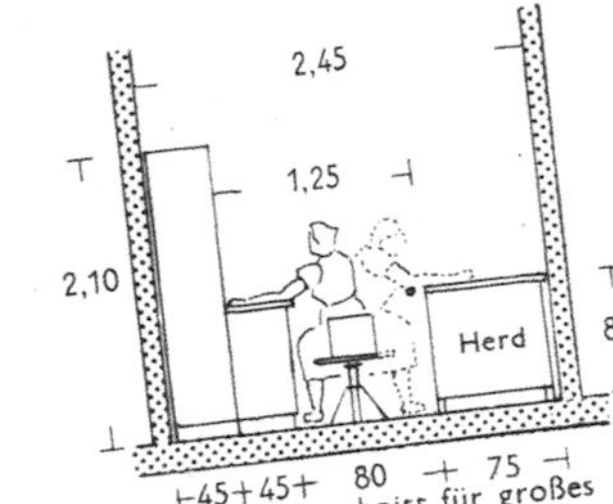
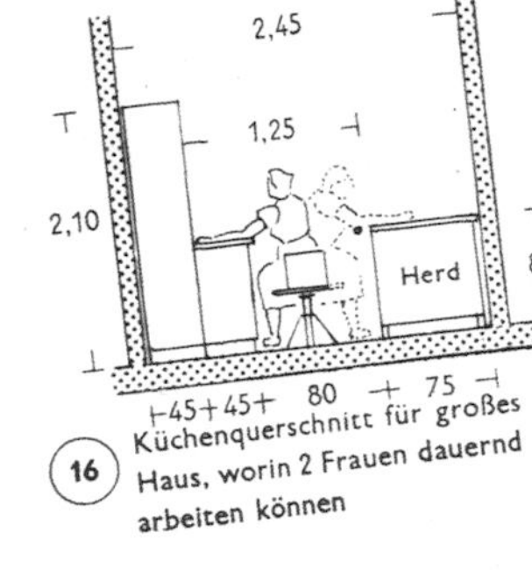

(16) Küchenquerschnitt für großes Haus, worin 2 Frauen dauernd arbeiten können

(17) Küchenquerschnitt für kleines Haus mit Platz für die Hausfrau und zeitweilige Aushilfe

102

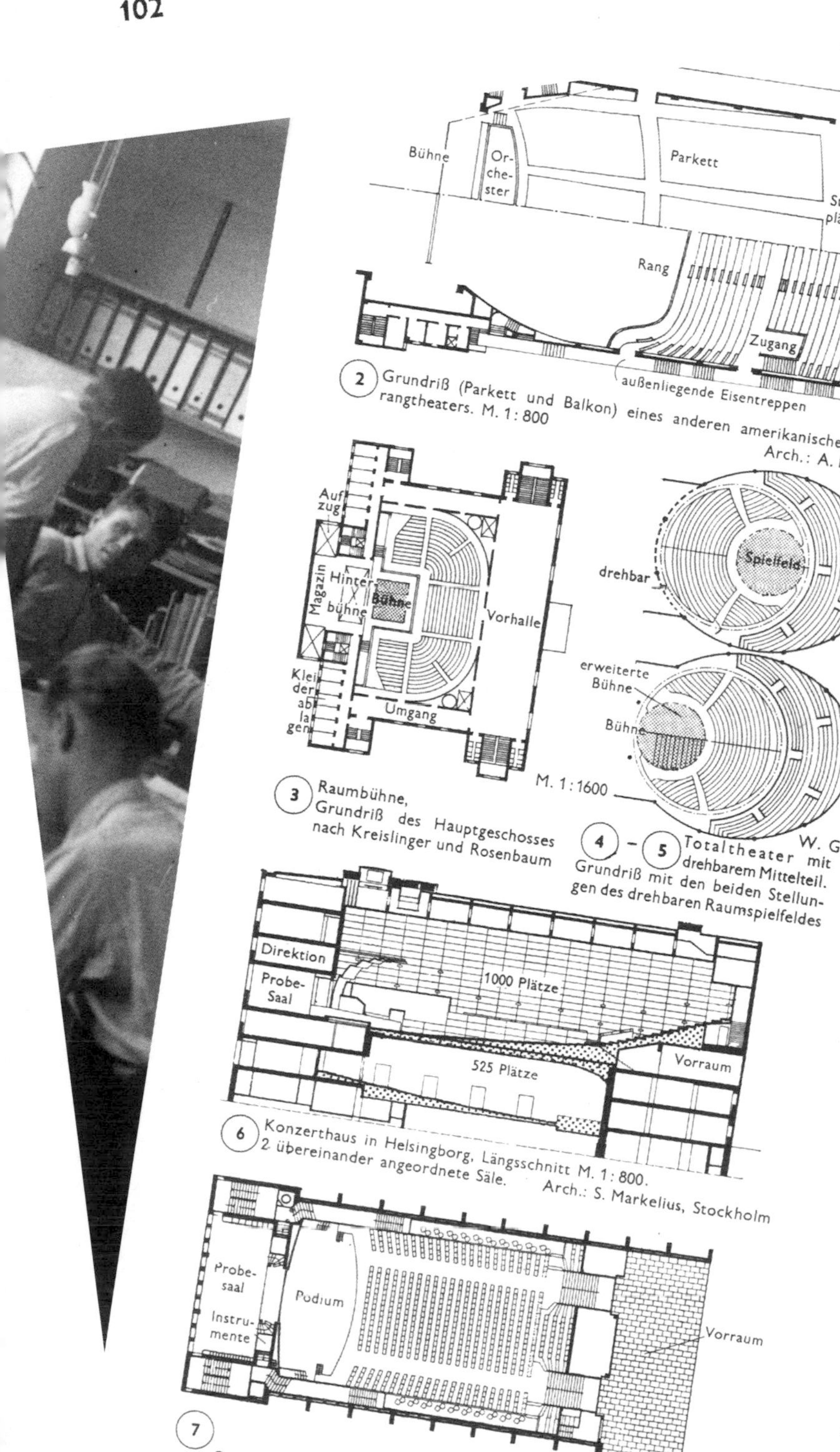

(2) Grundriß (Parkett und Balkon) eines anderen amerikanischen Einrangtheaters. M. 1:800 Arch.: A. D. Hill

(3) Raumbühne, Grundriß des Hauptgeschosses nach Kreislinger und Rosenbaum

(4)–(5) Totaltheater mit drehbarem Mittelteil. Grundriß mit den beiden Stellungen des drehbaren Raumspielfeldes nach W. Gropius

(6) Konzerthaus in Helsingborg, Längsschnitt M. 1:800. 2 übereinander angeordnete Säle. Arch.: S. Markelius, Stockholm

(7) Grundriß des großen Saales zu (6)

...LLENBAU...

...E WEGE UND Z...

...ut vorwiegend Ein... er dem baupolize... S. 224 (10) gerin... der Rangplätze aufwe... der amerikanischen Bauart durch ... Decke eine ästhetisch bessere Wirkung erzie... als bei der „drückenden" Decke (der oberste Rang ersche... eingepreßt) im deutschen Mehrrangbau. Die nachteilige La... der unter dem Rang befindlichen Parkettrücklage im Einran... theater ist durch Anordnung von Durchbrüchen in de... Parkettdecke und Anlage eines Umganges zu besser... ↪ (1) und (2).

Die **Raumbühne** ↪ (4)–(5) erstrebt eine innigere Verbindung von Zuschauer und Schauspieler und verlegt das Spielfeld in den Zuschauerraum, im Gegensatz zur Rahmen- oder Guckkastenbühne ↪ (3). Eine derartig neue Gruppierung würde eine Umwälzung des technischen Bühnenbetriebes nach sich ziehen. Verwendung des Films an stelle von Kulissen, senk-, heb- und drehbare Bühnen und Zuschauerflächen ↪ (4)–(5).

Bei **Hallenbauten** für verschiedene Zwecke ist die Konzerthalle der am häufigsten vorkommende Typ ↪ (6) und (7). In erster Linie sind dafür die Richtlinien für Akustik maßgebend ↪ S. 230. Wichtig ist die meist geforderte Unter... ...roßen Säle in kleinere (intime) ...e ↪ S. 63, und die Umwandlung ...h durch herausnehmbares Gestühl.

13

Dafür eignen sich bei gestuften Sitzreihen Hyan-Sessel. Raumbedarf für 1000 Stück zusammengeklappt: 3,0 × 4,0 = 12,0 m², bei 3,0 m Höhe = 36,0 m³.

Zur Bestuhlung von Tanzflächen eignen sich selbständig stehende Klappstühle (Theatromobilstühle) mit Abstand von ⌀ 1,0 m von V.-K. bis V.-K.

Raumbedarf für 1000 zusammengeklappte Theatromobilstühle: 20,0 m³.

Auch Tische haben für solche Fälle anklappbare Füße, die bei Gebrauch durch Schienen versteift werden.

Die auf S. 224–226 angegebenen Vorschriften über Bestuhlung sind neuerungsbedürftig. Nach Vorschlag von Professor S. Boljajew ↪ 📖 sollen auf 1 Ausgang ≦ 60 Sitzplätze kommen. Die Entfernung dieser Plätze von dem Ausgang soll begrenzt sein. In Rußland ist deshalb folgende Bestimmung Gesetz geworden:

Kein Platz darf diese **Grenzentfernung** überschreiten, die nicht nach Metern, sondern nach der Zahl der Plätze gemessen wird.

Die Grenzentfernung für diejenigen Plätzegruppen, für die die Saalausgänge nicht höher als 1 m über dem Fußsteig liegen, beträgt einschließlich des letzten Platzes:

1. für Theatersäle aus Holz . . . .
2. „ „ „ Stein oder offene . . . . 15 Plätze
3. „ andere Säle „ Holz . . . . 20 „
4. „ „ „ „ Stein oder offene . . . . . . 20 „

Liegt die Plätzegruppe höher als 1 m, so vermindert sich die Grenzentfernung um je 1 Platz und um je ei... Platz bei Sälen nach 1. und 2. ... bei Sä... 25 „ .

The Columbus House was operated briefly by the Woolworth Company, but its history thereafter falls into dispute. Balfour has mistakenly written that immediately after Hitler's election in 1933, the upper floors of the building were used as a detention center in the service of Hitler's campaign of *Schutzhaft* (protective custody) and implied that the building's functionalist facade eased this horrific division of its neutral floor plans, separated vertically by an elevator.[11] We can assume that Neufert included the plan of the Columbus House using the same architectural justification as Balfour's erroneous premise, seeing this flexibility instead as evidence of good design. Neufert's book depicts the drawing of a circle around the vertical circulation shaft for the staircase and the lift, leaving plenty of space for free use of a plan that is framed only by the columns of the building structure, thus allowing for multiple functions. When Neufert placed the plan of this building among his references in 1936, he certainly knew that Mendelsohn and his family had left and that his beautiful work had come under attack for demonstrating "Jewish traits."[12]

Another example that stands out in Neufert's 1936 edition is a housing project, the so-called Narkomfin House by Jewish architect Moisei Ginzburg, in Moscow. Ginzburg had collaborated with Hassenpflug on the competition for the Palace of the Soviets, and one can assume that it was Hassenpflug who had advised Neufert to include its plans in the volume.[13] The building was completed around the same time as the Columbus House in 1932.[14] Neufert presented all the plans and the section of the F-type apartment typology, unique for its vertical arrangements of low-ceilinged sleeping and sanitary rooms over three floors with double-height living rooms on two floors. With its emphasis on communal dwelling, the housing unit contained only communal kitchens and one dining hall, all in accordance with the Soviet ideology of the time.[15] It is surprising that such a visionary socialist "machine for housing" was still included in the hugely popular editions published at a time when German architecture was forced to embrace the *Heimatstil.*

On page 142, Neufert included plans by Alexander Klein, a Russian-Jewish émigré who in the late 1920s experimented with and studied housing typologies related to ideas about the *existenzminimum*. One of the last projects he realized before emigrating from Germany was a housing project he had begun with Gropius in Bad Dürrenberg, a town not far from Weimar. Klein and Gropius apparently fell out over the question of whether the roofs should be sloped or flat. For Klein the question of the roof and adhering to the strict aesthetics of Modernism were of minor concern, so he opted for the sloped version, as the client must have wanted, and Gropius withdrew his authorship. Neufert was keen to present Klein's schematic studies of movement in the minimal flat which aligned with his own interests, and we can assume that the two were friends. In 1933, when Klein wanted to leave Germany initially for the Netherlands, Neufert wrote a recommendation letter on his behalf to his former colleague in Weimar, Cornelis van Eesteren.[16] Luckily for Klein, he didn't get the job and left via France for Palestine.[17] In Neufert's section on kitchen design, the figures illustrating measurements throughout the book suddenly change from male to female. Among his own data regarding dimensions for cooking, storing, and cleaning, he mentions the Frankfurt Kitchen, a prototype designed in 1926 following studies of kitchen ergonomics by architect Margarete Schütte-Lihotzky. In 1930 Schütte-Lihotzky joined the office of Ernst May, who departed for the Soviet Union to help Stalin realize his five-year plans for housing projects. Neufert also published plans by the likes of Ludwig Hilbersheimer, Ludwig Mies van der Rohe, Max Taut, Fred Forbát, and architect couple Paula Maria Canthal and Dirk Gascard, all of whom—although not necessarily anti-Nazi in 1936—were forced to interrupt or end their practices and emigrate. In addition, Neufert included the plans of Gropius's Total Theatre.

This project had been developed in 1927 in collaboration with Erwin Piscator, a director who wrote political plays with radical left-wing positions that mainly addressed the revolutionary sentiments of the working class. For his performances Piscator used film projections along with optical and acoustical devices to challenge the staged illusions. Gropius designed a theater in which all these devices could be deployed on a mobile stage that could be shifted during the play to achieve the "total experience" of the performance. In 1931 Piscator traveled to the Soviet Union to shoot a film on a revolutionary uprising and was unable to return after Hitler came to power. Certainly Neufert was familiar with the Communist ideas promoted in Piscator's plays, made performable and viewable through Gropius's design.

The first architectural precedent in the book, on page 33, is Mies van der Rohe's Das Haus um 2000,[18] which Neufert long-windedly praises as the model for a new kind of architecture liberated from fears of adversaries, thieves, and demons yet open to life and nature. The next page begins with an introduction to a long chapter in which he explains the design process from draft to final plan. As an example, he uses a commission he must have received while finalizing the book: a house for Dr. Bruno Kindt, management board member and chemist of a glassworks factory in Weisswasser.[19] The house featured technological gadgets such as a four-meter-wide window that could be sunken into the ground, similar to those for which Mies had become known. To showcase the process of drafting and design, a task for which Neufert recommends reserving three to fourteen days, he sets his first draft of the house, titled "Haus-Vorentwurf mit Mängeln" next to a revised plan titled "Haus Entwurf ohne Mängel." In an almost fatherly manner he explains the disadvantages of the former as compared to the latter and elaborates recommendations about the relationship between architect and client.[20] The house was under construction in 1938 and its final plans were included in the 1939 publication, by which time its owner, Dr. Kindt, had already been killed serving as an ensign on a German submarine in October 1939, only a few weeks after the beginning of the war.[21]

14 Top image: Friends of the family with children in one of the upper bedrooms of the Neufert House. Middle and bottom images: The living room of the Neufert House was used to entertain and also as an architectural office after Neufert lost his teaching position.

This narrative, and indeed the inclusion of many of these case studies, opens the *Bauentwurfslehre* to questions regarding other aims and meanings behind publication, in contrast to the abstract collection of data for which the book has been praised. It seems that Neufert was trying to reach beyond rigid measuring systems and norms, something for which he was not yet willing to die.

Let's go back to Neufert's own house in Gelmeroda. This auto-experimentation, which stood on a one-hectare plot, was featured in the garden-design section of the *Bauentwurfslehre*. The large garden extended from the front terrace of the house to a running track that surrounded a local sports ground. Along the track various types of fruit trees were planted, while hedges marked the borders to the neighboring plot. An entire section next to the house was reserved for trellises supporting berry bushes and winter and summer vegetables, with specific areas for raspberries, gooseberries, and black currants. Other areas of the garden were purely ornamental, with functional aspects including a compost area, a stable, a swimming pool, and a system of six water sprinklers that irrigated the plants within their radius. Neufert's unusual sports-garden points to pedagogical principles employed at the time that aimed to balance physical development with educational and office work as well as self-sufficient housing concepts; these are principles he must have been familiar with during his work at the Bauhaus in Weimar and on his design for the school's building in Dessau. The home garden plan also reserved space for a building extension—an architecture school, a project he must have already considered while working as a professor at Bartning's school.

On a trip to the United States in 1936, shortly after the publication of the *Bauentwurfslehre*, Neufert met Frank Lloyd Wright, an architect who also had plans for an architecture school, at Taliesin. One can assume that Neufert considered staying in the United States, but he returned to Germany, where the first edition of his book had already sold out. On June 9, while still in New York, he authorized the second edition, believing the book would become an international bestseller.

Albert Speer, who in 1937 had become Generalbauinspektor für die Reichshauptstadt (General Inspector of Construction for the Capital of the Reich), a post Hitler created to enforce the megalomaniac planning of Berlin as a world capital, or "Germania," was thrilled by the book and even convinced that it could help systematize and speed up construction in an economy increasingly geared toward both major construction projects and war. Speer considered Neufert indispensible to his plans and, in 1938, assigned him a post overseeing the norms and standardization efforts for Berlin's housing production. Neufert accepted.[22] Whether this acceptance was tempered with hesitation or internal deliberation is not known. We cannot be certain whether it was an ideological or opportunistic move, but it seems from that moment on his work became more energized.

Neufert used this position as an opportunity to further develop his ideas on building norms, standardization, and building types based on the "octameter" system. These studies resulted in major texts, such as *Das Oktameter System* (1941), *Bombensicherer Luftschutz im Wohnungsbau* (1942), *Die Pläne zum Kriegseinheitstyp* (1943), and the book *Bauordnungslehre* (1943), which was prefaced by Speer.[23] In February 1942 Speer was appointed minister of armament and war production while remaining Generalbauinspektor.[24] In the same year the octameter system was declared the DIN norm, a key condition for the implementation of Neufert's guidelines for all construction projects in Hitler's Germany, including housing, public buildings, industrial buildings, and air-raid shelters in housing as well as military and logistical building types such as underground hangars and bunkers, for which Neufert developed blueprints in the last years of the war.[25]

The *Bauordnungslehre* builds on the collection of data and rules for standardization that Neufert had proclaimed in the *Bauentwurfslehre* in 1936 but lacks the references to architectural projects. In fact it becomes ensnarled in subliminal anti-Semitic comments when, for example, explaining that the number seven should be avoided in proportion systems. The last chapters of the book develop a bizarre proposal for a house-building machine, a *Gusshaus* or *Hausbaumaschine*,[26] in which standardized planning is automated. This was to be a giant railway-based machine that would build multistory apartment blocks in order to reconstruct the cities destroyed by the war, or—as Speer hoped—to colonize and occupy the new territories of a victorious Germany. In this project automation is revealed as the ultimate horizon of standardization. While much of Neufert's life and work during the war will probably remain unknown, this particular period attested to a rising technocratic ideology.

The archival records I consulted contain relatively little about Neufert's affiliation with National Socialism. After the war he presented these years as largely nonpolitical and mainly concerned with professional development. Apart from a short-term membership in a Nazi party motor club, which allowed him to go on a few boat tours with friends in Berlin's famous Wannsee, an affiliation he dutifully lists in his curriculum vitae after the war, he was not a member of any party.[27] We know very little about his collaboration with Speer's offices, for which he worked from 1938 to 1945, partially because Neufert sought to cloud this period. In his postwar curriculum vitae, Neufert mentions publications and lectures he presented in Helsinki (1943), Malmö and Stockholm (1943), and Kraków and Warsaw (1944).[28] Unfortunately there are no documents that testify on which subjects he lectured and whom he represented, but it seems difficult to separate the meaning of a lecture on architectural efficiency, norms, and technological advances from the war efforts. After the war Neufert also claimed that most of his archive had been burned in Berlin.

Indeed both his office in Lennéstrasse 10 and Speer's office at Pariser Platz 4 were partially destroyed in Allied bombing raids in 1945, but strangely many of his personal documents from before the war did survive. Did Neufert himself destroy this record in the attempt to build a career in the postwar Federal Republic of Germany?

Following the war Neufert immediately became a member of the board of directors of the Bund Deutscher Architekten (BDA), was appointed professor at Darmstadt Polytechnic College in 1945, director of the Institute for Standardization (Institut für Baunormung), and continued to work as a freelance architect. Today the archive of Neufert's work is divided between the Technical University of Darmstadt and the Archiv der Moderne at the Bauhaus-Universität Weimar, which holds documents contributed by the Neufert Foundation. Darmstadt's collection begins in about 1946, the year Neufert became a professor at the university. Weimar's archive holds documents from Neufert's early years at the Bauhaus, his time at the Bauatelier Gropius, his years as a professor at the Bauhochschule Weimar, as well as from his private life, including travel sketches and diaries. However, there is a ten-year gap.

The folders in the archive show Neufert's orderly filing system, along with the dates of his revisions and clearings, which he marks on each document. Among the documents from his estate in Weimar is a folder that Neufert labeled in 1982 with the words "Alter Kram" (old stuff). In a short note he asks his son Peter, with whom he had an office and to whom he entrusted his archive after his death, to judge whether or not it should be destroyed.

The folder contains correspondence related to the house in Gelmeroda between 1945 and '52, when Weimar was in the Soviet Sector and later in the territory of East Germany. It contains the sorts of things that historians of architecture might consider of minor interest but that promoters of microhistory, like Carlo Ginzburg, would delight at: complaints by tenants about noise, squeaking floorboards, hidden stashes, and leaks; questions about found objects, rules for sharing fruit and other harvested products from the garden, and leases; and apologies for late payments. While the folder may digress from the kind of historical sources usually of concern in architectural scholarship, it includes one of the only sources of evidence of Neufert's struggle with his own life and work under the Nazi regime.

Prof. Ernst Neufert
Darmstadt - Villenkolonie
Eberstadt,Hindenburgstr. 9

Darmstadt,am 6. Sept. 1945

Sehr geehrter Herr ████████!

Ihnen heutefolgendes zur Kenntnis.Ich lebe jetzt in Darmstadt,wo ich eine Professur an die TH angeboten bekam.

Ich wäre Ihnen außerordentlich dankbar,wenn Sie mir auf irgend einem Wege einen Bericht über mein Haus in Gelmeroda zukommen ließen. Leider konnte ich Sie in Weimar nicht selber noch einmal sprechen,aber ich hoffe das trotzdem alles zu beiderseitiger Zufriedenheit gelöst wurde.Die Ernte wird ja bestens ausgefallen sein,denn der Garten war ja mit aller Sorgfalt und großer Mühe bestellt.

Ich schrieb an meine Eltern,die in Mittweida,Sacheean leben,das sie, wenn es eien Reise nach dort erlaubt,sich Kartoffeln und Obst abholen können,also es ist unser Anteil,den ich an meine Eltern abtrete,da wir jetzt nichts aus dem Garten benötigen.

Sobald es eine Reisemöglichkeit in die russisch besetzte Zone gibt, werden wir nach Weimar kommen,um uns selbermit Ihnen über alles Wei - tere zu unterhalten.

Ich danke Ihnen bestens für Ihre Bemühungen,und hoffe recht bald von Ihnen zu hören.

Mit herzlichem Gruß,auch von meiner Frau,
und Ihnen alles Gute wünschend,
bin ich
Ihr

ERNST NEUFERT.

15

15 Letter from Ernst Neufert to Karl Zweimüller requesting that he manage the affairs of the house in Gelmeroda during Neufert's absence, September 6, 1943.

The house in Gelmeroda might have been the only personal object he valued, and he was forced to leave it behind to start a new life in the Western sector. Professionally he had lost touch with an exemplary project from his portfolio, with its timber structure, modular planning, and efficient management of space; personally he lost a beloved family home that was highly regarded by his colleagues and students in Weimar. Thus the building touches a sore spot and prompts him to speak.

Photographs from around 1930 show Neufert hosting parties at the house, his children playing in the nascent garden, and how the living room served as an architectural office with students and graduates of the Bauhochschule stationed at drafting tables. After he left Weimar and separated from his wife, Alice, Neufert's family remained in the house until 1932. Alice initially ran a theosophical school there, probably to generate some income. When she left, the house was divided and rented out to two parties.[29] In 1940 Rudolf Rogler, professor and acting director of the Hochschule für Baukunst und bildende Künste, and his wife moved into the house, but they soon thereafter left Weimar. During the war the house was taken over by the local government and used by the chief of agricultural production in the region, known for its fertile potato, onion, and cabbage fields much needed at the front. He fled on April 12, 1945, the day after nearby Buchenwald was liberated by American forces. The housekeeper, Frau Haupt, who had taken care of the home since the Neuferts lived there, writes that American soldiers, and later the Soviets, left it in a "disastrous state."[30]

After both his Berlin office and his apartment at Lennéstrasse, near the Tiergarten, were bombed, Neufert found temporary refuge in Mittweida, the town where his ex-wife and his children lived. On April 24, 1945, Neufert wrote a letter from Gelmeroda (we could presume he was back in his house), in which he gave a lengthy biographical account of his life and work during the war—facts for which only his second wife could provide testimony.[31] He probably met friends, colleagues, and delegates of the new authorities in those last days of the war. In June 1945 representatives of the new education authority—still under the control of the American military government—invited Neufert to become the director for a "new Bauhaus."[32] Neufert confirms later that he had been asked to run the school but turned down the position shortly after the Soviets assumed control of Thuringia in July to take a position at the Technical University in Darmstadt.[33] Before leaving Gelmeroda, his last order of business in this part of Germany might have been to engage a caretaker for the house. In September 1945 Neufert wrote from Darmstadt to construction engineer Karl Zweimüller, asking him to oversee the house, giving precise instructions on how to manage the rent and send fruit from the garden, precious at that time, to Mittweida and, later, all the way to Darmstadt.

Toward the end of 1945 a German family returning from Czechoslovakia rented the house. But they soon had to share it with a dentist who had moved into the ground floor after Zweimüller promised that the house would be made available exclusively for his family and medical practice. Soon the respective tenants began to argue, starting with the distribution of garden fruit and escalating, as was common in those days, into intense political polemics. In February 1946 the caretaker wrote to Neufert that the tenants believed the property was a "political property"—a category that in the Soviet-occupied zone allowed for its confiscation due to the status of an absent owner who was a suspected former Nazi. Neufert replied immediately in a series of detailed letters accounting for his wartime actions by affirming that they were purely professional in nature and reiterating his political neutrality.

These long letters were well composed, neatly typed, and copied, allowing the historian to reconstruct a nearly complete trail of correspondence in which Neufert gives long biographical accounts. In this same era he was compelled to write many such curriculum vitae as part of application forms, social insurance documents, and pension schemes, but whereas institutions requested these lists in bullet points the letters give a more detailed and intimate view of his adopted perspective on history than an institutional addressee would expect. Thus we have this type of account only for the house in Gelmeroda.

Clearly keen to defend himself, Neufert claims to be a victim of National Socialism, citing the loss of his professorship in 1930. He emphasizes that he was unemployed since he was not permitted to enter the Reichskulturkammer because of his affiliations with the Bauhaus, and that he wrote the *Bauentwurfslehre* because no secure position could be found for him in Germany.[34]

16

16 Roofing ceremony for Neufert House in 1929, photographer unknown.
17 Note about a dream from Ernst Neufert's diary, dated January 11, 1946.

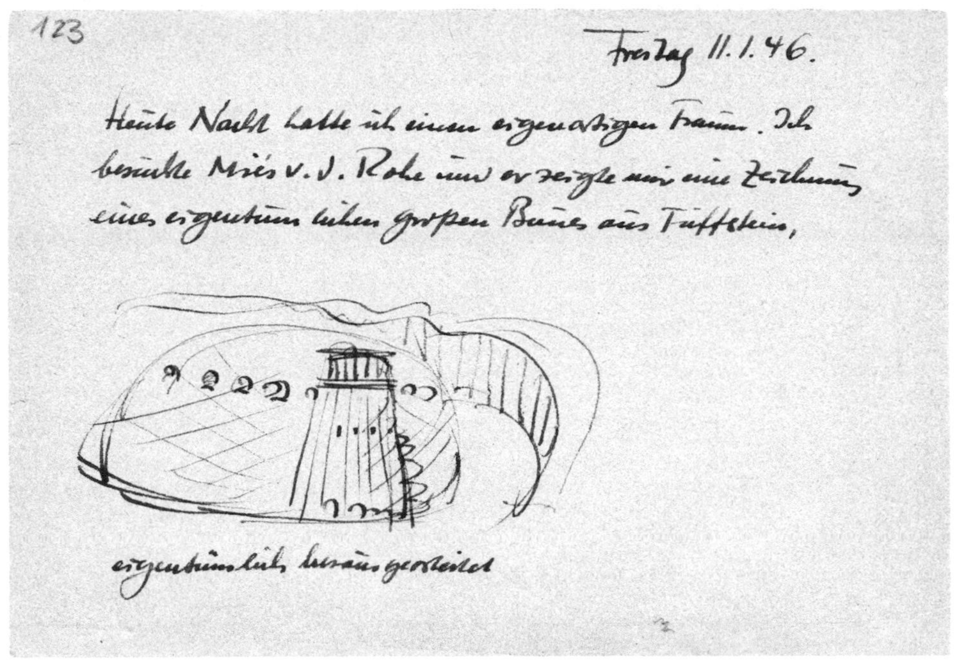
Freitag 11.1.46.

Heute Nacht hatte ich einen eigenartigen Traum. Ich besuchte Mies v. d. Rohe und er zeigte mir eine Zeichnung eines eigentümlichen großen Raumes aus Tuffstein,

17

In another letter he highlights that he published pieces in *Bauwelt Magazine* which belonged to the Jewish-owned Ullstein publishing house. He did not mention—or more likely he was ignorant of the realities around him—that in 1934 the Ullstein family was forced to emigrate after having their property expropriated with the publishing house "Arianized" and annexed to the Volk und Reich Verlag.[35] Neufert also emphasized his relations with other Jews: his assistant, Brigitte Bräuning, was "one-quarter Jewish" (in itself a Nazi designation), and he mentions his collaborator Konrad Sage, who was "half-Jewish," and whose deportation in 1943 "made him very angry."[36] He mentioned, of course, that in 1936, three years into Nazi rule, he published the *Bauentwurfslehre* with works by Jewish, American, and Russian architects, ignoring Nazi censorship. He did not mention the *Bauordnungslehre* or any of the works produced in Berlin for the ministry under Albert Speer.[37]

Soon the arguments between the tenants escalated further, and we read that the dentist thinks the other tenant is an "alcoholic who beats his children," that he would illegally "house his parents for long-term stays," and that he claimed to police that the homeowner was a former Nazi[38]—an accusation the dentist "despises" yet nonetheless obliges Neufert to respond with the long biographic letters.[39] Both parties ask for a proper contract, but it could not be arranged in the absence of the owner. In February 1947 the police searched the house and found a Nazi uniform in one of the cupboards. Even if Neufert wore such a uniform in his Berlin years, it couldn't have belonged to him. Finally, as the owner of the building was "absent"—being on the other side of Germany was legally considered thus—the house came under the "protection" of the administration of the German Democratic Republic, under a law released in 1952.[40]

After the reunification of Germany the house was returned to the Neufert family, who made it the basis of the Neufert Foundation, reconstructing its original features to the extent possible. However, the house is not well visited; it does not succeed in telling its own story, and there is so much to tell: the thick folder in the archive could be the source of a novel rather than an academic paper.

Afterword

Researchers also have access to Neufert's diary in the Weimar archive. In contrast to the orderliness of the rest of his documents, these personal notes are less coherent, consisting of index cards with notes for lectures, collections of citations of Goethe and Nietzsche, numerous drafts of CVs, and a few sketches.

Even in the best archives there are always things that do not fit into a particular organization system, even for an order fanatic like Neufert. The strange history of the house is certainly one such element that does not conform. Yet, as Michel Foucault taught us, it is precisely by looking at the thing that does not fit that one can understand the norm. And in a story about norms, it is precisely the nonstandard that may prove most relevant.

Among these loose document files I noticed another thing that, like the remarkable history of the house, seems to fall out of the archive's system of classification. On January 11, 1946, Neufert—who rarely got personal in his diary, which resembles more of a crossed-out schedule, and certainly never wrote about his dreams—recorded the following: "Tonight I had a bizarre dream. I went to see Mies v.d. Rohe and he showed me a drawing of a peculiar space made of tuffstone." The note goes along with a sketch in which we recognize vertical lines, perhaps a fence, and a stone tower with a small window, like a watchtower. The sketch is annotated with "strangely carved out."

I do not want to suggest a reading without access to a source that can confirm it. However, the note seems to indicate that his former colleagues were still on his mind, and that he may even have tried to get in touch with them. He also seems to have been familiar with the architecture of fences and watchtowers, and perhaps, like Mies, had other skeletons in his closet. But given the state of his archive and biographical notes, Neufert seems to have covered these tracks.

1 This paper was partially presented under the title "Alter Kram: Nachträge zum Werk Ernst Neuferts in Weimar," at the international symposium "Ernst Neufert in Weimar," organized by Jörg Stabenow and Ines Weizman at the Bauhaus-Universität Weimar, on April 29, 2014. I would like to thank Christiane Wolf and Petra Goertz, of the Archiv der Moderne at the Bauhaus-Universität Weimar; Nicole Delmes and Heike Sterner, of the Neufert Foundation; and architects Mrs. and Mr. Mittmann, who were kind enough to share their insights and documents on Ernst Neufert with me. Thanks also to Niclas Zimmer, who prepared a photographic essay for this research on the house in Gelmeroda, of which a selection accompanies this essay.

2 For more on the teaching curriculum, see Nader Vossoughian, "Standardization Reconsidered: Normierung in and after Ernst Neufert's *Bauentwurfslehre* (1936)," *Grey Room* 54 (Winter 2014): 34–55.

3 Michael Siebenbrodt, "Zwischen Tradition und Moderne: Haus Neufert in Gelmeroda 1929," in *Das andere Bauhaus: Otto Bartning und die Staatliche Bauhochschule Weimar 1926–1930* (Berlin: Bauhaus-Archiv, Museum für Gestaltung, 1996), 75–80.

4 In his later work and writing, while aiming to synthesize human measures and the metric system, he developed the octameter system—a measure that results from the division of a meter into eight and calculates at .125 meters.

5 N/55/66.4 II, Archiv der Moderne, Bauhaus-Universität Weimar.

6 See Ernst Neufert's curriculum vitae, N/52/66.4, Archiv der Moderne, Bauhaus-Universität Weimar.

7 *Bauentwurfslehre* was reissued eleven times before the end of the war and many times since 1945. The reference projects mentioned here were replaced by new projects in post-1945 revisions updating the data collections in the book. Neufert still oversaw the revisions of the book until shortly before his death.

8 Gustav Hassenpflug worked in Neufert's office between 1934 and '41 and participated in the revision and updating of its data. After his collaboration with Neufert he became known for furniture designs that would fit the standardized interiors in Neufert's housing plans.

9 Wolfgang Voigt mentioned some of these examples in Walter Prigge, ed., *Ernst Neufert: normierte Baukultur im 20. Jahrhundert*, (Frankfurt/New York: Campus, 1999), 23.

10 Alan Balfour, *Berlin: The Politics of Order 1737–1989* (New York: Rizzoli, 1990), 107–52.

11 Alan Balfour, "The New Berlin: A Haus, Not a Prison," New York *Times*, May 2, 1999.

12 The first edition of *Bauentwurfslehre* after the war, published in 1954, still retains the Columbus House as an example, though it was then half in ruins between the sectors, used by an East Berlin co-op, and the focus of the 1951 uprising. When the wall was built ten years later, it was caught in a no man's land and became a party spot for the punk scene of the 1980s. By that time it was no longer in the book.

13 In Summer 1932 Neufert had traveled to Moscow, where he gave a lecture about modern housing structures in timber. It is likely that he also visited the Narkomfin housing estate.

14 The Narkomfin Building still stands derelict today since Moscow's municipality has not put forth much effort to preserve this avant-garde design.

15 Whether Le Corbusier got the idea for this type of organization, which he used in his Unité d'Habitation, during his visit to Moscow in 1928 (when the building was just commissioned for construction) or from "the Neufert" is unknown.

16 Cornelis van Eesteren was professor of urbanism in Otto Bartning's Weimar school between 1927 and '30.

17 In Palestine Alexander Klein would become an influential architect for settlements and direct the architecture faculty at the Technion, in Haifa.

18 Mies's project for the House in 2000, a plan he presented in 1931 as the "Apartment for a Bachelor" at the German Buildings Exhibition in Berlin, is included in the book. Although it did not quite fit the ideas for building elements and minimal housing, it seems that Neufert was fond of the plan and wanted to pay respect to the third director of the Bauhaus. Perhaps he even aspired to living in such a house, for he was a bachelor at that time, too.

19 The commission for a house for Kindt, together with that for factory buildings and other housing projects, came from a recommendation by Wilhelm Wagenfeld, a former colleague of Neufert at the Bauhaus, later supervisor of the metal workshops at Bartning's Bauhochschule and from 1935, artistic director for the glass factory.

20 The book is dedicated to his sons, Peter and Ilas. Peter would also become an architect and collaborate with his father.

21 Helmut Maier, *Chemiker im "Dritten Reich": Die Deutsche Chemische Gesellschaft* (Weinheim: Wiley-VCH Verlag, 2015), 381.

22 In a biographical account written at Gelmeroda in April 1945, Neufert emphasized that he was not employed in the ministry but only worked as a freelancer and researcher, and that he never took commissions from the National Socialist party. In this letter he also claims that in all his time at the ministry he met "Professor Speer" only once, for five minutes. Letter from Ernst Neufert to Dr. Vogler, Gelmeroda, April 24, 1945, N/55/66.4 II, Archiv der Moderne, Bauhaus-Universität Weimar.

23 English translations: "The Octameter System," "Bomb-Proof Air Defense in Housing Construction," "Plans for a Wartime Unit Typology," and "Principles of Building Regulations."

24 In correspondence with Karl M. Hettlage, lead staff in the administration of Generalbaudirektor für die Reichshauptstadt, Neufert's freelance employment at the ministry is specified in that from January 1, 1942, he was only to take commissions from Professor Speer, Walter Brugmann, another manager in the administration of Generalbaudirektor, and Hettlage himself—all of whom had certainly participated in the expulsion of Jews in Berlin. Letter from K. M. Hettlage to Ernst Neufert, Berlin, September 29, 1941, N/55/66.5, Archiv der Moderne, Bauhaus-Universität Weimar. See also Susanna Schrafstetter, "Verfolgung und Wiedergutmachung. Karl M. Hettlage: Mitarbeiter von Albert Speer und Staatssekretär im Bundesfinanzministerium," *Vierteljahreshefte für Zeitgeschichte* 56 (2008): 431–66.

25 Neufert also worked as an architect for industrial and other planned structures (such as underground hangars and bunkers), which required not only an enormous workforce but also inhumane working conditions. One can assume that in 1943 he already counted on the manpower made available through forced labor. See Norbert Korrek's unpublished paper "...zumal ich sowieso als 'Bauhausmann' mit meiner Architektur als amerikanisch oder bolschewistisch verschrien war." "Ernst Neufert im Jahr 1945," from the international symposium "Ernst Neufert in Weimar."

26 *Bauordnungslehre* (Berlin: Volk und Reich Verlag, 1943), 471.

27 Letter from Ernst Neufert to Dr. Vogler, Gelmeroda, April 24, 1945, N/55/66.4 II, Archiv der Moderne, Bauhaus-Universität Weimar. Letter from Ernst Neufert to Dr. Th. Erich, 12.2.1947, N/52/66.4, Archiv der Moderne, Bauhaus-Universität Weimar.

28 N/55/66.4 II, Archiv der Moderne, Bauhaus-Universität Weimar.

29 Siebenbrodt, "Zwischen Tradition und Moderne," 79.

30 Letter from Mrs. Haupt to Ernst Neufert and his wife, 9.6.1946, N/52/66.4, Archiv der Moderne, Bauhaus-Universität Weimar.

31 Letter from Ernst Neufert to Dr. Vogler, Gelmeroda, April 24, 1945, N/55/66.4 II, Archiv der Moderne, Bauhaus-Universität Weimar.

32 Norbert Korrek, "Zur Bauhaus-Rezeption an der Weimarer Hochschule von 1945 bis 1979," in ed. Frank Simon-Ritz, Klaus-Jürgen Winkler, and Gerd Zimmermann, *Aber wir sind! Wir wollen! Und wir schaffen! Von der Großherzoglichen Kunstschule zur Bauhaus-Universität Weimar 1860–2010* (Weimar: Band 1, 2010), 179.

33 Korrek, "Zur Bauhaus-Rezeption." See also reference to a CV typed by Neufert, April 26, 1946, in Werner Durth, "Im Sog des Erfolgs. Biographische Verflechtungen," in Prigge, *Ernst Neufert*, 49.

34 However, in a 1947 letter to his tenant Dr. Th. Erich, Neufert writes that only when previews of his *Bauentwurfslehre* were published and widely welcomed in Germany in 1934–35 was he allowed to become a member of the Reichskammer der Bildenden Künste (Reich Chamber of Fine Arts). Rather than being produced "despite his exclusion," his work on the data collection allowed him to enter the establishment. Letter from Ernst Neufert to Dr. Th. Erich, 12.2.1947, N/52/66.4, Archiv der Moderne, Bauhaus-Universität Weimar.

35 In October 1933 the publishing house offered Neufert a voucher to travel to Great Britain. On the expropriation of the publishing house, see also Hermann Ullstein, *The Rise and Fall of the House of Ullstein* (New York: Simon and Schuster, 1943).

36 Letter from Ernst Neufert to Dr. Vogler, Gelmeroda, April 24, 1945, N/55/66.4 II, Archiv der Moderne, Bauhaus-Universität Weimar. Konrad Sage managed to escape a forced labor camp, and in June 1945 he became professor at the Hochschule für Bildende Künste in Berlin.

37 Durth, "Im Sog des Erfolgs."

38 Letter from Dr. Th. Erich to Ernst Neufert, 4.2.1947, N/52/66.4, Archiv der Moderne, Bauhaus-Universität Weimar.

39 Letter from Ernst Neufert to Dr. Th. Erich, 12.2.1947, N/52/66.4, Archiv der Moderne, Bauhaus-Universität Weimar.

40 Letter from Karl Zweimüller to Dorle Illgen (Neufert's mother-in-law), Weimar, 24.11.1952, N/52/66.4, Archiv der Moderne, Bauhaus-Universität Weimar.

"Art is situated exactly at this midpoint: it deals neither with origins nor with creation *ex novo* but with the distance traversed between the model and its modern repetition."

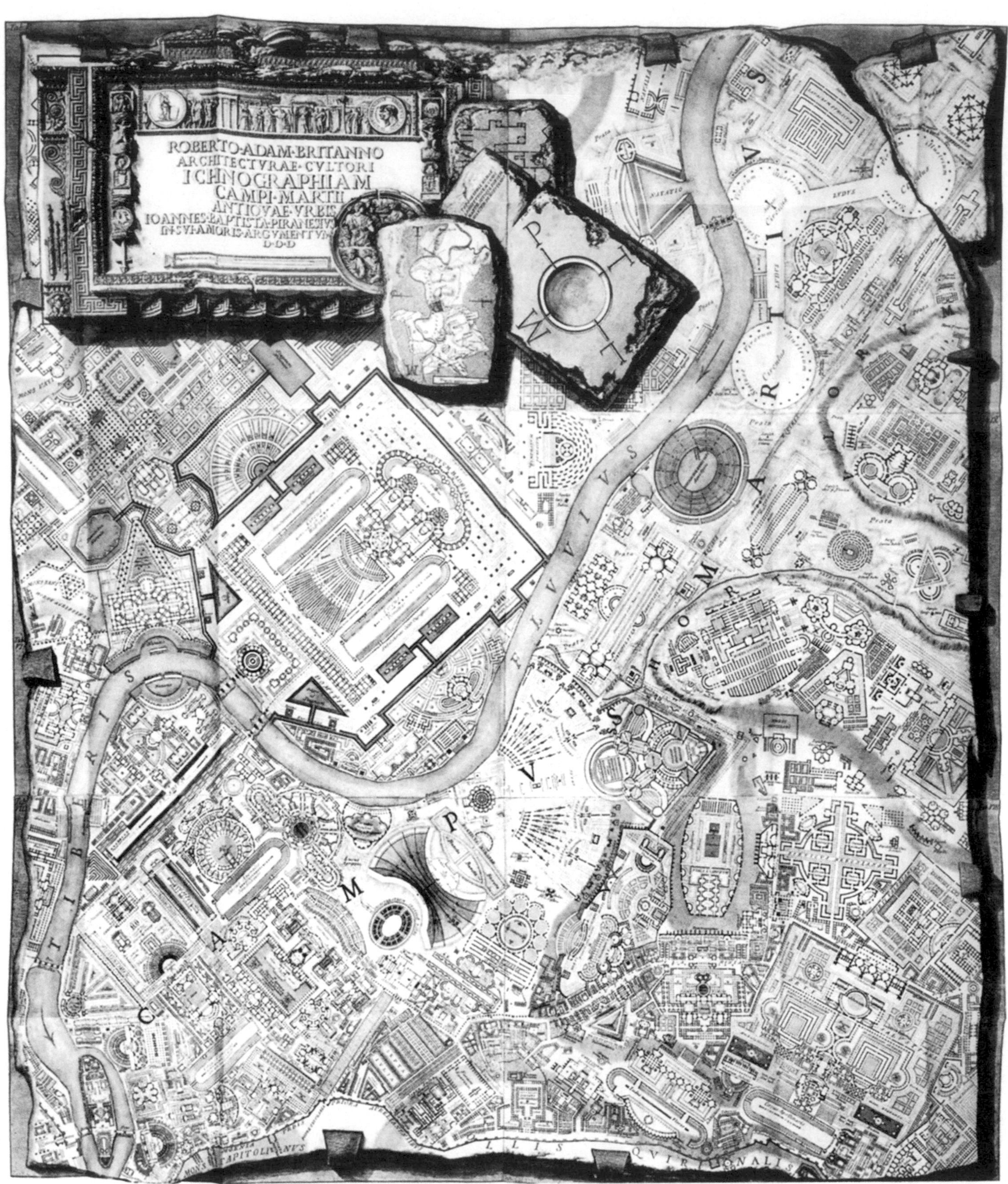

Giovanni Battista Piranesi, *Campo Marzio dell'antica Roma*, 1762.

Demetri Porphyrios

Art and Architecture as Palimpsest

> An artificial novelty is never so effective as a repetition that manages to suggest a fresh truth.
> —Marcel Proust
> *Remembrance of Things Past*

Quotation, imitation, representation, play, and recognition are not merely copies or second-rate versions. They all refer, in different ways, to educational and learning practices. "It is a rule of life that we should copy what we approve in others," Quintilian writes in his *Institutio Oratoria*. "Children copy the shapes of letters so that they may learn to write, musicians take the voice of their teachers, painters take the works of their predecessors... as models for their imitation."[1]

Aristotle writes in his *Poetics* that "imitation is natural to man from childhood [since] man learns at first by imitation ... The reason why men enjoy seeing a likeness is that they find themselves learning or inferring and saying perhaps, 'Ah, that is he.'"[2] It is this emotional delight that accompanies the pleasure of recognition of what is true *for us* that becomes the chief factor in the enjoyment of play and of the arts. Imitation (*mimesis*) seems to suggest, therefore, that art is a form of knowledge that serves to deepen our understanding of ourselves, and thus our familiarity with the world.

In what fashion does art speak to us? How does art disclose the truth of the world to us? Aristotle emphasizes the idea of likeness (*homeioma*) in art and thereby extricates artistic imitation from the notion of reduplication. This is an obvious point, and yet so often we tend to forget the necessary distance that artistic likeness demands. The identical repetition of a model can occur only in mechanical cloning, and for that reason it does not afford us pleasure. Instead artistic imitation "represents reality by means of an image," as Quatremère de Quincy writes.[3] The aim of art is not to deceive but to represent. In that sense, the difference between kitsch and art is that kitsch simulates as compensation for that which is not (Theodor Adorno), whereas art imitates in order to distance itself from that which is and thereby throw new light onto it. This distance is not a sign of ineptitude on the part of the artist but rather a crucial characteristic of artistic production. By distancing the artifact from its model, the artist invites us to see what we have never seen before, pointing out a relevance that might otherwise have gone unnoticed. The distance that art establishes between the world and the images it fabricates is at the very core of the experience of recognizing the new and relevant that art offers us. In this sense the Formalist theory of *ostranenie*, with its emphasis on the cognitive function of defamiliarization, is by no means incompatible with the aesthetics of imitation. The pleasure of recognition that art affords us is the very pleasure we feel when art opens up for us a new access to the world, free from simulation and all stifling commonplaces.

Aristotle frees artistic imitation from the burden of the literal transcription of material reality, to which Plato had tended to restrict it. Art must not only not imitate things as they are but also be concerned with things as they "ought to be." The example of the Maidens of Croton is pertinent here. When the citizens of Croton commissioned Zeuxis to paint a cult image of Venus, he chose not one model but the five most beautiful maidens of the city so that he could represent in his painting the most praiseworthy features in each of them and make, therefore, an image of Venus as "it ought to be."

This way the work of art may exist between the example and the precept. It represents a universal truth by imitating particular examples chosen for their typicality. This is not to say that a general idea is embodied in a particular example, but rather that the particular case is generalized by artistic treatment. No doubt this is what Goethe meant when he wrote that "a special case requires nothing but the treatment of a poet to become universal."[4] I must sidestep for a moment and respond to recent criticism of the aesthetics of imitation. Imitation, recent deconstructionists have argued, is essentially dependent on *doxa*, that is, on "points of view." Such points of view ultimately converge in common sense, formulate social identities, and thereby become prejudiced "plots" of legitimation.

The realization that art is always ideological is no news; Karl Marx and Friedrich Nietzsche have argued this point convincingly. What the deconstructionists underestimate, however, is that this point of view of ideology is the only access we have to social life. Without our own points of view the world around us would be unintelligible. It is one thing to criticize those who boast that their point of view is uniquely privileged and another to conclude that no point of view can ever be taken on account of paranoia of closure. At any rate, I know of no real achievement (I am speaking of the world of art) that was not based on some point of view. "And even if that were a failing, why is this failure always present when anything is achieved?"[5] Again and again we find that art does more than engage us in ideological debate. Art takes the point of view (*doxa*) of everyday life and gives us back fictional narratives (*mythos*) that have cognitive roles in social life. In other words, art questions the very assumptions of ideology by recognizing both its necessity and its pretentions. That is why art has more to do with freedom than with dogma. And that is the sense in which we can say that art tells the "truth" and never conspires to deceive.

Greek antiquity, from Aristotle to Isocrates, formulated both the pedagogic and artistic aspects of the theory of imitation. With the decline of Greece and the ascent of Rome, however, oratory, philosophy, and the arts had to deal with change. And though there was a clear sense that tradition must be maintained, this required innovation and therefore some degree of rejection. Dionysius of Halicarnassus was perhaps the first Greek author who, feeling a sense of cultural void, addressed the subject of the imitation of models. His view was that the poet/artist should imitate many models since no single model can ever embody all virtues.

The strongest argument in favor of imitating many models at once was that made by Cicero in *De Inventione*: "When I set out to write a book on rhetoric I did not choose one model... but after collecting all the works on the subject, I excerpted what seemed the most suitable precepts from each, and so culled the flower of many minds."[6] Poetic, and by extension artistic, works must always borrow and renovate quotations from other works. "Intellectual activity," Wilhelm von Humboldt writes, "is constantly diverted toward something already given."[7] The poet/artist "culls the flower of many minds" as a way to bridge the generational and cultural gap that loss and decay bring. Skills, ideas, and cultural values are transmitted from generation to generation through careful study and observation of precedents. And as Rome looked at Hellenic culture for its models, it set out to preserve and breathe new life into the threatened continuities.

Virgil's *Aeneid* is the highest achievement in the project of cultural reanimation. Following the sack of Troy, Aeneas escaped, carrying his father and household Gods, and eventually arrived in Latium. Years later his great-grandson Brutus, during his voyage in exile, founded the cities of Tours and Troynovant ("New Troy"), which King Lud was to rename London. Descendants of other Trojan princes followed the example of Brutus, founder of Britain and Brittany, in establishing various European nations. The tale of the Trojan descent had a clear advantage over the biblical story of the descent from Noah. Aeneas of Troy became the cultural ancestor of Europe exactly because he represented an origin that had to be destroyed, thus requiring the mediation of exile and reconstruction.

Or, consider the position Christianity adopted toward pagan artistic traditions. By the ninth century the iconoclastic movement that attacked the veneration of images was ultimately rejected. The decision to embrace once again the techniques of representational language gave a new impetus to Christian art, and was justified, in the eyes of the Church, because pictorial narration of the Bible made the Christian message accessible to the illiterate masses.

We may also look at the example of the Renaissance humanists. They stressed the claim of their poets to choose their own models from Greco-Roman antiquity and paraphrase rather than copy verbatim. In this way they set out to reconstruct an antiquity that suited the fifteenth century, thereby controlling the transmission of tradition. An awareness of discontinuity and the sense of loss of the past was a common element amid humanists in Italy and throughout Europe. Each new work, as it were, set out to bridge this gap and reconstruct its own antiquity.

In the educational treatises of Desiderius Erasmus, verbatim repetition is rated below paraphrase, but still higher is imitation, which alone can bridge the gap between antiquity and the Renaissance, thereby providing a model for continuity. For Petrarch, and later for Poliziano, imitation meant remembering but also modernizing and bringing antiquity up to date (*aggiornamento*). Thus Renaissance humanism distinguishes itself from antiquity and finds its own voice, emphasizing its distance from its precedent and by extension proclaiming its own modernity.

Another aspect in the Renaissance practice of imitation is whether to draw upon a single master or a number of select precedent works. Conscious as he was of the break between antiquity and the Renaissance, Poliziano proposed to integrate the style of multiple models of the past, emphasizing the creative freedom of imitation and thus advocating a restoration that points out its contemporaneity.

A parallel can be seen in Renaissance architecture. It is extraordinary how many architects—from Alberti and Bramante to Palladio—devoted years studying the ruins of Rome. Surely this was a preparatory exercise for designing their buildings, but it appears that the ruins had an inspiring effect as well. Giorgio Vasari mentions in his *Opere* that Filippo Brunelleschi "was capable of seeing Rome as it stood before it fell."[8] A century later, in his *Four Books on Architecture*, Andrea Palladio boasts that "though some of these [ancient] temples have very little to show above ground... I have made my conjecture about how they must have been when they were entire."[9] In the ruins of antiquity Renaissance humanists saw the new city to come. Surely Hegel, writing in his *Philosophy of History* centuries later, identifies a similar creative inspiration prompted by ruins: "When travelling among the ruins of Carthage, of Palmyra, Persepolis, or Rome... [we feel regret] but also at the same time the rise of a new life."[10]

Luigi Rossini, *Frontespizio delle Antichita Romane*, 1823.

L.F. Cassas, *Ruines D'un Arc de Triomphe a Palmyre*, 1799.

Hegel's claim that art is a thing of the past refers to the realization that, with the close of antiquity, art lost its divine authority and inevitably required justification. It is precisely because all men and women are rational, the Enlightenment argued, that they can exercise their own judgment unfettered by tradition and without recourse to any sort of authority. To invoke tradition or pay allegiance to authority, therefore, was seen by the Enlightenment as an entrapment in prejudice.

A similar fate awaited the tradition of classical antiquity. A useful convention of cultural history has been to have the Enlightenment begin with the *Querelle des Anciens et des Modernes* (Quarrel of the Ancients and the Moderns), a debate that questioned for the first time the normative status granted exclusively to the idea of natural beauty and the art and literature of classical antiquity. I say "useful convention" because this view grossly underestimates the contribution of other periods to the problem of break versus continuity with the ancients. Consider, for example, the practices of *inventio* in Roman oratory, of the *translatio studii* in Medieval scholasticism, of the Renaissance *renovatio* of antiquity, or of the sixteenth-century Ciceronian Quarrel. They all bear precisely on the question of whether absolute models can be selected from antiquity and to what extent tradition can be a source of inspiration or a futile constraint. In spite of these qualifications, it remains true that the Enlightenment differed from all these attitudes in one characteristic way: it decided everything before the judgment of reason and saw the authority of the ancients as a source of prejudice.

When Claude Perrault questioned the classical belief in "absolute beauty" and the authority of the ancients, he did not intend to provoke François Blondel and the architectural establishment, let alone the court of Louis XIV. In fact, it was Jean-Baptiste Colbert, minister in the king's court and purveyor of artisan production in France, who seemed to have given official support to the written and built work of Perrault. As a medical scientist, Perrault could not justify "the religious reverence of architects for works of antiquity,"[11] nor could he agree with the classical precept of absolute beauty. And since the architectural establishment eschewed any "rational" response to his critical challenge, he declared that "beauty has hardly any other foundation than *fantaisie*," that is chance, fancy, or custom.[12] By the second half of the seventeenth century no scientist or philosopher would doubt the authority of modern science over that of the ancients. Nicolas Malebranche, in his *De la recherche de la vérité*, found the authority of the ancients wanting since they "were men like us and of the same species as we."[13] From then on, in the sciences, only reason counted, not authority. The authority of the ancients was seen as a prejudice, and by the end of the eighteenth century the general feeling was that tradition was tainted by covert guile. Thus "quoting" an authority gradually became associated with making a false judgment—or at least it carried no weight other than the privilege of education and social provenance that name-dropping imparts to the beholder.

We must not forget, however, that judgment (*krinein*) is always a matter of dividing and selecting. In order to sift material under examination, we must form a preliminary view—a prejudgment (*prokrisis*). Such a prejudgment is not a false judgment. This is seen clearly in education when a student projects his or her own reading (prejudice) and thereby transforms the teacher's intended statement. All art and interpretation plays upon this oscillation between prejudice (prejudgment) and understanding.

The patterns of behavior and thinking we adopt in everyday life are ostensibly prejudgments on so many practical and theoretical issues. Such prejudgments are useful to us since they outline the conventions of our everyday life (social, artistic, linguistic, mathematical, scientific, historical). In art and architecture the study of conventions is based on analogy of form. When we formulate the question this way, two considerations become important: convention and originality.

It is clear that any building may be studied not only as an imitation of the world and of construction, but as an imitation of other buildings as well. Virgil thought, Alexander Pope reminds us, that imitating nature was ultimately the same thing as imitating Homer. Once we think of a building in relation to other buildings, we can see that a great part of creative design addresses the formation and transformation of conventions. All art and architecture is equally conventionalized, but we do not notice this because such conventions are always meant to appear natural and universal, otherwise their role as the binding "cement" of society would be undermined. In fact conventions can best be studied when one travels, for unless we are unaccustomed to the conventions of a country they do not stand out. The same is true with the conventions of art and architecture.

Today, however, the conventional element in architecture is elaborately disguised. Consider, for example, the early Modernist slogan "down with conventions, long live the free spirit of experimentation." Though such slogans were useful in the formative period of the early twentieth century, they became meaningless once Modernist architecture was established. There have been, of course, a few for whom modernity meant a permanent state of crisis, and according to this view architecture is always *in extremis*. And yet even the recent deconstructionist mood of transgression relies heavily on the conventional element and on quotation. In fact deconstruction does not deny the conventional element; it simply suspends the conventional meaning or introduces an ever-transforming state of "assemblages, rhizomes, or networks" that must always remain by necessity incomplete.[14]

There is another factor that disguises the importance of the conventional element in architecture today: copyright laws. It is by no means coincidental that the disciplines of art and architectural history appear for the first time in the period of post-Enlightenment modernity. Imitation (*mimesis*) had for millennia been the epistemological framework of classical culture, from Mesopotamia, Egypt, China, and the Greco-Roman world to Byzantium, the Middle Ages, and the Renaissance. We have seen how with the advent of the Enlightenment the "natural" practice of imitation progressively lost its epistemological strength. For the first time "borrowing" from the millennial human knowledge and experience had to be clearly identified as "quotation" lest the copy were mistaken for the original. Copyright laws were soon introduced to regulate and safeguard authorship, and thereby the inalienable "moral" rights of the artist.

As we all know, the market ethic of the original and the authentic is based on the pretense that every work of art is an invention singular enough to be patented. Ironically this state of affairs would make it difficult to appraise an architectural tradition that includes, say, Palladio, much of whose architecture is paraphrased from others, or Karl Friedrich Schinkel, whose buildings sometimes follow their sources almost verbatim. The comparison between the Villa Malcontenta and the Villa Stein, at Garches, comes to mind. And though this particular example might be admirable exactly because it is so far-fetched, Colin Rowe made us see that Le Corbusier's building remains in part unintelligible if we do not recognize Palladio in it. Similarly if we turn to poetry for a moment, I am reminded of John Milton, who asked for nothing better than to borrow the whole of the Bible.

Let me qualify this observation. Borrowing here does not mean reproducing. The distance between a new work and the model that has inspired it is indeed always the hallmark of creative talent, pointing out the contemporaneity of a work. An artist is said to be original exactly when he or she takes up the challenge of tradition and makes us see something more than we already know. Originality, and thus the modern itself, consists of this distance between the new and the model, as the new emplots itself within a tradition. Doubtless some would argue that the new has no tradition whatsoever. Derrida's *itérabilité*, for example, refers exactly to such an aimless "drift" inherent in all language.

Cut off from any sense of home base, language is meandering away from any origins and from all cultural and social meaning. Neither the forms of art nor the words of language, however, are "orphaned" (as Derrida would have them), but they always acquire parenthood in the context of the tradition that adopts them. Art is situated exactly at this midpoint: it deals neither with origins nor with creation *ex novo* but with the distance traversed between the model and its modern repetition. It is precisely this distance traversed between the model and its modern repetition that art quite consciously confronts and builds into the artifact. "You must ransack the old. But for a building," Ludwig Wittgenstein reminds us.[15] That is why art points to a dependence on the models it conditionally overcomes so that it may formulate its own modernity.

1 Quintilian, *Institutio Oratoria*, trans, H.E. Butler (Cambridge: Harvard University Press, 1922), 10.2.1-2

2 Aristotle, *The Poetics*, Ch. 4

3 Antoine-Chrysostome Quatremère De Quincy, *An Essay on the Nature, the End and the Means of Imitation*, trans. J. C. Kent (London: Smith, Elder and Co., 1837).

4 Johann Wolfgang Von Goethe, *The Wisdom of Goethe*, ed. John Stuart Blackie (New York: C. Scribner's Sons, 1883).

5 Hans-Georg Gadamer, *Truth and Method* (New York: Seabury Press, 1975).

6 Marcus Tullius Cicero, *De Inventione. De Optimo Genere Oratorum. Topica.*, trans H. M. Hubbell (Cambridge: Harvard University Press, 1949), 2.2

7 Wilhelm von Humboldt, *Linguistic Variability and Intellectual Development*, trans. G.C. Buck and F.A. Raven (Coral Gables: University of Miami Press, 1971).

8 Giorgio Vasari, *The Lives of the Artists*, trans. George Bull (Harmondsworth: Penguin Books, 1987).

9 Andrea Palladio, *The Four Books of Architecture*, trans. Isaac Ware (London: R. Ware, 1755).

10 Georg Hegel, *Lectures on the The Philosophy of History*, trans. John Sibree (London: G. Bell and Sons, 1914).

11 Claude Perrault, *Ordonnance Des Cinq Especes De Colonnes Selon La Methode Des Anciens* (Paris: J.B. Coignard, 1683).

12 Wolfgang Herrmann, *The Theory of Claude Perrault* (London: A. Zwemmer, 1973).

13 Nicolas Malebranche, *De La Recherche De La Vérité* (Paris: E. Flammarion, 1935).

14 Gilles Deleuze and Félix Guattari, *Mille Plateaux* (Paris: Éditions De Minuit, 1980).

15 Ludwig Wittgenstein, *Culture and Value*, ed. G. H. Von Wright (Chicago: University of Chicago Press, 1980).

"The invention of history does not seek to revive distant pasts but to establish instead a great leap forward, an ideal liberation."

Panayotis Tournikiotis

Quoting the Parthenon: History and the Building of Ideas

1 The Parthenon, 2010 preservation efforts, Athens.

2 The Parthenon reconstructed in

The Parthenon we know today was invented in the eighteenth century and rose to prominence in the Western political, historical, artistic, and architectural system of signification by early in the nineteenth century. Apparently the temple had been standing on top of the Acropolis from the fifth century BC and endured long enough to house the goddess Athena, the Virgin Mary, and a number of mortal princes for more than two thousand years—until it was blown to pieces in 1687, becoming merely an imposing ruin (fig. 1). However, its presence outside of its immediate location was culturally insignificant until then; all but a few words and even fewer inaccurate images can be found in the records. The writers of antiquity barely mention the Parthenon before Plutarch, who calls the works on the Acropolis "proud" and praises them as political achievements of Pericles.[1] The building was symbolically discarded in the Middle Ages, as was the whole world that created it. The Renaissance never turned toward the Parthenon, even at a time when classical sources were being read with the greatest passion; as an exceptional building or a masterpiece, it was all but ignored. By the time Brunelleschi was reinterpreting antiquity in the Duomo of Florence, Athens was a Florentine dominion ruled by the Acciaiuoli family, for whom the old temple served as the ducal palace. The situation did not change much until the end of the seventeenth century, in spite of the increase in European visitors to Athens as well as depictions of the building, all still dominated by the discourse of ancient sources.

The most important turning point in the perception of the Parthenon coincided with changing perceptions on humankind and its situation in the world. From the beginning of the eighteenth century, people cast light upon the obscure past, investing antiquity with the values they needed to justify both their position in the present and their desire to change the world. This resulted in a new order between words and things, and the outcome was a narrative of origins called *history*. This narrative lent ideological support to the political and social discourses of the Enlightenment, which allowed people to see *with their own eyes*, meaning *on their own*, and to decide who is their same and whose world might be the same too. In this *new world*, the emancipated individual constructs and interprets the past in retrospect as a foundation of the present. It so happened that the age that built

rt and Nicholas Revett, *The Antiquities of Athens*, vol. 2, London, 1789–1830.

3 Leo von Klenze, The Walhalla, 1821–42, Regensburg, Germany.

the Parthenon was singled out as a reference point for humankind's future, and the building was identified as the ideal expression of that time.

Of course, this inference did not take place in an instant; it belongs to the long duration of the passage between the seventeenth and nineteenth centuries, when discourse became interchangeable with reason. It emerged from the convergence and overlap of many different approaches in which the leading role was reserved for the sociopolitical, while the material and visible references in the narrative became the appropriate and necessary condition for the domination of discourse. The effective verification of history and the symbolic culmination of this era was marked by the literal transfer of material evidence before the very eyes of reason: transporting fragments of the Parthenon frieze to London and putting them on public display left everyone *speechless*—it *petrified* discourse. The words constructed those same things whose verification the new discourse had consolidated.

The famous sculptor Antonio Canova, who traveled to London to see the Elgin Marbles, is said to have declared at first sight, "It's real flesh," and later declared, "They were superior in style to everything else on earth."[2] Sir Henry Fuseli exclaimed, "The Greeks were Godes!" and Benjamin Robert Haydon concluded that the only way the Greeks could achieve such an effect was "by taking casts from life."[3]

With this accumulation of words, the Parthenon was promoted to the supreme work of architecture in history against which all later significant projects would be compared. This was understood as the "natural" culmination of those collective conditions that found their expression in the common perception of the nation, which included the social and political dimensions of liberty, equality, and democracy, notwithstanding the primacy of the excellent political man, a role that was undertaken by Pericles. The collective conditions of this culmination further included financial and military might, meaning the collective prosperity and power of the citizens, which was an outcome of liberty and democracy, by virtue of which the ancient Greeks were able to defeat the much more powerful yet illiberal Persians.

In Temple Stanyan's *Grecian History*,[4] the first significant historical narrative on ancient Greece (translated in French by Diderot),[5] we read that Pericles "restored and enlarged the

4 William Strickland, The Second Bank of the United States, 1818–24, Philadelphia. Photograph by Cervin Robinson.

Parthenion, or *Temple of Minerva* burnt by the *Persians*; which is said to be even at this Day, both for Matter and Art, the most beautiful Piece of Antiquity remaining in the World."[6] As explained by David Hume in the political essay "On Liberty and Despotism," this culmination was the result of liberty: It had been observed ... that all the Arts and Sciences arose among free nations, and that the *Persians* and *Egyptians*, notwithstanding all their Ease, Opulence and Luxury, made but faint Efforts towards a Relish in those finer Pleasures, which were carried to such Perfection by the *Greeks* ... It had also been observed, that as soon as the *Greeks* lost their Liberty, ... the Arts, from that Moment, declined among them, and have never since been able to raise their Head in that Climate."[7] Almost simultaneously Johann Joachim Winckelmann brought to the foreground the unbroken links between aesthetics, society, and politics in antiquity, describing an ideal synthesis of the arts and architecture with the cultural condition of the nation.[8] The eighteenth century and, even more, the beginning of the nineteenth saw the appearance of a multitude of political and historical treatises that contributed to the establishment of this new awareness. The free, independent, and sovereign Athenians, who decided about their own matters under the guidance of an enlightened leader elected among themselves, were thinking *well* by definition: They were wise and had reasonably developed philosophy. Moreover, they were just, and they were collectively governed by the rule of law, as proven in the case of Socrates. Furthermore, they were creative, freely and ideally expressing their principles in the arts—in poetry, theater, architecture, and sculpture—and excelling in all as a result of their collective condition. Therefore Periclean Athens was the supreme paradigm from the past within the modern narrative of history—the measure of any social and political comparison with the present and the future. The Parthenon was the symbolic culmination of an age, perfection itself standing majestically on top of the Acropolis hill; within that same narrative of history, it was the critical reference and the benchmark for perfect architecture of the future.

The most important and pressing matter then was the documentation and verification of this particular historical construct. Missions of experts would be sent to Athens to study the works of the ancients and bring back the necessary reports for the

5 Alexander Jackson Davis and Ithiel Town, United States Customs House, 1831–42, New York.

6 The Parthenon, Nashville, Tennessee. Built for the

thorough representation of the ideal buildings and, if possible, provide selected physical evidence of the art that would stand as irrefutable proof of its already accepted supremacy. From the mid-seventeenth century Greece, and particularly Athens, was visited by many French and English scholars, who brought back depictions and accounts of the antiquities, most notably of the Parthenon, which they published in monumental books.[9] The most critical contributions, however, were three.

The Englishmen James Stuart and Nicholas Revett stayed in Athens from 1751 to 1754, in the patronage of the Society of Dilettanti; their objective was to accurately measure and represent the *Antiquities of Athens*. Their systematic work was published in five volumes, the first printed in 1762 and the second, covering the Acropolis buildings and the Parthenon, in 1789.[10] Stuart and Revett provided excellent work: their drawings of all the important buildings of Athens were delivered in a succinct yet absolutely accurate manner of great artistic merit down to the smallest details. However, the authors lacked the formal training that would have allowed them to organize those buildings in series or to interpret them within the framework of a new historical narrative. What they provided to the audience instead was an original body of model illustrations that were republished and emulated in the whole of Europe (fig. 2). This model allowed Europeans to get familiar enough with the buildings that their faithful reconstruction, out of place and out of time, was now possible.

In 1755 French architect Julien-David Le Roy traveled to Athens and stayed for seven months. There he undertook the drawing and comparative study of only one type of building: temples. Those were serially classified to highlight the rational connection between the evolution of form and time of construction. The book Le Roy published in 1758 in Paris, *Les ruines des plus beaux monuments de la Grèce considérées du côte de l'histoire et du côté de l'architecture*, did not possess the accuracy of previous publications, neither was its objective to provide graphical models. His interpretation establishes the *history of architecture* with a global outlook, projecting the principles drawn from historical insight upon architectural practice; thus he introduces *history* in *architectural theory*. Within this comprehensive framework, the Parthenon prevails as supreme among all Greek monuments, following the criteria of an architectural history.

1897 Tennessee Centennial and International Exhibition.

7 Robert Mills, The United States Patent Office, 1836, Washington D.C.

The third critical contribution was made by Lord Elgin, ambassador to the Ottoman court of the Sultan in Istanbul: between 1801 and 1805 Elgin removed many sculptures and architectural details from the Parthenon and shipped them to London. The pieces were put on exhibition at the British Museum and were listed among its assets in 1816. This allowed European experts and the public at large to gain firsthand experience of the so-called masterpieces and their indisputable, unsurpassed quality, up to then mediated through the words and images of books. Accurate copies of the originals were acquired by museums and schools in major European cities, allowing for the instruction of art and architecture from the models. The impact was overwhelming, and the iconic Parthenon was fully established in the collective consciousness as an artistic, historic, and architectural ideal.

The invention of history as a retrospective construction of the past and the establishment of the Parthenon as the symbolic expression of the standard of perfection, against which the present would be compared as the projection of a desirable future, opened a vast field of referential creation. The emulation of models and the related anxiety of influence became the expression par excellence of modernity in contemporary art and architecture. In this radical environment—radical because it severs the continuity of the models and establishes prototypes in their place—the *quotation* becomes a structural element of the new architectural discourse. From now on, the reference to an order does not refer to an abstract Doric or Corinthian order but to a specific model in the Parthenon or the Temple of Olympian Zeus. These are precise buildings, with their own time and place of construction, symbolically bearing the social, political, and cultural weight of the people that created them. This was one of the most significant changes in the course of architecture, the result of the invention of history, and it *does not end* with the advent of Modernism—rather, it runs through its rise and decline *in a different way*.

Thus the quotation is a constituent of a new perception of the world, one that grounds the planning of the day to come upon the interpretation of its origin. This is history, either as the different repetition of the referent (a visible similarity) or as a set of fundamental principles that, repeated, produce a similar outcome. The explosive growth of "history" in the beginning of the nineteenth

8 Giovanni Antonio Selva, The Mausoleum of Antonio Canova, 1819, Possagno, Italy.

century and the dispersal of architects around the ancient world (first classical, then medieval, and at times even Islamic) entailed the close study of the originals and the publication of accurate studies illustrated with ideal depictions. During the course of very few years, this activity compiled a vast library and a particularly rich archive of forms, subject to grammatical and syntactic correlations, as well as original exhibits in the new architectural and archaeological museums.[11] These forms, meaningfully intertwined with their referential contexts, created a vast repository of signs that could be retrieved as quotations. Their positioning of buildings and their combinations spoke the contemporary language of history and symbolically expressed the respective ideologies of identity (of a nation, group, or community).

The Parthenon symbolically opened the way toward this direction, providing a wide range of socially, politically, and architecturally recognizable quotations in part or in whole: the portico, the sculptural and architectural details, the construction techniques, polychromy, and the basic principles of composition. I will cite selected examples of references to the Parthenon to highlight the ways in which history, as a discursive construction, changed our thinking about architecture. The first, and most impressive, references to the Parthenon concern the great number of differing repetitions—mostly regarding the interior—to its scale and sculptural ornamentation. These occurred on both sides of the Atlantic, albeit with substantial discrepancies among the things signified.

In 1817, only one year after the official reception of the Elgin Marbles in London and their display at the British Museum, the Parliament of Great Britain decided to erect a national monument in honor of the victories against Napoleon in Trafalgar and Waterloo, considered counterparts to those of the Greeks against the Persians. A proposal to rebuild the Parthenon on the site of Trafalgar Square was considered sensible and was granted approval by Parliament. It was debated extensively in the press and, although designs were made, the project never materialized, mostly for financial reasons.[12]

In 1817 the rebuilding of the Parthenon as a national monument was also prescribed in Edinburgh. In 1824 historian George Cleghorn had proposed placing an equestrian statue of King George IV in front of the monument, suggesting "resemblance, in

9 Henry Bacon, Lincoln Memorial, 1922, Washington, D.C.

character and association of objects, to the Athenian Acropolis, and the Roman Campidoglio."[13] Construction begun in 1826 and came to a halt three years later, mostly due to lack of funding. The architects, Charles Robert Cockerell and William Playfair, were soon called "Phidias" and "Callicrates." The incomplete edifice still stands today atop Calton Hill and is visible from the city of Edinburgh almost as the Parthenon is from the streets of Athens.

In Munich things were taken much further. From as early as 1807 there had been the idea of erecting a national monument to increase morale during the Napoleonic Wars. Interest was renewed after Napoleon's defeat at the Battle of Nations, on October 18, 1813; victory was again compared to the Greek victory against the Persians. In 1814 Carl Haller von Hallerstein sent straight from Athens his drawings for the monument in the form of a Parthenon upon a hill. Finally the edifice was named Walhalla and designed in 1821 by Leo von Klenze as an exact replica of the Parthenon, to be constructed on a hill by the Danube (fig. 3). The foundation stone was cast on October 18, 1830, and the building was inaugurated on the same date in 1842. The frieze displays scenes from German battles and the foundation of the German Confederation in 1815. Inside Valkyries coexist with busts of the most illustrious figures in German history, from Alaric I to Mozart and Goethe.

The almost simultaneous construction of Parthenon models in the United States is a remarkable phenomenon. In 1818 William Strickland won the competition for a building for the Bank of the United States; the project was completed in Philadelphia in 1824 and housed the headquarters and the market room (fig. 4). As explained in a 1827 book on the major landmarks of the city,[14] the structure is a different repetition adjusted to a new use. It should come as no surprise that a bank would emulate the Parthenon: the inner cell of the temple in ancient Athens was the site of the city treasury, later becoming the treasury of the Delian League, which was the confederation of the Greek cities under the tutelage of Athens. It is no coincidence that Benjamin Latrobe's entry for the same competition also proposed a Parthenon-type building.

The form of the Parthenon as a differing repetition was also applied to the Customs House on Wall Street, designed in 1831 by Alexander Jackson Davis and Ithiel Town, and built between 1833 and '42 with a circular hall in the middle (fig. 5). From 1862 to 1920 the building housed the U.S. sub-Treasury and after 1939, the

10 Gottfried Semper, the Doric order of the Parthenon, in *Die Anwendung der Farben in der Architektur und Plastik*, 1836.

DES YEUX QUI NE VOIENT PAS... 107

Cliché Albert Morancé. PARTHÉNON, de 447 à 434 av. J.-C.

faire mieux que l'adversaire *dans toutes les parties*, dans la ligne d'ensemble et dans tous les détails. C'est alors l'étude poussée des parties. Progrès.

Le standart est une nécessité d'ordre apporté dans le travail humain.

Le standart s'établit sur des bases certaines, non pas arbi-

DELAGE, Grand-Sport, 1921.

11 Le Corbusier, the Parthenon and the 1921 Grand Delage, in *Vers une Architecture*, 1923.

Federal Hall national memorial. The same architects designed the Indiana State House, completed in 1835 and demolished in 1877. In that case the building was a Parthenon with a dome over a central circular hall. The peak of these mutations was the construction of a carbon copy of the Parthenon as the centerpiece of the Tennessee Centennial and International Exhibition in Nashville, in 1897 (fig. 6). The building was restored using concrete in the 1920s, with the assistance of William Bell Dinsmoor, as an even more faithful copy of the original equipped with all the sculpture on the pediments and frieze.

The mutations of the Parthenon as quotations are revealing. Testament to its symbolic power is the fact that Parthenon imitations were built in Germany, Britain, and the United States. At the same time, we can trace the transition from the use of the Parthenon-as-quotation in national monuments at a critical juncture for its own self-awareness to uses compatible with particular aspects of the archetype: the storage of treasure (a bank), the seat of democratic government (a parliament), and as symbolic attraction in the zoo of commercial and historical values, as a peculiar lion in Tennessee.

The extraordinary replications of the Parthenon would be supplemented with a broad range of smaller-scale references confined to affixing one of its segments to buildings with different syntactic organizations together with quotations from other buildings. The most celebrated example is the Parthenon's octastyle Doric portico, employed to signify the entrance to various structures. We come across this portico in front of museums, courts of justice, universities, and even homes; it is called upon wherever there is a need for an appeal to higher values, such as those that culminated in the Parthenon of ancient Athens.

A Parthenon portico would lend grandeur to the entrance of the Glyptothek in Munich, whose designs were also sent from Athens by Haller von Hallerstein in 1813. A similar portico, designed by Cockerell in 1816, would grace the entrance to the palace of the Duke of Wellington; another would confer gravitas to the Court of Cassation in Paris—the Supreme Court building depicted in Theodore Labrouste's 1824 competition entry for the Grand Prix de Rome. In all three cases the quotation acquires meaning through the connotations of *history* that located the origins of the modern Western world in Greek and Roman antiquity.

12 Le Corbusier, Villa Savoye, 1929–31, Poissy.

Of equal interest are buildings that were designed with a Parthenon portico from the outset, such as the U.S. Patent Office, in Washington D.C., designed by Robert Mills in 1836 (fig. 7). This was conceived as a temple of ingenuity and resourcefulness, standing for the liberty and enterprise of the creative individual, the cornerstone of the industrial revolution and capitalism. Since the 1960s it has housed the National Portrait Gallery, a contemporary pantheon celebrating the icons of American identity.

The Parthenon portico was also used symbolically in the triumphal reconstruction of Moscow after the devastating fire of 1812, when Napoleon took over the city. In 1817 Domenico Gilardi redrew Moscow University with neoclassical features in place of the Palladian ones and a Parthenon portico at the entrance. Afanasy Grigoriev designed a Parthenon portico for the entrance to the new Razumovsky mansion, which became the Museum of the Revolution after 1917; today it houses the State Central Museum of Contemporary History of Russia. The image of the Parthenon as a quotation bridges insurmountable gaps because it conveys values less concerned with architectural form than with the ideas this form may reflect, at first or second sight.

Thus we may better understand the use of the Parthenon as an entrance for the Pantheon in Rome, as well as for national monuments and mausoleums. Such was the form proposed by Thomas Harrison, architect of Lord Elgin, for the national monument of Britain in 1815, and designed by Giovanni Antonio Selva for the mausoleum of sculptor Antonio Canova in Possagno in 1819 (fig. 8). Those visible references to the Parthenon reach down to the smallest details, recomposed as fragments in various buildings. Thus any association with the archetype can only be understood indirectly, by virtue of specific expertise or by subtractive powers. In this fashion, the meaning of form is enhanced with elliptical connotations. A typical example is Henry Bacon's Lincoln Memorial, in Washington D.C., finished in 1922: the Doric columns are exact replicas of those in the Parthenon, while other architectural features clearly allude to ancient Greek temples (fig. 9).

I won't elaborate further on the use of quotations in other buildings. The examples are countless, and their uses change over time; they are dispersed across space, becoming fragmentary and even ornamental. Of much greater importance is the establishment of the Parthenon in the historical and theoretical discourse on

13 Walter Gropius, American Embassy, 1959–61, Athens.

architecture in both the nineteenth and twentieth centuries. Within this discourse the Parthenon is promoted to the supreme reference as the ideal moment in a history where things that happened later, in other places and societies, could be just as exemplary. This is the condition enabling things to happen again in the present and the future, regardless of the similarity of forms, and most importantly, beyond any similarities. It is therefore understood that the Parthenon is the result of fundamental principles in society and architecture, albeit of a distant past. Applying the same principles to a different place, time, and society, the people of a new time—architects or master builders—construct a counterpart to the Parthenon that is just as perfect but does not and should not look the same as the prototype. The historical discourse attempts to ground its narrative on the affinity of ages that applied the same principles, with comparable intentions, and achieved corresponding results. However, the definition of the principles and intentions depends on the theoretical discourse about architecture's *being*, which respectively projects the selected past on the desired future. These definitions are a construct of present time authored by history and theory writers.

A typical case is Eugène-Emmanuel Viollet-le-Duc, who researched cathedral architecture and compared it to the Parthenon, aiming at the architecture of his time. The argument that the Greeks constructed the Parthenon because they were guided by reason and its subsequent principles led him to the conclusion that future times, with matching principles, had made or could make "Parthenons." What changes are the materials available, together with the social and climatic conditions that prescribe the methods of construction and the forms. Therefore the Parthenon could not have been built in nineteenth-century Edinburgh or Munich as an exact repetition; however, the twelfth- and thirteenth-century master builders in France, unconsciously working under the same principles as the ancient Greeks, built cathedrals that can be directly compared to the Parthenon. Applying the same principles to iron, the new material of their time, late nineteenth-century architects would have the opportunity to achieve comparable results. The Notre Dame in Paris is the French counterpart to the Parthenon because it was constructed on the same principles; those should also be the foundations of contemporary architecture.[15]

14 Mies van der Rohe, Neue Nationalgalerie, 1962–68, Berlin.

15 Alvar Aalto, Auditorium at the Helsinki

At about the same time Gottfried Semper brought up the Parthenon to support his theory of cladding, which gives primacy to the Renaissance over the Middle Ages but is similarly projected on the architecture of the nineteenth century. Semper visited Athens in 1831 to authenticate polychromy (fig. 10). His conclusion was that the ancients had gone as far as "dressing" the noble marbles of the Parthenon in an apparent external form to provide architecture with true meaning. His theory reaches as far as the primitive hut of the Caribbean, put on display at the 1851 Crystal Palace International Exhibition next to a Parthenon colored by Owen Jones, mirrored in the respectively colored iron-cast building of the exhibition space. The meeting of Semper and Jones in London at the debate on the polychromy of the Parthenon at the Crystal Palace Greek Court was not incidental; the two had already met in Athens and had similar views on the grammar of forms.[16] Besides, for Jones, "The Alhambra is at the very summit of perfection of Moorish art, as is the Parthenon of Greek art."[17] It is difficult to discern the Parthenon in Semper's architecture: the quotation is *invisible*, but it is there as the unquestionable foundation of architecture. At the beginning of the twentieth century this insight was confirmed by Adolf Loos, who asked his contemporaries to build like the Greeks (*Hellenen*) if they wanted to be modern, and he did so in the name of Semper.[18]

It seems commonplace to speak of the Parthenon in relation to Le Corbusier, who makes the comparison with the fast cars of his time. Remarkably his criteria were the same as those of Viollet-le-Duc, and the 1921 Delage Grand Sport in *Vers une Architecture* is the result of the same principles behind the Parthenon and Notre Dame, which would lead toward his own Modern architecture (fig. 11). The quotation is still invisible because it refers to principles and ideas; it is not, however, arbitrary in the sense that it is grounded on the comprehensive historical and theoretical discourse of Viollet-le-Duc and on Auguste Choisy's *History of Architecture*. This thorough narrative, published by Choisy in 1899 and read by most twentieth-century Modern architects, relies on the same principles as does Viollet-le-Duc's and showcases the Parthenon as the ideal foundation of both Gothic and contemporary architecture. The quotation is inevitable but radically unconfirmed because the resemblance is conceptual.

Technology, 1965, Otaniemi, Finland.

1 Plutarch, *Pericles*, 12–13.

2 *Gentleman's Magazine*, 1815, 624.

3 Marc Fehlmann, "As Greek as It Gets: British Attempts to Recreate the Parthenon," in *Rethinking History* vol. 11, no. 3 (September 2007), 363.

4 Temple Stanyan, *Grecian History: From the Origin of Greece to the Death of Philip of Macedon*. The first volume was published in 1707 and the second one in 1739, together with a revised edition of the original, in London.

5 *Histoire de Grèce*, three volumes, Paris, 1743, and Amsterdam, 1744.

6 Temple Stanyan, *Grecian History*, vol. 1 (1739), 313.

7 David Hume, "On Liberty and Despotism," in *Essays, Moral and Political* (Edinburgh: R. Fleming and A. Alison, 1741), 176.

8 See Johann Joachim Winckelmann, *Anmerkungen über die Baukunst der Alten* (Leipzig: Johann Gottfried Dyck, 1762), and *Geschichte der Kunst des Altertums* (Dresden: Walther, 1764). "The influence of climate on the mode of thought of a people—with which external circumstances, especially education, the form of government, and the manner of administering it, co-operate—is just as perceptible and conceivable as the influence of the same cause on the conformation. The mode of thought... is manifest even in works of art.... We must, therefore, in judging of the natural capacity of nations, and of the Greeks especially, in this respect, take into consideration, not merely the influence of climate alone, but also that of education and government." *The History of Ancient Art*, vol. 1, trans. G. Henry Lodge, James R. Osgood (Boston: James R. Osgood, 1873), 234, 236–37.

9 See Panayotis Tournikiotis, ed., *The Parthenon and Its Impact in Modern Times* (New York: Harry Abrams, 1996).

10 *The Antiquities of Athens, Measured and Delineated by James Stuart and Nicholas Revett* (London: John Haberkorn, 1762–1830).

11 See Werner Szambien, *Le musée de l'architecture* (Paris: Picard, 1988).

12 Andrew Robertson, *The Parthenon Adapted to the Purpose of a National Monument to Commemorate the Vic-*

The grand masters of the Modern movement would all make Parthenons in reinforced concrete and steel during the twentieth century. Many have thought that the Villa Savoye alluded to the ancient temple, but there is no explicit reference (fig. 12). Le Corbusier did clearly state that the crowning point of his Unité d'habitation in Marseilles indirectly quotes the top of the Acropolis. Indeed his oeuvre looks like a perpetual conversation with the Parthenon.[19] In 1956 Walter Gropius designed the United States Embassy in Athens as a peripteral temple that aspires to engage with the spirit of democracy and the Parthenon; the reinforced concrete is symbolically clad with the identical Pentelic marble (fig. 13). Mies van der Rohe started to build the glass-and-steel Neue Nationalgalerie in Berlin in 1962 as a temple of modern art and as "the Parthenon of the XX century,"[20] in a city pursuing democracy (fig. 14). In the Otaniemi campus Alvar Aalto designed a space of contemporary liberal education with local rationalism and direct allusions to the spirit of the Parthenon. The quotation remains invisible, concealed inside the body of architecture, but is clear on a seal on the central building bearing the Parthenon in relief (fig. 15); this is meant both as repetition, quality certificate, and pedigree. The quotation is invisible but highly spiritual in the classical Modernism of the former Athens airport, designed by Eero Saarinen in 1959, where the bare white mass of the huge concrete architraves and columns is made of Pentelic-marble-aggregate concrete, flesh of the flesh of the Parthenon![21]

Recourse to visible repetition of the Parthenon's elements became common architectural practice by early in the nineteenth century. Such quotations drew force from their resemblance to the original and became significant by virtue of historical interpretation. This practice was identified with neoclassicism in the same way quotations from other buildings, belonging to different historical periods, were identified with a number of respective "revivals." However, these were not in fact revivals: The invention of history does not seek to revive distant pasts but to establish instead a great leap forward, an ideal liberation. Buildings that look like the Parthenon, such as Walhalla or an American bank, pursue a completely modern world and announce a completely new order of things. The Parthenon and history itself are at once the flagship and the alibi of modernity—they are a construct of reason, they are *discourse*. Only in the land of the ancient Greeks, for the sake of this same historical discourse, did the construction of the past and the future have to take place simultaneously as restoration of classicism (antiquity) and creation of neoclassicism (modernity). Broken time had to be mended, and the *continuity of history* from ancient to modern times had to be invented and materialized in a completely new country called Greece.

The quotation is intertwined with modernity because modernity is an outcome of history. History is the discourse that conditions identity and difference, or else creates the continuum of all the past ages wherein the present can locate its origin. The present is unquestionably new, meaning *modern*, because those ages are old and, furthermore, they are the present's predecessors. Recourse to the past confirms the way to the future. The quotation is a structural and meaningful component of the discourse that establishes modernity. The different repetition of the models of an ideal past is much more than an imitation; it is a distancing and a radical renewal. This repetition challenges and rejects the substandard intermediate time—the immediate past. This is the reason why we encounter the same ideological use of the quotation at the beginning and the end of the nineteenth century: those were times of invention, consolidation, negation, and the recovery of history.

The explicit quotation is a statement that establishes a universe of connotations. This implies the visible similarities to be found in structures that cite the Parthenon or the Pantheon, Karl Friedrich Schinkel's Pinakothek, or Corbusian villas. However this is but one dimension of quoting, and it is not even the most important one. Besides the references that build forms, we should take interest mostly in those that build ideas—which means architectural theories that lead toward new architectures and bow to the Parthenon without any visible hint. Those are the most significant quotations because they overcome the limitations of an incidental cultural clustering, most clearly associated with neoclassicism, and extend all the way to our building of "Parthenons" in the modern and contemporary age. This transition from the different but visible repetition of the ideal model to its invisible transcript can be seen only with eyes wide shut: thus is contrived the relation between architecture's being and its meaning.

tories of the Late Wars; Proposed to Be Erected in Trafalgar Square or Hyde Park (London: Piccadilly, 1838).

13 George Cleghorn, *Remarks on the Intended Restoration of the Parthenon of Athens as the National Monument of Scotland* (Edinburgh: Archibald Constable and Co., 1824), 179.

14 *Views of Philadelphia and Its Environs* (Philadelphia: C.G. Childs, 1827), 76–84.

15 See Eugène-Emmanuel Viollet-le-Duc, *Entretiens sur l'architecture* (Paris: A. Morel et cie, 1863–72).

16 Owen Jones, *An Apology for the Colouring of the Greek Court in the Crystal Palace… and a Fragment on the Origin of Polychromy by Professor Semper* (London: Crystal Palace Library, 1854).

17 Owen Jones, *The Grammar of Ornament*, 2nd printing (London: Bernard Quaritch, 1868), 66.

18 "Are there still people who work in the same way as the Greeks? Oh yes! The English as a people, the engineers as a profession. The English and the engineers are our Hellenes. It is from them that we acquire our culture; from them it spreads over the entire globe." Adolf Loos, "Glas und Ton," in *Ins Leere gesprochen 1897-1900* (Paris: G. Crès, 1921), 66. English translation: "Glass and Clay," in *Spoken into the Void: Collected Essays 1897-1900* (Cambridge, Massachusetts: MIT Press, 1982), 35.

19 See Jean-Louis Cohen, "Vers une Acropole: d'Athènes à Ronchamp," and Panayotis Tournikiotis, "La résurgence de l'Acropole," in *L'invention d'un architecte: Le voyage en Orient de Le Corbusier* (Paris: Editions de la Villette, 2013), 376–93 and 394–405.

20 Francesco Dal Co, "Mies van der Rohe: *Grandezza della Modernità*," in *Casabella*, 692 (2001): 4.

21 See Susanna Santala, "Laboratory for a New Architecture: The Airport Terminal, Eero Saarinen, and the Historiography of Modern Architecture" (PhD diss., University of Helsinki, 2015), 27.

“Our intention is not to bind people to our own images and memories but to their own.”

Interview with Jacques Herzog

Archaeology

P49 You describe your creative process as a series of "discoveries," not revealing the old or the new, but rather the "world that exists." You categorize this methodology as neither anti- nor post-modern, but rather as "after-modern." Is the "after-modern" architect an author or archeologist?

JH Archaeology is fascinating because it very concretely excavates, re-creates, and reinterprets the physical remains of past cultures and societies. We always find it obvious and necessary to understand what we do now in the wider context of the given structures on a site—whether these are so called 'natural' or man-made topographies.

P49 With regard to the Serpentine Pavilion, the final design emerges from what was latent in the ground. How were the fragments selected, placed, curated, or otherwise "designed"?

JH We wanted to include structural remains from every single pavilion built in the years before, with no preferences whatsoever. We laid all the ground plans of these pavilions on top of each other, which created a fascinating maze of lines, kind of a pattern chart. We hoped to find some of their physical remains in the ground, but they all were eliminated and had been refilled with sand and earth. The holes of what once was a foundation had been refilled again and again, so in some way these past foundations were still there, as "ghosts." We immediately understood that this absence of physical remains would free us and open the door to a new landscape, which we could put together out of the virtual pattern chart of the forms offered to us by all our predecessors.

P49 Though the Serpentine Pavilion presents a collection of fragments, all of the elements below the roof pool are covered in cork. How do you reconcile the deliberate collage with this material uniformity?

JH It was easier to reconcile the different fragments in a material uniformity. We knew it should all be one material; only then would the new landscape work as a whole and not as a crowd of individual statements. Cork came very naturally as we had been studying new ways to use this wonderfully warm and soft material for quite a while. Its tactile qualities have certainly helped make the pavilion more attractive and friendly for the many visitors.

P49 Does this suggest that after the passing of time, artifacts and ideas fall out of the contexts for which they were designed and are subsumed into their new environment?

JH Time transforms and even destroys everything. Some things—artifacts or even ideas—survive a bit longer, but paradoxically only if they have a "transformative potential," i.e. if they attract coming generations to embrace them, transform them and make them their own thing.

Methodology

P49 While the Serpentine Pavilion presents collaged fragments of foundations and existing site elements, the Eberswalde Library multiplies images that are whole. Do these acts represent different attitudes toward context? Different attitudes toward presenting history?

JH We are not "presenting history." What might be a common element in those two, and in other projects, is that we try to find new ways to generate architecture. One way that we do this is to work with the projects "materiality." In both projects, you mention that we developed a specific building material that had never been used before: a mix of archeological fragments and new pieces, all in solid cork for the pavilion; historic photographs etched not on paper but into stone for the Eberswalde library. For the Eberswalde we really found a new technology which was going beyond other attempts of just painting and decorating a facade. The photographic images literally mutated into a building material shaping the entire building.

P49 We read another attitude in the presentation of your work when it is layered as transparencies, such as in the 1988 *Architektur/Denkform* exhibition in Basel. When your work is both seen and seen through, it embeds itself within the urban context. What is at stake in this superimposition?

JH *Architektur/Denkform* remains a very key moment in our biography. We always found architecture exhibitions boring and intellectually naive compared to art shows. Art is art and is made to be exhibited in galleries or elsewhere. Architecture is also just architecture but it is made to work on and for a specific given site. Architecture exhibitions cannot do that, so every show requires a big effort in order to inspire a convincing identity and beauty to the substituting elements: models, projections, texts, etc. In the exhibition you mention, we took the museum building itself—a modernist lantern-like building of translucent and transparent glass—and made it ours. We appropriated the museum, like a "found" object which reflected the urban context, its own structure, and our projects in an intrinsic way.

P49 In your work, the operation of quotation appears to always be linked to a material and its specific properties (cork, transparencies, concrete screen prints). What is the importance of materiality in revealing or undermining specific citations?

pages 168, 171–74
Serpentine Gallery Pavilion 2012.
Herzog & de Meuron and Ai Weiwei.
Kensington Gardens, London, UK. Project and realization 2011–2012, opening dates 1 June–14 October 2012.

page 169, top
Eberswalde Technical School Library.
Eberswalde, Germany.
Project 1994–1996, realization 1997–1999.
Photo Margherita Spiluttini,
© Architekturzentrum Wien, Collection.

page 169, bottom
Architektur Denkform.
Architekturmuseum Basel, Switzerland.
Exhibition 1 October–20 November 1988.

JH Citations, just like references, do not interest us. They may be an immanent ingredient in many of our buildings, otherwise you wouldn't keep asking… but as I said before, they may pop up or appear in the mind of people as they see the building, they appear as one of hopefully many other possible forms and interpretations. Our intention is not to bind people to our own images and memories but to their own.

P49 Is it possible to quote a particular craft or material usage to evoke a specific moment, place, or person? Or are the traditions inherent to architectural practice impossible to quote specifically?

JH The specific moment that an "author," be it an architect, fashion designer, or film maker has in his mind may be a driver, a kind of primary energy for the early phase of a project. The more you then work on it, the more that specific moment, that memory, etc., fades away and makes room for the new project that needs to be shaped. If a project doesn't succeed in "destroying" that memory it ends up being a nostalgic fart.

Legacy

P49 How could you return to the Serpentine? Is it a work in progress or is it complete?

JH As a project it is complete. As a concept it, like many of our projects, is a work in progress.

P49 How do you see the Serpentine Pavilion in relation to your work dealing with renovations, such as the Armory, the Tate Modern, or the House of Alfred Richterich?

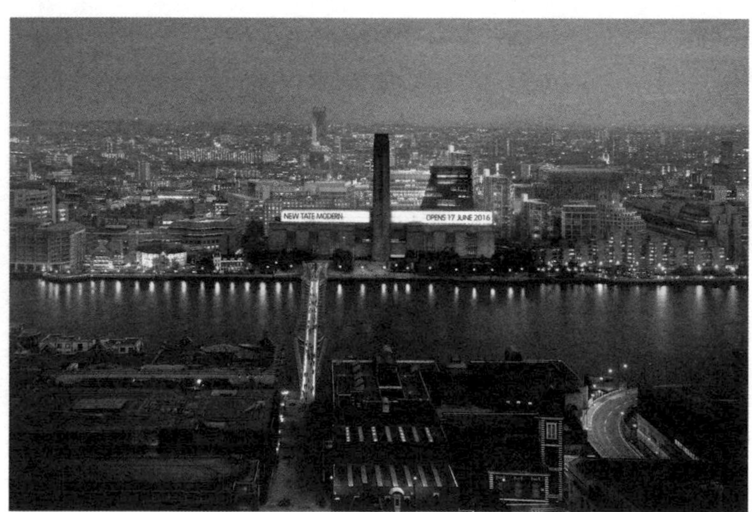

below
The Tate Modern Project.
London, UK. Competition 2005, project 2005–2016 (planned completion 2016).

JH Clearly, since our very early days, renovating, reconstructing, preserving, destroying, and simulating, etc., are key tools and methods for all our projects. Very consciously, we tackle a project as part of an existing specific and real world and not of an ideal one.

P49 Your partnership has served as a model for collaborative practice, whether it be with each other or with artists, curators, or collectors. Are there still traces of individual voices in the final product or are they subsumed in the transformation?

JH I am not aware of such traces. Experts and historians could perhaps trace back specific influences and obsessions, etc. of ours, or, eventually, of another involved partner.

P49 Might your work be so rich with reference that it itself resists appropriation and citation?

JH We have seen some rather awkward copies of some of our buildings which are a bit embarrassing, honestly. It is often more advisable to learn from strategies and methods than from finished form.

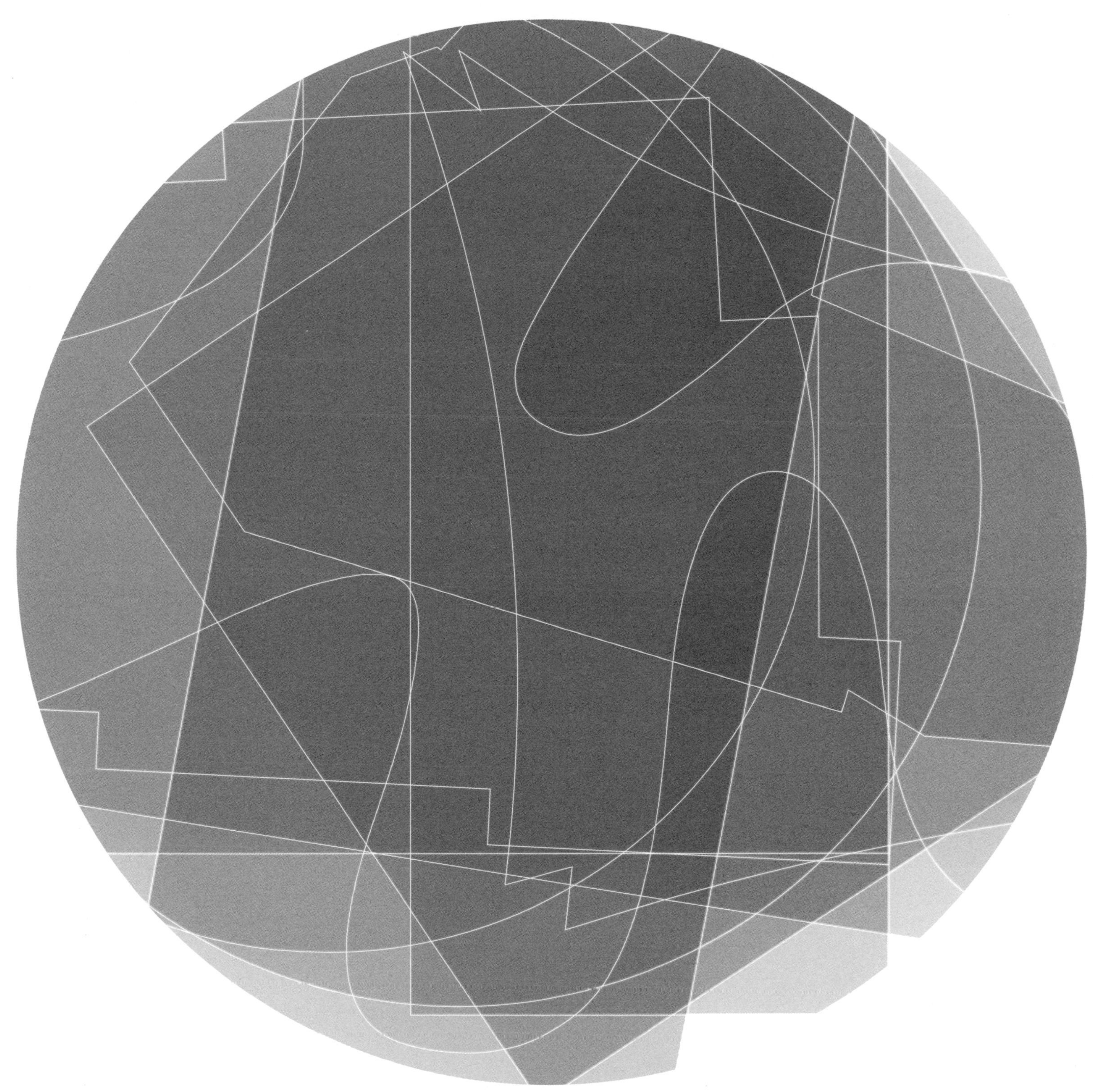

Serpentine Gallery Pavilion:
Traces of previous foundations

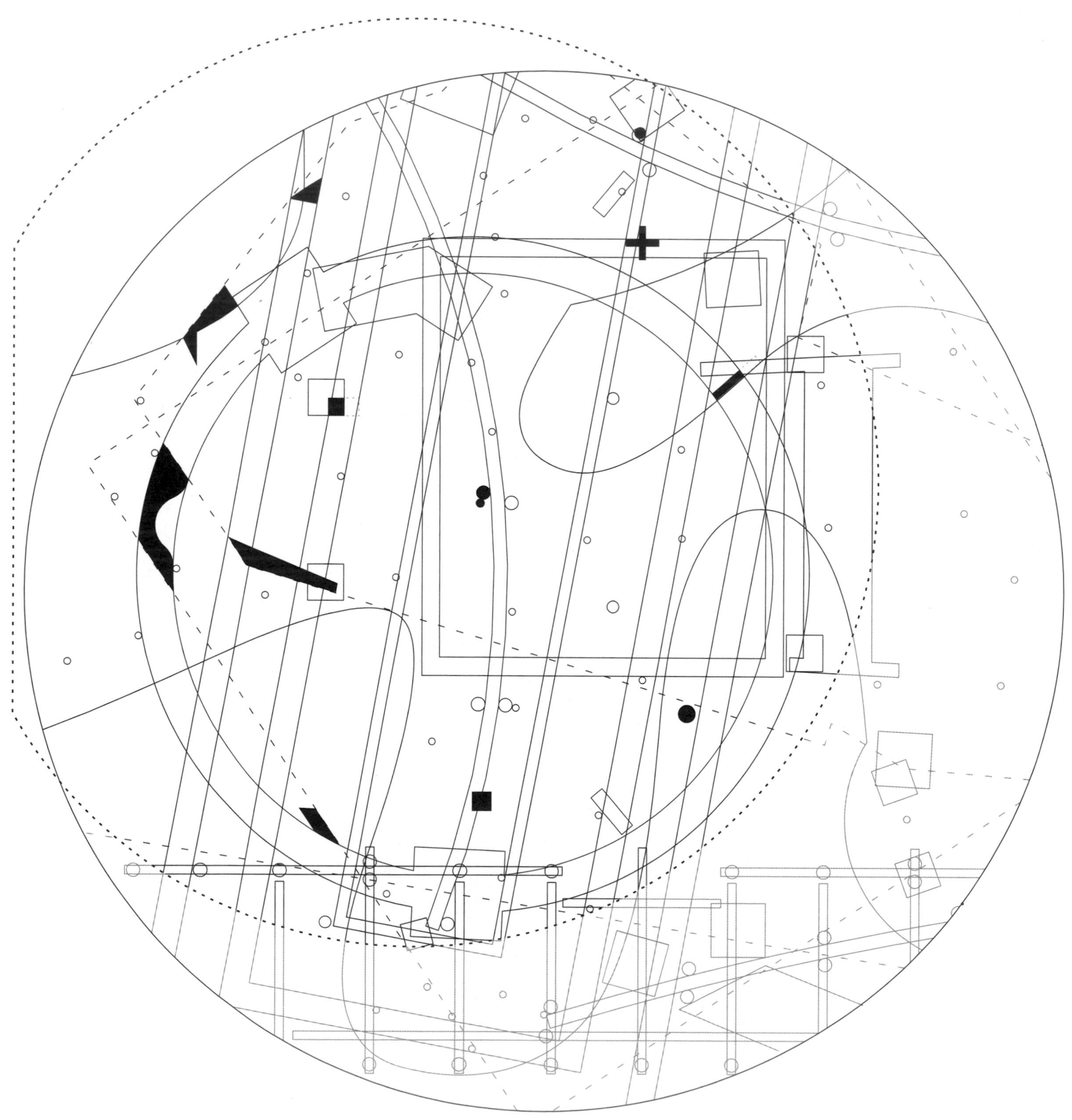

Serpentine Gallery Pavilion:
Cork landscape

Serpentine Gallery Pavilion:
Pavilion roof

"One might compare the situation to marriage versus free love."

†

George Hersey

Replication Replicated, or Notes on American Bastardy

This essay was originally published in *Perspecta* 9/10 in 1965, alongside a portfolio of photographs by John T. Hill. Constructing an architectural lineage between Richard M. Upjohn's Connecticut State Capitol in Hartford (1872–78) and the Brutalist architecture of the 1960s, Hersey argues that the "free replication" of style, scale, and building type is a uniquely American occurrence. While Hersey would go on to become a leading scholar in Renaissance art and architecture, "Replication Replicated" proved influential for a new generation of architects including Robert Venturi, Denise Scott Brown, and Steven Izenour, who cite the essay in *Learning from Las Vegas*.

REPLICATION REPLICATED, or Notes on American Bastardy *G. L. Hersey* / Photographs of the Connecticut State Capitol, Hartford *John T. Hill* 211

212  1

Richard M. Upjohn's Connecticut State Capitol (1, 2) in Hartford (1872-78) may look lumbering and overwrought to the Bauhaus generation, but to post-brutalists it ought to be an impressive sight. Upjohn, like the latter, enjoyed architecture that was ridgy, fissured, and anfractuous. Nor will a generation that is anti-purist, pro-expressionist, and soft on eclecticism mind the "stylistic ambiguity" Hitchcock has found in Upjohn's building.[1] One might even call the Hartford Capitol, with its spiked gables, its tall, faceted roofs, its squarely locked masses, and its big-volumed, downlit interior wells, a part of the *old* brutalism. As such it would belong to the nineteenth-century ancestry now revealing itself for postwar modernism. It would be part of the patrimony of Kahn and Rudolph.

The building is also of interest to art historians, for it proclaims with crude clarity a certain American concept of architecture. It is my purpose here to define this concept. I shall try first of all to identify it in general terms and to point out its presence in two predecessors of Upjohn's building. I shall then show how the concept was strengthened by the stylistic situation in Upjohn's period, how it afterward disappeared, and how it seems to be reappearing in the present wave of brutalism.

In its simplest form the concept may be described as follows: American architects, unlike their European colleagues, have seldom felt called upon to restrict the relationship between siting and outer shell, shell and interior, and scale and building type. In American building these pairs do not relate to each other according to any a priori framework at all. They link and unlink freely, whereas in Europe they are permanently shackled. One might compare the situation to marriage versus free love.[2]

I

As an example let us consider the siting and arrangement of buildings. In America this departed radically from tradition as soon as the first New England settlers built settlements.[3] In the East Anglian towns and villages from which these people came, the relationships between farmland, woods, and town center, between road, street, and lane, and between manor, cottage, church, and castle, were distinct and stable. The houses clustered together along the crooked streets in mutual support. Independent structures like the manor house, the rectory, and the church were clearly separate in style, siting, and function. Around this plastic nucleus stretched the flat enframing fields, separated here and there by roads and lanes (3).[4]

In this country the road swept straight into town from the open countryside and, often without turning aside, became the street (4). The town was merely an open configuration of houses along it.

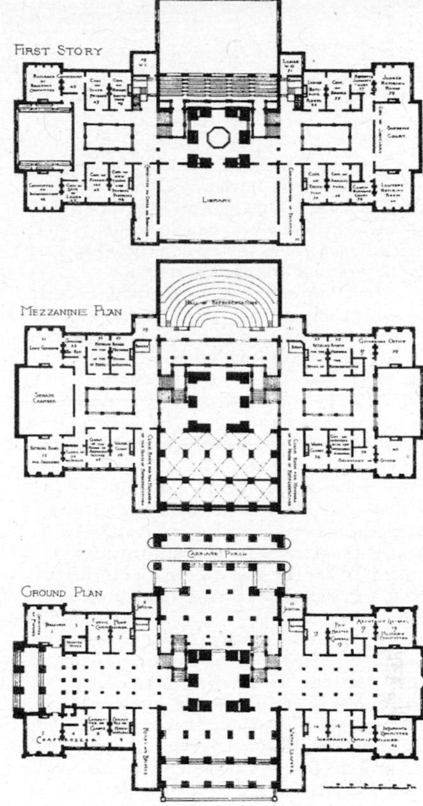

2-3

213

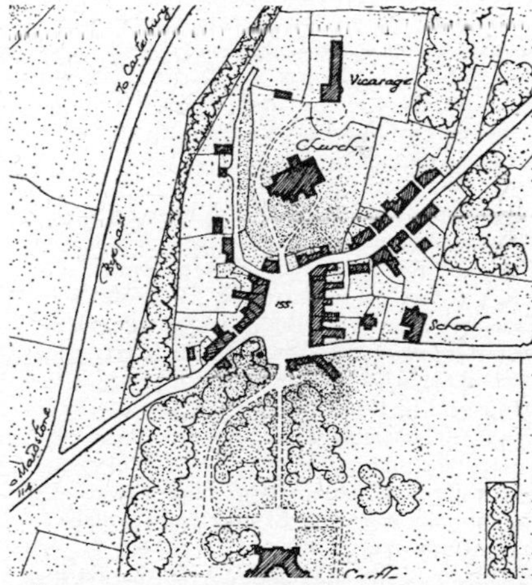

3-4

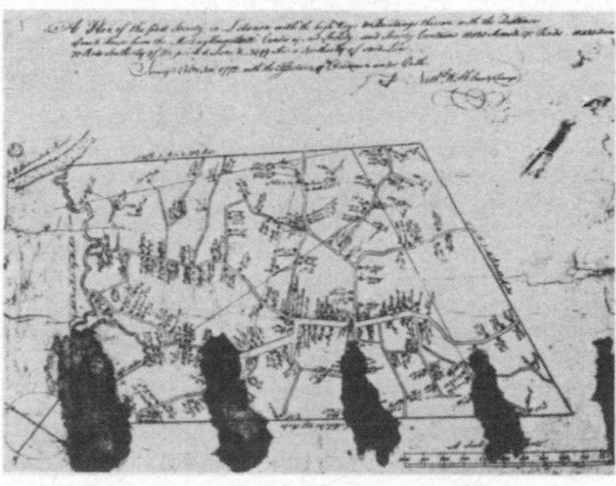

1.
Richard M. Upjohn, Connecticut State Capitol, Hartford (1872-78). John T. Hill.
2.
Connecticut State Capitol, plans of three main floors. From *Monographs of American Architecture. The State Capitol, Hartford, Conn.*
3.
Plan of Chilham, Kent. From Thomas Sharp, *Town and Countryside.*
4.
Nathaniel Webb, survey of Lebanon, Conn., 1772. Courtesy Yale Library.

1.
Henry-Russell Hitchcock, *Architecture: Nineteenth and Twentieth Centuries* (Baltimore, 1963), p. 195. Hitchcock's statement is part of a comparison between Upjohn's building and William Burges' Trinity College, Hartford. Whatever one thinks of Upjohn's Capitol, it ought not to be attributed to the architect's father, as it is by John Burchard and Albert Bush-Brown in the *Architecture of America* (Boston, 1961), p. 185. I must thank Charles Price for pointing out this slip to me.
2.
Or to the concept of "bound" as opposed to "free" variables in symbolic logic.
3.
See Christopher Tunnard and Henry Hope Reed, *American Skyline* (Cambridge, Mass., 1955), pp. 29-43. For a more detailed study of American town planning, in Connecticut, see Anthony N. B. Garvan, *Architecture and Town Planning in Colonial Connecticut* (New Haven, 1951), pp. 18-49.
4.
See Garvan, pp. 39-43, for a description of the differences between earlier English settlements and American villages. This was a difference as much of scale as of plan.

The houses were separated from each other by generous allotments of land, and behind each one stretched the long farm lot worked by the owner. As time went on and increased population burst the tight groupings of local New England villages, the towns spread out from their centers into amorphous townships even more lacking in clear divisions. Only the roads tied things together, not the sculptural cluster of buildings as in Europe.[5] Even in large urban centers the road, or street, was in command. The Reverend Andrew Burnaby in the eighteenth century, for example, commented on the spaced, nondescript character of American city buildings, which occupied a wide, powerful grid of streets leading off to the edges of town.[6] Jefferson's plan for the University of Virginia is another instance of a street-oriented arrangement of buildings (5). This also takes the form of a village street with connected houses on either side. The novel idea is explicit in Jefferson's name for the arrangement: "academical village."[7]

We have continued to warp the European relationship between the building and its context. The wilderness, which originally dictated this change, may still be responsible; for the wilderness has not so much been thrust back as tamed and cultivated. It has been turned into a farm, a garden, or a park. It often seems even to sweep through our
214 cities. The urban jungle, penetrated by its clear unrelenting grid of streets, is like a wilderness caged. Even Main Street has something of this. It is a tunnel of trees, flanked by houses, each of which is set like a cabin in a clearing. So great was the pull of this wilderness *Nachlass* that even our millionaires bowed to it. In Newport, Rhode Island, they made Bellevue Avenue into the Main Street of a plutocratic village (6).[8]

European forms still appear in unforeseen contexts in America. Eero Saarinen, in Stiles and Morse Colleges at Yale (1958-62), was following Jefferson, perhaps unconsciously, in creating an academic village (7).[9] But he also seems to have been thinking of recent European architecture that was evolved to take care of quite different problems. The Yale colleges resemble the wayward polyhredral housing developments designed by Italians who, in practicing the New Empiricism, burrow through masonry labyrinths of an ancient slum or build on the site of a peripheral village, and preserve or at least remember the old topography. Stiles and Morse are laid out like the INA-Casa housing on the Via Tiburtino, Rome (1950-51). The two Yale colleges have the same stepped pedestrian streets with jagged axes, and the same tall oblong wall forms with the slotted windows of other postwar projects of this type (8). The New Haven buildings even suggest the same Italian sunlight reflected from tall masonry prisms.[10] But Saarinen, unlike the Italians, created his crabbed topography out of his head.

Saarinen's buildings do not deserve the criticism that J. E. Cabot made of American architecture a hundred years ago in the *Atlantic Monthly*: "It is not bad taste we suffer from, – not plainness, not indifference to appearance, but features misplaced, shallow mimicry of 'effects' where their causes do not exist, transparent pretences of all kinds, forcing attention to the absence of reality, otherwise, perhaps, unnoticed."[11] Saarinen's unbending formalism, however, seems quite in the American tradition.

The normal European relationships between the shell and its interior can also be absent over here. Even with our earliest bursts of architectural ambition, the outsides and insides of our buildings have rarely had much to do with each other. The concept of "wrapped space" is an old one. It has been especially apparent in our classicizing architecture. One thinks for example of the Rotunda at Jefferson's University of Virginia 1823-26, (9). Here the exterior is resolute, unified, and classical. It has not been noticed before, I think, that a convincing prototype for it is a contemporaneous, baptistry project by a Grand Prix winner named Joseph Bénard[12], published in

5-6

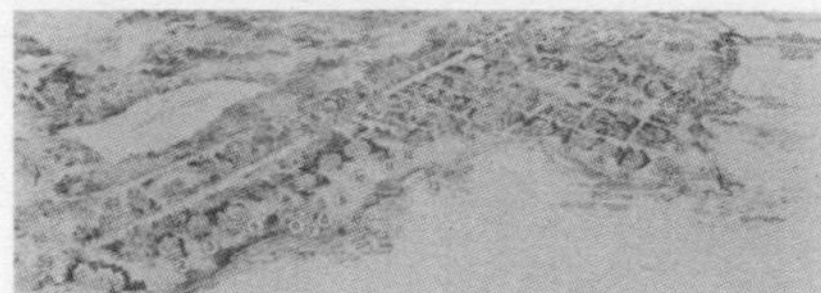

6-7

7-8

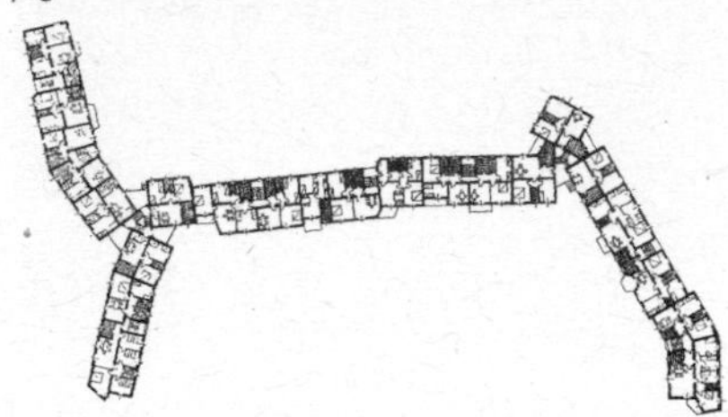

5.
Thomas Jefferson, plan of the University of Virginia, c. 1805. From I. T. Frary, *Thomas Jefferson, Architect and Builder.*
6.
Bellevue Avenue, Newport, R.I. From Mrs. J. K. van Rensselaer, *Newport, Our Social Capitol.*
7.
Eero Saarinen, plan of Stiles and Morse Colleges, Yale University (1958). From Eero Saarinen, *Eero Saarinen on His Work.*
8.
Ludovico Quaroni, Mario Fiorentino, Mario Ridolfi, and others, INA-Casa Housing, via Tiburtino, Rome (1950-51). From Leonardo Benevolo, *Storia dell'architettura moderna.*

5.
Besides the works cited above, see T. J. Wertenbaker, *The Puritan Oligarchy* (New York, 1947), pp. 2-16, for a discussion of East Anglian settlements, as well as an alternative origin for the American town plan (p. 42), and the distinction between the town, the village, and the manor, a distinction that disappeared in this country (p. 43).
6.
Andrew Burnaby, *Travels through the Middle Settlements in North-America* (2nd ed. London, 1775; Ithaca, N.Y., 1960), pp. 4-5, 53-54. Burnaby traveled in 1759 and 1760. In the mid 19th century James Fergusson again emhasized the importance of the grid. He claims graph paper was used to plan American towns, and says: "Whether the ground is flat or undulating – whether the river or shore on which [the town] is situated is straight or curved – whatever the accident of the situation, or the convenience of the traffic – this simple plan enables any man to lay out a city in a morning; and if he can do this, why should he spend weeks or months in carefully contouring the ground? Why proportion his streets to the traffic they are intended to convey? . . . Why, in short, think, when the thing can be done without thought?" James Fergusson, *A History of Architecture in all Countries, 4* (London, new ed., 1873), 499. See also John W. Reps, "Thomas Jefferson's Checkerboard Towns," *Journal of the Society of Architectural Historians, 20* (1961), 108-14, and Robert W. Winter, "Fergusson and Garbett in American Architectural Theory," ibid., *17* (1958), 25-30. Peter Collins, in "The Origins of Graph Paper as an Influence on Architectural Design," ibid., *21* (1962), 159-62, does not go into the question of town planning.
7.
Quoted by Frederick Nichols, *Thomas Jefferson's Architectural Drawings* (Boston, 1961), p. 8.
8.
Mrs. John K. van Rensselaer, *Newport, Our Social Capitol* (Philadelphia, 1905), pp. 39-54, and Maud Lyman Stevens, "Newport Streets," *Bulletin of the Newport Historical Society* (1928), 1-13.
9.
[Aline B. Saarinen, ed.] *Eero Saarinen on his Work* (New Haven, 1962), pp. 80-87.

9

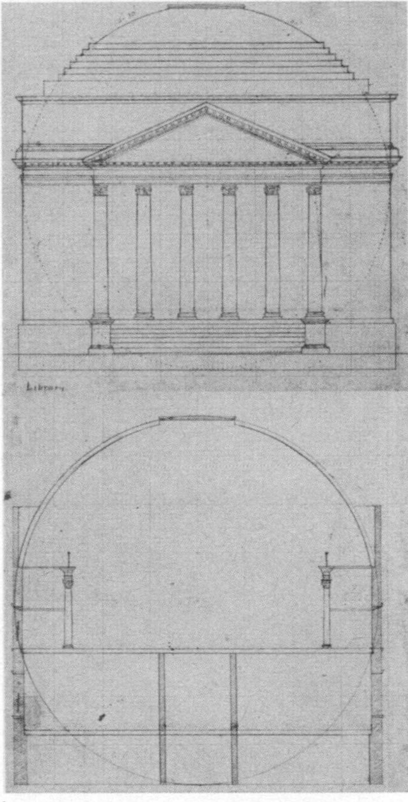

9.
Thomas Jefferson, cross-section and façade of the Rotunda of the University of Virginia (c. 1820). From *Arts in Virginia,* 1961.

1787 when Jefferson was in Paris (10). Both Bénard's and Jefferson's conceptions are sweetened restatements of the Pantheon, like Fragonard's adapting an antique Venus. The entablature has been enlarged to scale in a more orthodox way with the height of the Rotunda. The often criticized rectangular block behind the portico[13] has disappeared (although it reappeared in Jefferson's finished building), and the steps with their parapet have been restored.

It is in the interiors that the two projects differ. Bénard's is the reflex of his exterior: a big, domed, single room. But Jefferson has superimposed his shell, with all its obstinate academic beauty, on an interior honeycomb of offices, corridors, and bookshelves.[14] So unrelated were his conceptions of interior and exterior that he did not re-introduce the string courses of the original Roman prototype, which Bénard had omitted, and which in the Virginia Rotunda would have expressed the three stories within.[15]

II

But one cannot claim that this unintegrated formalism is characteristic of all American architecture. Alternating with it there is often a compulsive integration of shell, site, and interior. Phases of rigid imprisonment are balanced by periods when the shell is gratuitously broken through. The Stick Style began to articulate the outer shell into skeletal components in the 1840's.[16] In American wooden resort architecture of the 1870's and 1880's, flowing, breezy space-groupings were enclosed in a way that not only expressed but seemed to amplify this interior freedom.[17] Just as the houses were often anchored in sites that suggested dramatic landscape painting, so the interiors were planned in terms of descending volumes of light, with shadowy corners and with rising and falling horizontal surfaces, achieving in their own way the quality of landscape.[18]

Yet the Shingle Style, for all its integration, shows the conceptual freedom of American architecture in another way. In Europe not only were site, plan, and shell integrated with each other; building-type and scale were also subject to mutual control. Clear distinctions of size and form existed

10

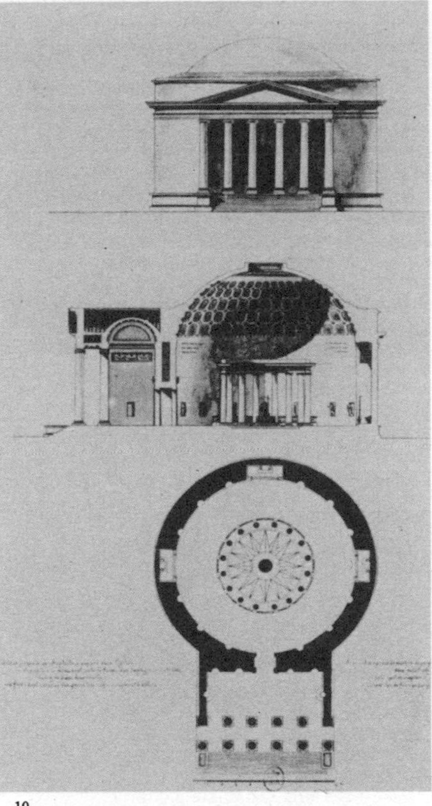

10.
Joseph Bénard, Project for a baptistry (1787). From *Architectural History,* 1960.

10.
For the New Empiricism in Italy see Giuseppe Vindigni, "Neueste Arbeiter-Wohnquartiere der INA-Casa ," *Werk, 42* (1955), 231-54, and Leonardo Benevolo, *Storia dell, architettura moderna, 2*(Bari, 1960), 945. For the movement's Scandinavian origins see Eric de Maré, "Antecedents and Origins of Sweden's Latest Style *Architectural Review 103* (1948), 9-10, and Benevolo, *2,* 882-901.

11.
James E. Cabot, "House-Building," *Atlantic Monthly, 10* (1862), 427.

12.
See Helen Rosenau, "The Engravings of the *Grands Prix* of the French Academy of Architecture," *Architectural History, 3* (1960), 163. I have been able to find no information on Bénard except that he was a pupil of P.–L. Moreau-Desproux (1727-93), *architecte du roi* after 1783, and the designer of the west front of St.-Eustache, Paris (1772-88). The Grands Prix projects were published in 1787, but Jefferson's architectural library does not seem to have contained a copy (*Collection des Prix,* Vol. I, Paris, 1787). See W. B. O'Neal, *Jefferson's Fine Arts Library* (Charlottesville, Va., 1956). Samuel A. Roberson has also kindly pointed out to me that the Mausoleum of Romulus, son of Maxentius, on the Via Appia, is an antique source far closer than the Pantheon.

13.
This block seems to be "correct" to those for whom the Pantheon is an integral structure, and "incorrect" to those for whom it is the result of remodeling. A.–B. Desgodetz, in *Les Edifices antiques de Rome* [1771 ff.] (Rome, 1822) p. 5, n. 3, and Carlo Fea, in *L'integrità del Panteon rivendicata a M. Agrippa* (new ed. ? Rome, 1820) passim, prefer to think of the building as a single conception, and refute those who attack the rectangular block with its false tympanum. Jefferson owned a copy of the 1779 edition of the *Edifices* (O'Neal, *Jefferson's Library,* p. 11). One should note that Jefferson's order is Corinthian, like the Pantheon's, and not Ionic, like Bénard's.

14.
The interior was made more "pantheonic" (i.e. two stories high instead of three) by McKim, Mead & White after a fire in 1895.
See P. A. Bruce, *History of the University of Virginia,* New York, 1921, *4,* 252-82.

15.
The temple shell which enclosed an office honeycomb became standard in American Greek Revival civil architecture. It probably originated with Jefferson's Virginia State Capitol at Richmond (1785-89). Almost all of Town and Davis' civic temples fall into this category (Fig. 13), as do Strickland's – e.g. the Philadelphia Customs House (1819). A notable example of the independent exterior and interior is Thomas U. Walter's Girard College, Philadelphia (1833-47). The specifications for this interior were written into the will of the founder, Stephen Girard. The temple shell was afterward designed at the insistence of Nicholas Biddle. Walter's task was therefore to reconcile these two unrelated concepts in a single building. See Cheesman A. Herrick, *History of Girard College* (Philadelphia, 1935), pp. 5, 20, 29, 108-12.

16.
See Vincent Scully, Jr., "Romantic Rationalism and the Expression of Structure in Wood. Downing, Wheeler, Gardner, and the 'Stick Style,' 1840-1876," *Art Bulletin, 35* (1953), 121-42.

17.
See Vincent Scully, Jr., *The Shingle Style* (New Haven, 1955), esp. pp. 91-129.

18.
I owe this suggestion, as I do many others, to Mr. Scully.

for cottages, farmsteads, manors, mansions, and palaces. Only the term "villa," in England, seems to have been ambiguous.[19] In America on the other hand, Shingle Style houses were called by a great variety of names.[20] No sense of the different function and scale of the European types was retained. And this ambiguity was justified, for actually many of these houses provided palatial living in terms of a cottage vocabulary.[21] They combined the look of Marie Antoinette's Hameau with the entertainment possibilities of the Petit Trianon. The *New York Sketchbook of Architecture* reveals this ambiguity in 1874 when it refers to such houses as "shingle palaces."[22] Here the ambiguity has become ironic hyperbole. One sees the same mock grandiosity in such modern locutions as "Dog City" or "Frank Palace" for roadside stands.

What gave rise to this incoherence may have been the immensity of the American environment. Emerson noticed how greatly his surroundings overbore the artifacts of his time (though he spoke in general, and not specifically in American terms): "Gravity, wind, sun, rain, the size of men and animals, and such like, have more to say than [the architect] . . . Beneath a necessity thus almighty, what is artificial in man's life seems insignificant."[23] The architect Calvert Vaux said the same thing: "Woods, fields, mountains and rivers *will* be more important than the houses that are built upon them.[24]

As if to make up for this insignificance, we were constantly trying to be grandiose. The normal thing in the eighteenth century was to deck out the façade of a farmhouse in the shrunken trappings of some much larger European prototype.
216 Emerson describes our rich men's houses in comparable terms, and adds that the houses of the poor were simply inadequate imitations of these.[25] Andrew Jackson Downing complained that even the builders of cottages imitated "all that belongs to palaces, castles, and buildings of princely dimensions."[26] "How ridiculous," exclaimed Samuel Sloan in 1869, "must be the figure our 'palatial' efforts represent to the eyes of reflecting Europeans."[27] This imitation of larger prototypes at smaller scale was what, in my opinion, obliterated the European distinctions between building types, and allowed an hyperbole of forms as well as names.

Civil architecture was the chief offender, being the kind that suffers most from insignificance. More than other varieties, it must embody the triumph of order and community. Civil Architecture should be the antithesis of the wilderness. In 1862 James Fergusson, in his *History of Architecture in All Countries,* concentrated a good deal of fire on the failure of our civic buildings.[28] Even our most doughty defenders seem to have felt the accuracy of such criticism. Sloan, for example, after quoting Fergusson at length, replied in a way that reveals his essential agreement: "with all our shortcomings, our capitol buildings are of convenient size," he says; then, later on: "And when their designs shall become distasteful to us, it will be something that our people will then have increased in numbers, taste, and wealth, and will feel able and willing to erect newer and better State buildings."[29]

It was not long after Sloan wrote (in 1869) that we actually did produce a number of extremely large, solid, and expensive civil buildings. They seem almost to have been intended to silence criticism like Fergusson's. But when one examines some of them, as we shall presently do, one is tempted to say that if before them American scale was too small, after them it was too large. The problem of the relation of scale to building type was still unsolved.

The kind of architectural thinking in which the relationship between siting and shell, shell and interior, and scale and building type are so fluid might be called "free replication." I use the term "replication" in Kubler's sense of the copy or adaptation of some principal work of art, or "prime object."[30] Kubler sees the history of art as consisting of "clouds" of replications around prime objects. We might think of these clouds as radiating series. Thus the Parthenon is a kind of transmitter, sending out an artistic signal that is picked up by lesser transmitters, which extend and modify the original signal. In the same way, Leyswood, the large Sussex house of 1868 by Norman Shaw, is introduced by Scully as a kind of prime object (though he does not use the term) for the Shingle Style.[31] One can call the Pantheon the prime object for the numerous replications that Meeks has recorded in eighteenth- and nineteenth-century Italy.[32] My point is that in Europe, for example, with Meeks' pantheons, the conceptions of site, plan, shell, scale, and function were mutually controlled. His buildings are pantheonic in all five categories: they are sited as mid-space objects, their rotundas house single spaces, they are impressively scaled, and they function as chapels or the like.[33] In this country Jefferson's Rotunda is pantheonic in only three of these categories – site, shell, and scale – and not in plan or function. The same could be said of most of our Greek Revival temples; and often they are temple-like in no way except shell, being sited like so many office blocks or row houses.[34]

As a result of this free replication, some novel effects, originally the result of a collision between desire and necessity, have been repeated out of sheer desire. A free replication can thus come to be a prime object. Returning to our parallel between marriage and free love, we can infer a lineage for Upjohn's Capitol that was illegitimate for two earlier generations.

III

Two other Connecticut state houses appear in this ancestry. The first, by Charles Bulfinch, was designed in 1792, built in 1794-96, and still stands on State House Square in Hartford (11).[35] This is a tall, long, narrow, hip-roofed block, with central porticoes on arcaded basements projecting from the long sides. In this it is strongly related to Bulfinch's other state houses in Boston (1795-98) and Augusta, Maine (1829).[36] The Hartford and Augusta buildings, in turn, are related more tenuously to the main façade designed by Pierre-Charles L'Enfant for the New York City Hall in 1788, when he transformed that building into Federal Hall. Bulfinch made a drawing of this façade, presumably when he visited New York in 1789 (12).

L'Enfant's building itself is fairly legitimate. It is, to be sure, a diminished variant of palace prototypes, since it refers back to Wren's work of the 1680's – notably, Hampton Court and Greenwich Hospital.[37] But the L'Enfant façade was an integrated proclamation of the interior, a two-story structure with circulation space and offices in the basement, and a single large assembly room on the *piano nobile.*

Bulfinch's building has been greatly altered inside. But it is still possible, with the help of Charles A. Place's reconstruction, to get an idea of what it was like.[38] Bulfinch, while insisting on

19.
J. C. Loudon, in his *Encyclopaedia of Cottage, Farm, and Villa Architecture* [1833] (London, 1846), pp. 1106 and 1112-13, emphasizes the categories of domestic buildings. But his follower A. J. Downing, in the 1853 edition of *Cottage Residences* (New York, 1842), uses terms like "cottage" and "villa" interchangeably (p.181); and Design XIV (p. 184) is called a cottage though it is a largish eight-room house. On the other hand, while Loudon is perfectly clear as to the differences in scale, plan, cubic space, arrangement of rooms, etc., between cottages and villas, the latter category in itself includes a great range of sizes (pp. 763-963).

20.
See the various names concocted for houses in the monthly architectural department by *Godey's Lady's Book* after 1870. I go into this to some extent in my "Godey's Choice," *Journal of the Society of Architectural Historians, 18* (1959), 104-11. The result was that building-types often became identified with styles – e.g. "Italian Villa" or "Gothic Cottage," so that the typal term lost its force. We now speak of the "Italian Villa Style."

21.
For example, the W. B. Howard House, Mt. Desert, Me., by W. R. Emerson (no doubt the same architect who entered the Hartford Capitol competition; see note 65.) c. 1883-84. But the most obviously magnified cottages of the Shingle Style were the hotels – for instance, the West End Hotel, Bar Harbor, Me., by Bruce Price (1878-79). Both these buildings are illustrated in Scully, *Shingle Style,* Figs. 82 and 39. Scully (pp. 77 and 110, respectively) appropriately compares them to mountains.

22.
See the *New-York Sketch-Book of Architecture, 1,* No. XII (1874).

23.
R. W. Emerson, "Art," in *Society and Solitude* [1870], *Works* (Boston, 1894), p. 45.

24.
Calvert Vaux, *Villas and Cottages* (New York, 1867), p. 67.

25.
"The houses of the rich are confectioners' shops, where we get sweetmeats and wine; the houses of the poor are imitations of these to the extent of their ability." Emerson, loc. cit., p. 108.

26.
A. J. Downing, *Rural Essays* (New York, 1853), p. 218.

27.
Samuel Sloan, "Architecture in America: Naissant and Renaissant," *Architectural Review and American Builders' Journal, 1* (1869), 612.

28.
Fergusson, *History of Architecture, 4,* 498-512.

29.
Samuel Sloan, "English Critics," *Architectural Review and American Builders' Journal, 2* (1869), 117.

the L'Enfant façade for both fronts, had, in fact, an entirely different program. He needed three large two-story assembly rooms for the Supreme Court, the House of Representatives, and the Senate. To get them he divided his building into quarters by transverse corridors running from portico to portico on each of the two main floors. He then disposed of the interior space in a way that had nothing to do with the façades. The uniform arcade of the basement story housed an asymmetrical interior, with a monumental two-story Supreme Court room on the east and an intricate arrangement of stairs and one-story offices on the west. On the main floor Bulfinch placed his two other large assembly chambers, separated by a modest corridor. There was no large room behind the portico. The third floor contained offices, but other offices and low-ceilinged rooms were located on the main floor as well. The only access to the third floor was a spiral staircase in the Secretary of State's office on the *piano nobile*. Bulfinch's State House, as planned and originally built, was therefore a thoroughly free replication.

Consciously or unconsciously, Upjohn incorporated many of these jarring effects into his building. Indeed, the 1872 Capitol is in some ways a blown up, "modernized" version of the 1792 one. Both lift the assembly chambers high up over the ground floor (though Upjohn has put his Supreme Court chamber not on the first but on the third floor). Both buildings provide intricate mixtures of one- and two-story rooms on the same floor. We might also add that the overscaled cupola on Bulfinch's building (though not erected until 1822, and not to Bulfinch's design) [39] matches the enormously tall dome on Upjohn's Capitol. Yet Upjohn's façade has no relation to Bulfinch's. The effects that were fortuitously created when Bulfinch forced his complicated program between two Federal Hall-like façades were here freely chosen. And the result, in Upjohn's hands, becomes subject yet again to free replication because of the increase in scale.

Another parent building was the small Doric temple designed in 1827 by Ithiel Town which stood on the New Haven Green until 1887 (13). It is hardly necessary to say that this is a typical column-wrapped honeycomb. More to the point is the siting. This had been carefully studied by the architect, as a number of his sketches, now in the Yale Art Gallery, make clear. From these, and from the finished building, it is obvious that Town saw his capitol almost as a garden folly not unlike Nicholas Revett's Doric temple at Hagley of seventy years earlier (14). Town cannot be accused of ignoring the relationship between his shell and his site, however much he ignored those between shell and plan, and between type and function. In fact, in order for him to achieve his aim, it was necessary to transform the Green (which had been a semi-private pasture) into a park.[40] Thus Town, like Saarinen after him, transformed the site to suit the borrowed shell.

In European terms the palatial silhouette of Upjohn's building would demand a rich urban context with subsidiary wings, avenues, and *ronds-points*. Instead, however, the Hartford Capitol rises amid the curving walks and swelling lawns of Bushnell Park. It, too, is sited as a summer house. But again an enormous change of scale is involved, completely transforming Town's effect.[41]

IV

Now we may look at Upjohn and at the architectural situation in which he found himself.

11-12

11.
Unknown, *State House Square, Hartford*, watercolor, c. 2⅜ x 4 inches, c. 1834. Courtesy Connecticut Historical Society, Hartford.
12.
Charles Bulfinch, façade of Federal Hall, New York (1789). From Place, *Charles Bulfinch*.

13-14

13.
Ithiel Town, Connecticut State House, New Haven (1827-31). Engraving. Courtesy Yale Art Gallery.
14.
Nicholas Revett, Doric Temple at Hagley Park, Worcestershire, England (1758). Country Life Photograph.

30.
George A. Kubler, *The Shape of Time* (New Haven, 1962), esp. pp. 39-53, 71-77.
31.
See Scully, *The Shingle Style*, pp. 10-11.
32.
C. L. V. Meeks, "Pantheon Paradigm," *Journal of the Society of Architectural Historians, 19* (1960), 135-44. I must here extend my thanks to Carroll Meeks for reading this article in manuscript and making many helpful suggestions.
33.
One exception is Palladio's diminutive domestic chapel at the Villa Barbaro, Maser. Here there is such a difference in scale between the prime object and the replication that one is tempted to accuse the architect of irresponsible freedom or even of toymaking. On the other hand, the sense of freedom and the sense of the miniature were the very qualities of villa life in Italy in the 16th century. Villas were miniature cities, as Palladio himself said: and if a miniature city, why not a miniature church? For this see Georgina Masson, "Palladian Villas as Rural Centres," *Architectural Review, 118* (1955), 17-20.
34.
E.g. Alexander Parris' St. Paul's Cathedral, Boston, 1819, or St. Andrew's (now St. George's Greek Orthodox) Church, Philadelphia, 1822-23, by John Haviland.
35.
See Charles A. Place, *Charles Bulfinch* (Boston, 1925), pp. 43-55; N. C. Brainard, "The Old State House," *Bulletin of the Connecticut Historical Society, 22* (1957), 19-22; and Sando Bologna, "Connecticut's Old State House," *Yankee, 25* (May, 1961), 30-31, 84-85.
36.
For this see Richard B. K. McLanathan, "Bulfinch's Drawings for the Maine State House," *Journal of the Society of Architectural Historians, 14* (1955), 12-17.
37.
The L'Enfant façade is even closer to the main front of Raynham Hall, Norfolk, a problematical building either by Inigo Jones or William Edge. But Raynham does not seem to have been available in published form as early as the 1790s.
38.
See Place, pp. 47-51.
39.
Ibid., p. 40.
40.
See Henry Peck, *The New Haven State House* (New Haven, 1889), p. 62, and engraving preceding p. 168.
p. 41.
41.
Designs by a certain Thomas McClunie for landscaping Bushnell Park, site of the Hartford Capitol, are now in the Connecticut State Library, Hartford. Their date is 1880.

Upjohn was born in England in 1828 and grew up in New York. He entered the office of his father, Richard Upjohn, at the age of eighteen.[42] This was in 1846, the year his father's famous Trinity Church was consecrated. In 1851-52 the young Upjohn spent eighteen months abroad. By then the first High Victorian Gothic building in London, All Saints', Margaret Street, was under construction and its outer shell well along (15). It is probable that the young architect saw it.[43] Also in 1852 L.-T.-J. Visconti was beginning his immense continuation of the Louvre, so that the first really significant monument of the Second Empire Style was also under way (16).[44] These completely opposed styles were to be crucial for the Hartford State Capitol.

Whatever young Upjohn saw of modern architecture in Europe in the early '50s, there is
218 little sign of it in the work turned out by the firm of Richard Upjohn & Son during the following years.[45] Such buildings as St. Peter's, Albany (1857-60), and the Central Congregational Church (now the Church of the Covenant), Boston, of 1865-68 (17), are couched in the demurely archaic vocabulary of A. Welby Pugin, or else in the spikier, balder manner of Pugin's English imitators of the 1840's (18). I have not been able to discover a single building by the American firm that shows any but the most timid approach to High Victorian Gothic, or any approach at all to Second Empire. This may have been due to the preferences of the older man, who retired in 1872 when the Hartford Capitol was on the drawing boards.[46]

As its basic documents make clear, English High Victorian Gothic was intended to be

15

16

17

15.
William Butterfield, All Saints', Margaret Street, London (1849-59). From *Builder*, 1853.

16.
L.-T.-J. Visconti, Pavillon Richelieu, Louvre, Paris (1852-57). From *Building News*, 1859.

17.
R. M. Upjohn, Central Congregational Church (now Church of the Covenant), Boston (1865-68). From the *American Architect and Building News*, 1879.

18.
Charles Lee and Thomas K. Bury, Christ Church, Battersea, Surrey, England (1846). From the *Illustrated London News*, 1849.

42.
For Upjohn see the *National Cyclopaedia of American Biography, 2* (New York. 1911), 245-46; the *Dictionary of American Biography, 19* (New York, 1943), 126-27; and the *American Architect and Building News, 79* (1903), 81-82. Upjohn was born in Shaftesbury (Dorset), England, and came to the United States with his widowed father in 1829. He spent four years as a student in his father's office (1846 to 1850). Immediately after his return from Europe he apparently tried to establish his own practice, but soon formed a partnership with his father. Aside from the many churches done by the firm, R. M. Upjohn is credited with the Mechanics' Bank, Wall Street, New York of 1858 (now destroyed), either the first or one of the first New York buildings with fireproof construction, i.e. iron floor beams on brick arches. The younger man may also have been responsible for the fantastic north entrance to Greenwood Cemetery, Brooklyn (1861). He was one of the original Fellows of the American Institute of Architects, and died in 1903.

43.
For All Saints' see *Builder, 11* (1853), 56, which describes the shell of the church as being nearly complete in January 1853. R. M. Upjohn was in contact with the Ecclesiological Society, which was sponsoring All Saints' as a model church, and visited their London headquarters in 1851. *Ecclesiologist, 13* (1852), 19.

44.
For the spread of High Victorian Gothic and Second Empire the standard accounts are in Hitchcock, *Nineteenth and Twentieth*, pp. 173-90 and 131-72, respectively.

45.
Everard Upjohn, in his biography of the older architect, says he has had difficulty in separating the hands of the two designers. Everard Upjohn, *Richard Upjohn* (New York, 1939), pp. 111-13, 124, 46.

46.
Ibid., p. 183. The formal resignation took place on March 19, just a week after the entries to the second and definitive competition for the Hartford Capitol went on display. Hartford *Daily Courant* (March 12, 1872).

18

flexible, machine-conscious, and democratic.[47] Its practitioners were almost religiously committed to it. It is colorful, asymmetrical, sharp-faceted, full of jumpy rhythms, and laced into irregular grids with polychrome bands. Weighty geometric solids are juggled into alternately tight and expansive array. In England the new style, in its most serious form, was often manifested in socially-conscious buildings: slum missions, clergy colleges, model housing, and the like. Its contacts with the past extend to the more whimsical kinds of Tudor, Italian, or Ottonian brickwork, to the formal compositions of Decorated Gothic, and, especially in the work of G. E. Street, to Spanish and North Italian medieval details.[48] High Victorian Gothic was consciously "modern," however, in its concern to imitate machine forms as well as medieval ones, to eliminate carving, and, through an elaborate program of architectural symbolism, to express the different functions and sites of individual buildings.

This was not the case in America. Here the first High Victorian Gothic building was probably the thickset, octagonal Nott Memorial Library, Union College, Schenectady, designed in 1856 by Edward Tuckerman Potter and built in 1858-76.[49] It would seem to refer to James Gibbs' Radcliffe Camera at Oxford, a completely non-High Victorian Gothic source to say the least. The library at Union led to William Alonzo Potter's Chancellor Green Library at Princeton (1872-73)[50] – a similar octagon, but with smaller flanking octagons connected to it. The First Church, Boston, by Ware and van Brunt (1865-67), and H. H. Richardson's Grace Church, West Medford, Massachusetts of 1867-68, are other examples. Though asymmetrical, they are timidly so by English standards. Such buildings as Richard M. Hunt's Yale Divinity School (1869) and Russell Sturgis' contemporaneous Farnam Hall, also at Yale (19), display a different aspect of the English style: its faceted simplicity of detail. But in Farnam Hall the basic idea is a system of regular repeats and modest shapes quite different from the abrupt syncopation and joyous dissonance in Butterfield's courtyard at Keble College, Oxford (20). The work of Peter B. Wight could vary between an essentially domestic Fine Arts Gallery at Yale (1864-67; Fig. 49), and a more archaizing pastiche of Venetian and Lombard elements in the National Academy of Design,

19-20

19.
Russell Sturgis, façade of Farnam Hall, Yale University (1869). Courtesy Yale University Library.
20.
William Butterfield, Keble College, Oxford, Quadrangle (1868). National Buildings Record.

47.
One can see this democratic and industrial side especially in A. J. B. Hope, *The Common Sense of Art* (London, 1858), and ibid., *The English Cathedral of the Nineteenth Century* (London, 1861). G. G. Scott, in *Remarks on Secular and Domestic Architecture* (London, 1857), pp. 267, 274, also emphasizes the architectural use of engineering forms.
48.
See his *Brick and Marble Architecture in the Middle Ages* (London, 1855).
49.
Hitchcock, *Nineteenth and Twentieth*, p. 191.
50.
In the *New-York Sketch-Book of Architecture, 1,* No. 3 (1874), Pl. 10. William Alonzo Potter was the brother of Edward Tuckerman Potter.

New York (1863-65).[51] The more significant career of Frank Furness, the only American with a vital sense of High Victorian Gothic, was just beginning in 1872.[52] So America actually had very little to offer Upjohn when he decided to break away from his father's manner and take up a style with more "vigor" and "go."

Psychologically and visually, Second Empire is very different from High Victorian Gothic. As the name implies, it proclaimed the authoritarian regime of Napoleon III. It is whitish, symmetrical, bulbous, and layered in appearance. It is classicizing and uniform. It is conceived in terms of long axes and long wings, regularly punctuated with arched, mansarded pavilions. Where High Victorian Gothic is primarily ecclesiastical or
220 charitable, Second Empire is primarily palatial and administrative. It relies heavily on rich sculptural extrusions, Baroque heraldry, trumpeting allegorical figures, and garlanded triumphal arches. It summons up not Antiquity but the "modern" patrimony of Francis I and his successors.[53]

The style appeared in this country concurrently with High Victorian Gothic. An early definitive attempt is James Renwick's Main Hall, Vassar, of 1860.[54] But the new mode quickly associated itself with government and commerce rather than with learning. In 1862-65 came the Boston City Hall by Gridley Bryant and Arthur D. Gilman, still a rather subdued building compared with what was to be built later (21).[55] Then in 1868 Thomas Fuller and Augustus Laver, both Englishmen and both earlier involved in the massive High Victorian Gothic parliament buildings in Ottawa, designed a New York State Capitol for Albany (22).[56] This fantastic dream seems to have sprung from both French and English roots. The detail is reminiscent of the New Louvre; but the silhouette is more like Cuthbert Broderick's Town Hall at Leeds of 1855-59 (23),[57] with its enormous central columniated tower. After this it was not hard to go on to the massive County buildings in Chicago by J. J. Egan (1872-75), the many post offices designed under the direction of A. B. Mullett, and Augustus Laver's own magnificent, if less roofy, municipal buildings in San Francisco (1870-94 and ff.). None of the more hugely exuberant members of this group, however, was in existence in 1872. The Hartford Capitol was therefore designed at the very beginning of the adventure in civic superscale that I mentioned earlier.

21

21.
Gridley Bryant and Arthur D. Gilman, Boston City Hall, Boston (1862-65). From Anonymous, *The City Hall.*

V

We now come to something else that was introduced earlier: the special importance, in this country, of free replication in the middle of the nineteenth century. At this time the relationships of stylistic motifs were as free as the relationships of site, shell, and interior. In Europe, throughout the nineteenth century, architectural styles were compared to languages and normally considered self-consistent, coherent systems.[58] Here, in practice, they were not. For us style meant aggregates of forms to be used without regard to their associations.

Critics of the time were quite aware of this American peculiarity. The *Ecclesiologist*, for example, complained in 1850 that American Episcopalians were using fourteenth-century English Decorated for their churches in all parts of the United States. The Ecclesiologists had urged this style for England for obvious reasons.[59]
But for those parts of America where the climate made it unsuitable, they recommended other more rational choices. North Italian was suggested for the South and Swedish for the extreme North.[60] The Americans were not persuaded that style need relate to climate, however. A blandly uniform English Gothic package was evolved and built everywhere. Gervase Wheeler commented on such unthinking mimicry: "The great evil of the present American architecture is that it . . . seems to have no laws, and express no meaning." [61] Even native critics sometimes agreed. James E. Cabot, writing in the *Atlantic Monthly* in 1862, attacked the "clever men who . . . dazzle and bewilder us with beauties plucked haphazard from all times and ages."[62]

In America, therefore, High Victorian Gothic and Second Empire were not competing but complementary modes. This can be shown in the work even of so responsible an architect as Richardson. Hitchcock has pointed out that in 1867 Richardson was building the High Victorian Gothic Unity Church and the Renaissance Western Railway Office in Springfield, Massachusetts, and creating an unsuccessful project that is fully Second Empire for the Equitable Life Insurance Building in New York. Richardson then went on, in the Springfield County Courthouse, actually to conflate High

---

51.
This is an excellent example of the difference between English and American High Victorian Gothic. The basic block of Wight's building was a modified Doge's Palace. In the center, at the head of a flight of steps, was a rich Lombard Gothic church portal. The building was completely symmetrical and covered with sculptured and polychromed ornament. Superficially it was a literal embodiment of some of Ruskin's precepts from *The Seven Lamps of Architecture* and *The Stones of Venice.* It was also thoroughly unlike typical High Victorian Gothic institutional building in England; in its basic mass it was almost neoclassical.

52.
Furness' first true High Victorian Gothic building was the Pennsylvania Academy of the Fine Arts, Philadelphia, of 1872-76. The Rodeph Shalom Synagogue, by the firm of Fraser, Furness & Hewitt (1869; demolished 1925) was not a true example of the mode.

53.
For a more detailed discussion of the sources of this style see Henry-Russell Hitchcock, "Second Empire avant la lettre," *Gazette des Beaux-Arts,* s. 6, *42*, (1953), 115-30. In its "modernity," Second Empire was like High Victorian Gothic. This sole likeness between the two is important. As Vincent Scully has pointed out in *Modern Architecture* (New York, 1961), p. 16, the 19th-century revivals appeared in roughly the same order as the styles that were being revived. In other words, the period was a capsule history of architecture. Second Empire and High Victorian Gothic, coming as they did toward the end of this series, are thus two self-consciously "modern" revivals which replace earlier antique and medieval ones. These "modern" revivals, in turn, give way to the Art Nouveau, which might be called *a*historical, and the International Style, which was *anti*historical. The whole period can thus be seen as an attempt to find a style by reliving the past, much as someone tries to find a lost object by repeating what he was doing when he lost it.

54.
For this see R. T. McKenna, "James Renwick, Jr., and the Second Empire Style in the United States," *Magazine of Art, 44* (1951), 97-101.

55.
See George I. Wrenn, "The Boston City Hall, Bryant and Gilman, 1862-65," *Journal of the Society of Architectural Historians, 21* (1962), 188-92.

22-23 221

22.
Thomas Fuller and Augustus Laver, project for the New York State Capitol, Albany (1868). From *American Architect and Building News*, 1876.
23.
Cuthbert Broderick, Town Hall, Leeds, Yorks, England (1855-59). From *Building News*, 1876.

56.
See the *American Architect and Building News, 1* (1876), 81-83, 93-94 ff.
57.
A project for which was published in the *Builder, 11* (1853), 690-91.
58.
English critics emphasize this over and over again. American writers also made the point, though in vain. Besides Downing, see D. H. Jacques, *The House: A Manual of Rural Architecture* (new ed. New York, 1867), p. 16. For an account of association theory as it relates to the idea of architectural grammar and language, see Loudon, *Encyclopaedia*, pp. 1-7, 1105-24.
59.
But they were not exclusively in favor of it as Sir Kenneth Clark maintains in *Gothic Revival* (3rd ed. London, 1962), p. 171.
60.
Ecclesiologist, 10 (1849), 203.
61.
Gervase Wheeler, *Homes for the People* [1855] (New York, 1858), pp. 5-6.
62.
J. E. Cabot, *Atlantic Monthly, 10* (1862) 431.

Victorian Gothic with Second Empire.[63] Unlike European architects, Americans seemed to be able to change gears stylistically without much compunction.

We find this once again if we look at some of the projects for the Hartford Capitol competition of 1872.[64] I have been able to find five of them in one form or another. These are by H. H. Richardson, George B. Post, Charles B. Atwood, the Boston firm of John H. Sturgis and Charles Brigham, and Upjohn. The program, as laid down by the building committee, was very specific, and the basic arrangement in all five projects is essentially similar. Each consists of a more or less cruciform block, with the arms devoted to Senate, Representatives', and Supreme Court chambers, and to an entrance foyer. The crossing space is given over to circulation. Around the outer parts of the arms are office blocks. Each project has either a dome or a tower.[65]

The most integrated design is Richardson's. It is discussed elsewhere in this issue by Charles Price, so here I need only say that although it is thoroughly Beaux-Arts in its symmetry, height, and simplicity, it is still something of a stylistic compromise. The general silhouette is more
222 church-like than legislative, for example. This quality, in the tower at least, must also have been apparent to Richardson, for, as Price notes, the final design of the tower of Trinity Church, Boston, is very like it. Also, the general silhouette of Richardson's Hartford project, a pyramid of clear, separate volumes, resembles the eastern view of a Romanesque abbey. This Romanesque and ecclesiastical character is emphasized by the zigzagging Auvergnat string courses and frowning round arches. In France, such a churchy flavor would have ruled this design out of court. There, Romanesque was acceptable only for ecclesiastical and charitable institutions.[66]

On the other hand, Richardson's heavy arches can equally well be read as *style massif*, the most austere and astylar kind of Beaux-Arts classicism. The *style massif* is derived from French Mannerism.[67] Also, Richardson's flat-headed windows are Late Gothic or Early Renaissance. There is therefore something in Richardson's project of the stylistic ambiguity Hitchcock found in Upjohn's completed building. Both compositionally and ornamentally, Richardson has trespassed across the European architectural language barriers. It is interesting to note that this project, which is one of the earliest examples of the mature style of our first great architect, is an essay in free replication. This might provide a key to the difficulty of relating Richardson, the Shingle Style, Sullivan, and Wright to the chronological and stylistic categories of European architectural history.

I have found only a rendering of Post's project (24). It is classic, of a heavily jointed, *encadré* sort, based on the vocabulary of J. I. Hittorf's Gare du Nord (1861-65) in Paris. But like Richardson's, Post's building is ecclesiastical rather than legislative in type, being composed like a Leonardesque church. Domed towers are set at the corners of a central square crossing capped with a tall parabolic dome. The arms, consisting of sub-basement, basement, *piano nobile*, attic, and pavilion roof, have cornices that are lower than the towers and higher than the office blocks that fill the corners of the arms. This produces a High Victorian effect of heterogeneous interlocked parallelepipeds. There is a tall exedral entrance at the top of a flight of steps. Being without porticoes and round-arched, Post's design is related to Richardson's Romanesque classicism as well as to a more properly Roman sort. Thus, in detail as well as composition, it is outside the usual canon for

63.
See Henry-Russell Hitchcock, *The Architecture of H. H. Richardson and His Times* (new ed., Hamden, Conn., 1961), pp.61-78. One could contrast this American mobility with the most famous English stylistic switch of the era. This was Sir G. G. Scott's abandonment of High Victorian Gothic for "classical" (not Second Empire but a very rich Early Victorian Renaissance) in the Government Offices competition of 1857. This apostasy was loudly bewailed, not least by the architect himself. It shows how wrong such behavior was felt to be in England. In this country it was so common as not to be worth mentioning. For the best account of the Scott affair, see Clark, *The Gothic Revival*, pp. 185-91.

64.
For this see the Hartford *Daily Courant* and the Hartford *Times*, which took opposing views, from January 1872 throughout the rest of the year. Of special interest are articles and editorials in the *Courant* for Jan. 3, 11, 12, and March 12. More general articles are found in ibid. (March 27, 1878), and in the *American Architecture and Building News*, *2* (1877), 295; *4* (1878), 174; and *5* (1879), 17-18. A more thorough but more biased source is the scrapbook, part MS and part clippings, "History of the New State House" at Hartford, Conn., compiled by J. G. Batterson in 1879, and now in the Connecticut State Library.

65.
Six architects were invited to submit to the first competition, held on January 1, 1872. Five did so. Three of them were Bryant and Rogers, Atwood. and Batterson & Keller. The deadline for the second competition was March 12. There were fourteen entrants. Besides those named in the first competition there were Upjohn, Peabody & Stearns, H. & J. E. Billings, John McArthur, George B. Post, J. Cleveland Cady, E. T. Potter, Griffith Thomas, W. R. Emerson, H. H. Richardson, Gridley Bryant, and Sturgis & Brigham. For the rigid program and specifications, see the Hartford *Daily Courant* (Feb. 1, 1872). Why the young Richardson (33) was chosen, or even the younger Atwood (23), is hard to say. Richardson had not yet won the Trinity Church competition, nor been commissioned to design the Phoenix Insurance Building in Hartford, nor had he undertaken any of his structures for the Cheney family in that city. He was presumably known through his Springfield work. Henry-Russell Hitchcock has been most helpful to me in making this tentative suggestion. As far as I know, Atwood had not built at all. Batterson & Keller were local builders.

66.
See Hitchcock, *Richardson*, pp. 30-31.

67.
For this see Louis Hautecoeur, *Histoire de l'architecture classique en France*, 6 (Paris, 1955), 152-57.

24

legislative palaces. It also has a diminutive character, enhanced by the formidable fanfare of Baroque ramps, stairs, and terraces, giving the impression of a mortuary chapel on some great estate. But on the whole, this project, out of all I have seen, is the most controlled replication. It looks forward to the compulsive correctness and European-ness of our later nineteenth- and early twentieth-century classicism, and is therefore an anticipation of its architect's later career.

When we turn to the three remaining competition entries we find a much greater freedom in the treatment of style. The very youthful Charles B. Atwood, who paradoxically was to be so imperially classical at the World's Columbian Exposition of 1893, submitted two designs (Figs. 25-28) which balance out High Victorian Gothic against Second Empire in a near-mathematical way. They also play with the free and restricted qualities of the two sites that were being considered (one downtown on a lot, and the other in Bushnell Park). It is almost as if the architect had assigned positive and negative values to the motifs and compositional effects of the two styles. The first design, for example (25, 26), obviously intended for the urban site, has an exterior that is completely symmetrical except for the low porch on the front. But inside, the plan is off center: The House of Representatives encroaches informally on the central hall; and the arrangement of offices and stairs is irregular. The other design was presumably for Bushnell Park (27, 28). Here, where there was more freedom of site, there was paradoxically more regularity of plan. And yet at

24.
George B. Post, project for the Connecticut State Capitol (1872). Courtesy Connecticut State Library, Hartford.
25.
Charles B. Atwood, "city" project for Connecticut State Capitol (1872).
26.
Plan of project in Fig. 25. Main (second) floor.
27.
Charles B. Atwood, "park" project for the Connecticut State Capitol (1872).
28.
Plan of project in Fig. 27. Main (second) floor. Figs 25-28 from *Architectural Sketchbook*, 1874.

25-26

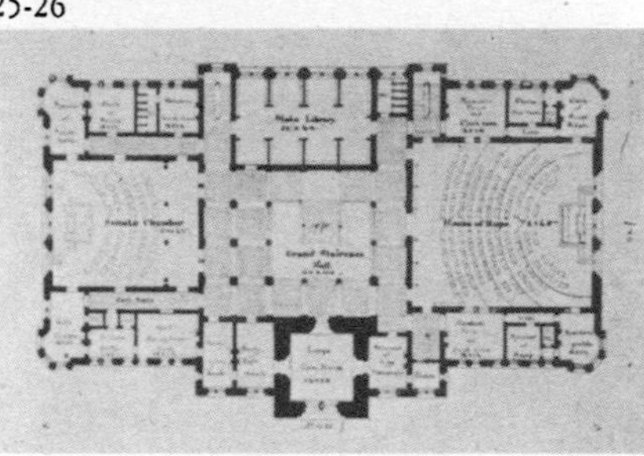

26-27

27-28

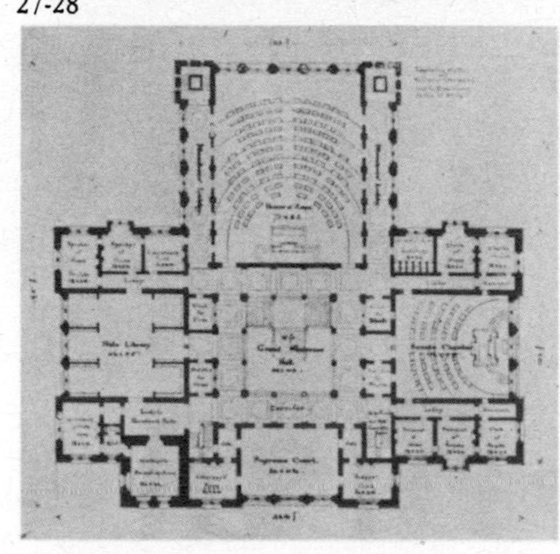

223

the same time, there are more separate roofs, there is more variety of cornice level, and as a result more plasticity of a High Victorian Gothic type. The tower is a striking asymmetrical "Gothic" accent.

One can even discern a calculation of secular as opposed to ecclesiastical factors. The detail of the park design is cruder and more fortress-like, more vernacular, than the detail in the other rendering. The relatively churchy plan is balanced, therefore, by Palazzo Vecchio-like qualities of wall and tower. The city design, on the other hand, is less churchy in plan but more so in detailing. Atwood's thinking is reminiscent of the way Neoplastic artists gave numerical values to the various elements of their compositions, and made them balance out to zero.[68]

224 29-30

31

Sturgis & Brigham's design shows the same thing in somewhat simpler form (29). Square pavilions flank a recessed gabled entrance with a rose window. Rising behind this is a higher gable, also with a rose window, and above this gable, at the crest of the roof, is a weighty square tower with a pyramidal spire. This centralized arrangement is varied by the introduction, on the left, of a square, pavilion-roofed chamber behind the outer front range. The angle pavilion on the same flank has a short turret rising from almost inside it. On the right a large chamber is housed in an impressive apse of the type favored by William Burges. Thus, around a static, processional center of rising tiers, are sets of outbuildings with more individual character. An authoritarian core is flanked by free subsidiaries, and the whole is covered with a fabric of High Victorian Gothic detail. Where Atwood had many smaller values balancing out, Sturgis & Brigham have used fewer, larger integers.

Upjohn also played mathematical games with stylistic motifs. But despite his freedom in this and in his use of sources, he also revealed a certain orderliness of mind. One of his presumably early projects (30)[69] called for the linking of a tall aspidal hall to the main building by means of a low arched gateway. The hall idea probably comes from Burges' project for the Law Courts of 1867. Burges himself re-used this feature in Trinity College, Hartford, designed in 1873, and we have just seen it also in Bryant's design for the Hartford Capitol. Linking two close-set elephantine masses by means of a low gateway was also an established High Victorian Gothic idea. But the uniformity of what I shall call the detail-grid in Upjohn's design, if not the detail itself, is classical, and this added classicism balances out the radical asymmetry of the massing.

Another variant, labeled "no. 2" (31), has an entrance porch set out from the main front of the building, a porch reminiscent of Scott's at St. Pancras' Station, London (1863-76). In the Upjohn scheme it serves as another radical mass. The detail in this project is, however, classical in form as well as disposition. But it is classical in a sliced-looking, schematic way. The ornamental system is reduced to a skeleton of tab-like pilasters and lintels that encase wall panels. The effect is almost that of a Chicago office building – e.g. William LeBaron Jenney's first Leiter Building of 1879 (32). The pointed arches of Upjohn's other designs have here been replaced either with round or flat-headed ones, and the scale of the subsidiary ornament has been increased. The tower is more barbarous, and the whole feeling is that of masons' vernacular, suggesting that Upjohn was giving to provincial classicism a

32

"Gothic" value, in the sense that it was coarse and wild. Compared to the other projects, therefore, in this design a less classicizing detail-grid balances a less Gothic mass.

VI

The winning design is more classicizing in every way than its predecessors (33). Like Atwood, Post, and Sturgis & Brigham, Upjohn has lifted his assembly rooms high up over an undercroft or basement. With Upjohn, however, not merely the crossing but almost the whole of the lower floor is given over to circulation space (2). Furthermore, this "basement" is so high and noble that it hardly deserves the name. At the edges of the building are tall office stacks, which are brought to a uniform height with the other interior spaces. But they are separately roofed and slightly recessed. In the center is a square crossing in which the massive tower piers are set close together. Flanking the tall well of the tower are secondary courts that rise to stained-glass skylights. The main façade is bilaterally symmetrical. There is a central frontispiece heavily inset with arcades and flanked by two stubby towers. Longer wings, set back from the main front, project from this grouping and end in lateral bays that take the form of tall gabled frontispieces, with hip-roofed pavilions set out, in turn, from them. As in Atwood's park design (27), the tower is located to the left of the main group. The one asymmetrical, Gothic element is therefore also the one vertical element and the one chiefly symbolic element. Upjohn thus lined up the values of classicism and

33

33.
Richard M. Upjohn, winning design for the Connecticut State Capitol. Courtesy Slide and Photographic Collection, Yale Art Library.

29.
John H. Sturgis & Charles Brigham, project for the Connecticut State Capitol. From *Architectural Sketchbook*, 1875.
30.
Richard M. Upjohn, project for Connecticut State Capitol, 1872. Side elevation. Courtesy Connecticut State Library.
31
Richard M. Upjohn, project "no. 2" for Connecticut State Capitol. Side elevation. Courtesy Connecticut State Library.
32.
William LeBaron Jenney, First Leiter Building, 1879, Chicago. Museum of Modern Art, New York.

68.
See Bruno Zevi, *Poetica dell'architettura neoplastica* (Milan, 1953), p. 42 (quoting Theo van Doesburg).
69.
There are a number of large folio volumes of Upjohn's Capitol drawings now in the Connecticut State Library. For permission to reproduce some of them here, I believe for the first time, I must thank Miss Virginia Knox, Acting State Librarian.

225

Gothicism neatly on either side of the fence. He did not let them mingle, as the other architects did. This is part of his orderliness.

Upjohn does not seem to have cared to disguise his borrowings. In a letter to the *Hartford Times* the well-known theologian, Dr. Horace Bushnell, pointed out that the tower came from Lockwood & Mawson's Bradford (Yorkshire) Town Hall, an engraving of which had appeared in the *Building News* in 1870 (34). Bushnell added that the American architect had misread the rendering, and had imagined that the tower rose from inside the building rather than from the outside far corner.[70] The fronts of Upjohn's pavilions apparently also came from an English source.[71] They are like those designed by Street for the Strand front of the Law Courts, and published in 1867 (35): gabled masses between slender turrets which have been sliced with rapid upright grooves, and which are supported on thin shafts that fall to massive molded bases.

226 34-35

Even this more classicizing design totaled up to a stylistic balance that was too Gothic for the building committee. In 1873 the Legislature asked for a dome instead of a tower. François I lucarnes also replaced the small triangular Gothic dormers (1).[72] But despite the essential classicism of the dome, it was detailed so as to maintain the old stylistic balance. As a shape, it was as much a tower as a dome, thus combining values from both styles. Furthermore, it has been ribbed and perforated into aggressively Gothic form. The idea of a Gothic dome need not have originated with Upjohn, since E. M. Barry had published one for his Law Courts project in 1867. And Alessandro Antonelli was building a tower-dome for San Gaudenzio, Novara, between 1840-88. It was only necessary for Upjohn to combine Antonelli's shape with Barry's brand of sculptured shell.[73]

The general massing of the Capitol as built is fully Second Empire except for this tower-dome (57).[74] Over the Second Empire masses Upjohn has put a layered classical detail-grid. The detail in itself is almost all High Victorian Gothic; however, it is most Gothic where masses beneath are most classical, and most classical where the masses beneath are most Gothic. For example, the central porches and the windows of the *piano nobile* are aggressively dressed with pointed arches, mosaics, and what not; and the complex pointed forms of the roofs are screened with flat, symmetrical Early Renaissance lucarnes. Thus there is a contrapuntal play between the values of the main masses and those of the detail-grid. Each stylistic motif is distinct as a number or expression in algebra. This concept of the exterior of a building as a set of masses (and later, of volumes) constrained by a taut grid was one that developed in Chicago. We have already noted the likeness of one of Upjohn's projects to Jenney's work, but the effect was developed into something beautiful in Sullivan's Wainwright and Guaranty buildings.

If the masses of the exterior are Second Empire, the treatment of interior space is High Victorian Gothic (36). One can also see the inside of the Capitol as a Shingle Style inner landscape brought up to monumental scale. It consists of three tall wells filled with light. Of these the middle well, the inside of the floorless dome, is the tallest and brightest. All three are united by lateral horizontal spaces which move squarely around them at various levels, and which, in turn, are defined by tray-like floors or mezzanines. In

36

34.
Lockwood & Mawson, project for Bradford, Yorks, Town Hall. From *Building News*, 1870.
35.
G. E. Street, Strand front of Law Courts. From *Building News*, 1867.
36.
Interior of Hartford Capitol. John T. Hill.

fact, the interior is somewhat reminiscent of Adolph Loos' concept of *raumplan*, for example in the Tristan Tzara house in Paris: the interior of a building as a hollow well filled with platforms at various levels.[75]

The idea of mass, so important on the exterior, disappears inside. The walls seem to have shrunk around a bony metallic armature of columns and beams (37). The stubby vertical members, at times socketed together end-to-end, and the encased beams create a set of cages from which the offices and assembly rooms seem slung. Ornament enhances the sense of machine or factory structure. The relief carving has blade-like ridges and resembles coils of metal shavings. The incised decoration consists of rosettes, like rivet heads, and broad bandings (38).[76]

Together, the open stairs, the balcony-like floors, and the tall wells create surfaces that rise and dip. One set of spaces passes through and over another. This complex landscape is punctuated here and there by statues, neoclassical in style but mannerist in scale and function.[77] They aid the effects of swift recession, incalculable gaps, and sudden returns, and form an alternative population to the human beings. In this they are like the small bands of plaster figures that Rudolph has set wandering through the Art and Architecture Building at Yale.

VII

We can see such an interplay of stylistic values in buildings that have been partly derived from Upjohn's. The Gothic domes that Calvert Vaux designed for a project for the 1876 Philadelphia

37-38

37.
Interior of Hartford Capitol. Main floor, John T. Hill.
38.
Interior of Hartford Capitol. Main floor. John T. Hill.

227

70.
Hartford *Times* (June 27, 1873). A view of the other side of the Bradford Town Hall, showing the tower projecting from the façade was published in the *Builder, 30* (1872), 907.
71.
This was noticed by a critic named Chetwood, writing in the *American Architect, 2* (1877), 295-96. He says the wings are like those of a certain public building recently erected near London. I do not understand the "near," unless he is trying to say that the Law Courts were not in the City but in Holborn. Chetwood also criticized the balustrade and the plainness of the lower-story windows as opposed to the upper. He tells us that Upjohn was not allowed to supervise construction. This was left to the unsuccessful competitor Batterson. Later on there was an enormous furor about the weakness of the dome piers. For this see the *American Architect, 1* (1876) ; *2* (1877), passim.
72.
American Architect, 2 (1877), 295. It was at this time that the balustrade was added. This may be yet another echo from the Bulfinch Capitol. See above n. 39.
73.
Barry's project was published in the *Builder* in 1867. Another possibly relevant Gothic dome is that by an unknown architect of Notre-Dame-de-Boulogne, Boulogne-sur-mer, France (1827-66), but I do not know that it was published. Antonelli's San Gaudenzio dome did not, so far as I know, appear in an English periodical before 1874. The project by the brothers Douillard for Sacré-Coeur calls for a dome that is the closest to Upjohn's of any I have found. But this project was for a competition that closed on June 30, 1874, well after the Upjohn dome was designed. Hautecoeur, *Histoire* 7, 212.
74.
One should here remark on the size and expense. The original building was to have cost $875,000. Contracts for this amount were signed in October 1872. By then the legislature had determined to build on land adjoining Bushnell Park, land then occupied by Trinity College (*Hartford Courant*, March 20. 1872, and *American Architect*, 5 [1879], 17-18). The ostensible reason for increasing the budget to $2,500.000 in 1873 was to make the building fireproof. Upjohn's drawings in the State Library show that the building is of marble, brick, and iron except for the wood trim. The Capitol is 300 feet long by 200 feet wide (at the crossing), and the masonry dome is 260 feet high and 56 feet in diameter. There was a long correspondence between readers of the *Courant* on the symbolism of the dome as opposed to the clock tower (*Courant*, Jan. 13, 1872 and thereafter, especially March 19).

75.
See Benevolo, *Storia, 1*, 402-03.
76.
The incised and stenciled interior decoration was designed and executed by the New York firm of Pottier & Stymus. Some of their designs are preserved in the Connecticut State Library with the Upjohn drawings.
77.
I do not know by whom. The *Genius of Connecticut* (1877), atop the lantern, is by Randolph Rogers, who also did the Colt Memorial (1862) in Hartford. An earlier plaster model for the dome figure is now located in the main floor (38). The twelve allegorical statues around the base of the dome are by J. Q. A. Ward. They symbolize Agriculture, Law, Commerce, Science, Music, and Equity, and the other six are duplicates, the result of an urge to economize. The statues of Sherman and Trumbull on the east entrance are from the hand of C. B. Ives. For Rogers, Ward, and Ives, see Lorado Taft, *The History of American Sculpture* (new ed. New York, 1930), pp. 159-70, 216-33, and 112-13. respectively. See also *American Architect*, *2* (1877), 396; and ibid., *4* (1878), 174.

Exposition are much like his (39). More generally, Vaux's scheme is another mixture of Second Empire and High Victorian Gothic values. It is a massive symmetrical design in which strongly High Victorian Gothic windows mingle with triumphal arches and pavilion roofs. One thinks also of Leopold Eidlitz and H. H. Richardson's 1875 project for the New York State Capitol (40). These architects had been called in with F. L. Olmstead when the original designers, Thomas Fuller and Augustus Laver, had exceeded their total budget merely in building the two lower stories.[78] Eidlitz and Richardson were apparently asked to design a building that would fit these foundation stories and cost as little as possible. The result was a design much like Upjohn's. It might even be described as a warping of the Hartford Capitol to fit Fuller & Laver's foundations. There is the same type of towered frontispiece, there are similar angle pavilions, and a corresponding relationship of the whole to the dome. It is an excellent example of free replication, by the way. It shows how the shell was understood as a hollow rubbery object to be stretched over the pre-existing "mold" of the interior.

228 39-40

In line with the general stylistic tendency of the era, Richardson and Eidlitz's conception is more classical than Upjohn's. The fenestration is more regular, and round arches, which are less overtly medieval than pointed ones, prevail throughout. In fact, the building moves upward through a kind of stylistic spectrum. It begins with an aggressively Baroque foundation story and rises through the moderate medievalism of *Rundbogenstil* main floors to Late Gothic-Early Renaissance roofs. It ends up with an octagonal dome like the one at Santa Maria del Fiore in Florence. The dome may have been intended as yet another stylistic compromise. But this series of transitions was in itself only a transition. The existing building, not finished until the '90s, is even more classicizing.

The concept of free replication, and with it the stylistic calculus we have been describing, passed out of sight with the onset of Beaux-Arts classicism in the '90s. I have already suggested that the latter was an attempt to root out the follies and inspirations of free replication. On the whole it was successful. We possess a great many Beaux-Arts buildings that are fully integrated in respect to siting, shell, interior, building type, and scale. They are as grandiose and iconologically indefinite as their European contemporaries. They represent the earliest American monumental architecture that is comparable to contemporaneous European work.

However, in our present period of brutalism there are renewed signs of free replication. Before it was completed, Walter McQuade warned that Rudolph's Art and Architecture Building (41-43) might wind up as a locomotive crash between Wright and Le Corbusier.[79] Such a combination of two entirely heterogeneous architectural languages is comparable to Upjohn's use of High Victorian Gothic and Second Empire. Indeed, Rudolph goes further than Upjohn, for his building has not only a Larkin aspect (44) and a Richards Medical aspect (45) but a Kenzo Tange aspect (46), a Georges Vantongerloo aspect (47), and even a Sir John Soane aspect (48).

And yet all these reminiscences are mere marginal reflections, a dim halo of associations. Perhaps because they are so numerous, the diverse

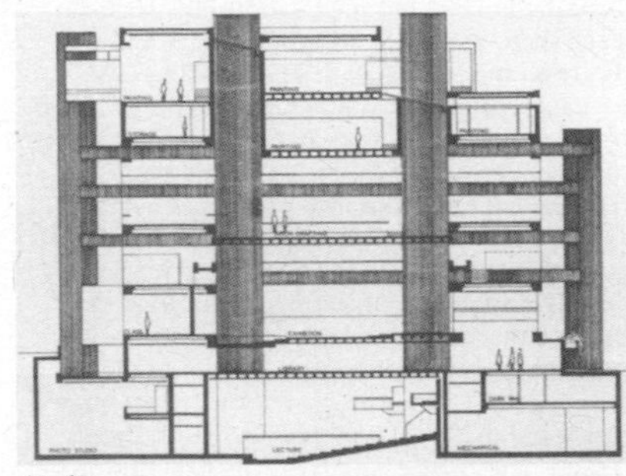

41-42

39.
Calvert Vaux and Frederick Withers, project for Philadelphia Centennial Exposition of 1876. From *American Architect and Building News*, 1874.
40
Leopold Eidlitz and H. H. Richardson, project for the New York State Capitol, Albany (1875). From *American Architect and Building News*, 1876.
41.
Paul Rudolph, Art and Architecture Building, transverse section
42.
Paul Rudolph, Art and Architecture Building, Yale University, New Haven. (1959-63). Transverse section.
43.
Paul Rudolph, Art and Architecture Building.
Cervin Robinson.
44.
Frank Lloyd Wright, Larkin Building, Buffalo (1904). From Arthur Drexler, editor, *Drawings of Frank Lloyd Wright.*
45.
Louis I. Kahn, Richards Medical Laboratory, University of Pennsylvania, Philadelphia (1957). Courtesy of Louis I. Kahn.
46.
Kenzo Tange, Prefectural Government Office, Takamatsu, Japan (1955-58). From *Kenchiku Bunka*, 1959.
47.
Georges Vantongerloo, *Interrelations of Masses based on the Ellipsoid* (1926), plaster, 47 x 40 x 26 cm. Present whereabouts unknown. From Georges Vantongerloo, *Paintings, Sculptures, Reflections.*
48.
J. M. Gandy, the Domed Crypt in Sir John Soane's Museum (1812), London. Watercolor, Sir John Soane's Museum.

78.
For this see Hitchcock, *Richardson*, pp. 167-71, and esp. p. 168, where the relationship to the Hartford Capitol is mentioned.
79.
New Statesman, 65 (1963); 125.

43

44-45

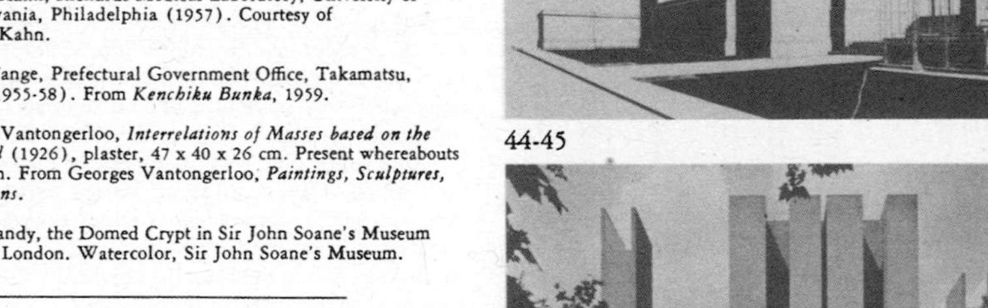

46-47

48

229

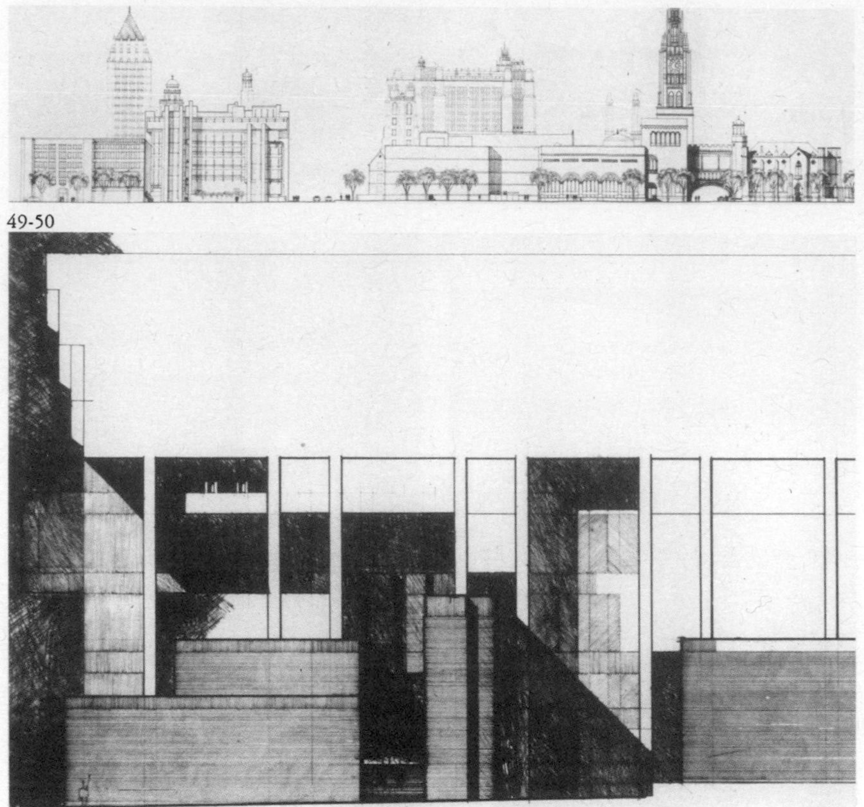

49-50

230 50-51

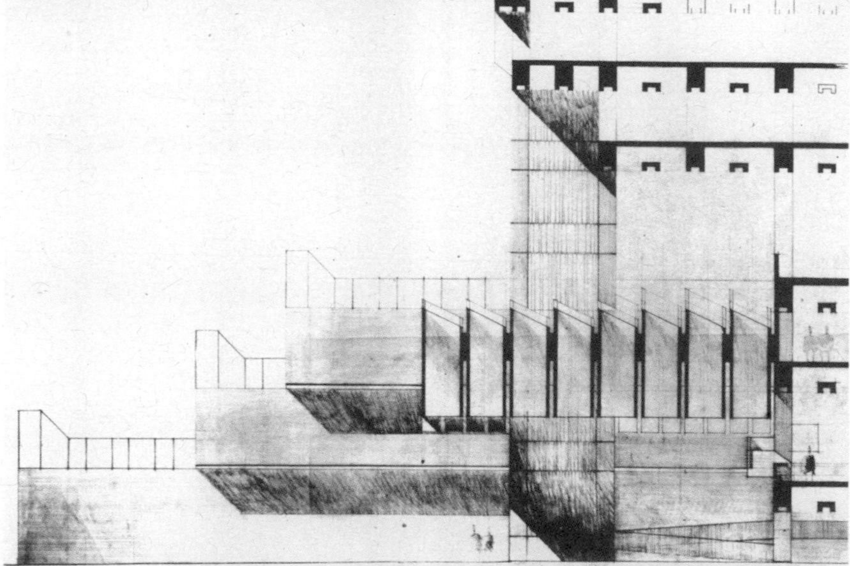

51-52

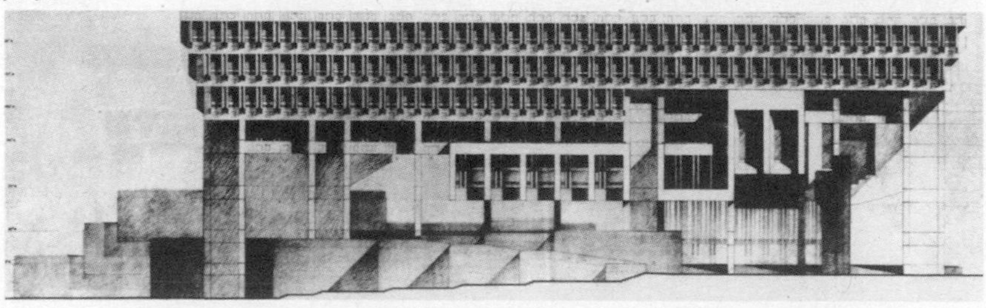

background styles coalesce in the actual building, resulting in something quite different from the mathematical distinctness with which Upjohn had played Second Empire against High Victorian Gothic. Not only is Rudolph's building stylistically unified, but the relationships between site and shell, shell and interior, and type and scale are all fully integrated. The building even takes up, amplifies, or comments upon the series of earlier art buildings along Chapel Street (49). It turns what had been a collection of good but heterogeneous buildings into a procession. It not only fits its environment, but gives a direction and force to that environment. Like the best houses of the Shingle Style, Rudolph's free replication has pushed on through its awkward stages of development to a new integrity.[80]

Another building still under construction speaks this same new artistic language: the new Boston City Hall by Gerhard M. Kallmann, Noel M. McKinnell, and Edward F. Knowles. It is dangerous to speak about buildings before they are complete. And yet one can know some things about this one that make it a contrast to Rudolph's. On first looking at the drawings (50-52), one sees a direct reference to La Tourette (53), and perhaps a lesser reference to the Palace of Justice at Chandigarh (54). The Boston building is also clearly related to a child of La Tourette, Sir Leslie Martin and Colin St. John Wilson's new structure at Caius College, Cambridge. Thus at first glance the Boston building, in contrast to Rudolph's, seems to make use of a self-consistent, delimited artistic language.

And yet looking more closely we see that this has not been the case. In an early project (50), the lean, nervous legs of the building are immured in a podium as inert and massive as the terraces of the Albany Capitol (22). In a later version (51) we see crudely introduced skylights from an equally different stylistic world, reminiscent of the looping "crystal skylight" of Aalto's Helsinki Pension Bank (55). Questions of site, scale, and type also arise. Le Corbusier's monastery is conceived as a shelf projecting from a hillside, like a sculptural ledge. The Boston City Hall will rise like a pagan temple in the midst of a wide urban square. And it will be gigantic in scale compared to La Tourette, as tall as the towers of Stiles and Morse Colleges at Yale.[81] To adapt a monastic prototype for a college, as Martin and Wilson have done, is a traditional procedure: it is what the medieval builders of Cambridge did. But to fill such a shell with secretaries and bureaucrats is more independent, more American. Thus the Boston building will probably include some of the typical after-effects of free replication: jarring stylistic dissonances, the impermanent look of having been transferred from some other site, and weird scale. But to the brutalist sensibility these effects are not necessarily undesirable.

The complex interior should be of interest as well. The offices are to be built around a large open court which may turn out to be reminiscent of the Hartford Capitol. Walter McQuade has described the effect, "blocks of enclosure . . . spotted in a seemingly random manner throughout the hollow volume,"[82] words which also describe the Hartford interior.

It may be that the architects of the Boston building will achieve results that are far more impressive and integrated than E. M. Upjohn's, but the essential process by which they do so, it seems to me, will be the same.

53

54

55

49.
Paul Rudolph, elevations of the art buildings on Chapel Street, including Street Hall (Peter B. Wight, 1864), the Old Art Gallery (Egerton Swartwout, 1928-31), the New Art Gallery (Louis I. Kahn, 1951-53), and the Art and Architecture Building.
50.-52.
Gerhard M. Kallmann, Noel M. McKinnell, and Edward F. Knowles, project for the new Boston City Hall (1962).
53.
Le Corbusier, Monastery of La Tourette, Eveux, France (1957-60). Wayne Andrews.
54.
LeCorbusier, Palace of Justice, Chandigarh, India (1956). Courtesy Slide and Photograph Collection, Yale Art Library.
55.
Alvar Aalto, National Pension Bank, Helsinki, Finland (1952-56). Great Hall with "crystal skylight." From Karl Fleig, ed., *Alvar Aalto.*

80.
So far the bibliography of this building is as follows: Preliminary schemes may be found in *Perspecta,* 7 (1961), 53-63. Then see: anonymous, "Design Jelled for Yale Art and Architectural School: Paul Rudolph, Architect," *Progressive Architecture. 43* (Jan. 1962), 62; anonymous, "Yale's New Art and Architecture Building, Paul Rudolph, Architect," *Architectural Record, 131* (Jan. 1962), 16-17; J. Barnett, "New Collegiate Architecture at Yale: Yale's School of Art and Architecture, Paul Rudolph, Architect," ibid., loc. cit., (April 1962), 125-38; Walter McQuade, "Building Years of a Yale Man: A. W. Griswold," *Architectural Forum, 118* (June 1963), 88-93; anonymous, "SOM, Rudolph, and Johnson at Yale," ibid., loc. cit., (Nov. 1963), 31-31; Jonathan Barnett, "A School for the Arts at Yale," *Architectural Record, 135* (Feb. 1964), 111-20; anonymous, "A & A: Yale School of Art and Architecture," *Progressive Architecture, 45* (Feb. 1964), 108-27, and editorial, p. 107; Ilse M. Reese and James T. Burns, Jr., "The Opposites: Expressionism and Formalism at Yale," ibid., pp. 128-29; the Series in *Architectural Forum,* 120 (Feb. 1964), 66-88: "Yale's School of Art and Architecture, Part I: the Building" (Walter McQuade), "Part II, The Measure" (Sybil Moholy-Nagy), "Part 3: The Builder" (Marshall Burchard), "Part 4: the Architect" (anonymous); Paul Rudolph, "Yale Art and Architecture Building," *Arts and Architecture, 81* (Feb. 1964), 26-29, 34-35, (with captions by Julius Shulman); "Art & Architecture Faculty Building, Yale" *Architectural Design, 34* (April 1964), 178-80; Vincent Scully, "Art and Architecture Building, Yale University. Architect Paul Rudolph." *Architectural Review, 135* (May, 1964), 325-332; Bruno Zevi, "Posano lo spazio su vassoi di cemento" *L'Espresso* April 12, 1964, p. 19. I must thank Robert A. M. Stern, the editor of this issue of *Perspecta,* for his assistance in compiling this bibliography, as well as for many useful suggestions.
81.
I should like to thank Thomas Bosworth for pointing this out to me.
82.
Walter McQuade, "Toughness-before-Gentility Wins in Boston," *Architectural Forum, 117* (Aug. 1962), 100.

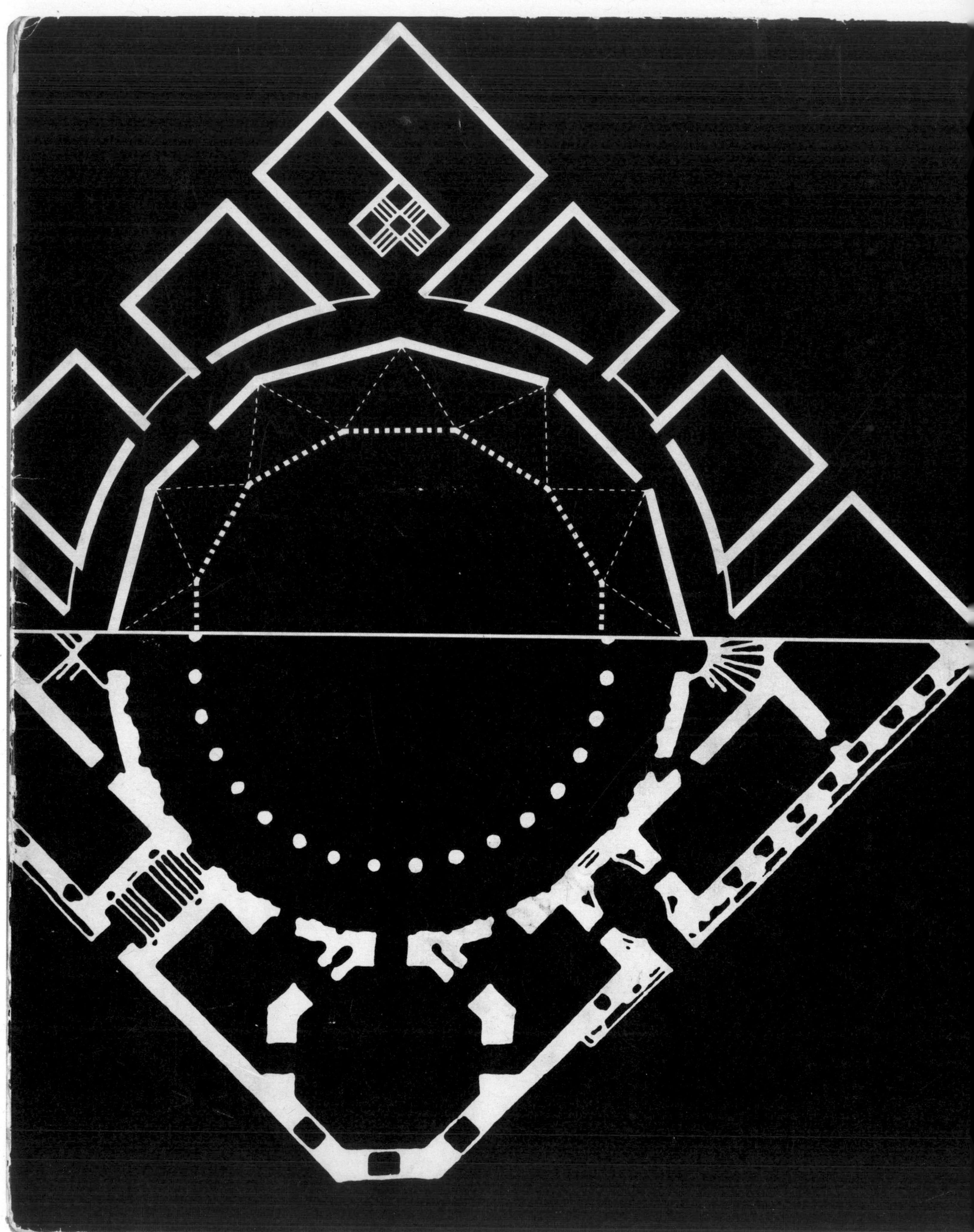

“There is both allure and menace in applying powerful references to build architectural identity.”

Xiahong Hua

Quotation and the Construction of Chinese Architectural Identity

Quotation, Authority, and Identity

Quotation is necessary and valuable only in a widely shared knowledge system. In such systems to quote is to establish or enhance one's own authority using already established authorities and to build or promote one's own identity using already distinguishable identities. Recognizable quotations—instances of borrowing in which both appearance and symbolic meaning are legible—can serve as a strategic podium to establish an identity in a field of other voices. This principle is near universal and is widespread in the history of cultural production, including in the architectural field.

For architecture, as for many other visual arts, this explicit repetition of precedents includes perceptible elements such as form, style, and material as well as intangible aspects such as concept and theory. In other words, architectural quotation is applied as both pragmatic design approach and theoretical paradigm. In the modern era there are at least two different layers in identity construction through architectural production. The first entails creating a built environment embodying the special character of a particular city, region, or nation. The second entails uncovering a unique aspect of architecture as a discipline and discourse, thereby conveying universal principles. Sometimes these layers coincide with each other, but more often than not they follow different trajectories. This situation is particularly true in modern China.

Chinese contemporary architecture tends to use quotation to establish recognition quickly, to achieve political capital, economic growth, social promotion, or cultural acclaim. This tendency results in phenomena ranging from "weird architecture (奇奇怪怪建筑)"[1] to successful regionalism. *Shanzhai* (山寨),[2] a Chinese term referring to the phenomenon of architectural pirating,

1 Mausoleum of Sun Yat-Sen, Nanjing (1929) by Lu Yanzhi.

2 Shanghai Park Hotel (1934) by L.E. Hudec.

has also aroused fierce debate around the world. The most notorious examples of this are displaced architectural landmarks, such as an Eiffel Tower in Hangzhou, Zhejiang, a U.S. Capitol Building in Minhang, Shanghai, a Ronchamp chapel in Zhengzhou, Hunan, and a Tiananmen in Suizhong, Liaoning. This piracy also extends to contemporary icons, such as Meiquan 22nd Century's copy of Zaha Hadid's Wangjing Soho, built in Chongqing (figs. 14, 15).[3] By contrast, Wang Shu's 2012 Pritzker Prize shows that Chinese architects' efforts to transform China's cultural heritage and vernacular resources into contemporary design has gained international recognition (fig. 10). Globally accepted conceptual rubrics for architectural practice, such as critical regionalism, are frequently used to differentiate this group of individual Chinese architects from the majority of local design agencies and their international counterparts.[4]

Modern versus Traditional: Enduring Anxiety

Since the middle of the nineteenth century, notably after the Opium Wars (1840–42 and 1856–60), there has been a pressing anxiety in China to reestablish a national identity independent of international interference. The search for a balance between modernization and tradition has constituted a "protracted war"[5] in many fields.

Although China boasts a rich architectural heritage dating back thousands of years, architecture as a modern profession is a relatively recent development based largely on imported systems from Europe, the United States, and Japan, where the first generation of Chinese architects were educated. Modern China's attempt to build an identity through architectural practice encompasses adapting ancient architectural vernaculars and philosophy for modern use, and incorporating global experiences into local development. Both history and regional context serve as sources for quotation, although the choice of historical periods, goals, references, focus, and criteria vary remarkably.

For the first three quarters of the twentieth century, the biggest challenge for all cultural fields was to define an identity for China as an independent modern nation-state. During the Republican Period (1912–49), when the entire country was subjugated by world war and colonization, architects' ambitions were generally consistent with broad political-economic demands. They had to rely on authorial precedent, both inherited and imported, to establish new systems of pragmatic and intellectual practice. By contrast, in the Maoist era (1949–76) ideological concerns gradually assumed primary importance. Before 1958 the Soviet Union served as the chief model for all construction, from its production-oriented development mode to its classical-revival architectural style. A popular slogan of Soviet origin during this time was "Nationalist in form, socialist in content."

After China's break with its Soviet big brother, Chinese architects fell into an embarrassing condition of collective aphasia. All architectural forms were to be judged according to their symbolic links with ideological significance. Buildings with traditional roofs were criticized as wasteful and dismissed as examples of Feudal Revivalism (封建复古主义),[6] while pure Modernist structures were blamed for getting caught in the "poisonous weeds of Capitalism (资本主义毒草)."[7] The institutional reorganization executed in this period pushed architecture into an objective technological domain in which production took the place of creation. Individual architects were assembled into engineer groups; collectivity replaced individuality.

Toward the late 1970s Chinese authorities stressed models of societal progress and liberation. Deng Xiaoping's statements, including "Development is the absolute need (发展是硬道理)"[8] and

3 Shanghai Exhibition Center, formerly the Sino-Soviet Friendship Building (1955) by Soviet architects and the East China Architectural Design Institute (ECADI).

4 The Great Hall of the People (1959) in Beijing designed by BIAD (Beijing Institute of Architectural Design Group: Zhang Bo, Zhao Dongri, Shen Qi).

"It does not matter whether the cat is black or white as long as it catches the mouse (不管白猫黑猫, 能抓到老鼠就是好猫),"[9] indicated a desire to build an open, advanced, and prosperous country, even if it meant loosening ideological constraints. In the architectural field various formal languages and theories including Post-Modernism and deconstructivism flooded in, responding to the fever for cultural revival and the thirst for cutting-edge experiences. As Modernism assumed nationalism's place, classical revival and cultural symbolism gradually lost their hegemony. After the Socialist market economy was established in 1992, there was a further boom in urbanization with the pace of demolition in the old districts becoming a physical manifestation of the zeal for modernization. When design competitions and private companies were legitimized, there was a corresponding increase in demand for architectural individuality and creativity.

After entering the World Trade Organization in 2001, China's relative rank within various global systems became a key criterion for judging achievement throughout the country, from building global cities to constructing first-class universities. Taking advantage of rapid urbanization, for which the 2008 Beijing Olympics and the 2010 Shanghai World Expo were the two most powerful engines, Chinese architecture has been able to attract worldwide attention. On one hand, ever greater numbers of international design firms keep active offices at the world's largest construction sites as foreign architects design signature buildings for Chinese cities at a startling pace. On the other hand, Chinese architects, especially those who were previously excluded from official communities,[10] began to seek international recognition by participating in exhibitions overseas. To distinguish themselves from international practices and large corporate firms, this group of Chinese architects has explored and used unique fragments of traditional heritage, vernacular resources, and everyday urbanism.

Quotation for Integration and Confirmation

The crisis of identity is a common symptom of an increasingly connected and rapidly changing modern world. As Yung Ho Chang summarized, "From the 1910s onward, modern architecture in China emerged as a series of adoptions, adaptations, and translations of architecture from elsewhere as well as from the past."[11] This journey toward architectural modernity has been made long and difficult by the extremely compressed time period of industrialization and urbanization, the frequent interruption of the modernization process by wars and political movements, the gap between physical and intellectual achievements, and the need to overcome thousands of years of feudal history.

For developing regions like China, integration into a global system of architectural modernity means relying on formal and technological advancements from the developed world. In the first half of the twentieth century Western classical revival, Art Deco, and Modernist buildings offered alternatives to traditional styles but never took hold as distinctly Chinese. From the 1950s through '70s national classicism was the authorized form for public buildings. Minimalist boxes were used for other functions, following Socialist ideology rather than the tenets of Modernism. In the 1980s and early '90s forms and theories of Post-Modernism and deconstruction were imported. When the culture of global capitalism flooded in, high-rises with curtain walls became the status symbols of an *internationalized metropolis* (国际化大都市)[12] just as interpretations of a so-called European Continental Style (欧陆风)[13] (fig. 12) came to exemplify Western lifestyles.

Meanwhile technological advancements have become faster and easier to import, imitate, and distribute; terms such as *BIM*, *LEED*, *eco-city*, *green architecture*, and *sustainability* are frequently mentioned in policy, branding slogans, and design

5 Fragrant Hill Hotel, Beijing (1982) by I.M. Pei.

6 Helouxuan (1986) in Fangtayuan, Songjiang, Shanghai by Feng Jizhong.

descriptions. However, due to the uneven geographical capacity for technological innovation and economic support across China, they are often deployed for conceptual consumption or as excuses for increased spending rather than to advance research or technology.

In contrast, in the developing world the incorporation of traditional or vernacular heritage into new building projects still serves as a reminder or confirmation of a culture's origins. For more than a century typical elements of Chinese classical and vernacular buildings such as curved roofs, brackets (斗拱),[14] and decorative patterns have been applied directly to modern structures. Strands of this new vernacularism have been present throughout China's modern history and are coming to the forefront once again. Traditional garden design, painting, calligraphy, philosophy, and other cultural pursuits are all seen as valid inspiration for modern designs, for both domestic architects and their foreign counterparts alike. Although the work of foreign architects is generally expected to exemplify the openness of contemporary China, their strategies often create linkages between modern styles and traditional cultural symbols, mostly from the remote past. Examples of the use of these motifs include lanterns, in OMA's scheme for the new National Art Museum of China (2010); porcelain, in Herzog & de Meuron's Beijing National Stadium (2008); and pagodas, in SOM's Shanghai Jinmao Tower (1999, fig. 8).

Ma Yansong's Shanshui City (山水城市)[15] (fig. 16) is another influential case study for the application of ancient images to modern form, in this case oriental philosophy related to the coherence of human beings and the natural environment. The architect has promoted it as a global manifesto of sustainable Chinese urbanism, in what was likely an attempt to shift focus from his strong formal connection to his mentor, Zaha Hadid.

Recognizable Quotation for Resistance and Differentiation

Assimilation and differentiation are two sides of the same coin. Throughout the process of building modern China's architectural identity, tradition has been seen as both inspiration and restriction, and modernization as both destination and threat. If integration and internal agreement are necessary first steps for a new nation-state to gain independent acknowledgment, then resistance and differentiation become more crucial in later phases of identity-building, as quotations are deployed to challenge the status quo. For long stretches of history Chinese architects' practices of resistance tended to serve the political or ideological agendas of the time. In the 1910s–40s they attempted to escape the shadow of feudalism with new forms and theories. In the 1950s–70s they adapted vernacular elements to undermine what they saw as capitalist pollution or Soviet control. In the 1980s–90s cultural revival movements applied Post-Modern historicism as a way to alleviate conditions of scarcity and catch up with the developed world.

It was not until the mid-1990s that a small group of young architects practicing outside of mainstream institutions struck out on their own. Under the umbrella of *Experimental Architecture* (实验建筑),[16] they applied concepts such as autonomy, criticality, and resistance to an academic manifesto that sought to liberate practice from ideological burdens, consumerist erosion, and institutional restrictions. The emergence of this Chinese avant-garde was seen as a milestone in moving the country's architecture community into an enlightened contemporary era. Concepts and strategies focused on architectural autonomy were imported and applied widely by Chinese experimental architects in order to incorporate resistance into architecture as an expression of opposition to external pressures. Abstraction became

7 Haining Youth Center (1989) by Wang Shu/ Amateur Architecture Studio.

8 Jinmao Tower Shanghai (1999) by SOM.

the main weapon used to fight the architectural eclecticism that had dominated the country for more than half a century.

Like their Western mentors, the new generation of Chinese experimental architects had initially shown more interest in concepts or paper architecture, installations, exhibitions, and publications than in real execution. Although it may have been the result of a shortage of opportunities to realize their schemes, this approach left space for experimentation. Furthermore, these architects were interested in redefining architecture itself, adopting terms such as *unusual architecture* (非常建筑)[17] and *basic architecture* (平常建筑),[18] both coined by Yung Ho Chang; *fundamental architecture* (基本建筑),[19] coined by Zhang Lei; and *building* (房子) emphasized by Wang Shu.[20] Instead of focusing on cultural symbolism, they advocated free geometric composition, space and materiality, conceptual clarity, and conscious expression. Deconstruction, especially Peter Eisenman's pursuit of an autonomous modern architecture, also attracted many followers. Wang Shu's first completed architectural project, a Youth Center in Haining (1989, fig. 7), is a typical example showing traces of deconstruction in its formal composition: three cubes of various sizes interlock with the main volume, a diagonally oriented five-story structure, with a series of frames forming the entrance placed at an angle to the main grid. The pure volume and its series of rotations reflect Eisenman's formal strategy, and the scattered red cubes recall Bernard Tschumi's Parc de la Villette.

By borrowing perspectives from contemporary Western architecture, these experimental architects succeeded in leading Chinese design beyond conventional national practices in the last decade of twentieth century. As critic Shi Jian observed, there was a "positional displacement caused by the dislocation of cultural context."[21] The concepts and formal compositions of Modernism became a new kitsch as a growing number of overseas-educated Chinese architects, together with their international counterparts, entered the architectural design market in China following the new millennium. Chinese avant-garde architects imported new terms and directions to establish an academic authority behind architectural modernity, including *tectonics culture*—highly valued since 2001, when Kenneth Frampton's theory was first introduced into China.[22] In addition, the international renown and similar geographic and cultural context of Japanese architects have made their practices and theories popular sources of quotation by Chinese contemporary architects. The evolution of formal quotation among this group of architects has, however, provoked some controversy.

After China's entry into the World Trade Organization in 2001 there was a boom in international exhibitions and publications on Chinese architecture and architects. Foreign curators and critics focused mainly on the uniqueness of Chinese architecture or the difference between Chinese and Western vernaculars. *Tumu* (土木), or earth and wood,[23] two dominant building materials in traditional Chinese architecture, are not limited to China, nor are they widely applied in its contemporary context. However *tumu*, together with variations such as low-tech and regionalist movements, became a symbol of resistance and differentiation. The term also came to represent Chinese architecture in general in 2001, when the exhibition *TUMU—Young Architecture from China*,[24] shown at the Architecture Forum Aedes in Berlin, used it as a conceptual umbrella.[25] The majority of the exhibited projects did not focus on these two special materials, except for Yung Ho Chang's Split House and the main installation, a collaboration between all the exhibited architects. Thus *tumu* was chosen intentionally to symbolize the collective identity of these Chinese architects, especially their "positions far from the architectural crowd."[26] The small-scale private projects in the exhibition consti-

9 Yuhu Primary School, Yunnan (2004) by Li Xiaodong.

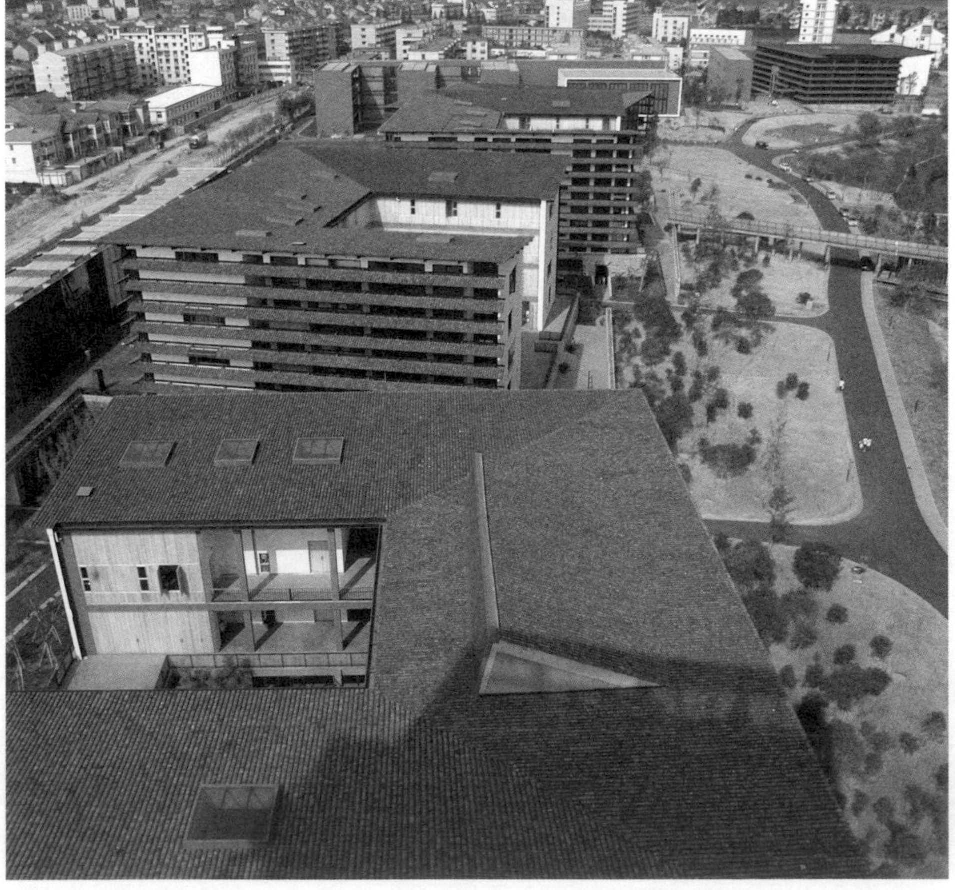

10 First phase of the Xiangshan School Campus, Hangzhou (2004) by Wang Shu/Amateur Architecture Studio.

tuted a contrast not only with mainstream domestic construction of large-scale projects for rapid urbanization and modernization but also with their Western counterparts. By moving the focus from form to materials and tectonics, it aimed to resist the formal symbolism prevailing in Chinese architecture in the 1980s–90s. On the other hand, by using traditional building materials, it aimed at differentiating their practices from prevailing commercial design paradigms. To some extent *tumu* also predicted the symbolic identity of contemporary Chinese architects and their academic focus on low-tech strategies. Wang Shu's 2012 Pritzker Prize brought even more recognition to its symbolism.

Thanks to China's geographical diversity, regional architectural practices have attracted increasing international attention, with buildings such as Li Xiaodong's Yuhu Primary School (2004, fig. 9), Li's Gaoligong Museum of Handcrafted Paper (2010), and Standard Architecture's series of tourist facilities in Tibet.[27] As a form of resistance to rapid urbanization under global capital, the use of natural resources, traditional crafts, and social engagement exemplify a paradigm for practice called "up to the mountains, down to the villages (上山下乡)."[28] In spite of the technological advancements sweeping through China, vernacular and low-tech design strategies are more popular than ever.

A Dilemma: Identity-Building or Self-Alienation

In 2003 the Japanese journal *Architecture and Urbanism* grasped the double face of China's architectural identity in a special issue entitled *Hundred Flowers Campaign* (《百花齐放》),[29] an issue in which "Fifteen glorious foreign flowers dwarf seven samples of tiny Chinese flowers."[30] If the glorious flowers, all large high-tech signature projects executed by international architects in cooperation with local design institutes, represent a national identity of progress and prosperity nurtured by rapid urbanization, then those tiny flowers, modest low-tech projects designed by independent Chinese architects, tend to reveal regional differences. Both sides involve the symbolic quotation of established images relating to particular typologies, forms, and materials. Although there has been a profound transformation in Chinese urbanism and architectural practice in the past thirteen years, as reflected in a newer issue of *Architecture and Urbanism*, titled *Contention of a Hundred Schools of Thought* (《百家争鸣》),"[31] these double faces haven't changed notably, for several reasons.

First, the nationwide anxiety regarding quick modernization has led to one-dimensional conspicuous consumption at the expense of fulfilling real requirements. This irrational fever has spawned the construction of internationalized cities competing for the distinction of having the world's biggest or tallest building. The pursuit of fast diversity and easy novelty may lead to a theme-park style emerging in the built environment, undermining a sense of community and recognition for local citizens. One radical and notorious case is One City, Nine Towns (一城九镇), initiated by the Shanghai municipality, in which nine suburban towns were to be built in the architectural styles of nine different countries.[32] Grand national theaters, stadiums, exhibition halls, museums, and other public cultural facilities became a standard set of amenities in these new administrative centers, many of which are mostly empty. Ephemeral monuments,[33] buildings quickly constructed and demolished, have been rather common in China in recent years as well. Under the pressure to compete for novelty, along with a low capacity for original design and low design fees, *Shanzhai*, or pirating, is prevalent.

By contrast, Chinese avant-garde architects who eagerly establish international fame by using traditional Chinese symbols are criticized as selling a new Chinatown culture.[34] Although

12 Huarunkanahugu, Ningbo (2007) designed by DC Alliance, an example of *Oulufang* or Western Continental Style.

13 Starchitecture in China. Collage by Pier Alessio Rizzardi.

there is plenty of potential in adapting traditional motifs for modern use, too much reliance on them is problematic. While in the 1950s and '80s the use of low-tech and vernacular materials was a result of economic limitation, in the 2000s it became a superficial aesthetic choice. Taking the scale of contemporary urban construction into consideration, the use of vernacular building materials such as rammed earth and wood is far beyond practical means, especially as industrial materials and technology are both largely available and economical. Moreover, many of these projects are examples of false regionalism. For example, an architectural style from the Yangzi Delta area is applied as the vernacular to Vanke 5th Garden, in southern China, where the local building tradition is totally different.

Billing the parametrically designed Shanshui City as an urban forest or artificial mountain can't disguise the fact that such overscaled structures ultimately symbolize global power and capital. This collage of symbolic traditional images and rapid urbanization has nothing to do with critiquing global modernization, rationalization, and technological supremacy. Instead it celebrates them to a new extreme. The slogan is commercially successful mainly because "this is a voice from 'the other' in the process of globalization."[35]

In an environment still lacking in accepted original theories, the citation of well-known references is a useful, inevitable, and effective strategy for producing and promoting architectural meaning. Yet while such a strategy may be a shortcut for success, it is not sustainable over the long term. Should winning international recognition be a priority? Can contemporary Chinese architects be satisfied with the position of "isolated carrots"[36] washed clean by international curators and critics? Should we be satisfied with being mainly an alternative voice on a global stage?

There is both allure and menace in applying powerful references to build architectural identity. Distinguishable labels are not equivalent to authentic identity, which must be the faithful expression of a particular context and relationship between people, objects, and place. Transplanting established authorities in an attempt to construct an identity can result in self-alienation. In the process of differentiating themselves in the mainstream global architecture community, Chinese architects may be ignoring complicated realities and the potential to solve major urban problems, precisely the areas in which contemporary Chinese architectural identity has the best chance to develop.

Transcending Quotation

Increasing numbers of Chinese architects, especially from the younger generations, see architectural identity as changing and dynamic, something that can be achieved by applying available and suitable forms and techniques to specific problems rather than using authoritarian quotation, either from inherited tradition or imported canons. They tend to stay flexible in different situations and gain inspiration from the complexity and contradiction of contemporary urban and rural contexts.

Pragmatic attitudes focusing on *now and here* (此时此地)[37] and *coping with reality* (处理现实)[38] are among the most influential strategies advocated by Liu Jiakun, a Chengdu-based architect. Local critics see a new critical pragmatism as the successor to experimental architecture in the new millennium.[39] Liu's recently completed project in Chengdu, West Village Basis Yard (2010–14, fig. 17), turned an enormous site surrounded by generic urban residential districts into a dynamic mixed-use complex. The impressive courtyard makes optimal use of the site's lack of scale. It was also inspired by the Mao-era spatial prototype of resi-

14 Wangjing SOHO, Beijing (2014) by Zaha Hadid Architects.

15 Meiquan 22nd Century (2014) in Chongqing.

dential courtyards serving as work units, meeting places where different activities took place.[40] The extremely long enclosing structure, including ramps and roofs, doubles as a floating jogging path. Open balconies face onto the divided yards, where fashionable sports fields are juxtaposed with bamboo yards and teahouses in the hopes that a new collective memory shared by diverse generations will soon crystallize.[41]

Urbanus, an architectural studio established in Shenzhen, sees chaotic urban economic, social, and cultural structures as motivations for design. For instance, the Dafen Art Museum (2007)[42] has successfully updated an urban village famous for producing counterfeit paintings into a cultural complex with galleries and studios without endangering original lifestyles or economic modes. The spatial composition and facade were both generated from related urban fabric.

In 2012 four design firms in Shanghai initiated the urban study program SH Project to examine everyday urbanism (fig. 18).[43] It aims to find new architectural principles derived from long ignored and largely neglected—sometimes banal, ugly, and even illegal—building activities and urban sceneries to challenge a mainstream design process largely rooted in Western architectural history and theories.

Atelier Archmixing, one of the participants in the SH Project, operates with what they call "unrecognizable systems (非识别体系),"[44] open to opportunities and resources from all available sources, employing all accessible and appropriate strategies, materials, and technologies to achieve a mixed and authentic built environment. In the past five years the studio has turned a series of minor urban facade renovations into positive experiments in everyday urbanism. One noteworthy case is a nursing home located in a dense residential area in downtown Shanghai. The original plan was poorly arranged, like a hospital without public spaces. The designer successfully persuaded the client to refocus the program from surface beautification to spatial intervention. Continuous balconies of varying sizes were built out from the exterior walls and glass meeting rooms were installed on the empty roofs, where seniors could watch TV, play cards, chat, or just sunbathe (fig. 19). These sunny new communal spaces, incorporating light and inexpensive structures and materials, resemble the informal additions and modifications taking place in the Shanghai urban context. Whether from the perspective of program or design strategy, these types of projects are not easily categorized, but they are exactly where a true architectural identity, both rooted in and benefiting the local quality of life, can be finally developed.

Indeed nothing comes from nothing. Transcending quotation is not about devaluating or eliminating existing references in the contemporary design process—which is neither necessary nor possible in an increasingly connected world. Rather it requires a new perspective, breaking disciplinary boundaries, seeking every opportunity, and employing strategies without a priori notions, thus achieving an active and diverse built environment in a context threatened by the hegemony of globalization and its homogenizing power. An authentic contemporary Chinese architectural identity will emerge and develop only from the solid soil of reality.

16 Narjing Zendai Himalayas Center (projected completion: 2017) by MAD Architects.

1 *Qiqiguaiguai jianzhu.* In recent years *weird architecture* has become one of the hottest buzzwords in Chinese architecture. After being coined by China's president, Xi Jinping, in his demand for "No more weird architecture like those Big Pants," [referring to OMA's CCTV Tower] it has invoked fierce debate among professionals as well as the public, both in China and around world. This statement was delivered at a forum on literature and art in October 2014. Xi went on to say, "Literature and art shall not be the slave of the market and get stinky with money"; art should "be like sunshine from the blue sky and the breeze in spring that will inspire minds, warm hearts, cultivate taste and clean up undesirable work styles." It was widely understood as a signal that China is moving into a new era of nationalism.

2 *Shanzhai* refers to imitation and pirated brands and goods, particularly electronics. Literally meaning mountain village or mountain stronghold, the term refers to the mountain stockades of regional warlords or bandits, far away from official control. Historically *shanzhai* has been used as a metaphor to describe bandits who oppose and evade corrupt authorities to perform deeds they see as justified. One example is in the story *Outlaws of the Marsh* (《水浒传》 *Shuihuzhuan*).

3 In this case, an extremely audacious copy of Zaha Hadid Architects' design for Soho China in Beijing was pirated in Chongqing and completed before the original.

4 Kenneth Frampton, "Towards a Critical Regionalism: Six Points for an Architecture of Resistance," ed. Hal Foster, *The Anti-Aesthetic: Essays on Postmodern Culture* (Port Townsend, Washington: Bay Press, 1983).

5 Mao Zedong. *On Protracted War* (《论持久战》 Lunchijiuzhan), 1938.

6 *Fengjian fuguzhuyi.* In the early 1950s, after visiting the Soviet Union and following the guidelines of Stalin's ethos "Nationalist in form, socialist in content," Liang Ssu-ch'eng advocated modern buildings with traditional features, among which a big roof is a distinctive characteristic. However, after 1955 this type of roof was seen as symbolizing backward forms that revived the ghosts of feudalism. Liang was severely criticized for celebrating historical landmarks, including the city walls of Beijing.

7 *Zibenzhuyi ducao.* "Poisonous weeds of capitalism" was a term coined in the 1950s that referred to thoughts and influences from the West, an enemy of the Socialist community. Since the form and ideas of Modernist architecture were borrowed from capitalist countries, they were also dangerous.

8 *Fazhan shi yingdaoli.*

9 *Buguan baimao heimao, neng zhuadao laoshu jiushi haomao.*

10 State-owned design institutes were organized in the early 1950s. Private firms and individual architects were marginalized in the design market since they had no official design licenses issued by the government.

11 Yung Ho Chang, "A Very Brief History of Modernity," *On the Edge: Ten Architects from China*, ed. Ian Luna and Thomas Tsang (New York: Rizzoli, 2006), 9.

12 *Guojihua dadushi.* This is a term widely used as a criterion of urban development in China in recent decades. It is seen as a symbol of a developed city with notable global influence. Since the central government equates the level of internationalization, such as absorbing transnational investment, with that of modernization and development, about 184 Chinese cities, many of them medium-sized, announced that they were developing into internationalized metropolises.

13 *Oulufeng.* This is actually an invented Western architectural style combining arbitrary classical and vernacular elements to promote social stature.

14 *Dougong.*

15 The concept of Shanshui City was defined by Qian Xuesen (or Hsue-Shen Tsien), sometimes called the Father of Chinese Rocketry, a scientist who made important contributions to the missile and space programs of both the United States and China. Shanshui City was first publicized in 1992 based on Qian's conception of an ideal city, initiated in 1984 with architectural professionals, which advocated constructing the Chinese metropolis as a garden city, with artificial mountains and water. This utopian city embodies both the poetic Chinese cultural tradition of dwelling and modern ideas of sustainable urbanism. Ma Yansong said he had been fascinated with the traditional Chinese cities filled with natural scenes since childhood. His design, which uses soft forms, is clearly more naturalistic than Modernist cubes. Ma has borrowed Qian's term to identify his designs and philosophy in recent years. For both Qian and Ma Yansong, Shanshui City was an abstract idea rather than a static form, and an alternative to the Modernist city.

16 *Shiyan jianzhu.* The term "Chinese experimental architecture" was devised by Wang Mingxian and Rao Xiaojun in the mid-1990s. It was first publicized in May 1996, when Mingxian organized the conference *Experiment and Dialogue May 18* for young Chinese architects. In June 1999, during the 20th UIA conference in Beijing, he curated the exhibition *Experimental Works by Chinese Young Architects*, showcasing work by eight marginal architects including Yung Ho Chang, Zhao Bing, Tang Hua, Wang Shu, Liu Jiakun, Zhu Wenyi, Xu Weiguo, Dong Yugan and his students. As the first

17 West Village Basis Yard, Chengdu (2014) by Jiakun Architects.

group show of Chinese experimental architecture, it provoked fierce debate in an architectural field dominated by state-owned design institutes.

17 *Feichang jianzhu.* Unusual Architecture is the name of a design company established by Yung Ho Chang and his wife, Lu Lijia, in Beijing in 1993, as well as the title of Chang's 1993–95 monograph *Feichang jianzhu* (Harbin, China: Heilongjiang Science and Technology Press, 1997).

18 *Pingchang jianzhu.*

19 *Jiben jianzhu.* This is also the title of Atelier Zhang Lei's 1998–2004 monograph *Fundamental Architecture* (Beijing: China Architecture and Building Press, 2002)

20 *Fangzi.*

21 Most of these experimental architects, including Yung Ho Chang, were educated in the United States or, like Zhang Lei, in Europe. Interested in the latest Western architectural trends, they absorbed and adopted more information from abroad than their colleagues graduating from national design institutes. The following comment on Yung Ho Chang by Shi Jian could also applied to the other experimental architects: "Although these are all perspectives borrowed from Western mainstream architectural fields, the positional displacement caused by the dislocation of cultural context successfully helped Yung Ho Chang accidently become the leader of Chinese experimental architects." Shi Jian, "'Unusual' Ten Years in the Context of Hyper Urbanization: Ten Year Review for Yung Ho Chang and Atelier FCJZ," *The Architect* (《建筑师》 *Jianzhushi*), no. 108, Special Issue on FCJZ (April 2004): 4–13.

22 Wang Junyang, "Reading the Tectonic Culture Research of Kenneth Frampton" (解读弗兰普顿的建构文化研究 *Jiedu Fulanpudun de jiangou wenhua yanjiu*), *A+D*, no. 1 (2001): 69–80; no. 2 (2001): 69–77. Kenneth Frampton, *Studies in Tectonic Culture: The Poetics of Construction in Nineteenth and Twentieth Century Architecture,* trans. Wang Junyang (Beijing: Chinese Architectural & Building Press, 2007).

23 *Tumu* included not only rammed earth but also bricks and tiles.

24 *TUMU* was the title of the first important exhibition abroad that represented Chinese architects as a group. The theme of *tumu* is also widely explored in the recent practices of some Chinese architects. The exhibition *TUMU - Young Architecture from China* was shown at Architecture Forum Aedes, Berlin, in 2001, and achieved a rather unexpected and enduring success. The six young architectural offices that were presented—Yung Ho Chang, Liu Jiakun, Wang Shu, Ai Weiwei, Ma Qingyun, and Nanjing University Architects—are the Chinese architecture icons of today and have left their mark in publications and exhibitions on Chinese architecture abroad. Thus the exhibition was a milestone for the emergence of individual architects in China on the global stage after 1952.

25 It was not only the first international exhibit for a group of young Chinese architects but also an opening for Chinese architects to build international reputations through exhibitions, helping small private practices through media exposure.

26 Eduard Kögel and Ulf Meyer, "Position Far from the Architectural Crowd," in *TUMU—Young Architecture of China* (Berlin: Aedes Gallery, 2001), 12–15.

27 The Yuhu Primary School, in Yunnan Province, designed by Li Xiaodong, won a UNESCO Asia Pacific Heritage Award in 2005. Gaoligong Museum of Handcraft Paper, designed by Hua Li, was nominated for an Aga Khan Award in 2013. Standard Architecture's Tibet series won the International Award Architecture in Stone, in Verona, Italy, in 2011.

28 *Shangshan xiaxiang.* This term, now applied to rural construction, is borrowed from a political program of the 1950s–70s. From December 1968 onward millions of educated urban youth (知识青年 *zhishi qingnian*) were mobilized and sent "up to the mountains and down to the villages"—to rural and frontier settlements. In these areas they were to be reeducated by the poor and lower-middle-class peasants. This relocation program was practiced first on a limited scale before the Great Leap Forward Movement, resumed in the early 1960s, and accelerated sharply by the late '60s. A recent issue of the Chinese journal *World Architecture* (《世界建筑》 *Shijie Jianzhu*, February 2015) adopted this term as a theme to focus on contemporary rural constructions.

29 *Baihua qifang.* A concept borrowed from a socialist slogan in the 1950s encouraging intellectuals to contribute different thoughts: "Let a hundred flowers bloom; let a hundred schools of thought contend" (百花齐放，百家争鸣 *baihua qifang, baijia zhengming*). *Architecture and Urbanism* published a new issue on this topic in April 2016 to record the changing scenery of Chinese contemporary architecture.

30 Hua Xiahong, "The Symbolic Consumption of the Starchitect," *The Architect* (建筑师 *Jianzhushi*) (June 2010): 122–30.

31 *Baijia zhengming.* This new issue featured twenty-six projects with varied functions and sizes designed by twenty-six local Chinese architects, most of them small private companies or individuals. These buildings range from newly built to various types of renovation program, located in metropolises like Beijing, Shanghai, and Guangzhou, as well as in the countryside. Although there are prominent projects with contemporary

18 Everyday urbanism/informal settlement in Shanghai.

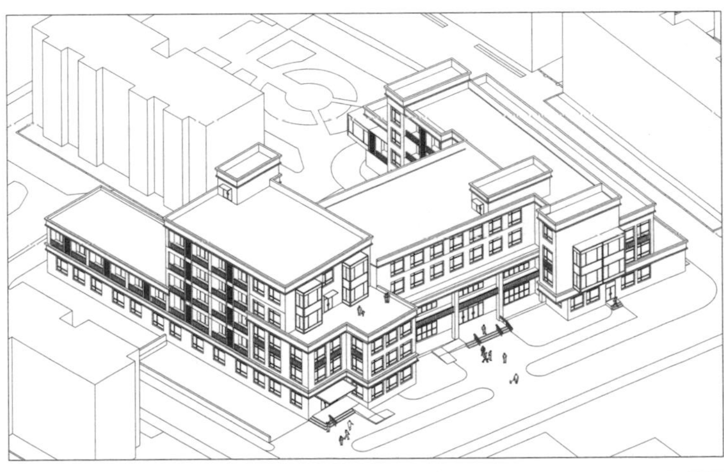

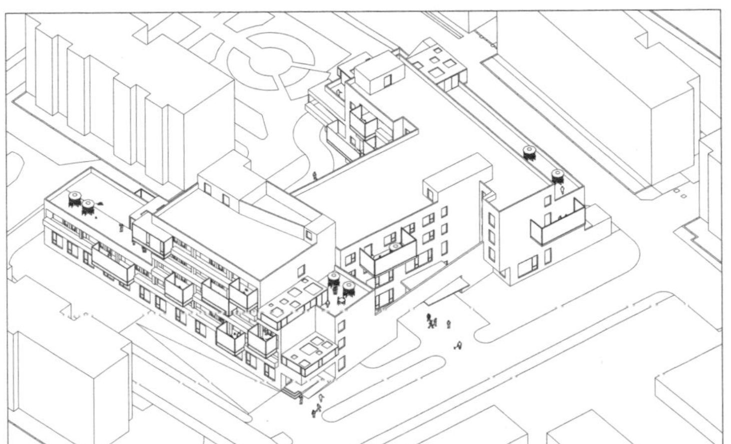

19 Longhua Elder Care Center, Shanghai (2016) by Atelier Archmixing (drawing: 2013).

forms that incorporate advanced technology—such as Atelier Deshaus's Long Museum on the West Bund, in Shanghai; MAD's Harbin Opera House; and Atelier Z+'s Sino-French Center, at Tongji University—the transformation of traditional form and low-tech craftsmanship remains an essential topic.

32 *Yicheng jiuzhen.* One City, Nine Towns is an urban-design program initiated in 2001 by the Shanghai municipal government. In order to build suburban towns with international standards and distinguished features, the government plans to use architectural styles from nine different countries, including China (Zhujiajiao), Germany (Anting), Italy (Pujiang), the Netherlands (Gaoqiao), Spain (Fengcheng), and the United Kingdom (Songjiang New City).

33 Zhou Jianjia and Li Dandeng, "Ephemeral Monuments: The Rapid Construction and Demolition of Architecture in China," *Time Architecture* (《时代建筑》 *Shidai jianzhu)* (2011): 36–39.

34 Chinese art critic Wang Nanming wrote several articles in the 2000s criticizing Chinese architects' symbolic application of traditional styles and materials. Wang Nanming, "The Chinese Architecture in the Exhibition Mechanism: An Honor of Post-Colonialism?" (展览机制下的中国建筑:后殖民荣誉 *Zhanlan jizhixia de zhongguo jianzhu: houzhimin rongyao*), *Mountain Flowers* (《山花》 *Shanhua*) (2004); Wang Nanming, "Ideology and Its Criticism of Chinese-Style Architecture" (中式建筑的意识形态及其批评 *Zhongshi jianzhu de yishixingtai jiqi piping*), *Art Observation* (《美术观察》 *Meishu guancha*) (2007); Wang Nanming, "Playing the 'Chinese Card' Back Home: On Yung Ho Chang's Panda Pavilion for the Venice Biennial" (把"中国牌"打回老家去--看威尼斯双年展中国馆(一)--张永和建筑--"熊猫馆" *Ba zhongguopai dahui laojia qu, kan weinisi shuangnianzhan zhongguoguan, zhang yonghe jianzhu, xiongmaoguan*), *Art Monthly* (《画刊》 *Huakan*) (2005).

35 Hans Ulrich Obrist and Lorenza Baroncelli, "Preface," in Ma Yansong, *Shanshui City* (《山水城市》 *Shanshui Chengshi)* (Guilin: Guangxi Normal University Press, 2014), 2.

36 Liu Jiakun, "A Response to Zhu Jianfei," *Time Architecture (*《时代建筑》 *Shidai jianzhu)* (2006): 67–68.

37 *Cishi cidi.*

38 *Chuli xianshi.* "Only by exploiting the reality do you have the chance to reverse and finally transcend the reality." Liu Jiakun, *Now and Here* (Beijing: China Architecture and Building Press, 2002).

39 Li Xiangning, "From 'Experimental Architecture' to 'Critical Pragmatism': Contemporary Architecture in China," *Architecture and Urbanism* (2016): 8–13.

40 The big courtyard and work unit are concepts taken from the Soviet Union.

41 West Village Basis Yard was selected as an exhibit for the 15th Venice Architecture Biennial in 2016.

42 Dafen Art Museum was selected as the Best Public Project in China in 2006 by *Architectural Record*, http://archrecord.construction.com/ar_china/BWAR/0804/0804_dafen_art/0804_dafen_art.asp.

43 This program was initiated by four Shanghai-based studios: Atelier Z+, Wuyang Architecture, Fan Wenbing, and Atelier Archmixing. They are interested in the constant addition and modification of projects year after year, and the phenomenon of informal construction.

44 *Feishibie tixi.* Zhuang Shen and Hua Xiahong, "Everyday Change and the Unrecognizable System," *New Architecture* (《新建筑》 *Xinjianzhu)* (2014): 16–19.

20 Long Museum West Bund, Shanghai (2014) by Atelier Deshaus.

"To narrate a tutorial video is to cast oneself as the star of a DIY reality show about computational mastery, digital savvy, and millennial-age entrepreneurial self-assertion."

Erin Besler and Ian Besler

Like So

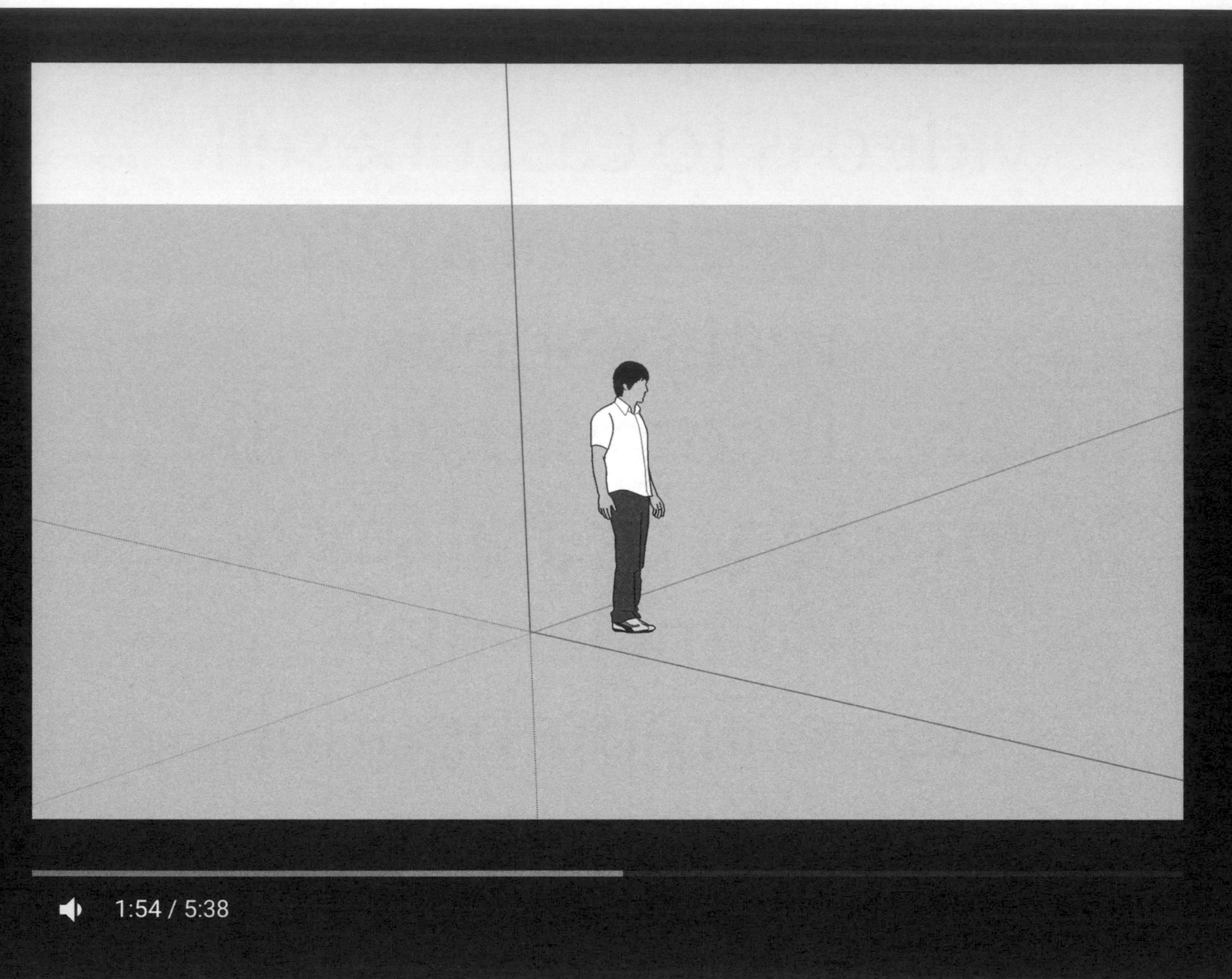

1 "Google SketchUp 7 Animation Tutorial—Beginners," posted by "Requiem Dissidia," 2009.

As is the case with so many artifacts in the realm of DIY, online tutorials can be more instructive and effective at capturing the viewer's attention when their production quality is either extremely high or, as is more often the case, excruciatingly low. More personable and narrative than the classic user manual, video tutorials have become not just a medium through which individuals learn to navigate software and operating system interfaces but also a meaningful way to enter, as producers and consumers, into the discourse of designed interactions and experiences. If one was to situate these videos somewhere along a graph in which audience attentiveness is a function of production value, we might find that they fit neatly into an inverted bell curve. After watching perhaps hundreds of online instructional videos (some of our favorites have been collected in a publicly shared YouTube playlist),[1] we have found that their capacity to hold our attention is lowest exactly at the point where performance, production value, and apparent competence or coherence are merely average. Videos

2 "Sketch UP—Library Space Demo," posted by "Brian Mathews," 2007.
3 "How to make a simple and good looking stair case in sketchup," posed by "mateo ardila," 2008.
4 "Google SketchUp 7 Animation Tutorial—Beginners," posted by "Requiem Dissidia," 2009.
5 "Google Sketchup—Easy To Use 3d Design Software," posted by "sydus," 2009.
6 "Sketchup Roof Tutorial," posted by "SuperPalarama," 2012.

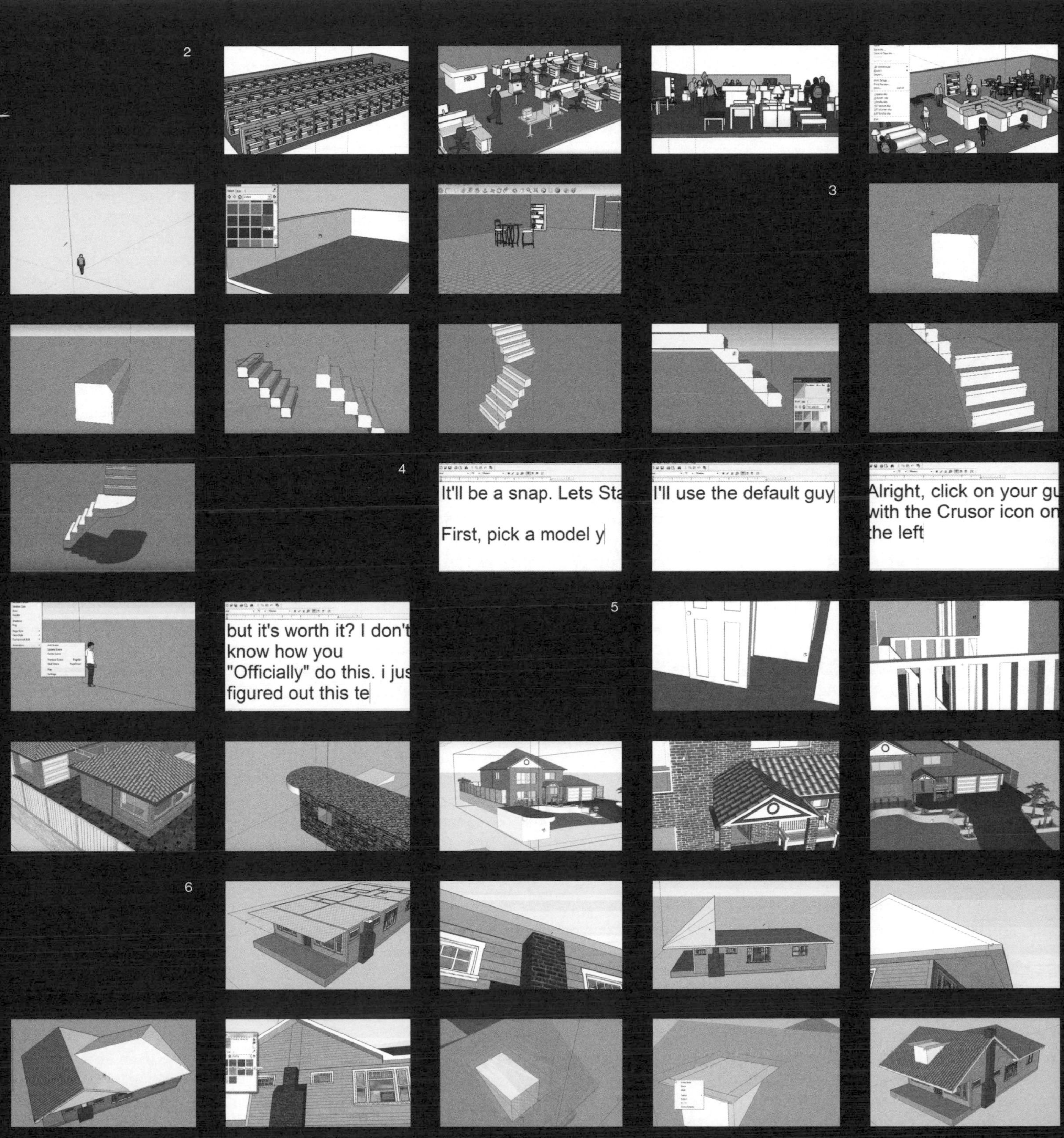

generated for paid subscription providers like Lynda.com or open online courses such as those produced for Khan Academy or Coursera generally fall to the extreme right side on this graph: clearly professional with relatively seamless production, verified expertise, and a coherent pedagogical trajectory. Those to the extreme left can often be found where all loose things on the Internet will eventually land, on YouTube.

While the professional has been distinguished from the amateur by reductive definitions based on economics and certifications of expertise—essentially professionals are licensed in some way and compensated for their work, whereas amateurs are not—the online software tutorial might provide an opportunity to rethink the limits of this differentiation and its inadequacy for other models of production.[2] The screen-captured video tutorials that are uploaded to YouTube and shared on social media provide a sense of dominion over the scripted digital processes that users negotiate on a daily basis. They turn the menu-drop, mouse-click, drag and scroll, and hot-key shortcut into a set of performative gestures—expressions of autonomy charged with meaning and marked indelibly with human intention—and represent an increasingly important, and often overlooked, space for users to convey authority in the otherwise detached and impersonal expanse of the digital workspace.

As a means of communication largely dependent on the spoken word, digital records of screenshots, audio tracks, and webcam files, along with platforms of playback and dissemination, the instructional video (like any other form of quotation) is entangled in the context of its capture, delivery, and repetition. The online software tutorial relies on the familiarity and functional capacity of both performer and audience as it pertains to uses of commentary (speaking over) and instruction (speaking to). In the case of YouTube videos, they make use of the capabilities of online video platforms: the step-by-step order of selections, tools, clicks, and drags can be reiterated through rewinding, complicated settings and instructions can be tediously copied while the video is paused, lengthy or mundane preambles can be skipped over, and further details can be requested in the comments.

The earliest examples of amateur software tutorials still found on YouTube date to around 2006, when the site had been in existence for only two years and was rapidly growing in popularity following its acquisition that year by Google. While many programs have accumulated attendant suites of user-made tutorial videos, Trimble's free 3-D modeling software, SketchUp (formerly owned by Google), provides a compellingly rich combination of qualities that bestows a particularly amateurish, uncontrolled, and improvised tone to the work produced and its accompanying tutorials. By comparison, tools in the Adobe Creative Suite, and most other video and photographic editing software, cater to a distinctly "prosumer" or "semiprofessional" mentality. The tutorial videos that accompany and affirm this posture tend to be predictably sober and task oriented. Distinctly by the book and thorough, they are strongly enamored with the "official" way of doing things and leave little room for improvisation and ad libbing.

On the other hand, SketchUp, with its stubborn insistence on ease of use, relatively low hardware requirements, and entry-level, community-oriented positioning, attracts a messier, more brazenly cavalier crowd to the task of instructional video making. "I don't know how you 'Officially' do this. i just figured out this technique so there it is," writes one video author in large on-screen captions.[3] "And, I mean, like I said in other videos, I mean, this is how I do stuff and not everyone will agree. But, whatever, people do it differently," insists a narrator near the beginning of another video.[4] This could be because SketchUp sets up, within its very existence, a fallacy around user participation and demonstrated expertise. A user would have to be crazy to think that her skyscraper design could be carried through the building process with only a cursory understanding of the software. But then why would a 3-D design software program—oriented toward "the people who shape the physical world"[5]—exist at all if not to invite and encourage the pursuit of participatory fantasy and performative urges?

If SketchUp seems to straighten the learning curve while blurring the line between software expert and software amateur, perhaps we can trace these destabilizing gestures in part to a sense of instability produced within the digital workspace, namely the 3-D Warehouse tool palette. Situated in the Toolbar near *View* controls such as pan and zoom, and next to a small map icon that allows users to geo-locate their digital model, the 3-D Warehouse palette presents the opportunity to add any of roughly three million publicly produced and available models to the SketchUp workspace or to upload any user-generated creation to the sharing platform. Anything from an ice-cream sandwich and a desk lamp to an international airport is available for appropriation and editing, suggesting open-source authorship and oscillation between acts of making and taking—if only to afford the possibility of pulling the shared model apart and gaining a better understanding of the specific components, layers, and groups involved in its creation.

Indeed some of the best online tutorials concern extremely specific subject matter or surprisingly narrow objectives—the imposition of procedures and step-by-step methods toward an end that one might not expect. In the case of SketchUp one can find entire genres of short clips, for instance, on creating interior details such as spiral staircases and exterior components such as hip roofs. Thus these videos encourage partitioning and selectively calling upon discrete information and skill sets. Unlike previous methods of learning, such as attending workshops and following guidebooks and instruction manuals, the video tutorial can be broken down and compartmentalized into searchable and selectable portions to make mastery appear attainable within a series of easily conveyed steps: from how to trace a floor plan and create walls to how to finish a roof—each method most likely being conveyed by a different video creator at different points in time in different parts of the world. In this manner the online instructional video series can suggest simultaneously a depth of understanding and a somewhat superficial ease of comprehension that otherwise would be irreconcilable. The software users and tutorial producers are able to claim command of complicated and advanced sets of knowledge without necessarily having a firm grasp of fundamentals such as how to work to scale or what each tool is called, in effect surpassing, confusing, and at times erasing the line between amateur and professional production and the criteria upon which these terms are predicated.

What's most compelling about online tutorial videos is the idea that, in their on-the-fly improvisational manner, they frequently oscillate from performative gestures to documents of an operational task. The best examples suggest the enactment of an inner monologue, almost like a Hollywood film director's commentary over software interface—a manifestation of the chatter that connects and mediates the threshold between our intentions as software users and the computational actions that our chosen systems carry out. These video tutors are, perhaps unknowingly, co-opting and appropriating the perceived command and authority possessed by the software being taught, and even its developers. Whether or not a given tutorial is less productive in an instructional sense, it effectively brings its creator into proximity with the people who created the software and the community of users who create with it. In her essay on the uses and implications of quotations both written and spoken, Marjorie Garber discusses the attachment or incorporation of authority that such external referencing can convey:

> This practice works well when the figure being quoted is eminent, recognizable, and honored; in fact, all three attributes then seem to attach themselves, in a rather ghostly fashion, to the present speaker, who appears in the act of quoting to have virtually incorporated the predecessor and to speak from the vantage point of the ages, as if the speaker were a Russian doll who had somehow swallowed up these articulate authorities and was therefore able to ventriloquize them from within. When the figure being quoted is less eminent or reputable, however, the old-style quote-unquote is deployed, but with a lawyerly edge, casting doubt on the veracity of the person quoted or underscoring the suspicious significance of the utterance.[6]

This issue of greater or lesser eminence in relation to quotations suggests how the act of incorporating can impact a reading in opposing or unintended directions. Occasionally videos are prefaced by defensive captions imploring viewers to refrain from abusive or negative comments: "Please don't comment unless you have someething productive, positive, or some USEFUL criticism," writes the user "Pizzscn" in an annotated note preceding one tutorial.[7] Indeed comment threads following many online tutorials scrutinize the purported benefits or deficiencies of a particular software or working method: "Sketchup is not bad for visualization but finally you cant MAKE any project (maybe except really small one) without autocad," user "Lukaszandzel" writes in the comments of one tutorial; regarding another, "subpolarity" writes: "should've assigned it to a group, brah."[8,9]

There is often a palpable sense of anxiety concerning how video makers position themselves in relation to the question of status, whether novice, amateur, hobbyist, or expert. YouTube refers to users who share videos simply as "creators."[10] The issue of credentials and experience in terms of the subject matter is most often simply left unaddressed, with few exceptions.[11] Viewers today look toward other factors to carry the weight of credibility: Which user has the most followers? Which video has the most views, the most thumbs up, or the most positive comments? Sometimes a video that is titled with the most concise description of the technique being taught gains the most credibility.[12]

The online tutorial space is a comparatively intimate one, and not only because the viewer often experiences the tutor's home desktop computer along with the atmospheric domestic sounds captured by its microphone.[13] And as a space cloaked in the anonymity of user names and logins, it allows freedom for sincere and informal admissions, like a digital confessional of amateur's remorse: "This is my second time using this ever," discloses narrator "sydus," referring to the software program that he is teaching in a 2009 tutorial on YouTube.[14] Another narrator comments: "They have a really good tutorial that demonstrates ... how to do this as well," exposing his insecurities as an instructor.[15] The video titled "How to make a slmple and good looking staircase in sketchup," by YouTube user "mateo ardilo," simply depicts the creation of the promised good looking staircase, accompanied by a soundtrack of Finnish death metal.[16]

These videos themselves manifest the soaring promises of software tools when placed in the hands of amateurs. To narrate a tutorial video is to cast oneself as the star of a DIY reality show about computational mastery, digital savvy, and millennial-age entrepreneurial self-assertion. Software programs such as iMovie, Photoshop, SketchUp, and Google Earth enable a stereotypically American brand of can-do spirit. Just as the selfie and photo-sharing platforms like Instagram and Snapchat have become conventional means to capture and broadcast one's identity and individuality online, the instructional video has become a common format for claiming a position as a maker, creator, and do-it-yourselfer. What sets the amateur tutorial apart from so many online formats is the infrequency of self-reflection and criticality toward the broader system of its production and circulation. If most memes and other viral agents rely on nuanced media literacy to achieve a sense of levity and effectiveness in their communication, the tutorial video seems woefully encumbered by the apparent weight of its purpose and subject matter. In fact these videos are often amusing precisely because of the excessive seriousness of their tone and the pedantic affectation of their narrators. This tendency might reflect a broader cultural perception of teaching as demanding sobriety, focus, and objectivity. But perhaps this is what drives the interest in this genre toward the amateur and improvisational—qualities that call attention to the tension between methods and outcomes at play in the tutorial.

To view these videos is to witness the blind optimism of versatile and curious practitioners who are unburdened from the implications of the problems that they engage. The immutable amateurism of the user-made tutorial is an unsteady performance of control, expertise, and mastery. These video makers walk a thin line between sincerity and parody, often conveying a vague sense of uncertainty along with varying degrees of information, while suggesting that performing a tutorial and sharing it is a claim of mastery over a toolset. In the process they push instruction into a practice that engages a dedicated and voluntary audience relieved from the fixed constraints that typically monopolize access to expertise.

The broad spectrum of online instructional videos—from the concise, deliberate, and coherent to the esoteric, bizarre, and endearingly inept—points to the potential that online media platforms possess for flattening previously recognized distinctions between amateur and professional creative, productive, and pedagogical practices. So much of the content that viewers and software users encounter online today is dictated by the vagaries of search algorithms, keyword combinations, and determinations of PageRank, which often privilege categories such as collectively derived *relevance*, *views*, *ratings*, and *recently uploaded* over credentials such as certification, seniority, and affiliations with governing bodies and professional institutions. They expand these discussions by reframing expertise as quantifiable, digestible, and communicable sets of discrete procedures and destabilizing the status of the expert in relation to experience and mastery.

Thus online tutorial videos, particularly those generated by self-taught amateurs, hobbyists, or dilettantes, suggest that foundational knowledge is no longer a prerequisite to expertise and that digital processes and software practices, once thought of as reserved only for high-functioning practitioners, might no longer be so strictly associated with an ordered accumulation of experience and familiarity. In doing so, they also call attention to the increasing importance of educational institutions in formalizing nonteachable skills while opening creative practices to broader groups of producers and participants.[17]

Um...Yeah. So that's it. Thanks for reading and let us know what you think in the comments section!

1 "Tutorials," YouTube playlist, posted by "Ian Besler," January 26, 2016, https://www.youtube.com/playlist?list=PLAv_YVkwqJRaFMKGynyxNvqDIUXXnWkPu.

2 Nick Salvato, "Out of Hand: YouTube Amateurs and Professionals," *TDR: The Drama Review* 53.3 (2009): 67–83, accessed February 7, 2015, [http://www.jstor.org/stable/25599494].

3 "Google SketchUp 7 Animation Tutorial-Beginners," YouTube video, 5:38. Posted by "Requiem Dissidia," June 23, 2009, https://www.youtube.com/watch?v=C_4LnXWV0dA#t=05m16s.

4 "Sketchup Roof Tutorial," YouTube video, 19:16. Posted by "SuperPalamara," October 4, 2012, https://www.youtube.com/watch?v=-cA060LkXps4.

5 "The SketchUp Story," SketchUp, accessed February 7, 2015, http://www.sketchup.com/about/sketchup-story.

6 Marjorie Garber, " " " (Quotation Marks)," *Critical Inquiry* 25, no. 4 (1999): 658.

7 "How to make a house-Trimble Sketchup," YouTube video, 7:48. Posted by "Pizzscn," May 16, 2007, https://www.youtube.com/watch?v=ITycE-25eV4c.

8 "How to make a simple and good looking staircase in sketchup," YouTube video comment posted by "Lukaszandzel," 2011, https://www.youtube.com/watch?v=DJ-Wtj2TOil&lc=ka-zY9fLE-S8U7DZzaytyJweium-LOtVjGyN-9K_OBkxk.

9 "How to make a second floor on Google Sketchup (efficient way)," YouTube video comment posted by "subpolarity," 2012, https://www.youtube.com/watch?v=9kPaaj1_aMo&lc=KbMMuXxb-S9e71Z44loRpehWfk-XBwoF0vHl2EWZY-zjY.

10 "Creator Hub, YouTube for Creators," YouTube, https://www.youtube.com/yt/creators.

11 "Simple Roof Design in Sketchup," YouTube video, 52:41. Posted by "Drew Murphy," November 23, 2013, https://www.youtube.com/watch?v=Y0A1Xjd9eL0.

12 Our gratitude goes to Andrew Kovacs for suggesting the relationship between view count, comments, search filtering, and the perceived credibility of the tutorial video.

13 "How to make a second floor on Google Sketchup (efficient way)," YouTube video, 1:34. Posted by "kepevipin9," February 13, 2010, https://www.youtube.com/watch?v=9kPaaj1_aMo.

14 "Google Sketchup—Easy To Use 3d Design Software," YouTube video, 9:48. Posted by "sydus," January 27, 2009, https://www.youtube.com/watch?v=S-Zqdfif64A#t=09m23s.

15 "Sketch UP - Library Space Demo," YouTube video, 4:18. Posted by "Brian Mathews," January 22, 2007, https://www.youtube.com/watch?v=plExqUKqQk4#t=2m58s.

16 "How to make a simple and good looking staircase in sketchup," YouTube video, 3:30. Posted by "mateo ardila," November 17, 2008, https://www.youtube.com/watch?v=-DJ-Wtj2TOil.

17 Our gratitude goes to Michael Osman for feedback and suggestions toward our concluding points.

“Quotation is by definition displaced: a migrant, ‘after belonging,’ nostalgic, and longing for another home.”

Δ Xenia Vytuleva

From Copy—to Trope: Secrecy, Quotation and Urbanism in Soviet ZATOs

> An accurate representation is in fact mathematically impossible.
> —Pavel Florensky

Off the Record

Nameless and entirely missing from maps, and today partially blurred on Google Earth, Soviet secret nuclear cities became sites of clandestine scientific and military research. Coded in early 1952 and officially announced as ZATO (*Zakrytoe administrativno-territorial'noe obrazovanie,* or Closed Administrative-Territorial Formation)[1] in April 1992, these secret cities shimmered on the surface of Soviet physical and intellectual landscapes and were listed under randomly changing numbers.[2]

Placed beyond the territory of any official or unofficial media, these secret cities could be traced only with fading pieces of information—gossip, rumors, fear, and sometimes with an odd code or a clink after a telephone call that would be immediately interrupted.[3] Inspired by imagined or ideal cities, based on military geometric plans, and articulated in the language of progressive Modernist architecture, Soviet secret cities were devised under strict KGB supervision behind the walls of Leningrad's Experimental Scientific Research Architectural Institute (VNIPIET).[4] This multifunctional architectural giant combined the features of a laboratory that produced knowledge and numerous publications, as well as specialization in designing and certifying copies of highly secretive industrial and military sites in the Soviet nuclear shield.[5]

In the short time span of 1946–47, ten urban clones were incubated with an identical ideological and spatial grid, armed with the standardized travel kit of politically charged architectural typologies: theater, school, city hall, sports arena, and cultural club. Ready to be distributed within the broader territories of the Eastern Block, the ZATO's primary focus was addressed to the remote areas of the Ural Mountains and eastern Siberia. The ultimate master plan of a secret city, however, very often featured minimum adjustments to local climate and geographical coordinates.[6] Architectural quotation and a radical cut-and-paste process became the central principles organizing the ZATOs' public spaces and strategic ideological domains. Thus a standardized mini-copy of Moscow's Bolshoi Theater, inaugurated with a rendition of the notorious ideological play *Happiness*, served as the center of the typical *matryoshka* doll design of these secret cities.[7] Another shocking example of the exact replication of design, cultural references, proportions, and color palette was the shared interface of the ZATOs' city halls: with their octagonal basements, slightly distorted arches, and open colonnades of a quasi-Corinthian order, along with a neo-Palladian cupola, all painted with a particular pale yellow pigment, these became an inevitable instance of déjà vu in these ghostly Soviet urban formations. Finally, the myth and the paradox of total displacement and the signature of the VNIPIET design were embodied in the unusually narrow Leningrad-style window frames of the privileged housing for the *nomenklatura* and well-established scientists. Even the small details of distributed domestication in media kiosks and propaganda monuments, with the iconographic figure of the bronze Communist leader stepping forward, left no space for urban inequality within the secret network. This urban mimicry ensured that a ZATO resident would feel equally at home and equally estranged in any location within the strategic nuclear shield. This rhetorical loop determines the zoning regulations and building codes of the ZATOs' architectural quotations while defining the predominant limits of the visual vocabulary of a secret city. Together these create a particular mythology: "living within quotation marks."

ZATOs are all about repetition. Total recall, comfort, and coziness in a well-known and therefore beloved bureaucratic environment, as well as the immediate orientation and the feeling of "having already lived through it,"[8] are the obsessive screen memories, by-products, and side effects of strategic military networks worldwide. However, vis-à-vis total catastrophe, and in close proximity to the limitless power of the radioactive particle, the logic of multiples was taken to a new extreme.[9] Due to Cold War political repercussions, the techniques of secrecy, the safety rules of uranium-based industry, and military restrictions, the scientific laboratories and sites of nuclear production had to be duplicated, triplicated, and multiplied, quoting each other also on a larger scale of copying entire urban settings, translating danger into the medium of architecture and urban design.[10] According to the military agenda for information recovery and survival in case of technological failure, Seversk could serve as a double of Novouralsk, while Ozersk was meant to substitute Sarov. As a phenomenon of the urban matrix and an extreme example of the "synergetic blur of military and urbanistic plans,"[11] the ZATO network allows the reframing of the format of architectural quotation as disintegration from the context, as in Walter Benjamin's expression, "to brush history against the grain."

Reinforcing the implications of this policy, architecture tends to incorporate radically different structural principles, not only based on ideological platforms and social and geopolitical conditions but following the pervasive logic of classified documents, files, and archives containing secret and carefully sealed information. One of the key ways in which architectural quotation and politics intersect is by means of the dual nature of VNIPIET as a machine for design and knowledge production and as the instrument of concealment, elimination, deletion, or rewriting the boundaries of fiction and reality. The VNIPIET institute would produce and authorize both true and false copies of a city master plan, distributing them through various paths, official and classified.

Silence as a plan, as a strategy, and as spatial significance becomes as powerful as vivid representation. The entire site of a nuclear city becomes a forbidden archive. This ambiguity of silence as a sign of both oppression and power reflects an important topos[12] in cultural anthropology, but it also signals an inevitable transference on the level of city as myth. Mainly it points to the possible meta-distinction: the transition from secular urbanism to sacral spaces, those that transcend the rhythms of ordinary life.[13] As Cornelia Vismann puts it, "Canceling endows a writ with authority and force of law [...] Deleting rather than writing establishes the symbolic order of law."[14] Remarkably we can even speak of a specific vocabulary while dealing with the simulation of cartography and unverifiable documentation. According to interviews with officials, the most popular expression in military lingo to identify the ZATO's location was "*lost in the thickness of a tracing paper.*"[15]

Quoting and Knowledge Production

Although initially proposed as a professional organization dedicated to producing buildings for military needs, Leningrad's architectural institute VNIPIET was also responsible for articulating the inner logic of these strategic domains and their spatial grid, and the conceptual framework of nuclear cities. Even the powerful linguistic representation of the ZATO, occasionally recognized in its logo or more often used as its motto, was crafted as part of the standardized master plan. And herein lies no paradox. The acronym itself suggests the essence of its hermeneutic status as well as the hierarchy of a secret society. It also points to a "process through which boundaries are determined on several different levels since these secret cities exist at the intersection of intellectual, geographical, cultural, social, legal, and political layers of information."[16] Perhaps it is true that on the official level "these four letters already communicate a sense of boundaries, demarcations, limitations, and circumscriptions on the social and political geography of the Soviet Union."[17]

In everyday life, however, the ZATOs were known as *pochtovy yashchik*, which literally means "mailbox" and incorporates the idea of a one-way communication media system—a network of storage under total control, a means of *cognitum* and survival in the face of political and economic realities. "I was born in the mailbox," one of the most common phrases among ZATO citizens, best describes the notorious claim that the reality of architecture is that of a media form.[18] Incoming mail, however, was addressed not to a geographical location but to a code (e.g. mailbox #XXXX) that did not necessarily correspond to the official postal code. Thus the name of the location was the box—an abstract notion and an indeterminate location. "Coming from a box" still signifies social status, privilege, and travel restrictions. I would argue that this vernacular wisdom of comparing the city, as well as the architectural studios designing weapons, aircrafts, space and military electronics, to hermeneutic boxes with sealed, controlled, and carefully selected information (and to the black box, the database that survives a catastrophe) changes the status of architectural quotation. It reveals a particular shift that allows architecture to follow a radically different narrative by likening cities to documents, multiplied and classified, that follow a distributive mode of direct quotations.

Copying and secrecy became the main components of the ZATO's architectural DNA, and the intersection of these components merits further exploration. While *copia* is connected via its Latin root to the word *copula*—meaning a tie, band, or fetter—and therefore to the words *copulate*, *love*, and *reproduce*,[19] copying is also the presentation of the *eidos*, or outward appearance, in a place where it does not belong and thus produces the trauma of the "no longer there."[20]

Quotation is by definition displaced: a migrant, "after belonging," nostalgic, and longing for another home. By reading the architectural and urban phenomena of the ZATOs in the discursive context of media studies, in terms of the dual nature of a secret space and a radical example of quotation, we can gain the sense of its potential power of "migrating aura," anxiety, hazard, and distance.[21]

On Perimeter

One of the key elements essential to understanding the logic of a closed and cloned city and the possible scenarios of living within quotation marks is the idea of a *perimeter*.[22] Dwelling beyond the perimeter has over time given rise to a de facto social and anthropological experiment: two generations born behind the wall have developed a specific ZATO-resident psychology. In a way, the perimeter became a sacred line—an altar boundary, a screen, and an interface between the ZATO and the other world. The ZATOs' perimeters enclosed an incredibly discreet fabric of strategic terrain: the city and the secret industry, with its own even more tightly secured perimeters—from the nuclear factory to the villages, woodlands, lakes, rivers, agricultural fields, and even secret ski slopes. Life within the perimeter acquires a different tempo and value; even talking about the idea of the perimeter creates anxiety. Serving as an official representation of the ZATO's boundary, the perimeter also transcends the features of the metaphysical border, preserving the status of uniqueness and isolation of these secret sites on the edge of demolition. Incorporated in the endless gray-green camouflage wall of prefabricated concrete blocks, it is a perimeter that frames the ZATO as an over-determined secret zone where the urban system operates in a particular fixed and controlled way.[23] The majority of ZATO residents are scared of losing their perimeter as a symbol of self-exclusiveness and an illusion of protection. The perimeter also serves as a warranty of familiar shapes of strategic terrain delineating architectural intimacy and serving as quotation marks on the margins of military sites.

1 Novouralsk petrol station, first introduced in 1967.

This is also the case with Sverdlovsk #44, today's Novouralsk, one of the first prototypes for the ZATO. A secret city with a population of more than one hundred thousand inhabitants at the height of the Cold War, it is located on the eastern side of the Ural Mountain range, fifty-seven kilometers to the north of Yekaterinburg (formerly Sverdlovsk).[24] For many years its territorial presence was concealed on official maps of the Soviet Union by a perfectly shaped blue lake—no traffic signs along the highway, no bus stops, no spatial or informational acknowledgment of its existence—just a narrow road camouflaged by taiga forests. Novouralsk was among the first cities in the nuclear shield of the USSR, and it remained secret until 1991. Its history began at the outset of World War II, with the establishment of a factory producing light metals for the military aircraft industry. Local residents, soldiers, German and Latvian refugees, and political and criminal prisoners built it upon the remains of the preexisting industrial settlement Verkh-Neyvinsk.[25] The Novouralsk perimeter still appears on the covers of ROSATOM brochures and serves as an endless facade for the entire city. Taking the example of the notorious Berlin Wall a decade after its fall in 1989, the authorities announced a competition for the best graffiti decoration of the perimeter. Unlike in the DDR, however, residents of Novouralsk worshipped their wall. Chosen to work for state projects with highly strategic goals and afforded the artificially comfortable conditions of life within, its residents comprised a roster of "voluntary prisoners."

Yet on closer inspection, the ZATO's urban structure embodies highly tectonic forms of quotation: three main official squares impaled by a monumental promenade packed with political slogans, ideologically charged flower beds, and propaganda statues. The monumental axis was meant to be the quintessential component of the Communist public space, the culmination of the whole urban scenario, and the stage for ceremonies and parades—"intended to underline a specific sense of moral centeredness and city unity."[26] This geometric pattern would be quoted accurately even in unclassified scientific centers, such as the Soviet *Atomograd*. Attested to in the charts of VNIPIET documents, the city was initially divided into three major districts according to durability and material makeup: a Permanent city (*Postoyanni*), a Temporal city (*Vremennii*), and a so-called Plywood city (*Fanernii*). The last one was considered to be even more temporal, hence the impossibility of surviving in local meteorological conditions. More significantly, this highly secretive urban activity coincided with the erecting of another kind of secret formation: the Gulag camp, or ITL# 27.[27] This formula of crisscrossing two urban zones according to their material matter and special temporality served as a typical inscription for Soviet secret cities, and in some cases still remains classified.[28] The coexistence and intersection of two highly restricted ghost urban networks on the territory of the Soviet empire, gulags and ZATOs, thereby raises several existential questions: how can the appearance of closed cities be mapped onto the previous trauma of Soviet/Russian topography? How can these extreme urban formations overlap and even quote each other? Can ZATOs be viewed as doppelgängers or a mirror image of the gulag camp network?[29] And most importantly, would a quote of an absent city imply reciprocity between critical liminal spaces and epistemic silences?

Threshold of Modernity

The urban planning of the ZATOs addresses issues of secrecy, the hierarchy and intersection of classified and unclassified territories, visible and invisible zones, and the informational vacuum around the architectural discipline. Today data analyses, budgets, geographical and architectural simulations, handwritten military notes and official political orders, civil records, declassified materials, oral histories, and photos from private archives and local museums serve as the primary sources of academic information on urban formations.[30] However, one of the most significant features of Cold War urbanism remains the production of a massive amount of simulations, legal/illegal materials, and fake documents whose essential goal was to verify the illusion of nonexistence, activating an ongoing argument with actual geographical coordinates. Disinformation, disorientation, blurring, and camouflage became the side effects, by-products, and parallel narratives, as well as the powerful determinations, of the period. The ZATO's architectural representation sought to embody the ambivalent nature of camouflaged spaces. This urban phenomenon can be seen as the most radical example of human geography in terms of spaces of otherness or heterotopias.[31]

Although this is not the place to expand on the topic, I would like to consider the origins and evolution of the concept of heterotopia in recent scholarship on the ZATO phenomenon. A term coined at the climax of the Cold War, *heterotopia* can be defined as a physical representation or approximation of a utopia or parallel space that includes undesirable bodies that make a real utopian space possible. Heterotopias always function in relation to other spaces by quoting them.[32] Michel Foucault underlined the initial geometrical impulse of heterotopias, as well as their military prototypes. Therefore the perimeter, with its characteristic forbidden spaces and layers of invisibility, as well the coded nature of the military verbal index, offers a solid metaphor for ZATO urban planning. Only the heterotopia is capable of creating an illusion by juxtaposing in a single real place several spaces, or sites, that are in themselves incompatible. Deleted from the official media and cartographic reality, obliterated from national statistics, and blurred on Google Earth, yet enlightened with the flash of utopian vision, these secret urban formations are neither here nor there. The sites of their existence are simultaneously physical and

ПО ЛЕНИНСКОМУ ПУТИ-К КОММУНИЗМУ!
Новый корпус ГСПТУ на 600 учащихся.
(Введен в 1975 году).

2 Detail of a mural showing boxers from the walls of the Kedr Sports Center, Novouralsk.
3 Vocational school for 600 students, 1975, Novouralsk.

4 Panorama of Novouralsk, 1940s.

5 Panorama of Novouralsk, 1970s.

mental and, as Foucault states, "reflect the space of a phone call itself or the moment when you see yourself in the mirror." Even in the jargon of lady telegraphers, the goddesses of communication during the Cold War, these secret cities were identified as *Punktirnye goroda* (dotted city) locations, due to the special clanging rhythm of these calls from "nowhere."[33]

The intention in recent years "to open up the closed cities" has created an active platform for cross-disciplinary discourse on Cold War aesthetics and visual culture, as well as forces to contextualize and decode one of the most astounding phenomena of multiplied architectural quotations. Today historic preservation probes not only the physical presence of this parallel Modernism but its historic and political complexity in order to rethink the significance of its architecture and the particular cut-and-paste production of these walled utopias.

Confronted with the twin concerns of environmental pollution and security risks, these secret cities face an uncertain future; some may survive and others may dissolve into urban formations within Russian suburbs. Eventually they will cease to exist either as metaphor or fact. A need to rethink the role of this political, ideological, and artistic gesture, as well as to explore its legal and metaphysical limits, has become more urgent with recent transformations of the empire and the crash of its postcolonial systems of sustainability.

Thus this format of a city as a direct quotation emerges at the critical edge of survival, security, biopolitics, and artistic practice at the aesthetic margin of theory and military strategy. While we must acknowledge the importance of the juridical-military-political discourse, the question of quotation in this case is not necessarily a legal or ethical one, in the strict sense of those words, but rather unveils the power and potentialities of reference, a sense of loss, and longing for home. "Living within quotation marks" does not suggest a continuous history—instead it confronts the breaks in tradition. This slowing down of time, this annihilation of memory and logical meaning, this ambiguous poetics of absence from maps to instead shimmer on the surface of the Soviet globe—even the verbal index of the ZATO, including its obsessions with coded reality—suggest parallel narratives to officially recognized histories of art and society by implementing an irrational logic for urbanism.

This research was made possible due to the generous support of the Graham Foundation and the Harriman Institute at Columbia University. Many thanks to my friends and colleagues: Oleg Genisaretsky, Dmitry Sladkov, Svetlana Boym, and Vitaly Komar for our inspiring conversations. I am grateful to Rosatom, the administration and the scientific society of Sarov, the administration of Novouralsk, and Oksana Zhidkova, the director of the local museum, for their assistance during my research trips to the local archives.

6 Novouralsk Library for Children and Youth.

7 A vehicle belonging to one of the nomenklatura drives past the Kedr sports center, under construction.
8 Mosaic glorifying science and learning.
9 Memorial to soldiers and victims of the Second-World War.
10 A house for one of the nomenklatura, Sarov.

11 VNIPIET plan of Novouralsk.

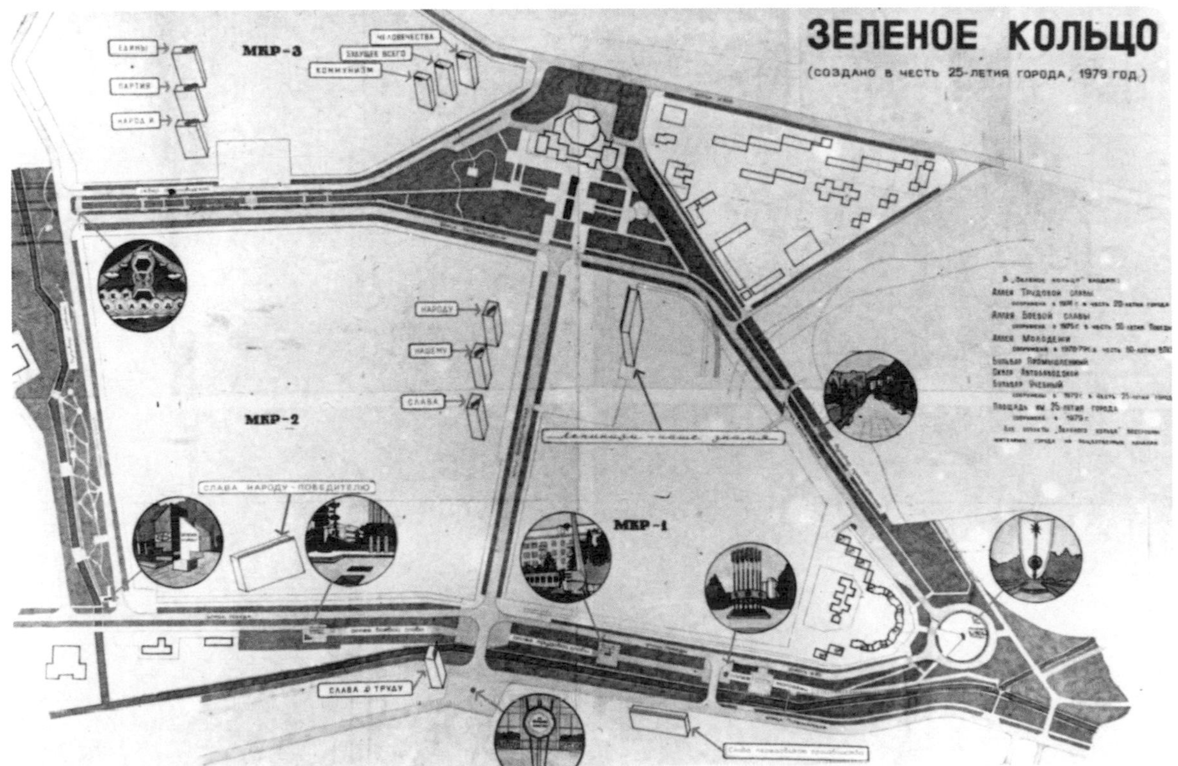

12 The program for the politically and ideologically charged "green ring" in the center of Novouralsk was created in 1979 for the 25th Anniversary of the Secret City. The architectural project is comprised of a system of memorial parks as well as other politically and ideologically charged architectural elements.

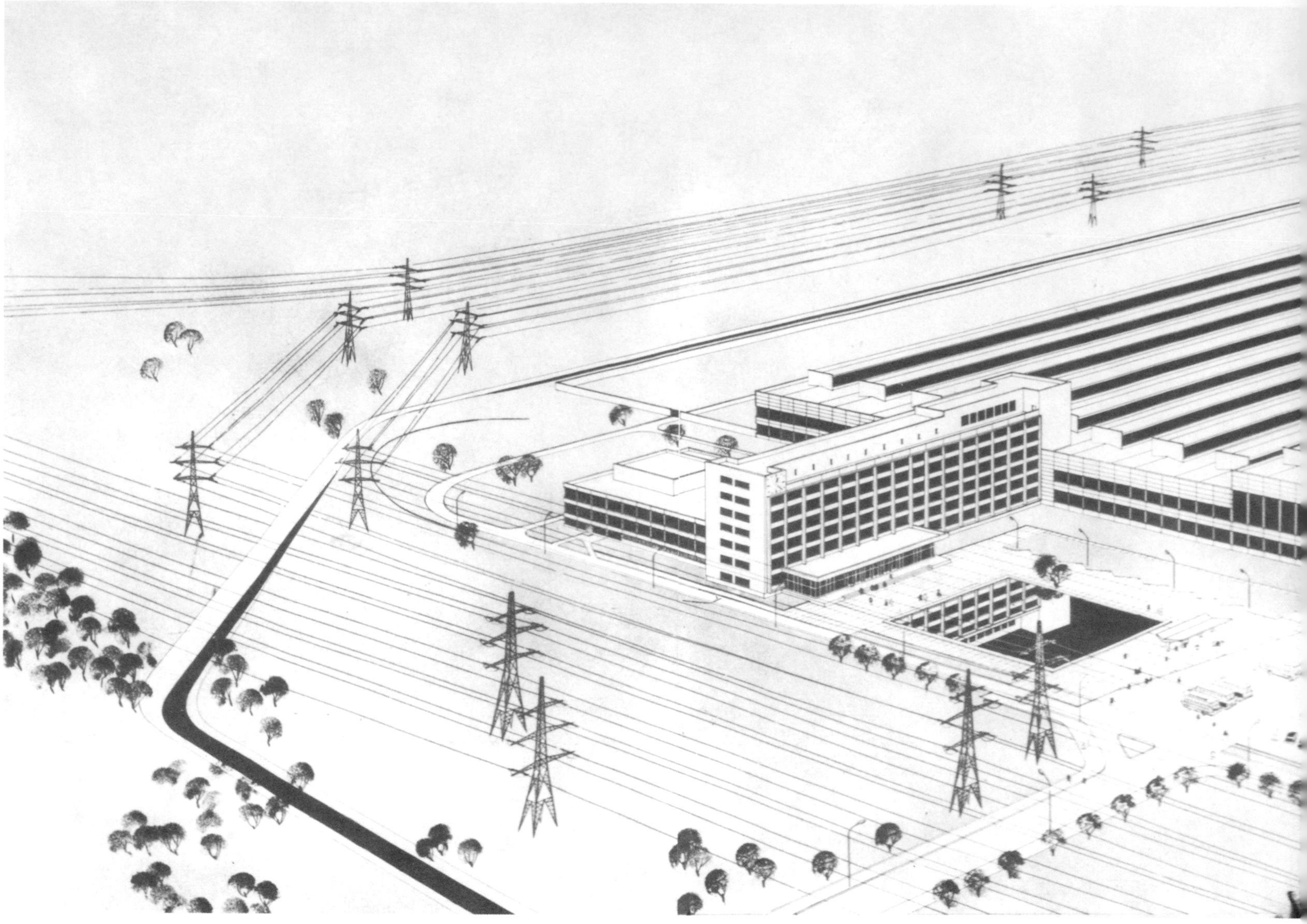

13 The Novouralsk SredMash Factory, designed by VNIPIET, an ultra-Modernist project with a mirrored pool as the culmination of the architectural ensemble. It was only partially realized and at the moment stands completely abandoned.

14

15

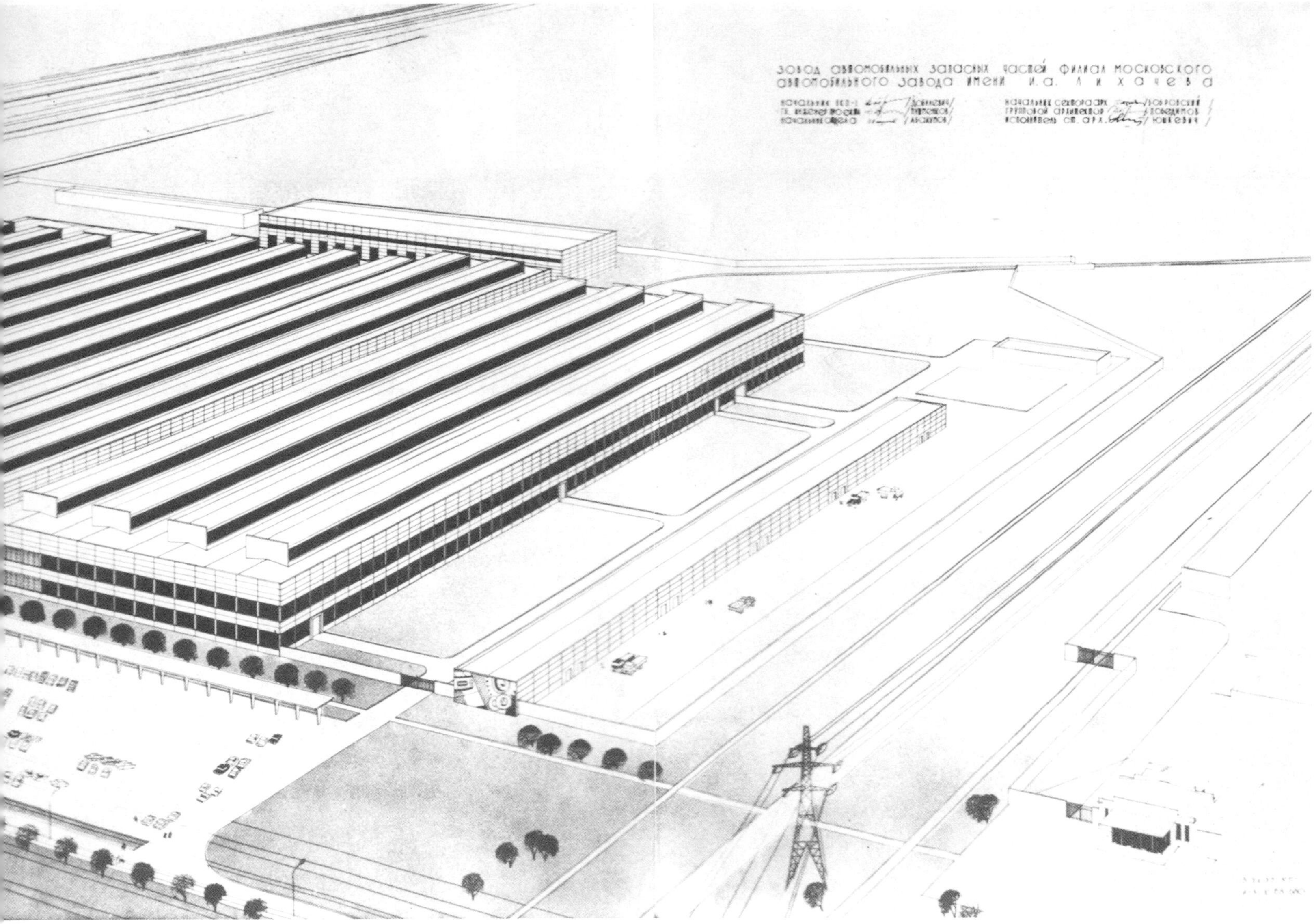

Зовод автомобильных запасных частей филиал Московского
автомобильного завода имени И.А. Лихачева

17

16

14 Modern Novouralsk.
15 View of early Novouralsk.
16 The Alley of the Glory of Labor, Novouralsk.
17 Cinema Neyva, 1971, Novouralsk.

18

19

20

21

22

23

18 Ozyorsk (Chelyabinsk-40, Chelyabinsk-65), ZATO.
19 Dudinka, closed city.
20 Lesnoy (Sverdlovsk-45), ZATO.
21 Novouralsk (Sverdlovsk-44), ZATO.
22 Novouralsk (Sverdlovsk-44), ZATO.
23 Seversk (Tomsk-7), ZATO.

24

25

26

27

28

29

24 Priozyorsk, Kazakhstan, ZATO.
25 Sarov (Arzamas-16), ZATO.
26 Novouralsk (Sverdlovsk-44), ZATO.
27 Seversk (Tomsk-7), ZATO.
28 Snezhinsk (Chelyabinsk-70), ZATO.
29 Zheleznogorsk (Krasnoyarsk-26), ZATO.

1 закрытые административно-территориальные образования.

2 Despite the lack of critical distance and the fact that the topic still lies partially submerged in the shadow of recent conflict, the secret cities of the Cold War are no longer entirely absent from historical accounts. They have undergone serious analyses from anthropological and sociopolitical points of view. Kate Brown, Michael Gordin, and Asif Siddiqi's work on the history of nuclear intelligence, national identity, and technical knowledge within the context of science, technology, and the history of the Cold War, as well as local investigations on economics, national statistics, and fake cartography by European scholars such as Ekaterina Emeliantseva-Koller, Katya Larina (U:Lab.spb), Victoria Donovan, and Chris Perkins, have created a rich background for professional dialogue. This article is focused on the significance of urban planning for the ten most classified and restricted nuclear cities of the USSR, the *Desyatka*: Tomsk 7, Arzamas–16, Severodvinsk, Sverdlovsk 44, Ozersk, Krasnoyarsk 26, Seversk, Znamensk (Kapustin Yar–1), Zeleznogorsk (Zaozerny, Krasnoyarsk 45), and Mirny.

3 Victoria Donovan, Ekaterina Emeliantseva-Koller, and Asif Siddiqi, in *ZATO: Soviet Secret Cities of the Cold War*, ed. Xenia Vytuleva (New York: Columbia University Press, 2011).

4 The state scientific research institute VNIPIET was formed in 1933 as an architectural bureau of the ministry of heavy industry specialized in military strategy and supplies. Before and during World War II, VNIPIET designed more than sixty military objects, standardized shelters, and small-scale urban sites. Its headquarters is located in St. Petersburg, formerly Leningrad, although at the eclipse of the Cold War branches were spread throughout the Urals and eastern Siberia. See N. Schadrin, *ZAVOD 813, Building the Isotope Reality* (Novouralsk, Russia, 2014), 115–209.

5 Schadrin, *ZAVOD 813*, 110.

6 See O. Zhidkova, *We Built Novouralsk* (Novouralsk, Russia: Novouralsk Press, 2013), 107.

7 In 1951 the ideological play *Happiness*, by Pyotr Pavlenko, was launched simultaneously in eight ZATO theaters. See Zhidkova, *We Built Novouralsk*, 346.

8 Hillel Schwartz, in his recent work on direct quotations discusses replication as a policy of insurance or an instrument of hegemony, guarding against dilemmas of replication, or disorders of repetition. "Is simulation a mode of insight or escape, recall or denial? Is replication a policy of insurance or an instrument of hegemony? Is repetition rutted or redemptive?" Hillel Schwartz, *Culture of the Copy: Striking Likenesses, Unreasonable Facsimiles*, revised and updated edition (Brooklyn, New York: Zone Books, 2013).

9 This research is primarily focused on the Soviet experience of architectural significance in the ZATO's nuclear sites. To compare it with the U.S. experience, see Kate Brown, *Plutopia, Nuclear Families, Atomic Cities, and the Great Soviet and American Plutonium Disasters* (Oxford: Oxford University Press, 2014).

10 On the architectural restrictions of isotope-based technology, see Schadrin, *ZAVOD 813*, 116–19.

11 This expression is borrowed from Stanislaus von Moos's article "Ruin Count: Le Corbusier and European Reconstruction," *Perspecta* 48 (2015): 146.

12 Jean Jamin provides a detailed interpretation of the interlocking sacral/secret spaces and the attributes of power within tribes. See Jean Jamin, *Les lois du silence: Essai sur les fonctions sociales du secret* (Paris: Les Éditions François Maspero, 1977).

13 The intersection of the secret/sacral and the potentiality of the "military trans-rational" is a subject of further research. See Xenia Vytuleva, *Military-Trans-rational*, forthcoming.

14 Cornelia Vismann, in *Files: Law and Media Technology* (Stanford: Stanford University Press, 2008), 26.

15 Xenia Vytuleva, from an interview with a ROSATOM bureaucrat in 2013.

16 Asif Siddiqi, "The Secret Cities," in *ZATO: Soviet Secret Cities*, ed. Xenia Vytuleva (New York: Harriman Institute, Columbia University, 2011), 8.

17 Ibid., 6.

18 "Born in the mailbox" appears as the most popular phrase, a red dotted line among twenty-five interviews with local citizens in 2013–14 in the Urals and Siberia.

19 On the copy as love, see Marcus Boon, *In Praise of Copying* (Cambridge, Massachusetts: Harvard University Press, 2010), 83.

20 Boon, *In Praise of Copying*.

21 This potential extension was inspired by Jacob Moore, "Origin and Development of a New Tradition: *Space, Time, and Architecture* in the Translation Zone," *Future Anterior*, vol. 12, no. 1 (Summer 2015): 32–44, and Amanda Reeser Lawrence, "Preservation through Replication: The Barnes Foundation," *Future Anterior*, 1–15.

22 Even though the term was used mainly to articulate a shape of fortification already found in ideal cities of the early Renaissance, its military sense of "boundary of a defended position" was formalized in 1943 for the identification of concentration camps as restricted territories for execution and biological experiments. See Guido Beltramini, *Andrea Palladio and the Architecture of Battle: With the Unpublished Edition of Polybius' Histories* (Venice: Marsilio, 2010).

23 Perimeter also defines the special landownership conditions of the ZATO. Most of ZATO land and property is owned by the state, though it is being transferred to municipal control in an ongoing process. Until recently all the programs of socioeconomic and spatial development of the ZATO had to be coordinated by the special council for federal regulations. See Kosenkova, "Industrial Cities," also U:Lab.spb and Katya Larina in *ZATO: Soviet Secret Cities*.

24 Anna Zvezdina, "A New Life for a Closed City," *Project Russia* 2 (1996).

25 U:Lab.spb and Katya Larina, in *ZATO: Soviet Secret Cities*.

26 From urban-planning manifesto; see Leningrad master-plan bureau, from RGALI Archives.

27 In 1946, in accordance with the nuclear shield program of the Soviet Union, the party started building the new secret industrial complex with the code name "Industrial factory #813." The highly enriched uranium for the first Russian nuclear bomb and the alternative "Lunar Program" were produced there.

28 On the significance of the USSR Prison Science Systems, see the works of Asif Siddiqi.

29 Here I am referring to the article by Ines Weizman, "Architectural Doppelgängers," *AA Files* 65 (2012): 19–24.

30 In a still more concrete manner, the problem of placement arises for nonexisting ZATOs in terms of their demographic data and statistics.

31 This text, "Des espaces autres," published by French journal *Architecture/Mouvement/Continuité* in October 1984, was the basis of a lecture given by Michel Foucault in March 1967. Although not reviewed for publication by the author, and thus not part of the official corpus of his work, the manuscript was released into the public domain for an exhibition in Berlin shortly before Foucault's death. Translated from the French by Jay Miskowiec.

32 For a productive discourse on the "Heterotopian Nature of ZATOs," see the Princeton Media and Modernity event "Secret Cities during the Cold War," with Jean-Louis Cohen, Michael Gordin, and Xenia Vytuleva, at the Media and Modernity Archives, November 2012.

33 Arlen Viktorovich Blium, "Forbidden Topics: Early Soviet Censorship Directives," in *Book History*, trans. Donna M. Farina, vol. 1 (Baltimore, Maryland: Johns Hopkins University Press, 1998), 268–82.

"Quotations are actually ways of transferring credibility."

Fake Industries Architectural Agonism, Córdova Canillas, and MAIO

On *Rooms: No Vacancy*

One of the more interesting proposals for the 2014 MoMA PS1 Young Architects Program shows a series of rooms filled with hedonistic partygoers, jazz musicians, and piles of powder against a backdrop of blank white walls and isometric grids. The project, *Rooms: No Vacancy*, was the work of Fake Industries Architectural Agonism and MAIO, along with other collaborators. It is distinctive not only for the anti-iconicity of its architecture, but also for the plentiful visual and verbal quotations—a text by Edgar Alan Poe, a still from the film *Spring Breakers*, and a work by Urs Fischer, among others—found in the magazine produced for the project, designed by Córdova Canillas. This magazine, along with spread-by-spread commentary by MAIO and Córdova Canillas, is printed in the following pages.

The *Perspecta* editors sat down with Fake Industries Architectural Agonism founders Urtzi Grau and Cristina Goberna at 10:30 pm on the evening of January 25, 2016, to discuss their practice, the magazine, and the conceptual and practical uses for quotation in architecture.

AA AJ Artemel
UG Urtzi Grau
CG Cristina Goberna
VS Violette de la Selle
RL Russell LeStourgeon

AA **Could you give us a brief history of your practice and its major goals?**

UG We are usually so good at refusing to answer that type of question!

CG It all started with a series of disagreements that resulted in the name of our practice as the combination of two singular entities with different, yet not irreconcilable, interests. Fake Industries Architectural Agonism is not a practical name—something that we actually enjoy.

UG The conceptual logic of our practice is that rather than a resolution or a synthesis, we are more interested in productive disagreement, and this itself becomes the structure in which we keep producing. The name is something arrived at by chance, post-conceptualization, and actual disagreement—a beautiful manifestation of how we work. You can look back at the history of names in architecture practices, starting with the logic of the Beaux-Arts era with offices being attached to a specific architect's name, the almost classical logic of an artist who creates with his own signature. Corporate practices in the 40s and 50s take names from acronyms like SOM, which both encapsulate the practice and also echo abstractions like stock exchange symbols. These evolve again in the 70s for groups that were more manifesto-like to names like Archigram or OMA. This type of name playfully reclaims the acronym, but it becomes a manifesto, Office for Metropolitan Architecture. Now, a name like BIG is empty of any manifesto and becomes basically the name of an app—a catchy one that pops but doesn't necessarily mean too much. Well, given that context, we like a name that is impossible to use.

CG I would also point out that from the beginning we were interested in the false, the fake. For example, something we've been doing through the years is constructing voices and characters who would write articles for us. We've always been very interested in the role of agonism in the history of art and architecture and we try to re-conceptualize what a practice is—how an office works, how to rethink architectural communication, how to prevent being recognized as a brand.

VS **So that's the agonism in the name of your practice: constantly reconceptualizing your office for every project?**

CG One figure that deeply interests us is the public intellectual and the idea of the contrarian: someone who has a public voice, who is not building an opposition per se, but who finds the themes that need to be discussed at a certain moment in time.

RL **It seems you disagree with the expected norms of architectural presentation. You prepared plans and sections of the project, but were hesitant to include them as part of this magazine.**

CG We certainly do not reject more orthodox forms of architectural communication. We make plans and sections of our projects. But we are very much interested in literature as a medium to explore how we can write about architecture without limiting ourselves to descriptive texts. We explore this issue through different kinds of publications and genres as fictions and interviews for the books we design for our projects. We also publish copies of articles from the *New Yorker* in other magazines, which we slightly modify so they talk about the current conditions of our field.

VS **That seems very liberating: you have to make it believable, but you are actually floating further away from the real because you're exploring another imaginary—an Imaginary that we don't necessarily have access to in architecture.**

CG Architectural language is quite pragmatic. It has a purpose, which is to communicate in an effective manner and, unfortunately, it sometimes ends up as not very interesting writing.

UG We like to imagine ourselves as conceptually contextual, so with this magazine and the PS1 competition in general, we're aware that we're talking with a jury of people—curators of a museum, people that are connected to art, people that have sensibilities that are really specific—so we provide a range of architectural representations to appeal to their various sensibilities. That doesn't mean that we just say, "Oh, what do you want?" We actually examine how you seduce and construct a voice, how you operate with a multiplicity of authorships in that context.

CG The question that the PS1 YAP raised for MAIO and us was, of course, if architecture could trigger or enhance a party. We understood how the tradition of legendary parties in New York operated: that is, normally taking place in a multiplicity of interior spaces and rarely accompanied by iconic architecture. So in order to avoid being a quote framed in the corner of a yard, you have to do something different, something triggered by the public and not the other way around—something that shows respect to the users by transforming them from passive observers to active users.

RL **How did all these elements play out in the presentation? How did the jury react?**

UG You go, you are given a room, and you do whatever you want.

CG You have fifteen minutes to set up the place. You are supposed to bring a model and the drawings of the proposal.

UG I think the only mandatory thing is a presentation and a model. But we also did the movie, this magazine, and a silver shelf with small models. We decided to do all these things, assumed that they were all fragmentary—none of them show the entire project. Each of them has its own life and the jury had to piece them together. We gave this magazine to the jurors and said that they should keep it. We had to produce a document that they would want to keep after the presentation, so it had to have a trigger to make them think, "Oh, this is good." It's probably the document that had, in relationship to the jury, the longest life span. And it was quite successful; they kept almost all of them.

CG Here's how the PS1 YAP competition process works: the MoMA curators ask deans of different schools, other curators, editors, et cetera, for recommendations. If you are named you have to submit a portfolio. If you are selected (and they only select five), then you have the opportunity of doing the entire proposal. We were invited, and we wanted MAIO to be co-authors. And it was a total pleasure that they accepted; it worked very well. And then some other fabulous collaborators came (very generously) from other places: Luis Urculo, a visual artist and architect, came from Madrid to direct the film, Daniel Fernández Pascual and Pol Esteve came from London, because one is an expert in parties in Berlin and has this fantastic project title, Partytopias, and the other did research that mapped back rooms in Barcelona's gay clubs. The competition was a party of friends indeed. *Una maravilla.*

AA It seems that this sort of collaboration, the writing of articles under other bylines, and changing the *New Yorker* articles are all attempts to challenge authorship. Is that how you think of it?

UG There is a confusion between the concept of originality and authorship that falls within the history of architecture itself and which hasn't been challenged much. In a nineteenth-century paradigm you have to be original and that's what we are taught in schools. You cannot show up in school claiming that the value of your work is that you've copied something. In any other creative field—art, music, film—it would be completely valid, one of the possible approaches. Interestingly enough, art and music haven't necessarily challenged notions of authorship through the question of originality. Copying has become one of the possible ways authors express themselves. There has been discussion around the death of the author since the 70s, but it tends not to be about the direct connection of the trace, but more about the ability to control the meaning of the work. So the death of the author is the fact that usually when you produce something it gets its own life and it operates differently separated from your intent. This idea of the author as the one who inserts meaning into a work is the one being completely destroyed, but architecture has never been like that. Buildings don't have meanings that are stable; they operate. Similarly, we like the idea that someone will take this magazine and make sense of it without having to put it back into the context of a project. It operates as it is. I don't think copying destabilizes authorship at all, and we live surrounded by examples that prove that: people that just copy and are famous for it. Kenneth Goldsmith is the most important case right now in New York.

AA Yes, we saw him give a reading at a symposium about law and art.

UG Law is more interesting in terms of copying, but it doesn't destabilize authorship conceptually, it destabilizes it legally. And architecture is one of the fields that hasn't developed a legal structure around intellectual property. It's there, but it's not implemented. There's too much blurriness and architects don't like it much. And besides, we operate by presenting a lot of work, allowing other people to use our knowledge, and it's probably going to change because there's so much pressure from legal entities. There is so much money in trying to implement the idea of intellectual property in architecture. But that's a completely different thing—it doesn't really relate to artistic authorship, it belongs to a legal discussion about money. Being able to read differences between authorship, intellectual property, and originality is really important to clarify questions that in other fields are much more clearly defined.

AA Does that lack of definition leave more room to operate?

UG Well, the work of architects does fall more in the space of invention. We live surrounded by blogs and magazines that reproduce our work, from details all the way to plans and elevations, so architects love to see other people use the documents. Architectural products are not pure creation but a weird mix of technology, politics, and societal relationships, so they probably come closer to something like invention and therefore would fall into the realm of the patent. We have a project to patent architectural projects and we try, but it's difficult.

AA But someone like Buckminster Fuller, for example, he's patented inventions, and he even gets to the architectural scale with some of his patents.

UG But those patents, like the Apple stores, are technical details. And Apple is able to patent by using a really nice trick: they patent the technical definition of the glass and the structure, and then they claim they patent the pavilion that they are able to build with those technologies.

VS But we were talking about how in fields other than architecture there is a framework for, and a clearer conceptual definition for, the author, the original, the copyrighted. Why start *Rooms: No Vacancy* with an unattributed text? Is that the analog of the Pictures Generation maneuver on photography? Is the argument that actually this piece printed here is in a different context, is no longer Poe?

CG This piece is like a replica of "Pierre Menard author of El Quixote" by Borges. Should you consider it a literal copy or a creation? It actually was another collaboration with a friend of ours, Albert Fuentes, who is a translator and a writer. This magazine is also of course co-authored with MAIO and with Córdova Canillas, the designers with whom we worked very closely. For example, Córdova Canillas selected the jokes and produced all the photomontages.

VS So was the team working on all the different pieces?

UG Different people did different things.

CG Everybody touched everything, more or less.

VS So Córdova Canillas knew the plan of the pavilion?

CG No. They knew the concept.

UG But we didn't know about their images when we were doing the plan.

CG We didn't see those images until the day that we got the magazine.

VS So it's completely sincere.

UG Well, I don't know if sincere is the word but...

CG We talked intensively about film references and they showed us a couple of small samples, but it was a creative collaboration. We definitely didn't direct them.

VS So you're the impresario because you invited people to share the idea?

CG Impresario... I don't know if it is an accurate term.

VS You're a host.

UG Host is a better one.

CG Yes, host.

UG Dinner host is a good comparison. Dinner hosts are interesting characters because if they're good they are able to seat people for three hours in the right places and provide the right amount of food and drink so the conversation flows.

CG And they are the authors too, as opposed to how architectural practices normally operate.

UG But I want to say something about this first text, because there's a significant difference between a *quotation* and a *transcription* and I think this is a transcription. "Pierre Menard" is very important; there is a beautiful section of the story where we go and take a quotation from the original *Don Quixote* and a quotation from the *Quixote* that Pierre Menard has written and they're exactly the same, and it's beautiful because you have one paragraph, and then the same paragraph, and obviously they are completely different. The second one, first of all, has to deal with the fact that the *Quixote* already existed when it was written, and also has to deal with the fact that, between Cervantes's time and Menard's time, everything has happened. It's been three hundred years, there have been wars, so each of these words in the text has completely transformed its meaning. There's no way they mean the same thing; there's no way those words are the same as the other ones because they are filled with the passage of time. If the first one is specific and completely necessary for the time it was written, the second one requires more explanation. I think this text operates like that: it could be recognized as a well-known tale by a famous writer, but it could also be a description of the project. And it's both at the same time, of course, but it's not a quotation in the way that quotations usually work, especially in academic fields where quotations are actually ways of transferring credibility. You insert them in a text to actually share in the credibility of the original author.

VS But because you don't name an author...

UG "Oh, this important person that everybody recognizes said it, so I have that value behind me, that's why it stands." We don't need that. Of course, people might recognize the text, but if not, it's ok, it works.

VS If Cervantes writes *Don Quixote*, he takes a huge risk, he doesn't know how it will be received, but if Pierre Menard rewrites it, it's already an iconic text. So if you take Poe but you don't say that it's Poe, you assume the risk all over again: no one will know that it's accepted already because it doesn't have that important signature.

CG Also, the text could be iconic at one specific time, but not twenty years later or one hundred years later.

UG But Borges writing "Pierre Menard," uses exactly the opposite logic. He says that, written in 1615, *Quixote* is a necessary text. It's the only thing that Cervantes could have written at that time. It's obvious; it's the text that has to happen at that moment. Everything fits. But to rewrite it right now is the most difficult task because the author has to make sense of those words in the present. How can you actually make the same claims that Cervantes did three hundred years ago, and make them make sense? Can you actually take the Poe story and make it make sense in a party in Queens in 2014? On one hand it's completely impossible, but at the same time we are completely sure that those are the words to describe the project.

AA It's interesting that you turn to this page because Hans Ulrich Obrist is the ultimate contemporary author who's not an author. He's interviewing everyone, he's everywhere, and he's putting all these things together. Why did you include him?

CG We are interested in the interview as a format and in its different modalities. There is HUO's method of asking a set of rather general questions that are repeated and that allow the interviewees to talk about their childhood or what they are doing at the moment. Then you have Enrique Walker's model of proving a specific point. You also have the type of interviews from the *Paris Review* that build situations. And then you have the Djuna Barnes method, which is based in the total construction of a character up to the point that you never directly hear the voice of the person that is being interviewed. We didn't go to that extent... it would have been actually easier to do this with quite a short text, the typical architectural dry, laconic, pragmatic text—but how can you deliver more information? How can you get the feeling of moving through the spaces? How can you talk about fame, and success, and failure in a more seductive manner? Architecture gets too serious. I am interested in Lydia Lunch's motto, "Pleasure is the ultimate rebellion." It seems that architects have forgotten about pleasure so this is something that we try to recuperate in our work and in how we operate.

UG We think the interview is a literary style, and therefore it belongs in a series of exercises in style.

AA And interviews are among the most heavily edited thing you'll see.

UG One of the most famous books of interviews is *Hitchcock-Truffaut* (1966), and it's basically a conversation that happened I think over the course of seven years in twenty-five different places and you read it as a single conversation. You can construct an interview by Obrist and you realize that it's actually a series of literary devices that you're using.

CG In the past we also published a series of "Agonistic Interviews" where we would interview the characters that were involved in specific architectural polemics, by taking the role of the critic. But going back to this piece in *ROOMS*: this was a very short exercise in how to contradict the aura of fame around the PS1 competition which is big in New York but almost microscopic anywhere else.

AA Another issue that raises is how, with this magazine and various competitions, you're working with art and the idea that art is trying to pull architecture into the museum. How do you see architecture in relation to art?

UG It's a charged question. Architects are operating more and more like artists. Starting in the 70s, being an artist in the US might have required an MFA degree and a type of training as an artist that implies knowledge of the history of art and art theory. That leads to a series of conceptual practices that are constructed through that type of knowledge. But the other side of MFAs is that they produce professional artists aware of certain ways of making money: not only the art market, but also grants and residencies. Architecture has been entering this territory for a long time.

CG But to identify ourselves as an art-related architectural practice could be limiting. We are definitely interested in the design and construction of buildings too.

UG For several generations architects in New York have operated with the understanding that you don't need to actually build a building to be relevant. But in Europe, in other places in the world—South America for example—that is a really strange position. The incipient entrance of architecture into this market can be tracked through the explosion of Masters of Architectural Curation. There is an increasing number of people who call themselves architectural curators. A lot of friends of ours do that. But what does it mean? Barry Bergdoll mentioned the other day that probably the moment in which being an architecture curator is the equivalent of being an art curator at MoMA will be the end of architecture. Why? Because when you're an art curator at MoMA, if you hang a painting, you know that you're shifting the values. You're playing with millions of dollars. You hang this painting, the value of this painter grows exponentially. You put a model of a building in MoMA and nothing changes. Compare that with the amount of money you deal with if you change a painting at MoMA, and how it actually destroys the ability to make judgements. Because for a curator of art right now, his judgement is so constrained by economic value while taking decisions around exhibitions in architecture is comparatively easy. You can have a decision-making process that makes a little bit of sense. It's an interesting space. I think at the time it's actually not so dangerous because architecture is still valueless. Both for good and bad.

VS Baudrillard lamented that "the Pompidou has escalators, it's a shopping mall, this is the end of culture," and is Barry Bergdoll now saying the same thing? If everyone knows the difference between a Rem Koolhaas building and a project someone out of university did for fun on the weekend, it's all over?

UG Well, it's not exactly like that. Barry Bergdoll was claiming that architecture curators don't make sense, that professional curators are useless, that a curator by definition has to be someone who is not professional, someone who has a position, not a profession. So it's a nineteenth-century conception of a connoisseur who actually has taste which validates their position, rather than someone who has the knowledge to take on any exhibition. You call and say, "Hey, I need an exhibition on Le Corbusier." "Yes, I'm a professional curator." That's what it is.

VS That used to be him.

UG But if someone goes to him and says, "I need to make an exhibition on Bofill," he would probably say, "No, thank you." He's a historian, not a professional curator.

CG Not necessarily. The idea is that they can conceptualize and crystalize the moment in culture in which they live and observe, so that they make things visible. I think that curators could have a very relevant role. They are also trained by professional programs to be cultural managers which might be a different story.

RL We've been discussing the distinction between the curator, the author, and the editor, and how one person could be all three. You mentioned before the importance of being a host. It seems like that should be another category in this matrix: the host, who is an author that also curates the conversation.

VS Yes, someone more generous than the curator because you give people their own voice.

UG And you provide dinner.

CG A host is generous, and different from an organization that invites you to do many things but doesn't pay you or an architect that invites you to do things but doesn't credit you.

AA With this document and this collaborative model, how did you envision sharing the credit with the collaborators were you to win? Would one have to enumerate this long list of contributors?

CG Yes. From the very beginning we said and we repeat again, that this project is by MAIO and Fake Industries Architectural Agonism, and then different pieces of the puzzle are authored by other people. MoMA was not necessarily used to this way of operating. Architects don't often invite other people to jump in to share authorship. We had to insist so that everybody was credited correctly in the different media where the project was published and to the different institutions where it was (and still is) exhibited.

AA What's the difference between fake and real? It's not the same as copy and original.

UG Usually the definition of fakeness is something validated by an original, or copies that refer back to an original—you know it's a copy *of* something. So, the fake we're interested in is a fake that doesn't refer to anything but is fake by itself. There are a bunch of people who have been working on developing the fake in philosophical terms, from Nietzsche in *The Gay Science* to Deleuze talking about *F for Fake* by Orson Welles. In *Cinema 2*, Deleuze has an entire chapter on the powers of the fake. Both Deleuze and Nietzsche try to imagine that possibility, a fake that builds off its fakeness, not with a relationship with something that is true—it transcends notions of essentiality in a way. Duchamp was really playful with these things, and he got to those problems through humor and that's something that we also admire. Humor helps a lot.

CG Not only humor. Another thing that interests us about Duchamp is his rejection of work. This has something to do with the ready-mades, of course, but also with the concept of the false. I'm not saying they don't require work—of course they do. But there's this current obsession with super-production which is perhaps unnecessary.

UG But again his laziness, or what he playfully constructs as laziness—producing one work in 30 years—was carefully worked out and required an incredible amount of effort. And humor has another aspect which is that it cannot be explained too much, because the moment you explain then it stops being funny. Humor also requires the audience to participate. They have to want to be part of the joke.

AA Again, you bring up the audience and in this project the audience is very clearly the people who make the project by filling the space with activity. The actual architecture is blank. In the magazine, the rooms themselves are represented with either a white wall or with a grid only.

UG There are three different kinds of audience in this project. One is the audience that's constructed through collages and narratives, the audience that will fill the rooms—sometimes chickens, sometimes ladies from *Spring Breakers*, sometimes our fantasy about an amazing party happening in these rooms. There is a second audience which is the jury of the competition. It's a literal audience. We are telling the story through six different documents, and they are listening and have to enjoy it. And there is a third audience which is the audience for each of the documents when they flow around after the competition.

VS Us!

UG Yes. We try to be extremely aware of those three audiences—they are particularly different, and they are all operating under different fantasies of truth. And for each you have to reconfigure the project differently, but the reconfiguration happens in the audience, not with us. We put these documents in front of you and you have to imagine what happens in these rooms. Each of the documents is an attempt to imagine how these spaces operate as cultural products that circulate around architects and the general public, as certifications of the technical project that has to be constructed, and also as documents that have to be seductive to a jury of peers or curators.

AA What about film as precedent or turning to other media for inspiration?

UG If I had to complain about something in the architectural field right now, it would be that it's a field that produces mainly images, documents, but I witness an incredible lack of a culture of images. Renderings have become this transparent medium in which you assume that a rendering shows an actual building when we know renderings, like any other type of architectural document, are constructed. They refer back to images, so you're not producing a new image of a new building. You're producing an image that is framed and static. And how do we deal with that? Well, there's a history of images that we should be aware of; we should also be aware that we're operating in the larger culture.

RL It seems like you use collage as an architectural tool. Is that a way around the notion of a singular image?

CG We have an anecdote from the Guggenheim competition. In one of the collages that we produced for the second stage, we used an image of a recent exhibition. The exhibition designer called the organizers of the Guggenheim Helsinki Competition claiming that she was the real author of the image. The image was part of a collage and had been post-produced; in many ways it was a new work. But the organizers of the competition let us know that they couldn't use that specific collage and therefore in the boards they covered it with a black square. So we were angry at the beginning and then we realized that it was such a fantastic opportunity because the jurors might project their fantasies of what was underneath. Also, we were surprised that they didn't censor more images from our submission.

UG Collages are fast, first of all, and they force you into clear decision making. In terms of readability and understanding what we're trying to do, this clarity helps. In our project for the Guggenheim, we proposed a museum that is constructed around changes in temperature and atmospheric conditions. Those are really hard to draw and we didn't want to put mist everywhere because it would have been terrible, so we end up having collages. They're not blurry.

CG I think there is another argument. As the Gallagher brothers used to answer when they were asked about their copy of the Beatles: if it's been done already, why do it again? It's already there.

UG Right. For the Guggenheim project we have a couple of collages that are not collages; they are basically projects that are built.

CG The first competition that we won actually included a collection of the works of previous winners.

AA Are the techniques and media of graphic design increasingly being adopted in architecture?

UG Architects have been doing graphic design forever, and dealing with publications. Beatriz Colomina's hypothesis for the modern movement is that it's not about white walls, but rather about engaging with media in a different way. Every master of architectural modernity started by doing magazines and then eventually built things. It's not so problematic. In any case, we are learning to learn from people that know graphic design rather than architects because architects tend to be quite terrible at it. Also, instead of asking graphic designers to choose the type, we ask them to do the collages. Because if we do the collage, we know how it's going to look, but if they do it it's going to be unexpected. I mean the people we worked with—Córdova-Canillas, Naranjo-Etxeberria, Numa-Merino—they are amazing. But we still believe in our ability to produce. In fact, architects are good at producing documents that a lot of people can appropriate. That doesn't mean that everybody understands what they're about but they can mobilize discussions. Suddenly a politician shows up holding a rendering, and shows how something could look. I think that's not just graphic design, it is a mix of things. And I think that's specific to architecture. At the same time, because it's specific, it's probably fragile and always shifting.

ROOMS:

FAKE INDUSTRIES ARCHITECTURAL AGONISM AND MAIO 2014 YAP P.S.1

NO VACANCY

CÓRDOVA - CANILLAS

FOR

FAKE INDUSTRIES ARCHITECTURAL AGONISM

AND MAIO

2014 YAP P.S.1

It was a voluptuous scene that masquerade. But first let me tell of the rooms in which it was held. There were seven --an imperial suite. In many palaces, however, such suites form a long and straight vista, while the folding doors slide back nearly to the walls on either hand, so that the view of the whole extent is scarcely impeded. Here the case was very different; as might have been expected from the duke's love of the bizarre. The apartments were so irregularly disposed that the vision embraced but little more than one at a time. There was a sharp turn at every twenty or thirty yards, and at each turn a novel effect. To the right and left, in the middle of each wall, a tall and narrow Gothic window looked out upon a closed corridor which pursued the windings of the suite. These windows were of stained glass whose color varied in accordance with the prevailing hue of the decorations of the chamber into which it opened. That at the eastern extremity was hung, for example, in blue --and vividly blue were its windows. The second chamber was purple in its ornaments and tapestries, and here the panes were purple. The third was green throughout, and so were the casements. The fourth was furnished and lighted with orange --the fifth with white --the sixth with violet. The seventh apartment was closely shrouded in black velvet tapestries that hung all over the ceiling and down the walls, falling in heavy folds upon a carpet of the same material and hue. But in this chamber only, the color of the windows failed to correspond with the decorations. The panes here were scarlet --a deep blood color. Now in no one of the seven apartments was there any lamp or candelabrum, amid the profusion of golden ornaments that lay scattered to and fro or depended from the roof. There was no light of any kind emanating from lamp or candle within the suite of chambers. But in the corridors that followed the suite, there stood, opposite to each window, a heavy tripod, bearing a brazier of fire that protected its rays through the tinted glass and so glaringly illumined the room. And thus were produced a multitude of gaudy and fantastic appearances. But in the western or black chamber the effect of the fire-light that streamed upon the dark hangings through the blood-tinted panes, was ghastly in the extreme, and produced so wild a look upon the countenances of those who entered, that there were few of the company bold enough to set foot within its precincts at all.

ROOMS, NO VACANCY

4

— THE STEAMY ROOM

6

— THE EMPTY ROOM

8

— THE JAM ROOM

New York Parties, an Urban Legendary Approach

Probably one of the most remarkable features in the history of New York City is its rich and long tradition of parties, celebratory events and other kind of festivities. There is a myriad of notable examples: Dutch beer gardens in New Amsterdam, Shakespearean theatres brought by the British Empire, balls and waltzes of the New World aristocracy, all kinds of speakeasies or gay underground fantasy venues*. Yet if there is one common denominator throughout this chaotic trajectory of celebratory gatherings, it is that they were largely hosted in interior spaces. Furthermore, from the Cotton Club to the Chelsea Hotel, from the Mudd Club to Union Pool, we can assure that the success of these legendary spots was fostered by a spatial configuration made of rooms that in its variation, allowed a multiplicity of different events to take place in the same location. We could perhaps confirm other features common to these premises: They were not overdesigned (and some even spatially banal) yet they were skillful in activating the public who became its most relevant component aside from any iconic architectural presence. The project Rooms: NO VACANCY to be built this summer at PS1's courtyard, seeks to introduce its Saturday's Warm Up parties precisely to this same tradition though an argument based on two points: The recovery of the idea of New York Parties based in a collection of interior spaces, some surprise object- trouvé environments and darker secret rooms; and in the relevance of the subject over the object, that is, the public over the built artifact. In doing so, MoMA will add to PS1's excellent musical programming an architectural intervention that will not make the public passively admire its shape, but that will give them the possibility of adventure, secrecy, fantasy and surprise.

*some of which were famously site specific like Harlem's rent parties, beat gatherings in Columbia apartments, folk shows at the Village, loft happenings in Soho, exclusive dance clubs in Midtown, Meat Packing District sex trunks, punk gig bars at the Bowery and a long etcetera.

— That's not even funny

— THE DUNE ROOM

— THE POOL ROOM

Willkommen

Ladies and Gentleman, welcome to NO VACANCY. But please, there is no need to look up, this is a party spot, not a monument square. Instead we invite you to go through our collection of spaces. Yes, spaces, rooms to be more precise. Do you want to get separated from your partner? Come to our cloud room, you will get refresh and distracted. Do you want to dance? Go straight ahead, there is plenty of room for that. Do you feel nostalgically adventurous? Climb a mountain with a stranger, follow her or him under a tree with a cocktail in your hand. Are you up for a group conversation? Join us in our bedroom. Is it too hot? Visit our lake and enjoy your wet t-shirt. But I warn you Ladies and Gentleman, there is more here than what meets the eye. There is no vacancy nor vacant spaces here. On the contrary there is a collection of secret capsules, fantasy-filled dark rooms commissioned to guest artist in case you are feeling wilder today. No. I shall not tell you their location, discovery, as you know, is a universal charm. Of course, in every corner of our premises you will be able to enjoy today musical program, and if you want a milder experience we are open the rest of the week. Now, leave your preoccupations behind and have a most enjoyable celebration.

—Perhaps it should have remained on the discourse level

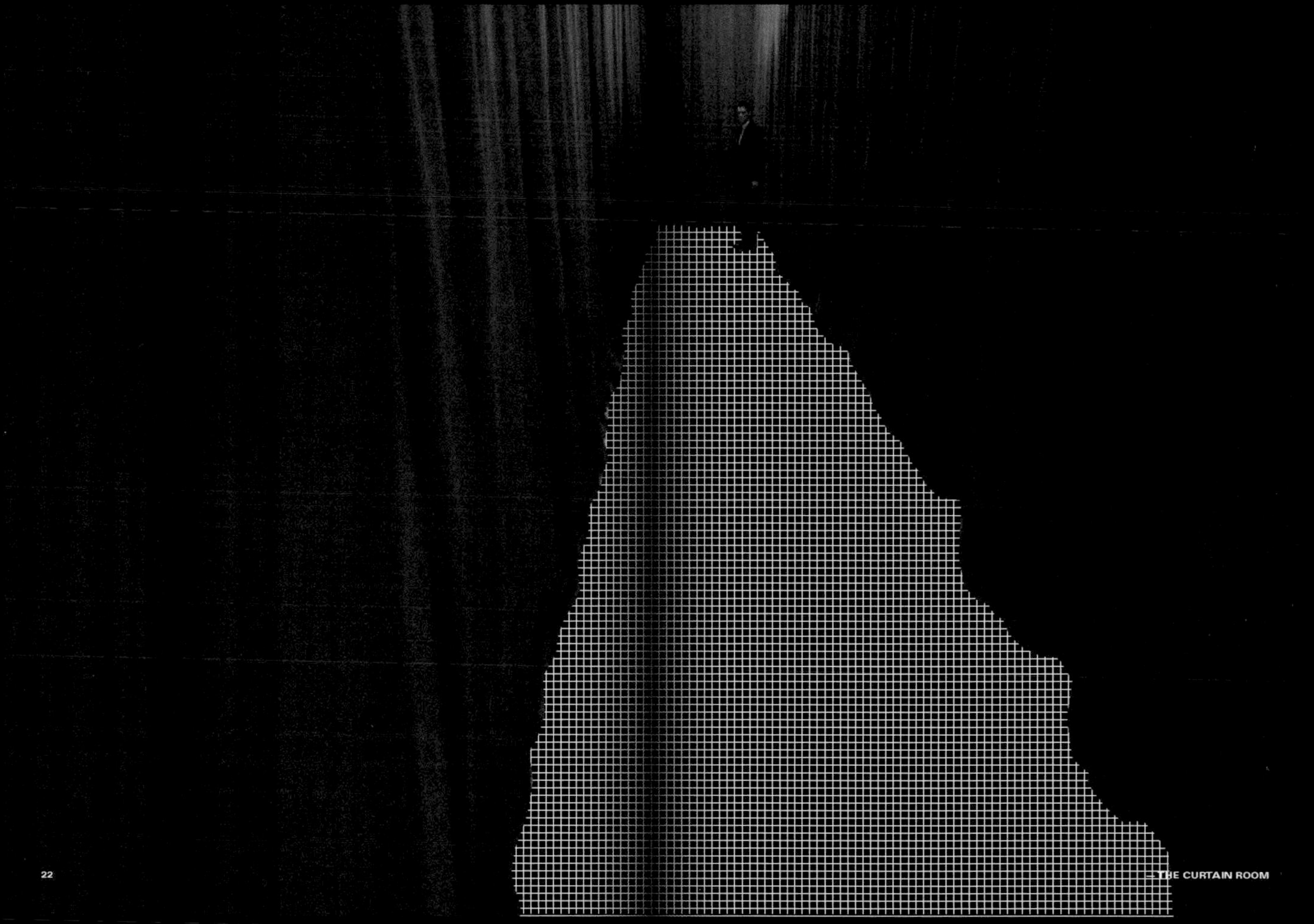

22

— THE CURTAIN ROOM

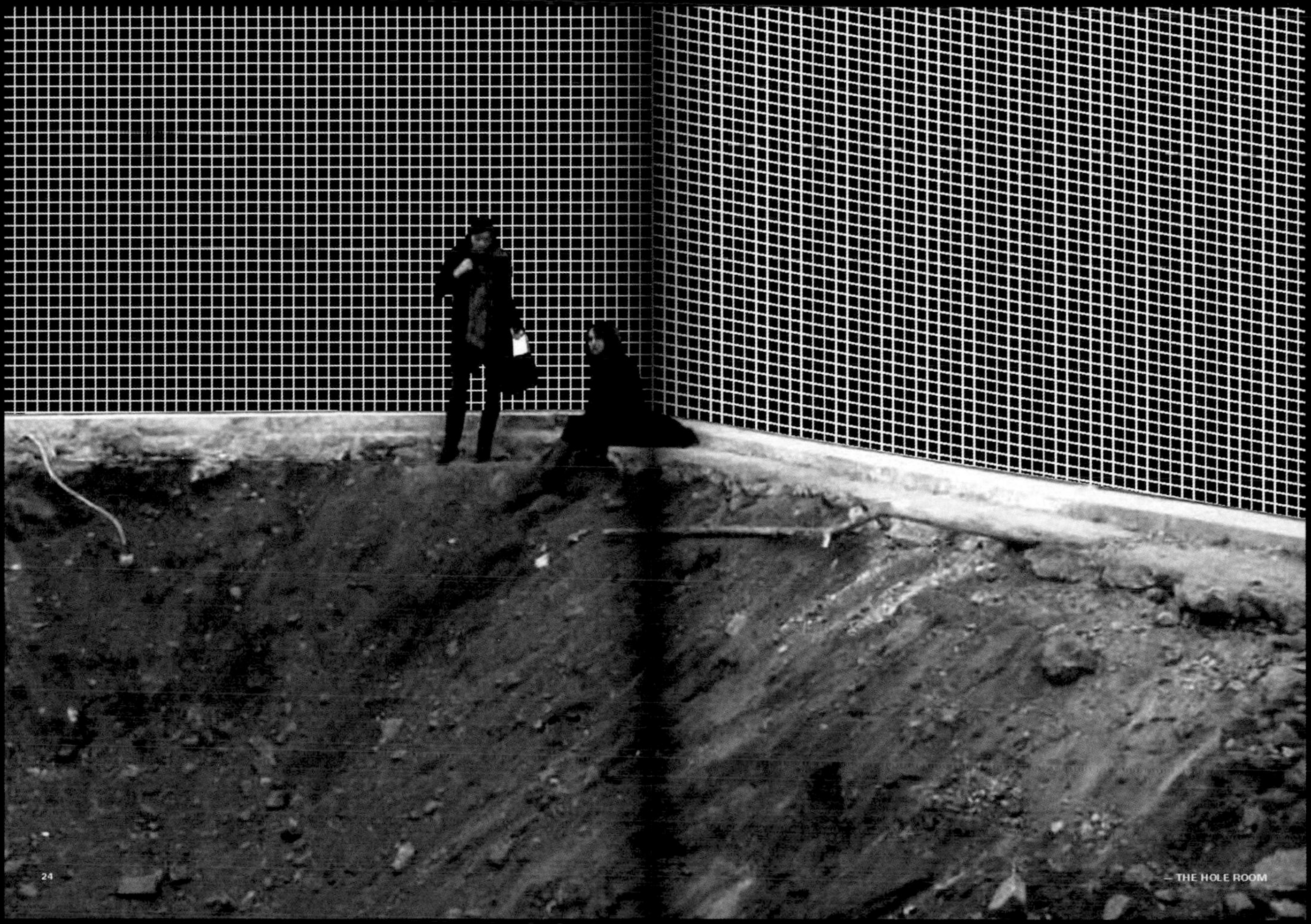

24

— THE HOLE ROOM

The Donor and the Beast

-Hello
-How do you do?
-It is nice here, don't you think?
-Do you mean at the PS1 in general or at this MoMA's donors party?
-I mean at this year's YAP installation
-Oh, I haven't seen it all, I went straight to the donors' event that takes place at the Jam or Piano Room, I'm not sure about the name. I'm starting to explore the rest of the spaces now. It is difficult to abandon them once you are inside to be perfectly honest.
- I understand…I have been here for ten hours and it seems that I have been partying a whole week.
-What do you mean?
-Well, different people, different environments, secret rooms... hiding spots…you know. I have broken up with my partner and got back together three times since noon.
-Oh I see…are you single now?
-Technically speaking…I think so, yes.
-This donors' thing is boring, why don't you show me around?
-Sure. Are you are connected with MoMA?
-In a sense…and you?
-Not really, I'm a journalist from The New Yorker, but I know the architects who did this (pointing his finger around). Crazy bastards.
-So, what is this thing made of?
-Oh, they wouldn't tell you. They only want you to see the surface…but I heard rumors. It is just some sort of scenery built with dry wall.
-Do you mean cheap construction dry wall? That is not as quite sophisticated as I expected.
-That is the point I guess. An affordable, easy and practical construction that will not leave any trace, it is recyclable and renders invisible.
-Interesting. Don't you miss a more object-like installation?
-And losing all this fun? Oh no, I really needed a divorce. Have you heard about the hairy room?
-Not at all. Where is it?
-This way, follow me.
(…)
-Oh, so this is one of the secret rooms. Delightful. Private and soft. What were you saying about the installation?
-Well, iconic objects are of easy consumption. You admire them for five minutes, then you go for a cocktail and forget them as easily. At the end of the day, variation and a collection of strange yet familiar elements in rooms make the party more exciting.
-Do you think there is an architectural argument behind the design?
-Mmm…yes. I heard something about replicas, agonism… But you know, all this profound conversation is giving me a headache, I need another drink before the last call… Good bye, it was nice to meet you.
-Good bye… it was my pleasure. (…) Do you know how to get out of here?…Hello?

— THE PIANO ROOM

30

— THE TABLE ROOM

CHAPTER IV: THE ARCHITECT

HUO interviews MOMA 2014 YAP P.S.1 Winners

HANS ULRICH OBRIST (HUO) — So this is our first interview and I think it would be great to begin at the beginning. I would like to ask you how it all started. Can you tell us was your epiphany with architecture?

THE ARCHITECTS (TA) — (looking at each other in stupor) we don't remember. All these days of partying in NO VACANCY have seriously damaged our memory. No, seriously, don't you prefer to talk about this installation now that we are here?

HUO — Yes, but it will be interesting to hear a little bit more about your influences first.

TA — Well, all of us obviously have different influences that go from famous art and architecture forgers to general culture of the XXII century, from avant-gardes from the 10' and the 60' to public intellectuals or infamous contrarians. In terms of architecture the list would be too long. We are hopeless collectors of useless information. (Should we talk now about ROOMS?)

HUO — I have mentioned on a number of occasions that it seems that the concept of memory implies a certain radicalism right now. As Rem Koolhaas once said, information doesn't necessarily produce memory. Amnesia seems widespread in the digital age. I would like to ask you about the kind of memory implicit in ROOMS: NO VACANCY and how it is reflected in its design

TA — We are quite interested in the history of hedonistic festivities, especially in New York. To be more specific, we are fascinated with the role of architectural typologies and other devices to either provoke them or make them successful. In that sense we could differentiate two categories: Parties that happens in wide spaces like big scale discotheques or raves, where the technologies that are used are mostly atmospheric (light, sound...) or had to do with our bodies (drugs), and those that occur in medium, small or very reduced areas (apartment parties, bars or dark rooms) where architecture has a more direct role and sometimes the walls become activating devices characterized by their different materiality, transparency, holes (or glory holes) etc. In NO VACANY we applied both concepts. It is a collection of pseudo-identical spaces with punctual atmospheric variations and surprises, but where the walls become active technologies that curate the visitor's orientation, view and even touch in intimate spaces.

— THE EMPTY ROOM

But these other apartments were densely crowded, and in them beat feverishly the heart of life. And the revel went whirlingly on, until at length there commenced the sounding of midnight upon the clock. And then the music ceased, as I have told; and the evolutions of the waltzers were quieted; and there was an uneasy cessation of all things as before.

—UNBELIEVABLE!

Interview with MAIO and Córdova Canillas

P49 Editors of Perspecta 49
CC Diego Córdova, Córdova Canillas
MAIO Anna Puigjaner, MAIO

P49 **Could you give a brief history of your practice and its goals?**

CC We are a design practice founded in Barcelona in 2011. We specialize in editorial and content design, although we have worked for clients in many different fields.

MAIO MAIO is an architectural office that works on flexible systems where notions such as variation, ephemerality, or ad hoc permit theoretical positions to materialize. Founded in 2005, it is currently led by Maria Charneco, Alfredo Lérida, Guillermo López, and Anna Puigjaner, architects based in Barcelona who combine professional work with academics, research, and editorial activities.

We are currently in charge of running the magazine *Quaderns d'Arquitectura i Urbanisme* and are teaching at the Barcelona School of Architecture (ETSAB/ETSAV). We understand our practice as a flexible system so we are used to collaborating with different offices. In the case of the MoMA PS1 competition, we were invited to join by Fake Industries Architectural Agonism, with whom we have collaborated on several occasions.

P49 **How can a narrative replace an architectural drawing?**

CC Narrative is, in a way, an architectural tool used to convey an experience. We can say that our vision has definitely changed after getting to know Archigram's projects; they are pure narrative.

MAIO If we understand architecture as a wide form of cultural production, then modes of representation and narration can be interchangeable. The representational logic of this project aimed to be coherent with its fragmentary content. The rooms were qualified by means of variations and specific interventions. Inside the set of rooms, the visitor could never have a picture of the whole intervention, but only a polyhedral sum of fragments to be reconstructed while crossing the spaces.

P49 **What was your process for creating this book?**

MAIO Since we wanted a fragmentary presentation of the work in order to allow the beholder to reconstruct it, we invited some artists and designers to produce their own vision. In the case of the book, we explained the general idea and produced the textual contents, but gave freedom to the designers to propose a specific approach from their point of view. Everything worked like that.

[Spread 1]

P49 **What was the intention behind rejecting a cover image?**

CC It gives the document an aura of confidentiality, while at the same time opening it up to infinite possibilities within. The phrase "No vacancy" is also very suggestive; for us it evokes the neon language of highway motels.

MAIO This was a decision taken by the designers. Nevertheless it follows the general guideline of stressing an understanding of the publication as a set of spaces—chapters or rooms—so that multiplicity would end up building a whole overview, which was part of the general strategy we've mentioned above.

P49 **Does "No Vacancy" help summon a mental image to substitute for the missing cover image?**

CC We were looking for something poetic that would conjure up an image with a personal meaning, different for every reader.

MAIO The name has to do with two principal decisions. The first aims to render visible the idea of the "generic" linked to that kind of highway building including the language of other similar ordinary/anonymous references. The second is more complex and has to do with a very important issue, which is the image of architecture. In the case of this project, there was no "image", unlike in many of the other proposals. This sign—a text, by the way—aimed to render visible the interior system and at the same time to conjure an image.

[Spread 2]

P49 **What is the nature of authorship for the document? How does this align with more general thoughts on authorship in your practice and in your discipline in general?**

CC With the internet, authorship is very blurry nowadays and it is losing its relevance. The narrative itself has now become the protagonist.

MAIO This project departs from an idea of collective and collaborative construction and gives freedom to the different collaborators, who somehow became authors themselves (designers Córdova-Canillas and artist Luis Úrculo). We created some guidelines that amount to a conceptual system that can be materialized in several ways while maintaining a global coherence (as happens with the proposal itself) and the invited collaborators act as authors of a specific approach (book, video, etc.).

As for the second part, authorship is, more and more, a very fragile concept constantly redefined. Nevertheless, more than in "authorship" we believe in "responsibility," which includes a broader sense of commitment and dissolves any romantic idea of individuality. This is something important for us since we work in a group of four by means of mutual agreements.

P49 **Is this text meant to set up the basic theme of the project?**

CC No, although it functions as a poetic statement to support it.

MAIO Somehow it does. The narration and narrator accompany the visitor through a set of rooms where action takes place.

P49 **Is text better at conveying affect than plans and sections?**

CC We think it is.

MAIO As we mentioned before, it is precisely the sum of these documents that can provide a specific mood and outline a precise intention, but this can also be achieved by means of relatively independent complementary processes.

P49 **How does using Poe's voice here add to or change the project itself?**

CC It is almost a description of the project.

MAIO Poe's quote allowed us, among other things, to recover the idea of a set or scenario that allows things to happen. We created a stage where life—the party and other uncontrollable things—could happen. A space of possibilities.

P49 **Why not cite this text in the publication?**

CC Because it is not relevant. The text could be written by an anonymous author and it would be just as effective.

[Spread 3]

P49 **What is the function of the grid?**

CC It gives a sense of scale and represents the human's instinctive search for structure in infinite space, or maybe nothing at all.

MAIO This was, again, a decision of the designers, but has to do with the fact that the grid is the background to the important thing: it allows the party to happen. The grid aims to transform the space of a museum into a generic one. That is the starting point of the display designed by MAIO. The grid also allows the construction of a rational yet maze-like space, where the labyrinthine perception arises by means of a strict repetition.

P49 **This collage technique recalls work from the 1960s, such as No Stop City or Exodus. Was this intentional?**

CC They are indeed references; collage is very useful when visually transferring subjects into a different context.

MAIO It was a decision of the designers, but of course their imaginary is aware of those references. The grid acts as a base sustaining variations on it, creating a family of related drawings where variation is the basis of the collage.

[Spread 4]

P49 **Does this depict the project or a generic gallery space?**

CC More than depicting the project itself, it depicts emptiness as experience.

MAIO It is a generic space. Introducing humor and this kind of supplement allowed us to stress the idea of split chapters and characters—different visions of the book.

P49 **Is this a photograph of a model?**

CC Yes, it is a photo of a model we built.

MAIO A model we prepared for the designers. They took the picture. All of us wanted a partial view.

P49 **Is there an anti-architectural theme here?**

CC Perhaps it is anti-anti-architectural.

MAIO Not really. It was about the architectonic elements (doors, etc.) and objects (the mountain) that configured the space with a very tight view.

[Spread 5]

P49 **The grid here is different. What does that mean?**

CC The grid works as spatial reference; it lets us define the feeling of the space in a rather abstract way. A smaller grid conveys the sensation of vast space while a larger grid gives it a closer, more intimate feel.

MAIO This little variation stresses the change of distance of the viewer with regard to what happens inside each of the rooms. But in general terms it remains coherent with the entire description of the ambiance.

P49 **This spread seems to speak to a long tradition of collage in architecture, but reduces it to its minimum: a subject, a ground, and a background. How does collage reveal (or hide) architectural intent?**

CC In a way it is an art direction decision; we have designed the collage by its architectural implications, in a manner that reveals the pure architectural intent.

MAIO This collage in particular depicts the radical and plain elements of the project: walls, floor, doors, windows. It was about architecture, but specifically about how it can enhance a party.

P49 **Here a blank floor is added to the wall grid. Why was it important to distinguish these elements?**

CC It was added to intensify the feeling of the experience, as if the spectator were in the same room.

MAIO In order to reproduce different situations. Some rooms appear crowded while some others just show a single element or activity going on. So here the floor appears.

10 11

New York Parties, an Urban Legendary Approach

[Spread 6]

P49 **Why this image in particular?**

CC We wanted to use an image of a New York party different from the collage scheme used in the rest of the publication to communicate the perspective of an author as chronicler. We found this interesting 1929 lithograph by Mabel Dwight that depicts a "rent party," a kind of house party that was popular during the Harlem Renaissance.

MAIO It links our proposal to a New York party tradition. "Home sweet home" connects the party with the domestic sphere. Both public and domestic spheres converge here, as happens with parties.

P49 **Do you have any speculations on why New York has such an interior-based party culture?**

CC Most likely because the weather is cold during most of the year. Maybe also because of the Dutch heritage from the first settlers who founded New Amsterdam.

MAIO From the party point of view, and unlike what happens in some Mediterranean cultures where parties and urban spaces are boldly linked, in New York, maybe due to laws, climate or culture, interiors have become the place for celebration.

P49 **To some extent, what was once underground in New York is now above ground. Parties have moved from interiors out to the PS1 courtyard. Is this project nostalgic? Trying to turn back time?**

CC In a way it is trying turn it back to its original nature.

MAIO It is not nostalgic at all. We believe in anachronism as a form of newness. Learning from the past can be done without nostalgia. It has to do with understanding the underlying criteria that remain. Instead of trying to go back in time we would like to think of it as going back to future.

P49 **Your collection of diverse interiors also resonates with OMA's City of the Captive Globe. What about New York generates this type of architectural thought?**

CC New York is a city of cities: as an island with very clear boundaries, a vast amount of situations are concentrated in a relatively small space, where different spheres collide, ending up with unexpected results.

MAIO Koolhaas understood very well that the grid of the city allowed variations and difference to take place.

P49 **How would you define interiority? Do you need a ceiling or walls?**

CC Not necessarily: interiority could be defined as the appropriation and delimitation of a space. Ceilings and walls are nothing more than cultural references.

MAIO There are at least three ways of producing effects in a party: external technologies (architecture), ambient technology (lights, sound), and interior technologies or technologies of the body. The three of them generate a space—an ambiance, an atmosphere. We like to think of architecture as a sum of these.

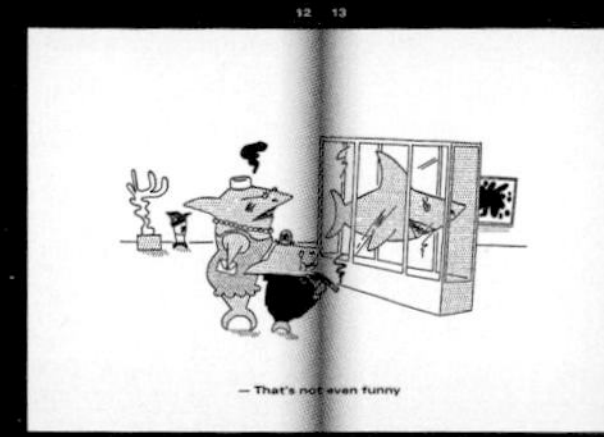

[Spread 7]

P49 **The stillness of the art objects here contrasts with the activity in preceding images. Is a critique of art implicit in this project?**

CC More than a critique of art, it is a critique of the gallery system.

MAIO Of course there's irony. Being a curator and thinking of a party inside the museum is somehow problematic. Where are the limits? That's a question we often thought of while doing the project.

P49 **What is the role of this cartoon specifically, and humor generally, in this publication?**

CC To generate pauses in the narrative and to guide the perception of the reader.

MAIO Humor is always necessary. Even more when you think of parties.

[Spread 8]

P49 **Formlessness hugging form. What does the dune represent? How does such a mass act on urban space?**

CC In this case it represents an unexpected stimulus in a sequence of spaces, and through its scale it also works as a force of attraction.

MAIO The mountain allowed us to signify a room in particular and, by means of the formal opposition between it and the grid, produce dysfunctional results of unforeseeable actions.

[Spread 9]

P49 **Why suggest a pool through attire without showing the actual pool?**

CC Here, the importance of the pool does not lie in its architectural qualities; it is more of a situation or an attitude.

Willkommen

[Spread 10]

P49 **Why German here?**

CC We interpret it as a reference to tourism. In Spain we are used to hearing and seeing German expressions of hospitality in touristic areas, since Germans are very fond of visiting our beaches.

MAIO It was a nod to the Berlin party scene. We collaborated with Daniel Fernández Pascual from Cooking Sections. He had an incredible analysis of Berlin Partytopias.

P49 **How many rooms are there, in final count? Are they all devoted to a singular atmosphere or are some more multifarious?**

MAIO There are 44.

P49 **Here architecture is the frame around activity. Metaphorically, then, is architecture a sort of quotation mark?**

CC Yes, it is.

MAIO Sometimes. Here it is.

[Spread 11]

P49 **Is that a Malevich on the wall?**

CC Basically 90% of contemporary art practices.

MAIO A cartoon. Nothing transcendental, quite the opposite.

P49 **Who drew these cartoons?**

CC We have borrowed from Samuel Nyholm's website. We think they're quite charming.

[Spread 12]

P49 **Many of these images are stills from videos/film. What is so special about this medium? How does it relate to architecture?**

CC It relates to architecture in many ways, either as a backdrop or as the main subject. We chose stills to portray situations through cultural references.

MAIO Maybe it has to do with recalling a certain imaginary.

[Spread 13]

P49 **The hole is spatial but not architectural and definitely picks up Urs Fischer's critique of the gallery "scene." On what level did you intend this image to function?**

CC On a human level.

MAIO Well, here the hole is supposed to be a folly inside the system. So it can be understood as another layer accompanying architecture. Nevertheless, it could be in another context an architectural device. Quoting Hollein: "Alles ist Architektur."

P49 **What activities did you envision in the hole?**

CC Dog fights.

MAIO We did not think of specific actions. The follies were just invitations to use them in an open way.

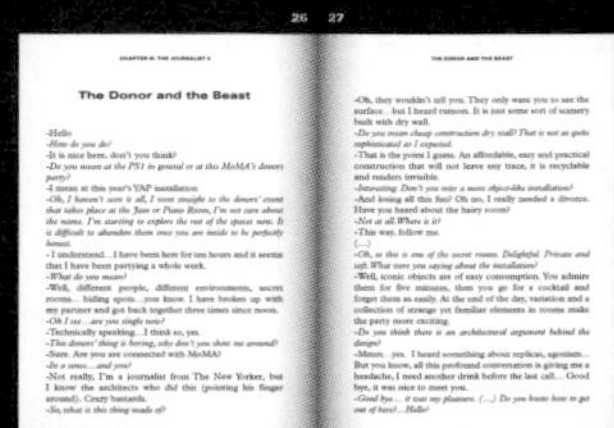
The Donor and the Beast

[Spread 14]

P49 **This seems to be the most direct description of the project, but also rejects its own intentions. What is the role of time in the project?**

CC Time is a sequence of actions that trigger other actions.

MAIO Time is the project. Time allows things to happen. Architecture is an alibi.

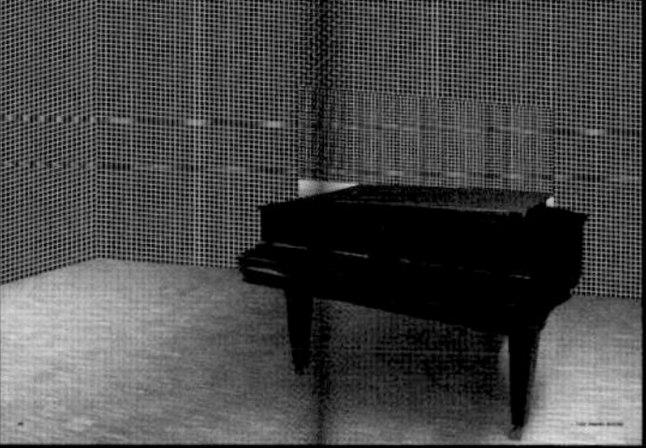

[Spread 15]

P49 **Here the grid is at its most spatial yet, but the activity that fills it is the most inert. Is that the trade off you're exploring?**

CC Indeed. *Rooms* is about the balance between human interaction and space.

MAIO No. It's casual.

[Spread 16]

HUO Interviews MOMA 2014 YAP P.S.1 Winners

[Spread 17]

P49 **Is HUO difficult to quote? Or a spirit to be invoked?**

CC For us he's a bit like David Letterman but a Swiss, artistic version. We're big fans of HUO so he is, obviously, a spirit to be invoked.

MAIO It is obviously a joke. We wanted to introduce a final provocation.

P49 **This sidesteps the question of influence. What is the role of influence in the project? What is the relationship between influence and source material, as in collage?**

CC Collage works as a graphic resource, in this case, with cultural references.

MAIO This is a really difficult question to answer. I am not sure we can really quantify it. Nevertheless, we cannot hide our sympathies for Italian radicals from the 60s such as Superstudio, where the conceptualization of architecture was a capital issue.

P49 **Why have a Fake HUO quote Rem?**

MAIO Rem Koolhaas is right when he says that "Information doesn't necessarily produce memory." It is a good quote that captures what we were thinking about.

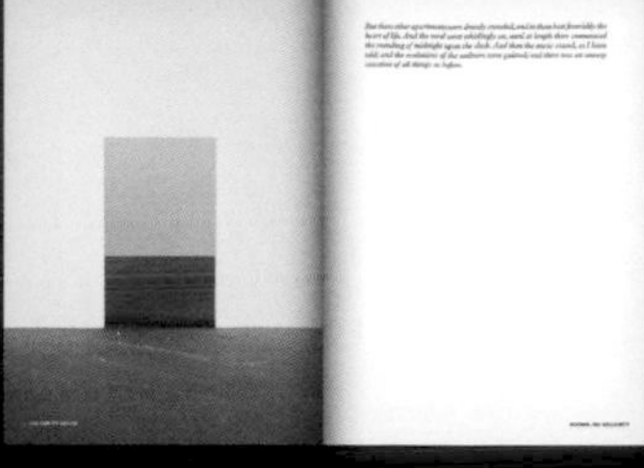

[Spread 18]

P49 **A room with plenty of vacancy?**

CC Yes.

MAIO Some rooms remained empty, as generic spaces.

[Spread 19]

P49 **Self-reflection seems to play a big role in this project, or at least this publication. What is the difference between quoting others and quoting oneself? Why displace your voice onto fictional characters?**

CC Because it is more dramatic, more theatrical. The narrative was placed in the future and the editorial structure was created for it.

MAIO It is a mechanism to show the project through multiplicity. It's not about a point of view but about the infinite perspectives the project will allow. We thought a lot in "Instagram-like" points of view.

P49 **We've come to the end, but haven't seen any plans, sections, or other traditional architectural representations. What is the intent of this? After some reflection, do you think a publication like this is just as adept as architectural drawing at describing space?**

CC In our opinion, a publication without drawings can unquestionably be more architectural than a plan or section, since it can transmit underlying concepts and values that can't be represented solely through measurements.

MAIO The plans were presented apart. The display, as mentioned before, used different media.

P49 **What are you working on now? Where do you see quotation in the future?**

CC We are working on various projects; one them is our self-initiated modern erotic monograph titled *MORENA*.

MAIO MAIO has recently produced an installation for the Chicago Architecture Biennial and is currently finishing a housing block in Barcelona. Recently we designed an urban square—using a grid—and designed an exhibition for MACBA entitled Species of Spaces that has a lot to do with the MoMA PS1 project.

"A story retold is the essence of literature, the artifact is the underpinning of Art."

∞ Elia Zenghelis

Perpetually Quoting—The Architectural Project: Abstraction, Essence, and Metaphor

> The real voyage of discovery consists not in seeking new landscapes but in having new eyes.
> —Marcel Proust

In *Le Temps Retrouvé (Time Regained)*, the seventh and last book of *A la Recherche du Temps Perdu (In Search of Lost Time)*, Proust formulates his clearest vision of the role, meaning, and instrumentality of Art, a concern that haunted him throughout the entire work; haunted by "the extreme difference that exists between the true impression we have of a thing and the false impression that we give ourselves when we voluntarily try to represent it." Art, he realizes, reveals the truth of things, because it bestows the ability to understand the unchanging essences behind fleeting experience.

In the closing parts of the book, the narrator goes to a matinée at the princess of Guermantes's; along the way, the recurring awareness of his inability to be a writer, an anxiety that has been afflicting him through all the preceding books of the *Recherche* wells up in him; while he waits in the Guermantes's library for the end of a musical performance, the sound of a spoon, the stiffness of a towel, trigger in him an intense pleasure that he had felt on a number of occasions in the past—when seeing the trees of Hudimesnil from the train, for instance. It strikes him that what these sensations had in common was that they were experienced simultaneously in the present and in a distant moment, so far as to cause the past to encroach on the present and make him wonder in which of the two he found himself: "the creature in me which at that moment tasted this sensation, was tasting it in what it held in common with a bygone day, and now, in whatever extra-temporal sense it had, a creature that only appeared when it could be found in the only environment where it could live, enjoy the essence of things, [...] outside time."

This *creature* had never come to him in "real time," but it only appeared each time that the "miracle of an analogy" made him escape the present. This time he decides to investigate his impression, to "elucidate the secret of this trance," to decode the sense of this "bedazzling and indistinct vision" and to realize why certain spontaneous sensations give him such happiness; he finally understands that only *involuntary memory* can resurrect and *recreate* the past; what's more, he sees in this artificial recreation the potential properties of a work of art; and in the end, the narrator discovers the meaning of life in art and literature: it is the work of art that enables him to live what he considers to be a "real life."

The characteristic trait of the experience activated by involuntary memory is that it is more intense than the original; through its being *resurrected*, or because of it—because of its *artificiality*—it gives him a pleasure that he did not experience initially, and he can therefore draw the conclusion that it is invested with a quality which stems from this transformation—and which, in the process, decrees the reconstructed, or the *synthetic*, as superior to the real. The palpability of this reconstruction takes on a certain *objective* physiognomy that can be considered in its own right and thus assumes the qualities of a work of Art.

Art generates a critical distance from everyday actuality: "only through Art can we walk out of ourselves, know what someone else sees in a universe which is not the same as ours, in landscapes that would have remained as unknown to us as those that might be on the moon"; far from the mundane, the work of Art can *recapture* the *lost*, save it from oblivion and abolish the limits imposed by Time. And at this juncture, the hero is finally ready to create a literary work (which, incidentally, is none other than the book we are reading).

This he was now determined to "prepare meticulously" and with "perpetual force, like an onslaught," "to support like a fatigue, accept like a rule, construct like a church, follow like a diet, overcome like an obstacle, conquer like a friendship, nourish like a child, create like a world, without leaving aside those mysteries that probably have their explanation in other worlds and whose premonition is what moves us most in life and art."

Art reveals the truth of things because it bestows the ability to understand the unchanging *essences* behind fleeting experiences. The *essence of things* is the objective of Proust's research and emotions are the catalysts—aesthetic emotions that become the muses of art. These essences are abstract and unchanging quantities that lie behind transient experience and are intrinsic to it; they are "ideal forms" waiting to be extracted; they are not immediately manifest on the surface of things and it is the writer's task to uncover them. This task is accomplished by the work of art, which at the same time communicates the meaning of life: "truth—and life too—can be attained by us only when, by comparing a quality common to two sensations, we succeed in extracting their common essence and in reuniting them to each other, liberated from the contingencies of time, within a metaphor." In conclusion, the medium that carries the liberated message of the consummated essences is the *metaphor*.

In the resulting work, the narrator recreates a condition of worldliness that is drawn not from his present reality, but from the fabrication of an artificial world recalled by memory, reshaped, transformed, and with its banality redeemed, in line with his own individual vision of the human condition, a kind of *recreation* that is meant to transcend and to outlast the past: "the truths that intelligence derives directly from reality have no depth... because they have not been recreated."

A story *retold* is the essence of literature, the artifact is the underpinning of Art. The story in *A la Recherche du Temps Perdu* is, if looked at dispassionately, a banal story of debility, self-doubt, lost love, jealousy, greed, callousness, and depravity—within the framework of a fin de siècle Parisian society, a declining and impotent aristocracy, a rising and unscrupulous bourgeoisie, and a duplicitous worldliness. Eminently boring as a story, it becomes, as *retold* by Proust, one of literature's richest discourses and greatest masterpieces—a work in which the trivial becomes extraordinary.

But apart from being a paradigmatic work of literature, it is a didactic text and an invaluable reference book, as it also is a prescription for Art itself, a prescription that additionally owns up to Art's legacy; in Proust's words, "a book is a great cemetery where, on most of the graves, one can no longer read the wiped out names."

The *Recherche* is didactic for architecture too, given that of all the arts, with its sensual materiality, architecture is the most demonstrably object oriented. Like a book, a work of architecture must incorporate its own inheritance, distilled within its projected newness.

Proust's ground rules incorporate the axiomatic rejection of any search for *invention*: "to write this crucial book, this single true book, a writer doesn't have, in the ordinary sense, to invent it, since it already exists in each one of us, but to translate it. The duty and the task of a writer are those of a translator."

One can correspondingly argue that whatever was to be invented in architecture (as distinct from technology) was invented more than 4,500 years ago: if literature rests on the translation of "the great book of our coexisting sensations within ourselves," architecture rests on the translation of its own makeup, which intrinsically exists within itself. Architecture has a syntax and a language that is dynamic and evolving, but nonetheless inherent to its constitution, and *existing outside time*. This we can call the *essence* of architecture.

In fact, the idea of *essence* in architecture comprises two components: first, the "extra-temporal" and immutable consistency, the *idem* that is intrinsic to architecture and is, by the "miracle of an analogy," recognizable as such throughout its history, the "ideal form" that lies outside Time and is waiting to be extracted; and, second, the kind of progressive *essence* that is necessarily embodied within an envisioned architectural project, within a *design.* This is what is commonly referred to as the concept: when we talk of a *concept*, we refer to the idea, or guiding principle, which will steer the design and will remain a reference to all decisions in the process—and which may or may not become a visible feature; but, notwithstanding the complexities involved in the parameters of the architectural project, *it is the essence* that has to be embodied in the design. In a sense, this proceeds from the first component like a ghost, in that the extra-temporal, analogical essence is also ingrained within the concept.

In architecture, too, we can, by comparing the common qualities that we recognize throughout the nearly five millennia of architectural history and right up to our present day, extract their common essence and, liberated from the contingencies of time, reunite them to each other, as *permanent, ideological abstractions*: when we do this, architecture becomes the metaphor of ideal form—and we create the new, perpetually quoting.

All of the text in quotation marks is extracted from Marcel Proust's *Le Temps Retrouvé* (Paris: Editions Gallimard, 1927) and translated by the author.

pages 258–259
Dogma with Elia Zenghelis, *The Runway*, competition project, 2004, Hellenikon Park, Athens. Characters from Resnais's *L'année dernière à Marienbad* give the defunct airport infrastructure a new use.

"In architecture as in life quotation is really all that matters, and no transcendental individualism can ever replace the richness of a world full of reference, nuance, and allusion."

Thomas Weaver

LOOSE SALLY

In one of Reyner Banham's less celebrated architectural homilies the English critic anointed Le Corbusier's *Towards a New Architecture* as "The only piece of architectural writing that will be classed among the 'essential literature of the twentieth century'." Despite the fact that this testimonial is printed on the back cover of all English editions of the book it goes somewhat overlooked, never referenced or quoted. Perhaps one of the reasons for its relative obscurity is the measure by which Banham was appraising Le Corbusier—*Towards a New Architecture* was not being invited into an art historical, intellectual or philosophical pantheon, but a literary canon.

There is something interesting in this association, not least because among all the glorious and vainglorious platitudes typically bestowed upon an architectural work ("most important", "most harmonious", "most original"), the idea that an architect can write beautifully—"most literary"—has never been among them. The cynical onlooker would point out that this omission simply reflects the fact that so few architects write well, yet for a discipline that since its inception has been presented to us as a language, this disregard for writerly finesse still seems a significant lacuna. Paradoxically, there is also something deeply uncorbusian about Banham's estimation, for it adjudges Le Corbusier by the single quality that he had consistently denied—style. Accordingly, the radicalism of his testimonial is that Le Corbusier should be venerated less for what he was saying than for the compelling ways in which he said it.

One of the most obvious registers of the power of this style is the fact that Le Corbusier is so quotable—a quality made easier by the lyricism of his prose (or more particularly, the excellence of Frederick Etchells' original English translation). In fact, it is actually harder to find ordinary, undistinguished sentences in *Towards a New Architecture* than it is to highlight those that are memorable or repeatable. In almost every line one can find a quote. The book, in this sense, is less an architectural polemic than it is a kind of dictionary of aphorisms, even if the only person Le Corbusier ever quotes is himself.

And yet in architectural historiography's embrace of Le Corbusier these literary associations are somehow suppressed, and *Towards a New Architecture* is sold to us only through the unambiguity of its message—a book of lyricisms presented instead only as a rallying call. More presciently, in terms of the way future architects learnt to articulate their ideas, the fundamentalism of its voice also became the yardstick by which subsequent practitioners established their influence. Architects, it seems, only ever aspire to write manifestos, now the *de facto* architectural text, whose monotheism panders to all of architecture's less endearing qualities and none of its intrinsic charms. As a result, architectural discourse now articulates itself as a kind of holy war, rather than as a contrasting Algonquin Round Table of witticisms and allusions that you would imagine a discipline predicated on quotation, reference, style, and association would be more naturally suited.

Indeed, if these are the characteristics through which architecture should better promote itself—being both more adept at quotation and more quotable—then there is a mode of writing ideally suited to the task, and it is not the manifesto (for no one can write like Le Corbusier) but the essay. First pioneered by the French writer Montaigne in the late sixteenth century, the essay was invented as a way to test complicated ideas in a literary form that was simple and clear—something reflected in its etymology, for the word derives from the French *essayer*, meaning to try or to attempt. And so in contrast to the assuredness and confidence of the manifesto, an essay revels in its self-doubt, or at least in an essay what structures the narrative is the meditative questioning of a set of ideas rather than a treatise which provides only declarative answers. An essay is also relatively short, stripped to the exposition of a single idea; is never broken down into sub-sections or chapters; its title should typically provide some sense of reference, or at least humour; and there should never be any footnotes. As a piece of writing, not typing—to borrow Truman Capote's distinction—an essay must also have ambitions towards a certain lyricism, for essays are mellifluous and free-flowing, and sell their ideas as much through the compelling choice of words as through what is actually being said. Ultimately, though, the only true rule of essay writing is a commitment not to observe any rules—an inbuilt sense of mischief that characterises most definitions of the essay form, and certainly that of Aldous Huxley: "the essay is a literary device for saying almost everything about almost anything."

For an architect whose professional responsibilities demand a level of propriety (a building has to stand up after all), the essay therefore offers a form of relief, a chance at nonconformity by constructing a work through an opposing set of registers. Such an opportunity is even engrained into the dictionary definition of the essay, in the form of a quote from Samuel Johnson. "An essay," he said, "is a loose sally of the mind, an irregular undigested piece: not a regular and orderly composition." In this sense, an architectural adoption of the essay reorders Vitruvius'—that is, architecture's—value system, elevating *venustas* or delight above any obligation for *firmitas* or solidity.

In the history of ideas, the appeal of Montainge's invention was immediate, and soon crossed over into the Anglo-Saxon world through the appropriation of the essay by the author and philosopher Francis Bacon. His own enthusiasm then established a self-informing cast of English intellectuals, dilettantes and connoisseurs—Milton, Johnson, Hazlitt, Lamb, Ruskin, De Quincey, Pater, Chesterton, Strachey, Woolf, Huxley and Orwell—all of whose criticism was written not as treatises, tomes, or papers but only and ever as essays. Equivalent lineages emerged in the French-speaking world, culminating with the wonderful essayist Roland Barthes, and in Germany with the man Theodor Adorno referred to as "the unsurpassed master of the essay form," Walter Benjamin. Adorno even canonised the essay in its own kind of ironic treatise, his essay "The Essay as Form", which is riddled with apposite little subversions, oppositions and quotations: "the essay is both more open and more closed than traditional thought would like"; "the essay resists the idea of a masterpiece, an idea which itself reflects the idea of creation and totality"; "the effort of the essay reflects a childlike freedom that catches fire, without scruple, on what others have already done."

Adorno wrote "The Essay as Form" in 1958, a moment that now seems to be the high-water mark of the essay's popularity, not only in terms of philosophical, cultural, and art historical writing, but crucially also in architecture. As evidence, one need only look at a quintet of English architectural historians whose key works were only ever anthologies of essays. Despite their shared nationality and mode of writing, what is additionally distinctive about these thinkers is that each of them presented a different facet of the good essayist. For the first of them, John Summerson, and in particular his collection of essays, *Heavenly Mansions*, it was in the clarity, accessibility, and didacticism of his writing, as much as his ability to preach on the value of architecture not just through its tectonics but through a whole assemblage of cultural artefacts. His successor, chronologically, if not intellectually, Colin Rowe, was also at his best in the essay form, but his words are characterised by their first-person narrative—Rowe writes as he speaks (*As I Was Saying* is the fitting title of his three-volume collected works), and it is a kind of speech made more compelling by its indiscretion, innuendo, and iconoclasm. Just a year younger than Rowe was Alan Colquhoun, an incredibly rigorous and precise scholar, someone who never thought of presenting his ideas through the philosophising treatise, but only the razor-sharp essay (his collection, *Essays in Architectural Criticism*, being the best of them). A further year younger than Colquhoun was Banham himself. To read any one of the hundreds of short texts in his posthumous anthology of writings, *A Critic Writes*, is to appreciate a historian fully in command of both his popularism and expertise. The last of this collective was Robin Evans, who arrived a little later, more than twenty years Banham's junior, but who died tragically young, and who wrote as he thought—figuring things out as he went along. Evans also has perhaps the single best opening line of any architectural essay: "Ordinary things contain the deepest mysteries," from "Figures, Doors and Passages" in *Translations from Drawing to Building and Other Essays*.

The essay is a literary device for saying almost everything about almost anything.

An essay is a loose sally of the mind, an irregular undigested piece: not a regular and orderly composition.

The effort of the essay reflects a childlike freedom that catches fire, without scruple, on what others have already done.

The essay can be seen as a small part of the history of rhetoric, dating from the Renaissance, ... from the hands of specialists to the hands of “all educated people”

Quotations in my works are like robbers by the roadside who make an armed attack and relieve an idler of his convictions.

Sermoniser, raconteur, scholar, populist, autodidact—this, then, is a group of historians who have collectively defined not only the way we think about architecture, but the form through which these thoughts appear to us. And yet despite all their quotations and the enduring resonances of their legacy, each of them was strangely bashful about their contribution, or at least about the unifying form in which they all presented their work. Perhaps to elaborate would have been undignified, or simply to state the obvious. The only tiny fragment of self-analysis can be found in the unpublished correspondences of Colquhoun, who on June 15, 2011, just a year before his death aged 91, wrote to his friend and fellow architectural historian Jacques Gubler a letter headlined "Some Thoughts on the Essay". To read it is to finally be able to peer behind the curtain and see the inner-workings of a methodology. "The essay," Colquhoun writes, "is not merely a quirky Anglo-Saxon genre, puzzling to all continental Europe. It is an important agent of the Enlightenment . . . combining 'learned' ideas with popular expression . . . But also—more remotely—the essay can be seen as a small part of the history of rhetoric, dating from the Renaissance, which moved knowledge (both reason and understanding) from the hands of specialists to the hands of 'all educated people'."

The sad thing about almost all architectural writing now, both by practitioners and commentators, is that hardly anyone writes in the essay form. For a brief moment in the 1990s there was Sanford Kwinter and Robert Somol, delivering short and punchy texts in New York's *ANY* magazine, and before them, Michael Sorkin, as architectural critic for *The Village Voice*, who got closer still to the irreverent standards of a good essayist in publishing numerous funny little vitriolic blasts against contemporary architecture. But today the best thinkers and writers about architecture—people like Vidler, Forty, Forster, Picon, Cohen, Bergdoll, Colomina, Hays, and Frampton—never write essays, only books. And yet if we imagine for a moment a history of, say, American architecture through a means of expression more expert both in its own voice and that of others, then the legacy of its works could have been sharper, wittier, more astute, more easily disseminated, more quotable even. Ludicrously narcissistic autobiographies by Sullivan or Wright could have been instantly improved; ground-breaking exhibitions but mind-numbing catalogues, such as Hitchcock and Johnson's *The International Style*, could have been really profound; the cultivated inner workings of Eisenman's alternating neo-classicism, mannerism, and parametricism could have been de-cluttered and made accessible; and the subtlety of the argument buried deep within *Complexity and Contradiction* could have come to the fore, far outreaching the crudity of its architecture. Think, even, of what such a re-imagination could do to the American academy and the attendant effect such a recasting would have on the drudgery of the term paper, or that rotten old vessel of bad sentences, the PhD. Not only would the long-entrenched apartheid between making architecture and writing architecture be dissolved, but one would hope that ultimately many more architectural works would be considered *essential* to literature's canon.

In a nice piece of post-modernism, the entry for *quotation* in the *Oxford English Dictionary* itself features a quote, Ralph Waldo Emerson declaring that "quotation confesses inferiority." It goes without saying that Emerson is clearly wrong, for in architecture as in life quotation is really all that matters, and no transcendental individualism can ever replace the richness of a world full of reference, nuance, and allusion. Inscribed into the dictionary, and the lexicon through which language defines itself, an alternative citation should be Benjamin's observation that "quotations in my works are like robbers by the roadside who make an armed attack and relieve an idler of his convictions." We therefore need to wilfully give ourselves over to such criminality, even over indulge in quotation to such an extent that it no longer leaves a mark.

Contributors

Erin Besler and Ian Besler are cofounders of Besler & Sons, a Los Angeles based practice that works across multiple sites of production. Their work has been published in *Log*, *Pidgin*, *FutureAnterior*, *Project*, and *San Rocco*. Erin holds a Bachelor of Arts from Yale University and a Master of Architecture with Distinction from the Southern California Institute of Architecture. She is a Lecturer at the University of California Los Angeles in the Department of Architecture and Urban Design, where she was the 2013–2014 Teaching Fellow. Ian holds a Bachelor of Science in News-Editorial Journalism from the College of Media at the University of Illinois at Urbana-Champaign and a Master of Fine Arts from the Media Design Practices program at ArtCenter College of Design in Pasadena, where he was the 2014 Milken Family Foundation Post-Graduate Design Fellow. He is a Lecturer of Design at the University of Southern California.

Córdova Canillas is an art direction and design practice based in Barcelona founded by Diego Córdova and Martí Canillas. The duo met in 2010 and have been working together on editorial projects since founding their own studio in 2012. The studio's approach is defined by a collaborative network that allows them to integrate graphic design, art direction, photography, communication, and strategy to develop projects for commercial and institutional clients focused on contemporary culture.

Fake Industries Architectural Agonism (FKAA) is an entity of variable boundaries and questionable taste that provides architectural tools to mediate between citizens, institutions, the public sphere, and disciplinary knowledge. Created by Cristina Goberna and Urtzi Grau from their headquarters in New York, Sydney, and Barcelona, FKAA bridges the professional world and the environments of architectural academia to reclaim the architect's role as a public intellectual—that is, someone who earnestly risks his or her credibility to question hegemonic beliefs. The practice has recently completed the Superphosphates! Masterplan in Cáceres, the OE House in Barcelona, and is currently working on the New Velodrome of Medellín. In 2014 FKAA won the AIA NY New Practices Award and was shortlisted for the MoMA PS1 YAP and the Art Basel-Miami Beach Design pavilion. In 2015 FKAA was a finalist for the Guggenheim Helsinki Competition and represented Australia in the Chicago Architectural Biennial with the Indo-Pacific Atlas.

Formlessfinder was founded by Garrett Ricciardi and Julian Rose in 2010. The studio was selected as a finalist for the MOMA/PS1 Young Architects Program in 2011 and received the 2012 AIANY New Practices award. Formlessfinder's design work, ranging from residential additions to public pavilions, has been exhibited at institutions such as the Museum of Modern Art in New York, the MAXXI in Rome, Storefront for Art and Architecture, Design Miami, and featured in publications including *Architectural Record*, *Domus*, *Surface*, *Metropolis*, and *W Magazine*. Ricciardi and Rose have lectured on their work at The Cooper Union, Princeton University, University of Chicago, and other universities, and published their *Formless Manifesto* with Lars Müller in 2014. Formlessfinder's recent clients include Design Miami, the Museum of Art and Design, the Museum of Modern Art, the AIANY Center for Architecture, and Blue Hill Restaurant.

George Hersey (1927–2007) was Professor Emeritus of History of Art at Yale University. His scholarship focused on Italian Renaissance architecture and nineteenth-century architecture and art in Europe and America. Hersey was the author of thirteen books, including *Pythagorean Palaces: Architecture and Magic in the Italian Renaissance* (1976), *The Lost Meaning of Classical Architecture: Speculations on Ornament from Vitruvius to Venturi* (1988), and *Architecture and Geometry in the Age of the Baroque* (2002). He was a visiting scholar at the Warburg Institute in London, Villa i Tatti in Florence, and the American Academy in Rome.

Jacques Herzog established Herzog & de Meuron with Pierre de Meuron in Basel in 1978. He studied architecture at the Swiss Federal Institute of Technology Zurich (ETHZ) from 1970 to 1975 with Aldo Rossi and Dolf Schnebli. He was a visiting tutor at Cornell University, USA in 1983. With Pierre de Meuron, he is visiting professor at Harvard University, USA (1989 and since 1994), professor at ETH Zürich since 1999, and co-founder of ETH Studio Basel–Contemporary City Institute since 2002. In 2001, he was awarded the Pritzker Architecture Prize together with Pierre de Meuron.

Xiahong Hua is an associate professor at the College of Architecture and Urban Planning, Tongji University. She earned her PhD in Architectural History and Theory from Tongji University in 2007, and was a Visiting Fellow at the Yale School of Architecture from 2014 to 2015. Her academic interests include contemporary architecture in consumer culture, Chinese architects and their practices in modern and contemporary periods, and L.E. Hudec's architecture in Shanghai. She has co-authored five books, co-translated two books, and published more than 25 articles in Chinese academic periodicals. As a Chinese registered architect since 1999, her award-winning design work has been widely published and exhibited. She is also the cultural consultant for Atelier Archmixing and a part-time editor of *Time Architecture* magazine.

Steven Lauritano is an art and architectural historian and a PhD candidate at Yale University in the Department of the History of Art. He is currently completing a book project on the Prussian architect Karl Friedrich Schinkel and the models of history that emerged through his experimental work with re-incorporated antique remains. Lauritano is a former fellow of the Berlin Program for Advanced German and European Studies at the Freie Universität Berlin and a recipient of the Carter Manny Award for Research granted by the Graham Foundation for Advanced Studies in the Fine Arts. His writings have appeared in *Pidgin Magazine*, *Circo*, and *306090 Books*.

Sylvia Lavin received her PhD from the Department of Art and Archaeology at Columbia University and published her first books, *Quatremère de Quincy and the Invention of a Modern Language of Architecture* and *Form Follows Libido: Architecture and Richard Neutra in a Psychoanalytic Culture,* with the MIT Press. Other books include *Kissing Architecture* and *Flash in the Pan*. Lavin is an active curator and recent exhibition venues include the Canadian Center for Architecture, the Graham Foundation, and the Yale School of Architecture, where *Everything Loose Will Land: Art and Architecture in Los Angeles in the 1970s* was shown in 2014. She is the Director of the Critical Studies MA and PhD Program in the Department of Architecture and Urban Design at UCLA, where she was Chairperson from 1996 to 2006. Lavin is the recipient of an Arts and Letters Award in Architecture from the American Academy of Arts and Letters.

Amanda Reeser Lawrence is an assistant professor at the School of Architecture at Northeastern University. She holds a PhD from Harvard's Graduate School of Design, a Master of Architecture from Columbia University, and a BA Summa Cum Laude from Princeton University. Her book *James Stirling: Revisionary Modernist* (Yale University Press, 2013) was funded by the Graham Foundation and the Paul Mellon Center for Studies in British Art. Her work has also been funded by the National Endowment for the Humanities, the National Endowment for the Arts, the J.M. Kaplan Fund, and the American Institute of Architects. Her essays have appeared in *Log*, *Architectural Theory Review*, *OASE*, *Journal of Architectural Education*, and *Future Anterior*. A licensed architect, Lawrence is founding co-editor of the award-winning journal, *Praxis*.

Mari Lending is a professor of architectural history and theory at the Oslo School of Architecture and Design, and a senior researcher in the research projects *The Printed and the Built: Architecture and Public Debate in Modern Europe* and *Place and Displacement: Exhibiting Architecture*, run out of OCCAS (the Oslo Center for Critical Architectural Studies). Her book *Monuments in Flux: Plaster Casts as Mass Medium* on nineteenth-century plaster cast collections is forthcoming. She recently published, with Mari Hvattum, *Modelling Time: The Permanent Collection, 1925–2014* (Torpedo Press, 2014), drawing on the exhibition *Model as Ruin* at the House of Artists in Oslo.

Adam Lowe created the multi-disciplinary workshop Factum Arte in Madrid in 2000 and the Factum Foundation for Digital Technology in Conservation in 2007. An exact facsimile of the burial chamber of Tutankhamen was installed at the entrance to the Valley of the Kings in 2014. His approach to both monitoring the condition of "at risk" sites and to creating exact copies is transforming heritage management and transferring skills and technologies to local teams. He has worked with many institutions and museums including the National Gallery (London), the Museo del Prado, the Musée du Louvre, the Vatican Museums, Fondazione Giorgio Cini (Venice), the Church of San Petronio (Bologna), the Royal Collection, Sir John Soane's Museum, and many other public and private institutions.

MAIO is an architectural office founded in 2005. It is currently led by Maria Charneco, Alfredo Lérida, Guillermo López, and Anna Puigjaner, architects based in Barcelona. They are currently in charge of running the magazine *Quaderns d'Arquitectura i Urbanisme*, teaching at the School of Architecture of Barcelona ETSAB/ETSAV, and building ongoing projects, ranging from installations to housing.

Ana Miljački is a critic, curator, and Associate Professor of Architecture at Massachusetts Institute of Technology, where she teaches history, theory, and design. Her research interests range from the role of architecture and architects in the Cold War-era Eastern Europe, through the theories of postmodernism in late socialism to politics of contemporary architectural production. Miljački was part of the three member curatorial team, with Eva Franch i Gilabert and Ashley Schafer, of *OfficeUS*, the United States presentation at the 2014 Venice Architecture Biennale. In 2013, with Lee Moreau and Sarah Hirschman, she produced *Project_Rorschach* for the Boston Design Biennial. The exhibition *UnFair Use*, which she co-curated with Sarah Hirschman, was on the view at the Center for Architecture in New York in the fall of 2015. Miljački's book *The Optimum Imperative: Czech Architecture for the Socialist Lifestyle 1938–1968* will be published with Routledge in 2017.

Eeva-Liisa Pelkonen is an Associate Professor at Yale School of Architecture, where she teaches design, history, and theory. Her scholarly work deals with the genesis and meaning of form in various geographic and historical contexts. She is the author of three books: *Achtung Architektur! Image and Phantasm in Contemporary Austrian Architecture* (MIT Press/Graham Foundation, 1996), *Alvar Aalto: Architecture, Modernity and Geopolitics* (Yale University Press, 2009), and *Kevin Roche: Architecture as an Environment* (Yale University Press, 2011), and a co-editor of *Eero Saarinen: Shaping the Future* (Yale University Press, 2006) with Donald Albrecht. She is currently working on a documentary anthology of twentieth-century architectural exhibitions entitled *Architecture, Exhibited* to be published by Phaidon in 2017.

Demetri Porphyrios is founder and principal of Porphyrios Associates and has an international reputation as an architect and theorist. Dr. Porphyrios was educated at Princeton University where he received his Master of Architecture and PhD in the History and Theory of Architecture. He is currently the Robert A.M. Stern Visiting Professor at Yale School of Architecture. He is the recipient of the prestigious Driehaus Prize and the Arthur Ross Award. He is Trustee of the Saint Catherine Foundation, Archon of the Ecumenical Patriarchate, Member of Europa Nostra, and Member of the Society of Architectural Historians. His books include *Studies on Alvar Aalto*; *On the Methodology of Architectural History*; *Classicism is not a Style*; *Building and Rational Architecture*; *Classical Architecture*; and monographs: *Demetri Porphyrios: Selected Buildings and Writings*; *Porphyrios Associates: Recent Work*. His new monograph *Porphyrios Associates: The Allure of The Classical* will be published in September 2016.

Richard Rogers is an architect best known for such pioneering works as the Centre Pompidou in Paris, the headquarters for Lloyd's of London, the European Court of Human Rights in Strasbourg, and for large-scale masterplanning schemes in London, Lisbon, Berlin and Shanghai. Since creating his first practice with Norman Foster, Team 4, he has continually worked in collaborative settings establishing Piano + Rogers with Renzo Piano and Su Rogers, and Richard Rogers Partnership, since evolved into Rogers Stirk Harbour + Partners. He was awarded the Legion d'Honneur in 1986, knighted in 1991, and made a member of the House of Lords. He was the 2007 Pritzker Architecture Prize Laureate.

Sergio Muñoz Sarmiento is an artist and arts lawyer interested in the analysis of property and structures, in both tangible and intangible forms, through legal and cultural discourses and practices. Sarmiento received his BA in Art from the University of Texas-El Paso, an MFA in Art from the California Institute of the Arts, and a JD from Cornell Law School in 2006. He has lectured and performed in a wide range of institutions, including Harvard University, Cornell Law School, Yale Law School, Columbia Law School, Fundación Cisneros (Caracas), Universidad de los Andes (Bogotá), Cour de Cassation (Paris), McGill Faculty of Law, RISD, and the Walker Art Center. He has also published texts in *Law Text Culture, Unbound: Harvard Journal of the Legal Left, Texas A&M Law Review, Yale Journal of Law and the Humanities*, and *The New York Times*. In 2010 Sarmiento founded the Art & Law Program, a philosophical think-tank on law and culture. He maintains a private practice and currently teaches art and law at Fordham Law School.

Panayotis Tournikiotis is the professor of architectural theory at the National Technical University of Athens, School of Architecture. He has studied architecture, town planning, geography and philosophy in Athens and Paris. His research focuses on critical history and theory, and the way understanding the past may contribute to the interdisciplinary setting of design strategies in architecture and town planning. He has authored many books including *Adolf Loos* (1994), *The Historiography of Modern Architecture* (1999) and *The Diagonal of Le Corbusier* (2010). His recent work explores the legacy of Le Corbusier in Greece and the reinvention of the city centre in metropolitan Athens.

Xenia Vytuleva is an architectural historian, theorist, and curator. Born and raised in Moscow, she studied in Moscow and in Cambridge, UK. Her scholarship is focused on new modes of conceptual preservation, the intersection of art, science and politics, as well as Cold War architecture. She is currently teaching at the Columbia University Graduate School of Architecture, Planning, and Preservation in New York. Dr. Vytuleva writes extensively on the interconnection of architecture, contemporary cultures, and new media. Her recent curatorial projects include *Music on Bones* (MAXXI, Rome), Experimental Preservation: Venice CCCP Observatory 2014, and "Straying: the Book of Instructions" at the Slought Foundation in Philadelphia. A recipient of various grants and awards, most recently from the Graham Foundation for the project *Cold War Secret Spaces*, she is currently working on a manuscript titled *An Atlas of Untold Territories*.

Thomas Weaver is an architectural writer, teacher, and editor. He has taught architectural history at Princeton University, architectural design at The Cooper Union, New York, and has also acted as editor of ANY magazine and various architectural monographs. Since 2007 he has worked at the Architectural Association School of Architecture in London, where he manages all of the AA's publications, including editing the long-running journal *AA Files*.

Ines Weizman is professor of architecture theory at the Bauhaus University, Weimar, director of the Bauhaus Institute of History and Theory of Architecture and Planning, and director of the Centre for Documentary Architecture. Her books include *Architecture and the Paradox of Dissidence* (Routledge, 2014) and *Before and After: Documenting the Architecture of Disaster* with Eyal Weizman (Strelka Press, 2014). In 2015 she edited a volume of *Future Anterior* with Jorge Otero-Pailos. Her writing has been published in books, magazines, and journals such as *AA Files*, *ADD METAPHYSICS*, *ARCH+*, *Bauhaus Magazine*, *BEYOND*, *Displayer*, *JAE*, *Harvard Design Magazine*, *Perspecta*, *Volume*, and *The Sage Handbook of Architectural Theory*. Research and exhibition projects include *Celltexts: Books and Other Works Produced in Prison* with Eyal Weizman, first exhibited at the Fondazione Sandretto Re Rebaudengo, Turino (2008, 2009, 2014, 2014, 2015); celltexts.org; and *Repeat Yourself. Loos, Law and the Culture of the Copy*, first presented at the Venice Architecture Biennale in 2012 as part of the *Museum of Copies* curated by FAT, shown also in Vienna and in New York in 2013.

WikiHouse New Haven was founded by Yale School of Forestry and Environmental Studies student Peter Hirsch in 2014. As a local chapter of the WikiHouse Foundation, WikiHouse New Haven joined a global network of architects and amateurs contributing to the open-source design of low-cost, self-built houses. WikiHouse New Haven completed the construction of the first permanent WikiHouse in the United States, a shelter on the Yale West Campus Urban Farm in West Haven, Connecticut.

Elia Zenghelis is an architect and educator dividing his time between Greece, Switzerland, the UK, and the USA. He studied and taught from 1956 to 1986 at the Architectural Association School of Architecture in London. He is one of the original founders of OMA (the Office for Metropolitan Architecture) in partnership with Rem Koolhaas, Zoe Zenghelis, and Madelon Vriesendorp. In 1987 he established Gigantes Zenghelis Architects in Athens, Greece with Eleni Gigantes. In practice he has received a number of distinctions including the Mies van de Rohe Award and the Eternit Award for Checkpoint Charlie (Berlin, 1989). A committed educator, he continues to teach at many schools in Europe, Asia, South America and the United States. In 2000 Zenghelis received the Annie Spink Award for Excellence in Education from the Royal Institute of British Architects.

Image Credits

The editors greatly acknowledge the permissions granted to reproduce the copyrighted material in this publication. Every effort has been made to trace the ownership of all copyrighted material and to secure proper credits and permissions from the appropriate copyright holders. In the event of any omission or oversight, all necessary corrections will be made in future printings. Unless otherwise noted, all images are courtesy of the author.

Page 1: The Metropolitan Museum of Art, Gift of the artist, 1995 (1995.266.4) Walker Evans Archive, The Metropolitan Museum of Art. Image source: Art Resource, NY. Courtesy David Zwirner, New York, Simon Lee Gallery, London, Jablonka Galerie, Cologne; page 4: Eléonore Goblé; page 272, top: The Royal Pavilion and Museums, Brighton & Hove; page 272, bottom: Jerzy Survillo.

Pelkonen
Fig. 1–2, © The Museum of Modern Art/ Licensed by SCALA/Art Resource, NY; fig. 3, Glass Skyscraper Project: © The Museum of Modern Art/Licensed by SCALA/Art Resource, NY; fig. 4, Willis, Faber & Dumas: © Nigel Young/Foster + Partners; fig. 5, © Studio Passarelli; fig. 6, Alley Theater: Michael E Johnston, CC BY-SA 2.0.; Watergate: Wikimedia user Nick-D, CC BY-SA 3.0.; Rudolph Garage: Seth Tisue, CC BY-SA 2.0.; Sea-Tac: Steve Mohundro. CC BY-SA 2.0.; Marina Baie: Thomas Leth-Olsen, CC BY-SA 2.0.

Lawrence
Fig. 1: Library of Congress, Prints & Photographs Division. HABS CAL, 38-SANFRA, 160; figs. 2–3, pages 33–34: Julius Shulman, © J. Paul Getty Trust. Getty Research Institute, Los Angeles (2004.R.10); figs. 4, 6–16: © Frank Lloyd Wright Foundation, Scottsdale, AZ. All rights reserved. The Frank Lloyd Wright Foundation Archives (The Museum of Modern Art | Avery Architectural & Fine Arts Library, Columbia University); fig. 5: Library of Congress, Prints & Photographs Division. LC-USZ62-111252.

Miljacki
All images courtesy of the author.

Lavin
Page 41, © Billy Al Bengston; page 42, 35 mm slides courtesy of www.environ mentalcommunications.info; pages 43–45, © GEHRY PARTNERS, LLP; pages 46–47, © Estate of Evelyn Hofer; pages 48–50, © **Ed Ruscha**.

Sarmiento
Page 58: Yale School of Architecture; page 59, right: Russell LeStourgeon, CC BY-SA 3.0; page 60, left: Lower Manhattan Development Corporation; page 64: © Carey Young. Courtesy Paula Cooper Gallery, New York; page 66: © 2016 Estate of Gordon Matta-Clark / Artists Rights Society (ARS), New York.

Rogers
Figs. 1, 2, 4, 5, 7, 10: © Rogers Stirk Harbour + Partners; fig. 3: © Rogers Stirk Harbour + Partners / Renzo Piano Building Workshop; fig. 6: © Renzo Piano Building Workshop; figs. 8, 9: © Richard Bryant/ARCAID.

Lending
Page 80, top: Flickr User fmpgoh, CC BY-NC-ND 2.0; page 80, bottom: The Metropolitan Museum of Art, Rogers Fund, Transferred from the Library, 1941; page 81: © Factum Arte; page 82, top: Chris Brown, CC BY-SA 1.0; pages 82, bottom: © Griffith Institute, University of Oxford; pages 83–85, 87: © Factum Arte; page 86: © Griffith Institute, University of Oxford.

Lowe
Pages 92–94: All photographs © Factum Arte; pages 91, 95–96: All photographs © Tarek Waly Studio.

Formlessfinder
Page 100: Wikimedia user timsdad, CC BY-SA 3.0; page 101: © Habrda; page 102: A.J.P. Artemel, CC BY-SA 3.0; page 103: © Tennessee Valley Authority, CC BY 2.0.

Lauritano
Figs. 1, 8–10, 15: CC BY-SA 3.0 DE; figs. 2–7, 11–14: Courtesy of the author; fig. 15: Hans Peter Schaefer, CC BY-SA 3.0 DE.

Wikihouse
All images: Peter Hirsch, WikiHouse New Haven.

Weizman
Pages 134–135: All images © Niclas Zimmer, 2014; page 136, top left: © Niclas Zimmer, 2014; page 136, middle: Bauhaus-Universität Weimar, Archiv der Moderne / Neufert Stiftung, signature N/63/66.16; page 136, bottom: Bauhaus-Universität Weimar, Archiv der Moderne / Neufert Stiftung; pages 138–139: Bauhaus-Universität Weimar, Archiv der Moderne / Neufert Stiftung, signature N/63/66.2; page 141: Bauhaus-Universität Weimar, Archiv der Moderne / Neufert Stiftung, signature N/52/66.101; page 143: Bauhaus-Universität Weimar, Archiv der Moderne / Neufert Stiftung, signature N/53/66.4; page 144: Bauhaus-Universität Weimar, Archiv der Moderne / Neufert Stiftung, signature N/52/66.101_10_F2; page 145: Bauhaus-Universität Weimar, Archiv der Moderne / Neufert Stiftung, signature N/52/66.113.

Porphyrios
Page 150, top: German Archaeological Institute, University of Cologne; page 150, bottom: © Delft University of Technology.

Tournikiotis
Fig. 1: Aleksandr Zykov. CC BY-SA 2.0; figs. 2, 10–11, 15: Courtesy of the author; fig. 3: Flickr User Rexness. CC BY-NC 2.0; fig. 4: Library of Congress, Prints & Photographs Division, HABS PA, 51-PHILA, 223–42; fig. 5. Library of Congress, Prints & Photographs Division, HABS NY, 31-NEYO, 53–33; fig. 6: Mayur Phadtare, CC BY-SA 3.0; fig. 7: Library of Congress, Prints & Photographs Division, HABS DC, WASH, 503–4; fig. 8: Wikimedia User Alupus, CC BY-SA 3.0; fig. 9: Library of Congress, Prints & Photographs Division, HABS DC, WASH, 462–11; fig. 12: Rory Hide, CC BY-SA 2.0; fig. 13: K. Megalokonomou, Courtesy of the author; fig. 14: Fabio Candido, CC BY-NC 2.0.

Herzog
Page 168, © Iwan Baan; page 169, Eberswalde Library: Photo Margherita Spiluttini, © Architekturzentrum Wien, Collection; page 169, Architektur/Denkform: © Herzog & de Meuron; page 170, © Hayes Davidson and Herzog & de Meuron; pages 171–174, © Herzog & de Meuron and Ai Weiwei.

Hersey
Reprint courtesy of Yale School of Architecture.

Hua
Page 202, left: Wikimedia Commons user Airunp, GNU FDL; page 202, right: Wikimedia Commons user WiNG, CC BY 3.0; page 203, left: © Architectural Society of Shanghai; page 203, right: Diego Delso, CC BY-SA 3.0; page 204, left: Wikimedia Commons user Gisling, CC BY 3.0; page 204, right: © Liu Yichun, 1999; page 205, left: © Zhuang Shen, 2015; page 205, right: Wikimedia Commons user Shizhao, CC BY-SA 3.0; page 206, left: © Wang Meijie, 2014; page 206, right: Courtesy of Amateur Architecture Studio; page 207, left: © Lu Hengzhong, 2008; page 207, right: © Pier Alessio Rizzardi, from *The Condition of Chinese Architecture* (Shanghai: Tongji University Press / Chinese Architectural and Industrial PRESS, 2015); page 208, left: © Yang Cailiang, 2014; page 208, right: © Su Yingkui, 2015; page 209: Courtesy of MAD Architects; page 210: Courtesy of Jiakun Architects / ARCH-EXIST; page 211, left: © Tang Yu; page 211, right: Courtesy of Atelier Archmixing; page 212: © Su Shengliang, 2014.

Besler
YouTube and the YouTube logo are registered trademarks of Google Inc. used with permission.

Vytuleva
Pages 222–229: All images courtesy of the author or the Novouralsk Museum of Local History; pages 230–231: Spread developed by *Perspecta* 49 Editors. Page 230, clockwise from top left: Wikimedia user ScriptMaster, CC BY-SA 3.0; Wikimedia Commons, CC BY-SA 3.0; courtesy of author; courtesy of Seversk ZATO Administration, seversknet.ru; courtesy of author; Wikimedia Commons user Xabre, public domain. Page 231, clockwise from top left: Wikimedia Commons user Orinoko1973, public domain; © Alisa Tagina; public domain; © http://www.tipazheleznogorsk.narod.ru/english/index.html; Wikimedia Commons user MikhailOrlov, CC BY 2.5; courtesy of author.

Fake, CC, MAIO
Pages 241–254: Courtesy of Fake Industries Architectural Agonism, MAIO, and Córdova Canillas.

Zenghelis
Pages 258–259, © Dogma with Elia Zenghelis.

Weaver
Illustrations by Martha Kang McGill and Min Hee Lee.

Perspecta, The Yale Architectural Journal is published in the United States of America by the Yale School of Architecture and distributed by the MIT Press.

Massachusetts Institute of Technology
Cambridge, MA 02142
http://mitpress.mit.edu

ISBN: 978-0-262-52942-6
ISSN: 0079-0958

10 9 8 7 6 5 4 3 2 1

Perspecta
The Yale Architectural Journal
No. 49: Quote

Editors
A.J.P. Artemel
Russell LeStourgeon
Violette de la Selle

Designers
Min Hee Lee
Martha Kang McGill

Printer
Conti Tipocolor
Florence, Italy

Typefaces
Neue Haas Grotesk is a recent redrawing of arguably the most copied typeface of the past century, Max Miedinger's Helvetica. Designed by Christian Schwartz and released in 2010, Neue Haas Grotesk is a revival of the original letterforms, before they were compromised by repeated translations for different typesetting technologies.

Optima Nova was designed by Hermann Zapf and Akira Kobayashi in 2002. It is a redesign of Zapf's well-known typeface Optima (released 1952–1955), which was itself an interpretation of Roman monumental capitals.

The old fellows stole our best ideas.
—Frederic Goudy

Acknowledgments

Just as authors are indebted to those from whom they quote, we are indebted to the myriad people who have supported our efforts and contributed to this issue.

Our most sincere thanks to the donors that make the production of *Perspecta* possible:
Marc F. Appleton, '72 M.Arch
Hans Baldauf, '81 BA, '88 M.Arch
Austin Church III, '60 BA Family Fund
Fred Koetter and Susie Kim
Elizabeth Lenahan
Cesar Pelli, '08 DFAH
Robert A.M. Stern, '65 M.Arch
Jeremy Scott Wood, '64 BA, '70 M.Arch
F. Anthony Zunino, '70 M.Arch

We would like to thank the members of the *Perspecta* board for their direction, guidance, and trust:
Peggy Deamer
Sheila Levrant de Bretteville
Keller Easterling
Gavin Macrae-Gibson
Cesar Pelli
Emmanuel Petit
Alan Plattus
Harold Roth
Robert A.M. Stern

Special thanks to Dean Robert A.M. Stern for his caring tutelage and constructive advice. John Jacobson, Richard DeFlumeri, Lillian Smith, and Rosemary Watts at Yale School of Architecture were instrumental in facilitating the production of this issue.

Our deepest gratitude to our exceptional designers, Martha Kang McGill and Min Hee Lee, for their commitment and keen eyes. We thank Cathryn Drake for her careful copyedits. We must also thank Christine Savage, Justin Kehoe, Erin Hasley, and Victoria Hindley at MIT Press for their oversight and help navigating the publishing process.

We thank our mentors and colleagues whose advice and support have been invaluable: Samuel Medina, Dr. Christiane Wolf, Petra Goertz, Mario Carpo, Ryan Carter, Lu Wenyu, Ralph Valanzuolo, Clandestino, Blanca Nieto, Margo Stipe, Mac Brydon, Christina Jentsch, Robbi Siegel, James McKee, Martino Tattara, Chelsea Weathers, Michael Cohen, Chris Rawson, Florinda Gomes, Shayari de Silva, Alice Tai, Jo Murtagh, Jennifer Goldsmith, Jessica Svendsen, and Alisa Tagina.

We greatly appreciate the unwavering support and patience of our families and friends. We thank the previous editors of Perspecta for their insights, especially Aaron Dresben, Teo Quintana, Ed Hsu, Andrea Leung, and Joseph Clark.

Finally, it was an honor to work with our esteemed contributors. Thank you for enriching our issue and and stimulating an ongoing discussion.

following page
John Nash, Kitchen of the Royal Pavilion, Brighton, 1816.
Hans Hollein, Austrian Travel Agency, Vienna, 1979.
Robert Burton, *The Anatomy of Melancholy*, 1621.

We can say nothing but what hath been said, the
composition and method is ours only, and shows a scholar.